Second Edition

Making Sense of Your World

A Biblical Worldview

W. Gary Phillips
William E. Brown
John Stonestreet

Foreword by Norman Geisler

Sheffield Publishing Company

For information about this book contact:
    Sheffield Publishing Company
    P.O. Box 359
    Salem, Wisconsin 53168
    262.843.2281
    info@spcbooks.com
    www.spcbooks.com

ISBN 1-879215-51-9
ISBN 978-1-879215-51-1

Printed in the United States of America

14 13 12 11 10

To our parents
Bill and Mildred Phillips
Joe and DeLois Brown
Jim and Pat Stonestreet
who first gave us our worldview
which we have at various times over the years
embraced, questioned, rejected, reexamined, and
now eagerly explore

WILLIAM E. BROWN is President of Cedarville University. A graduate of the University of South Florida, he holds a master of theology degree and Ph.D. from Dallas Theological Seminary. As a nationally recognized expert in worldview, Brown has authored three books (*Making Sense of Your Faith*; *Where Have All the Dreamers Gone?: Observations from a Biblical Worldview*; and *Making Sense of Your World* with Gary Phillips and John Stonestreet) and more than a hundred articles for journals, magazines, encyclopedias, and newspapers. He has also lectured internationally in Europe, the former Soviet Union, and South America. Dr. Brown and his wife, Lynne, are the parents of two children, April and Alex, and they reside in Cedarville, Ohio.

W. GARY PHILLIPS is pastor of Signal Mountain Bible Church in Chattanooga, Tennessee. His degrees are from Vanderbilt University (B.A.), Dallas Theological Seminary (Th.M.), and Grace Theological Seminary (Th.D.). He was Chairman of Biblical Studies at Bryan College, where he taught for twenty-four years, and was named by the trustees "Distinguished Professor of Biblical Studies." He has received six teaching awards, has published articles and books (including *Making Sense of Your World* with W. E. Brown and John Stonestreet, the first edition having been nominated for Christianity Today's "Reader's Choice" book of the year), and has served as an officer in both the Evangelical Theological Society and the Evangelical Philosophical Society. Most recently he contributed several articles for *The Encyclopedia of Theology* (Baker) and wrote a commentary entitled *Judges and Ruth* (Broadman & Holman, 2004). In 1985 Dr. Phillips planted a church on Signal Mountain where he served part-time for sixteen years while teaching at Bryan, and in 2001 became its full-time pastor. He and his wife, Betsy, have three grown children, David, Beth, and Rebecca.

JOHN STONESTREET is the Director of Programs for Summit Ministries, a ministry dedicated to training Christians to understand and live from a biblical worldview. He is a popular speaker around the country and internationally at camps, schools, churches, and conferences. He ministers to thousands of parents, teachers, and students each year on topics such as biblical worldview, comparative worldviews, education, apologetics, leadership, and cultural issues. John holds a B.A. in Bible from Bryan College, an M.A. in Christian Thought from Trinity International University, and has been on the Christian Studies faculty at Bryan College since 2002. John and his wife, Sarah, have two daughters, Abigail and Anna, and they reside in Colorado Springs, Colorado.

CONTENTS

Index of Graphics   vi
Foreword by Dr. Norman Geisler   vii
Preface   ix
Introduction   xi

Part One: The Difference a Worldview Makes   1

1	When Worldviews Collide	3
2	The World of Worldviews	19
3	Putting Worldviews to the Test	61

Part Two: A *Biblical* Worldview   91

4	The Essentials of a Biblical Worldview	93
5	Why a Biblical Worldview?	111
6	What's Wrong? The Problem of Evil and Suffering	145
7	Who's Right? The Problem of Pluralism	171

Part Three: So What? A View *Of* and a View *For*   195

8	A View *of* and *for* the Self	197
9	A View *of* and *for* the Family	219
10	A View *of* and *for* the Church	239
11	A View *of* and *for* the World	257

Appendix: Case Studies for Each Chapter   281
Index of Subjects   295

INDEX OF GRAPHICS

Diagram 1.1
   The Worldview Triangle   **8**

Diagram 2.1
   Living Backwards: The Worldview Triangle Reversed   **20**

Diagram 2.2
   Classifying the Major Worldviews   **23**

Diagram 2.3
   Comparing the Worldviews   **40**

Diagram 2.4
   Theistic Distinctives   **41**

Diagram 2.5
   Comparing the Three Great Theistic Religions   **47**

Diagram 2.6
   Postmodernism   **51**

Diagram 6.1
   The Beginning and the End   **165**

FOREWORD

The truth is that everyone has a worldview. The tragedy is that many people think and live by their worldview and do not take the time to analyze what it is or even whether it is true.

The truth is that a worldview is like colored glasses; it colors everything at which we look. It is a grid through which one views all of life. As such it helps form our thoughts, values, and decisions. The tragedy is that most people do not even know what their worldview is, how they got it, and how important it is in their lives.

The truth is that not all worldviews are true. Opposites cannot both be true, and if one worldview is true, then all opposing worldviews must be false. The tragedy is that most people think that all worldviews are true, and it does not matter which one you believe.

The truth is that there is a distinctive Christian worldview. That is, there is a uniquely Christian way to think and act. The tragedy is that a recent Barna survey revealed that only eight percent of all evangelical Christians have a Christian worldview. It is a further tragedy that only half of Christian leaders have a Christian worldview.

The truth is that we have our work cut out for us. And the tragedy is that more people do not know about this excellent book on worldviews by two of the people in the country most qualified to write on the topic.

Making Sense of Your World was not only one of the first on this subject, but it is one of the best. It comes from experts in the field who have decades of experience in teaching worldviews on the college level in two of the best Christian colleges in the country.

Having spent nearly a half century defining and defending a Christian worldview, I can heartily recommend this book. It not only covers the major worldviews, but it defends the uniqueness of the Christian worldview. It stands for absolutism in a world of relativism; supernaturalism over against naturalism, and exclusivism in face of a growing pluralism.

Making Sense of Your World does just that. It demonstrates that the only view that really makes sense is the biblical worldview. This it does, not only in an intellectual way, but also in a practical way. From the thoughtful questions at the end of each chapter, the suggested readings, and the helpful charts, this book reveals that it is a product of men who have spent untold hours in the classroom helping to mold young minds and motivate eager hearts.

If we are going to make sense of our world, we must study worldviews. And if we are going to make sense of the contemporary smorgasbord of worldviews, this book is an insightful way to sort through them. Without the material presented here in defense of the uniqueness of the Christian worldview, Christian belief is a defenseless faith. In the marketplace of ideas, *Making Sense* makes great sense.

Given the state of our post-Christian culture, there is a growing and desperate need for worldview apologetics. There is no longer a Judeo-Christian basis for our society. Objective truth has all but vanished. Moral absolutes are nearly non-existent, and the prevailing philosophy is secularist. If Christianity is to survive, worldview education is no longer an option; it is an absolute necessity. For in our pluralistic, relativistic, and naturalistic culture the very preconditions for understanding the Gospel have evaporated. The revision and reprinting of this valuable tool in transforming our culture for Christ is more than welcome.

Dr. Norman Geisler, Dean
Southern Evangelical Seminary
Charlotte, NC
Winter 2007

PREFACE

My worldview "teeth" were cut on this book. I transferred to Bryan College as a second year student in the fall of 1994. My decision to transfer was based on sports, and I had little knowledge about the school itself or its emerging emphasis on biblical worldview. What I discovered was an institution committed to a worldview approach to education and to training Christian leaders in all areas of life. This commitment was due in large part to the vision and leadership of its president, Dr. William E. Brown.

Bill is one of those rare college presidents whom students love to hear speak in chapel. In fact, students rarely skipped chapel when he spoke. I learned from Bill the importance of understanding and engaging culture, that I could not withdraw from the world that I was trying to reach with the Gospel, and that people were never my enemy. Bill's invitation a year after I graduated from Bryan to return and lead the "Worldview Team" ministry that he had started essentially put my life on its current trajectory.

Dr. W. Gary Phillips was the first professor I encountered at Bryan—the class was called "Biblical Worldview." At the time, I had no idea what the word "worldview" even meant, but the class was life-changing for me. I learned that Christianity was to be applied to every area of life and culture, and that thinking was a Christian thing to do.

I went on to take several more classes from Gary, and I left each one changed. In most of his classes, I kept two sets of notes: one for what I needed to know for the test and another for what I knew I never wanted to forget. His classes awakened my mind and forged the basis of my worldview.

It would be hard for me to quantify the extent to which these men have shaped my thinking. Now I teach on biblical worldview at Bryan College, at Summit Ministries programs, and in other contexts whenever I can. More than once over the last several years, I have supposed myself to have stumbled onto some new revolutionary truth, only to remember later that I had actually heard it first from Gary or Bill.

This is why I did not hesitate when Gary asked me about being involved in an update of this book. There is an extensive, and growing, body of evangelical literature on worldview, but in my view, this book remains unique. There are excellent books that *compare* worldviews (i.e. Jim Sire's *The Universe Next Door*), there are excellent books that *contrast* the biblical worldview with other worldviews (i.e. David Noebel's *Understanding the Times*), and there are a few excellent books that help one *construct* a biblical worldview (i.e. Nancy Pearcey's *Total Truth*).

ix

What *Making Sense of Your World* offers is a basic, accessible introduction to biblical worldview that covers *all* of these aspects of worldview thinking. Part One *compares* the basic worldviews, Part Two *contrasts* (and seeks to defend) the biblical worldview with the others, and Part Three *constructs* a biblical worldview in four key areas. This book is an overview; the Christian thinker is invited to continue his or her study through the recommended readings at the end of each chapter—an ongoing task Paul labels the "renewing" of our minds (Romans 12:2).

For those who have used the earlier edition of this book, there are several ways that this edition has been updated. First, for clarity and due to the recent emergence of Islam on the world scene, we separated the examination of the biblical worldview from the examination of theism. This resulted in an overall structural change (from two parts to three) which we hope will help the reader better follow the argument of the book. Second, we sought to update wherever necessary and to remove any outdated material. Thus, we have added material on Islam (including a case study) as well as an extended examination of postmodernism. Several of the chapters have been "tightened" from the first edition, and the case studies have been updated (and were moved to the appendix). Finally, we have added a much needed chapter on evaluating worldviews.

My thanks go to Bill Brown and Gary Phillips, and the many others who have been sharpeners in my life toward proper biblical thinking. My thanks, love, and admiration go to my wife Sarah who models a consistent biblical worldview to me in more ways than I could adequately describe.

John Stonestreet
Winter 2007

My thanks go to John Stonestreet for his diligent work in revising *Making Sense of Your World.* My involvement has been comparatively minimal, mainly because John is on the cutting edge of worldview thinking. His proven excellence as a teacher and his practical experience in communicating worldview material (to a variety of audiences and ages) have made this edition more complete and usable for those who desire to "give a reason for the hope that is within them." (2 Peter 3:15)

My thanks also go to Steve Nelson of Sheffield Publishing Company, who encouraged this revision. His consistent graciousness and patience are deeply appreciated.

W. Gary Phillips
Winter 2007

INTRODUCTION

"There is no longer a Christian mind."

With this proclamation, Harry Blamires begins his book *The Christian Mind: How Should a Christian Think?*[1] Blamires points out that there is a Christian ethic, a Christian practice, and a Christian spirituality, but that consistent thinking on the part of Christians does not exist. The fragmentation of American culture has found its way into the very heart of American Christianity. The resulting spiritual schizophrenia provides a poor reflection of the rich heritage of historical Christianity in this area and a sad model for the coming generation of Christians who must forge a Christian agenda for tomorrow.

It is time to recover the Christian mind. While some lament the nonexistence of the Christian mind, American Christianity charges full speed ahead in its course of incessant activity, indomitable individualism, and irrepressible pragmatism. "Doing the work" and "getting results" are the all-consuming objectives of the Christian church, leaving little room (or time) for tough-minded contemplation of the role of the Christian mind. This approach to ministry has led to sanctified versions of the Fortune 500 (the largest churches and ministries), the top forty ("Christian Contemporary Music," complete with its own award show and a Christianized version of *The Next American Idol)*, and self-help books. The "feel-good" religion that Christianity has become casts a jaundiced eye toward anything that smacks of "intellectual pursuit." Historian Mark Noll quips, "Comprehensive and coherent Christian thinking has never been a major part of religious life in America."[2]

Society in general gives little evidence of thinking about ultimate questions and important issues. The resulting self-indulgent values permeate every strata of social interaction. Many in higher education lament the shift away from altruistic ideals to an obsession with "having it all." The well-known study by the American Council on Education and the Higher Education Research Institute at UCLA revealed that over three-fourths of college freshmen feel that being financially well off is an "essential" or "very important" goal. A key reason for their decision to attend college was "to make more money," while at the same time only

---

[1] Harry Blamires, *The Christian Mind: How Should a Christian Think?* (Ann Arbor, MI: Servant, 1978), p. 3.

[2] Mark Noll, "Christian World Views and Some Lessons from History," in *The Making of a Christian Mind*, ed. Arthur Holmes (Downers Grove, IL: InterVarsity, 1985), p. 29.

thirty-nine percent of freshmen put any emphasis on developing a meaningful philosophy of life.[3]

Without a well-developed philosophy of life, students are not prepared for the ethical and existential dilemmas they will face. They face what some have called a "quarter-life crisis,"[4] questioning who they are and why they exist, despite having the degree, career, and lifestyle that they always desired. As one Duke University student put it: "We've got no philosophy of what... it is we want by the time somebody graduates. The so-called curriculum is a set of hoops that somebody says students ought to jump through before graduation. Nobody seems to have asked, 'How do people become good people?'"[5]

Christian higher education is not immune from this mercenary approach to education and life. As formal institutions of education, the Christian college, even more than the local church, must set the agenda for Christian thought. For this reason, setting forth a biblical worldview is not optional for institutions that desire to be distinctly Christian in their educational philosophy. The presentation and defense of a biblical world-view must be aggressive in its engagement with alternate worldviews; it must be well-rounded in its integration with the full scope of truth. Carl F. H. Henry delivered this charge: "Just as the Enlightenment in its revolt against biblical theism sought to explain law, religion, science, ethics, and all aspects of culture without reference to miraculous revelation and redemption, so Christian supernaturalism must bring into its purview every sphere of reality and activity. It will involve all the disciplines of a liberal arts education."[6]

Developing a biblical worldview involves both a *mindset* and a *willset*.[7] The former includes the essentials of a biblical view *of* the world. How does the Bible explain and interpret my life and the world around me? Once this question is answered and accepted, the latter

[3] Reported in "Freshmen Found Stressing Wealth," *New York Times*, 14 January 1988, p. A-14.
[4] See Alexandra Robbins and Abby Wilner, *The Quarterlife Crisis: The Unique Challenges of Life in Your Twenties* (New York: Tarcher/Putnam, 2001). Their work has led to an online support community (www.quarterlifecrisis.com) which has attracted over 80,000 registered users.
[5] Quoted in Steven Garber, *The Fabric of Faithfulness: Weaving Together Belief and Behavior During the University Years* (Downers Grove, IL: Inter-Varsity, 1996).
[6] Carl F. H. Henry, *Twilight of a Great Civilization: The Drift Toward Neo-Paganism* (Westchester, IL: Crossway, 1988), p. 121.
[7] Ibid., p. 19.

aspect of a biblical worldview presents the challenge to put this view into practice. This is a biblical view *for* the world. My values, plans, and decisions are informed by—even prescribed by—the worldview perspective given by the Scriptures.

This two-fold description of a worldview drives the approach of this book. Part One describes the nature of worldviews in general and examines the major views *of* and *for* the world that compete with Christianity. In Part Two, we focus on the biblical view *of* and *for* the world. As part of the examination of the biblical worldview, we will confront the challenges to it and seek to give adequate answers to those challenges. The purpose of Part Three is to sketch out the significant applications of the biblical worldview for four key areas: self, family, church, and society.

The primary goal of any exploration of worldviews is the attainment of truth. Let us begin by exploring the world of worldviews.

PART I:
THE DIFFERENCE A WORLDVIEW MAKES

What the meaning of life may be I don't know; I incline to
suspect that it has none.

H. L. Mencken

The tragedy of modern man is not that he knows less and less
about the meaning of his own life, but that it bothers him less
and less.

Vaclev Havel

Is life worth living, or is it a meaningless absurdity?

How one answers this question sets the stage for how (and even
why) one chooses to live. Disagreement about how to answer this question, and whether it is a question even worth caring about, cuts deeply
into the fundamental differences among religions and philosophies.

Mencken's way is by far the easier path to travel. A meaningless
existence requires nothing from anyone. There is no need to check for
bearings along the way, no need to justify one's choices, values, or goals.
Life is a lark at best, a tedium at worst. Such a philosophy agrees with
Brendan Gill, who once quipped, "Not a shred of evidence exists in favor
of the idea that life is serious."

On the other hand, despite our attempts to ignore these sorts of
issues, there exists a "quiet desperation" that drives humanity to think
about the question, "Does life have meaning?" Deciding that life does
have meaning is not the end but the beginning of a quest. Life becomes a
continual pilgrimage to find, affirm, and reaffirm a philosophy of life.
One may join a church (or leave a church), change religions, switch jobs,
get married, get divorced, or make any number of changes in an attempt
to find meaning and purpose.

This is the stuff of worldviews.

The tragedy in American culture is that thinking has been trivialized
by distraction, pragmatism has replaced principles, and "how" has
displaced the more profound question, "why?" Robert Bellah describes a
woman whose worldview epitomizes many: "I just sort of accept the way
the world is and then don't think about it a whole lot."[1] The results of

---

[1] Robert Bellah et al, *Habits of the Heart: Individualism and Commitment in
American Life* (New York: Harper & Row, 1985), p. 14.

1

this approach are the autonomy and individualism that are so much a part of current American public thought.

A vital corrective for Christians is that we learn to think in terms of worldviews. Raising the basic questions addressed by worldview inquiry is imperative in the face of New Age irrationality, Islamic extremism, scientific dogmatism, and existential sensuality. Christianity must present an alternative that sweeps away stereotypes and speaks to the central longings of man's existence.

Some argue that God merely requires a childlike faith and that a breadth of understanding of worldviews is unnecessary, but this confuses "childlikeness" with "childishness." As a child is unusually focused on his own needs and desires, so many Christians brandish a commitment to a biblical worldview that goes little beyond a "moralistic therapeutic deism", believing in a God who only exists to enhance their personal behavior and well-being.[2]

If a superficial knowledge of a biblical worldview continues to dominate the evangelical community, we cannot expect that community to stand unblemished against the onslaught of other worldview choices. David Wolfe wisely cautions, "Our ungrounded belief is easily swayed and abandoned, even though it may be correct."[3]

Christians are to put away childish thinking (1 Cor. 13:11; 14:20) and boldly confront the world with the full message of Christ. This involves knowing the essentials of a biblical worldview, the basic tenets of the alternate views, and where these views both agree and disagree. A person often finds it helpful to understand what he believes by knowing what he does not believe, and why. To this end we begin by exploring the difference that worldviews, including a biblical one, actually make.

---

[2] The phrase "moralistic therapeutic deism" was coined by Christian Smith and Melinda Lundquist Denton in their important book *Soul Searching: The Religious and Spiritual Lives of American Teenagers* (New York: Oxford, 2005).

[3] David Wolfe, *Epistemology: The Justification of Belief* (Downers Grove, IL: InterVarsity, 1982), p. 15.

1
WHEN WORLDVIEWS COLLIDE

Worldviews: Making Sense of Life
Worldviews: What Are They and How Do They Work?
    The Definition of a Worldview
    The Elements of a Worldview:
        Confronting God
        Confronting Humanity
        Confronting Nature
Worldviews: The Cultural Mold
    What Is Culture?
    Culture and Worldview
Worldviews: The Biblical Perspective

Worldviews: Making Sense of Life

This is a book about worldviews. If the average person were asked to describe their worldview, their response would be a blank stare. If they asked what the question meant, our response would result in glazed eyes. But this does not make the question any less relevant. Everyone has a worldview, whether they know it or not.

The events of September 11, 2001, the devastation of a tsunami, the assassination of a world leader, the evils of ethnic cleansing—all these tragedies elicit a certain type of response. Ask about one of these realities and most people will have an opinion on not only what happened, but why it happened and what it means. On the other hand, the wonderful things in life—the birth of a child, falling in love, witnessing an act of heroism—also bring about a response. When we are confronted with the great events of life, we tend to become armchair philosophers, wrestling with the deeper reasons and meaning of the events and life itself.

Some believe there is no particular reason. "Things just happen," some say. Scientist Richard Dawkins put it this way:

> In a universe of blind physical forces and genetic replication, some people are going to get hurt, other people are going to get lucky, and you won't find any rhyme or reason in it, nor any justice. The universe we observe has precisely the properties we should expect if there is, at bottom, no design,

3

no purpose, no evil and no good, nothing but blind, pitiless indifference....[1]

Others believe that there is a personal God who is constantly involved in the affairs of people. Helen Young Hayes, a securities analyst from Denver, survived the 1989 crash of United flight 232 in the cornfields near Sioux City, Iowa that killed 111 people. She believed God took her through the crash for her own personal benefit. She claimed, "I think I went through this for a purpose—to show that God can still be seen and felt and glorified in the face of this tragedy."[2]

Still others postulate that events result, sometimes unwittingly it seems, from the "positive or negative psychic energy" that we all express. Feng Shui consultant Marie Diamond says, "The Secret means that we are creators of our Universe, and that every wish that we want to create will manifest in our lives."[3]

A coincidence . . . a personal God . . . cosmic forces? These different interpretations represent more than just isolated opinions. They reflect differing worldviews and different understandings about the basic makeup of the world, how it works, and why things happen the way they do.

A worldview has been compared to a pair of glasses through which we see the world. Without these glasses, the world would appear as an unfocused, meaningless blob of people, places and ideas. Our worldview puts the world in focus and shapes how we make sense out of what we see; and, like glasses, it will either help us or prevent us from seeing the world as it really is.

Everyone has a worldview—whether they realize it or not. It is not only a human prerogative, but a human necessity. Some people embrace a well-defined worldview, chosen carefully after examining the various options, and they can articulate it clearly as their "philosophy of life." Others possess a worldview that is not so systematically arranged—at least not consciously—yet it still serves to give direction and meaning to their lives. Theirs may be more of a "whirled-view" made up of a smorgasbord of contradictory, but personally satisfying and culturally popular, ideas. Either way, our worldview is our way of making sense of the world and our lives.

---

[1] Richard Dawkins, *River Out of Eden: A Darwinian View of Life* (New York: HarperCollins, 1996), p. 113.

[2] Quote taken from *Life*, September 1989, pp. 29-35.

[3] Quoted in Rhonda Byrne, *The Secret* (New York: Atria Books, 2006), p. 113.

Our existence in the world screams for answers. Our minds question our existence and crave to know what this life is all about. The individual knows this is not *his* world and that he did not create himself, yet he has the frightening task of trying to make sense of it all. Where did we come from? What is our purpose? Is there anything after death to look forward to or to fear? How should we live while we are alive? Who are we?[4]

Even the nonreligious recognize that man has a "crying need" to make sense out of his life. Humanist Deane Starr writes, "Humans find their most complete fulfillment, whether real or imaginary, in some sort of intimacy with the ultimate."[5] The inability of many to find some reason for living results in an array of emotional and behavioral aberrations. Anthropologist Paul Hiebert concludes "to lose the faith that there is meaning in life and in the universe is to lose part of what it means to be human."[6] Bruno Bettelheim adds, "Our greatest and most difficult achievement is to find meaning in life. It is well known that many people lose their will to live because such meaning evades them."[7]

All around us, people desperately try to make sense of their lives and put their worlds together. Many, without ever really consciously thinking about it, accept popular views about life because they are fun, glamorous, or easy. Worldview evangelists are everywhere: the New Age actress, the internet religious "expert," the television scientist, the libidinous teenagers in the latest Hollywood youth movie, the conveniently religious politician, and even the characters on Saturday morning TV cartoons.

Amid the din of varied views clamoring for attention, the real issue is often overlooked: Which worldview is the "correct" one? Which view actually represents reality? Which one adequately explains the events in the universe and the experiences of a person's mind and emotions? We must always keep in mind that it does not matter whether or not a particular worldview suits *us*; the question is, Does it suit *the world*?

---

[4] These feelings of insecurity and dependence are what Reinhold Niebuhr calls man's "natural contingency." See Reinhold Niebuhr, *The Nature and Destiny of Man* (New York: Scribners, 1941), vol. 1, *Human Nature*, p. 178.

[5] Deane Starr, "The Crying Need for a Believable Theology," *The Humanist*, July/August 1984, p. 13.

[6] Paul Hiebert, *Cultural Anthropology* (Philadelphia: Lippincott, 1976), pp. 355-56.

[7] Bruno Bettelheim, "Reflections: The Use of Enchantment," *The New Yorker*, 8 December 1975, p. 50. Bettelheim also notes that some people do attempt to live "from moment to moment" without giving any thought to their existence. For such people, finding a "meaning in life" is not important.

Christians believe God has spoken and revealed the essentials of a worldview that is genuine and objectively true. Through His creation (the universe) and His Word (the Bible), God has shown man how to make sense of his world and his life. God explains why He made the world and where He is leading it. In Scripture He unveils the nature and structure of reality, the cause of suffering, the remedy for evil, and the ultimate end of all things.

The purpose of this book is threefold and corresponds to the three parts of the book. The first is to offer an honest, though admittedly Christian, exploration and analysis of the world of worldviews. An understanding of worldviews is absolutely essential if one is to navigate the marketplace of ideas that have shaped history and are at the root of what many have termed the "culture wars."

A second purpose of this book is to describe and defend a distinctly biblical worldview. To gain further insight into the nature of the biblical worldview we will compare and contrast it with competing worldviews. James Orr, who was one of the first to champion the Christian worldview, said:

> He who with his whole heart believes in Jesus as the Son of God is thereby committed to much else besides. He is committed to a view of God, to a view of man, to a view of sin, to a view of redemption, to a view of the purpose of God in creation and history, to a view of human destiny, found only in Christianity.[8]

A third purpose is to take the biblical worldview and apply it to life. If a biblical worldview is true, then what difference does it make in the way we live? How should one view himself, his family, church, job, society, government, and world?

First, we shall lay the groundwork for our discussion by defining and clarifying what we mean by the term "worldview."

---

[8] James Orr, *The Christian View of God and the World* (New York: Scribner, 1897; reprint, Grand Rapids, MI: Kregel, 1989), p. 4.

Worldviews:
What Are They and How Do They Work?

"The goal in life is to survive; you gotta keep out of trouble. You know, party and have a good time, but don't overdo it and hurt somebody."

Most prison inmates I talk with have no problem articulating their worldview—whatever it might be. Harry was no exception. He told me his story of how the world works and what is important in life.

"So you survive," I asked, "What happens then?"

"You die," he replied matter-of-factly.

"And after that?"

"Nothing." He looked insistent. "When you die, you die."

"You mean there's no God or life after death?"

"Nope," he responded. Then he looked away and sighed. "If there is, I'm in big trouble."

The Definition of a Worldview

Harry recognized that the choices he made in his lifestyle reflected his basic views of God and immortality. His rejection of God and life after death were a part of his worldview. Before I left, he had narrated his own story about the existence of the world and man's purpose in life.

We all have a "story," a description of what life is about, why we are here and where we are going. This helps us see where we fit into the world and how to get the most out of life. In one sense, our story is our worldview; and our story is made up of the basic beliefs we have about life and the world.

The concept of worldview has been defined in various ways: philosophically, culturally, theologically. While it is helpful to talk of worldviews in formal terms, Nancy Pearcey correctly reminds us that worldviews "(are) not the same as a formal philosophy; otherwise it would be only for professional philosophers. Even ordinary people have a set of convictions about how reality functions and how they should live."[9] Pearcey highlights here two key aspects of any worldview. First, it is a particular perception of reality. Second, it is the basis for one's decisions.

---

[9] Nancy Pearcey, *Total Truth: Liberating Christianity from Its Cultural Captivity* (Wheaton, IL: Crossway, 2004), p. 23.

It is this two-fold perspective that will serve as the parameters for our working definition of worldview in this book. A worldview is *the framework of our most basic beliefs that shapes our view **of** and **for** the world and is the basis of our decisions and actions*. It is a blueprint, or a map, for reality: first, it helps me to explain and interpret life and the world; and second, it is the starting point from which I apply my view to life through my decisions and actions (see Diagram 1.1: "Worldview Triangle: Why Worldviews Matter"). The beliefs that we are referring to as basic here are the beliefs we hold about life's biggest questions. These beliefs shape our worldview. We call them "basic" since they are fundamental to all of our other beliefs and are the assumptions upon which we build our lives.

Diagram 1.1
The Worldview Triangle:
Why Worldviews Matter

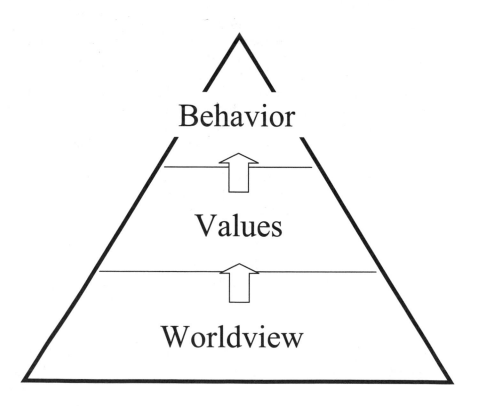

The Elements of a Worldview

Worldviews are never passive; they are by their very nature a confrontation of our presence in the world. Before he became a Christian, Russian novelist Leo Tolstoy listed six questions he had to answer:

> Why am I living?
> What is the cause of my existence and that of everyone else?
> Why do I exist?
> Why is there a division of good and evil within me?
> How must I live?
> What is death—how can I save myself?[10]

These "ultimate questions" of life confront every human being. They include questions about *origins* (Where did everything come from? Is there a God? What is the nature of ultimate reality?); *meaning* (Why is there something rather than nothing? What is the meaning of life? What is our purpose?); *morality* (Is there a right and wrong? Why does it seem that the world is not as it should be?); *destiny* (What happens after we die? Where is history going?); and *identity* (What is a human being? Who am I? Why am I here? How do I fit?)

The answers we embrace to these ultimate questions, whether consciously or subconsciously, shape our assumptions about the three major concepts of human existence: (1) *God*, or the concept of ultimate reality; (2) *humanity*, or the reality of human existence and self-consciousness (my own as well as that of other persons); and (3) *nature*, or the existence and purpose of the world around me, both physical and spiritual. These upward, inward, and outward assumptions form the framework for my worldview.[11]

---

[10] Stephen Zweig, *The Living Thoughts of Tolstoy* (Philadelphia: David McKay, 1939), p. 4.

[11] These three aspects of man's existence became the focal point of many nineteenth- and twentieth-century theological inquiries. Schleiermacher's theological system utilized man, nature, and God as a framework; see Friedrich Schleiermacher, *The Christian Faith*, ed. H. R. Mackintosh and J. S. Stewart (Edinburgh: T. & T. Clark, 1928). See also William Temple's *Nature, Man and God* (London: Macmillan, 1934).

Confronting God

One's view of God is the starting point for all worldviews. Mortimer Adler, in the Great Books series, comments, "More consequences for thought and action follow the affirmation or denial of God than from answering any other basic question."[12] When *confronting God*, I come face to face with that which is of ultimate concern. An atheist may merely shrug off the existence of God, or he may face it with more sincerity than many Christians. In whatever way he arrives at his atheism, he still must confront "God." It is not optional.

If I deny the existence of God, I still must explain certain qualities of man and the world that have been traditionally answered by appealing to God. Why does humanity even have the idea of God if no such being exists? How did the universe come into existence? How do we account for the apparent design and purpose within nature? Why is there a sense of right and wrong in the heart of man, across cultures and histories?

Denying the existence of God usually results in a worldview that focuses on the more immediate concerns of humanity rather than on "ultimate" questions. A "God-less" philosophy of life generally emphasizes the "here and now" because there is no "out there and later." We shall explore the implications of a worldview without God in chapter two.

If I take the step to acknowledge the existence of God, I am forced to answer several questions about Him. Is He a personal being or an impersonal force? Is He actively involved in human events? Is He a moral God who will judge His creation? Is He a "he"? Can He communicate with man? Does He desire to communicate with man?

If I believe that God is the Creator of all things, I move myself from the center of my universe and see God as the most important being. I ask Him the crucial questions, "Why did you make me?" and, "What do you expect from me?" If He is the final judge, then I desperately need to know by what criteria He will judge me and what I must do to avoid His displeasure. A belief about God is really a belief about everything else.

Confronting Humanity

"Man," wrote Reinhold Niebuhr, "has always been his own most vexing problem. How shall he think of himself?"[13] In confronting humanity I am laying the foundation for my worldview. Why? Because

---

[12] Mortimer J. Adler, *Great Books of the Western World*, ed. Robert M. Hutchins (Chicago: Encyclopedia Britannica, 1952), 2:561.

[13] Niebuhr, *Human Nature*, p. 1.

whatever I decide about humanity's place in the world affects me; it is my worldview. I am setting the agenda for my life.

I am me. How did I get to be "me"? Further, I see other people who all have this same concept of personal identity. They are like me, but they are not "me." What is my responsibility to them? What is their responsibility to me? Confronting ourselves is a difficult and unnerving task. We are both the subject and the object of the investigation.

Whatever I decide about my purpose and future will set the values I place on my family, my work, and all my relationships. If I conclude that life has no purpose, then I will live accordingly. If I reason that human existence has some meaning, then I will conform my life to that purpose (or at least I *should*).

The question "What is a human being?" is a key question any civilization must address, and history is full of examples of the devastation that results from answering this question in a way that elevates some races and people groups, and denigrates the rest. This will be discussed in chapter eight.

Confronting Nature

A final aspect in the development of one's worldview is the *confrontation with nature*; or, as Redfield puts it, "man" confronting "not-man."[14] To possess a *world*view, I must have an explanation that includes all the elements of the universe—one that first describes the origin of the world and explains its apparent design.

How am I related to the physical universe? At times I am the master of nature; at other times I am its slave. Is the natural world friendly, hostile, or indifferent to man?

In times past, the confrontation with nature was often the major influence in man's comprehending his place in the world. His understanding and response to nature set the agenda for the life and practice of his culture. Some of the earliest worldviews saw man and nature as partners in the universe. There was a personal relationship with the world that emphasized a need on the part of man to be in harmony with his environment. For example, to the early Egyptians, two central events in nature helped to shape their worldview: the triumphant daily

---

[14] Robert Redfield, *The Primitive World and Its Transformations* (Ithaca, NY: Cornell U., 1953), p. 92. It is important to note that Redfield included beliefs about God and spirit beings in his category of "not-man." However, this confrontation with "not-man" is first of all a confrontation of that which makes up the physical universe. It is in this sense that we refer to his term.

rebirth of the sun and the triumphant annual rebirth of the Nile River.[15] Their confrontation with nature led them to assume a regularity in the universe. Nature was a friendly and benevolent partner in the cycles of life. For this reason, the people of Egypt considered themselves to be the special object of care by the gods of nature. The word *human*, in fact, was used by the Egyptians only to refer to themselves.

The ancient Mesopotamians, on the other hand, did not have the benefit of the Nile River or the somewhat predictable seasonal changes of Egypt; rather, they were overwhelmed by the power within natural events. The cosmos seemed capricious, often antagonistic. To the Mesopotamians, nature was a hostile, degrading feature of life. This may have led to their strong emphasis on submission and authority within society as a whole.[16]

The confrontation with nature by these ancient societies resulted in a different understanding of man's place in the world. It is no wonder then that the Egyptians built to themselves impressive monuments that still stand today. The monuments of the Mesopotamian civilizations, in the words of the prophets, "have become heaps."

Unlike ancient cultures (and many non-Western cultures today), Western societies do not generally confront nature with the same sense of respect. For us, the physical realm of "not-man" is indifferent to man. Nature is lifeless and spiritless, operating according to predetermined forces. It exists for man to harness for his own purposes. There are no gods to appease, no magic formulae to recite. Science and technology probe the cosmic machine for clues to increasing the well-being of humanity. We do not conform to the universe, rather we seek to conform the universe to us or our needs.

In spite of this indifference, there is another dimension in the confrontation with the created world. Is there a realm of reality that cannot be seen with physical eyes? Are there nonhuman personal beings who populate the universe? The belief in spirit beings permeates the worldviews of ancient civilizations. In their view of the universe, Persian, Greek, Jewish, Egyptian, Asian, and Roman cultures included demigods, angels, demons, and other beings.

Various mythologies ascribed certain powers to unseen personalities. Some were godlike beings and traveled between earth and the heavens, manipulating humans and circumstances for their own purposes. Other mythologies considered the unseen world populated with

---

[15] John A. Wilson, "Egypt," in *The Intellectual Adventure of Ancient Man*, ed. H. and H. A. Frankfort et al (Chicago: U. of Chicago, 1946), p. 36.

[16] Thorkild Jacobsen, "Mesopotamia," ibid., p. 202.

less powerful beings of questionable character, or the spirits of the dead that remained to "haunt" the living.

The modern mind, which drinks heavily at the well of naturalism, has no room for the existence of spirits. Metaphysical "objects" cannot exist in a materialistic scheme. Belief in angels, demons, and spirit beings is considered a remnant of archaic and superstitious thinking.

But the possible existence of a spirit world cannot be so easily dismissed. In spite of the great and numerous strides made by science and technology over the past two centuries, the scientific enterprise has not eradicated belief in another realm beyond the physical. In fact, interest in "the spiritual world" is on the rise. To admit to the possibility that unseen entities may exist opens a flood of possibilities in the worldview arena.

My response to the confrontation of God, humanity, and nature gives much of the basic shape of my worldview. How many of us consciously examine our lives at this basic level to arrive at our worldview? The fact that we all see life through the lens of our worldview has significant implications. We ought to be intentional about our worldview. The question is not "Do I have a worldview?"; but "Which worldview do I have, and is it the one I ought to have?"

Worldviews: The Cultural Mold

While worldviews are personal perspectives, they are rarely isolated perspectives. In fact, Charles Kraft defines worldview in a corporate sense, as "the central systematization of conceptions of reality *to which the members of the culture assent (largely unconsciously)* and from which stems their value system."[17] One of his points is that worldviews are often shared perspectives of life that become part of the culture. A particular worldview thus pervades a culture and is passed on to succeeding generations as a "social inheritance."[18] In other words, I may have my particular worldview primarily because it was the prevailing one of the environment in which I was raised.

---

[17] Charles H. Kraft, *Christianity in Culture*, (Maryknoll, NY: Orbis, 1979), p. 53.

[18] Linton refers to culture as man's "social heredity." (See Ralph Linton, *The Study of Man: An Introduction* [New York: Appleton-Century, 1936], p. 76.)

What Is Culture?

When we say a person has "culture," we usually have in mind a refined individual who enjoys the "finer things in life. " But in the broadest sense of the term, everyone has culture—at least *a* culture, because it is essentially the social environment in which one is raised.

A group of people within a particular locality will generally adopt certain behavior patterns that become normative for the group. These accepted forms of conduct are passed on by teaching and modeling. For this reason, culture is often described as our "social and intellectual heritage."[19] One's culture, then, is "the integrated system of learned behavior patterns which are characteristic of the members of a society and which are not the result of biological inheritance."[20]

Suppose a friend walked up to you, smiled broadly, and then spit on your chest. As an American, you might not be pleased with such a greeting since men generally shake hands when they meet. But if you lived among the Siriano of South America, you would smile and spit back, the normal manner of greeting. In Mexico, they embrace; whereas in parts of Europe, they kiss one another on the cheek. None of these behaviors is "right" or "wrong." They are merely the culturally accepted (and expected) modes of conduct within a particular group.

Our culture takes a visible form in everything from the institutions of society (government, schools, churches, etc.) to eating and sleeping patterns (midnight meals, siestas, etc.). Economic, social, and religious institutions reflect what the group considers important. This is also seen in what the group chooses to commemorate through rituals: weddings, funerals, graduations, and other rites of passage. When and how these rituals are carried out (including religious worship) become a matter of cultural agreement.

Culture and Worldview

How is a worldview related to culture? The visible aspects of a culture are to some extent a reflection of an underlying ideology or worldview, which gives the reasons for the customs. Kraft notes, "Thus, in its explanatory, evaluational, reinforcing and integrating functions, worldview lies at the heart of a culture."[21] *Culture* suggests the way a

---

[19] James F. Downs and Herman K. Bleibtreu, "The Evolution of Our Capacity for Culture," in *Cultural and Social Anthropology*, ed. Peter B. Hammond, 2d ed. (New York: Macmillan, 1975), p. 4.

[20] E. Adamson Hoebel, *Anthropology: The Study of Man*, 4th ed. (New York: McGraw-Hill, 1972), p. 6.

[21] Kraft, *Christianity in Culture*, p. 56.

group of people may appear to an anthropologist; *worldview* suggests how the universe looks to the group.

A worldview, as the heart of the culture, is passed from generation to generation. For example, we see a pantheistic view of God dominant in the Eastern world, whereas a theistic view prevails in the West. These views are certainly not genetic; an Asian child can be reared in Western society (or an American child in the East) and will adopt the cultural views of his social environment. In other words, the earliest worldview I accepted was the prevailing view of the culture in which I was raised—it was an "accident of birth." In the same way that culture gives us the impression that our way of doing things is the "right way to behave," the worldview of our society instills within us an overwhelming sense that our outlook is the "right way to believe."[22]

From the beginning of human history man has confronted the issues of God, humanity, and nature and constructed worldviews that attempt to interpret life. Worldviews have been adapted, modified, embedded, and enshrined in various cultures. Now, in the information age, a smorgasbord of worldviews confronts us as we explore our global village. How are we to sift through all these views and determine which (if any) reflects true reality?

Worldviews: The Biblical Perspective

Father Brown, the clergy-sleuth of G. K. Chesterton novels, often solved crimes by putting together the evidence in a creative manner that baffled the experts. Sometimes, investigators would view the scene of a crime and make elaborate guesses as to how the crime was committed. Father Brown would usually sigh and remark, "There are many explanations that may fit the evidence. What we want to know is, which one is right?"

In the same way, many different worldviews seem to fit the evidence found in our world. Atheistic naturalism seems to fit the view of the world as we investigate it by the scientific method. On the other hand, a pantheistic view of the world seems to explain the spiritual realities that

---

[22] This of course does not mean that a person's worldview cannot change. Through the process of growth and adaptation, one's worldview does modify slightly. Drastic changes often occur when one is confronted with a worldview that is radically different from his own. At such a time, a decisive choice may be presented either to affirm one's own worldview or to embrace the new. This is what happens in evangelism, for example, especially in cross-cultural missions.

are common to our experience. More and more new worldviews clamor for attention. With all these competing claims, what we, like Father Brown, want to know is, Which one is right?

Man's attempts to explain his existence are just that: *man's attempts*. Within the world, man's experience and perceptions of the infinite universe are limited and inadequate. We need help from the "outside." This is what a biblical worldview claims to be: help from the outside. It acknowledges that God, the Creator and controller of all things, has given light in the confused darkness. He has not given us all the answers, but He has supplied us with information sufficient for our need.

As we mentioned earlier, a worldview can function as a pair of glasses through which we observe and understand our world. Everything we perceive must come through these glasses. If such glasses have "Christian" lenses, then everything we observe will be "tinted" Christian. We will explain the universe and life's events from a Christian perspective. We will not understand why others do not see the world as we do—it is so obvious to us.

The same is true for those who wear atheist glasses or Buddhist glasses. They will "see" the same world, but it will be understood differently. Their "glasses" (worldview) do not shape reality nor do they ensure a correct perception, but they do determine a person's *explanation and interpretation* of life and the world.

A biblical worldview is thus a perspective that sees everything through the "glasses" of Scripture. Rather than allowing culture or experience to determine a worldview, it allows the Bible to make that determination.

Claiming that the Bible gives a perspective of reality that is uniquely true sounds narrow-minded and obscurantist. Immediately challenges to such a position arise.

> Is not the Bible just one of many cultural attempts at piecing together a worldview? After all, the biblical writers were merely reflecting their own cultural worldview, were they not?

> What allows the Bible to dictate the answers to my life? Do I not have a say? It presents such a mental straight-jacket; I am not free to sort things out for myself.

> How can an ancient book speak to our situation today? The Bible does not address our modern technological society. Times are changing; the Bible does not.

We will not sidestep these (and many other) difficult challenges to a biblical worldview. Essentially, these challenges concern the nature of the Bible. Does it have the authority to dictate the correct worldview? Are we being foolish in allowing it to do so? We will take up these challenges in chapter four.

However, before a person dismisses a biblical worldview, he should be honest enough to consider the Bible's claims and its comprehensive view of reality. The question is: Does a biblical worldview fit the actual world? If it does not, then it may be discarded onto the heap of misguided philosophies. If it does, then a careful search into its implications and consequences is the only reasonable response.

Where does a biblical worldview start? Two basic truths are at its heart: (1) God exists; (2) God has uniquely revealed His character and will in the Bible.

Both of these statements are more complex than they first appear. We hope to demonstrate that they can be accepted with genuine intellectual integrity. If both statements *are* true (in the sense that we will define them), then we are driven to the conclusion that the Bible holds the answers to man's basic questions and longings about life. We will allow the Bible to give us a view *of* the world by detailing the answers to the ultimate questions of life. Then we will discuss how we should allow the Bible to determine both our view *for* the world and how we ought to live *in* the world.

Obviously, not everyone agrees that the Bible should be man's guide to truth. Many worldviews claim the right to be called "the way." What are these worldviews? How does a biblical worldview compare with them? In the next chapter, we will explore the world of world-views.

DISCUSSION QUESTIONS

1. Why do people search for meaning in their lives? In what ways is this universal search evident?
2. Discuss Mortimer Adler's statement: "More consequences for thought and action follow the affirmation or denial of God than from answering any other basic question."
3. Turn to Tolstoy's ultimate questions on page 23. Give as many plausible answers as you can for each question.
4. Why do you think Western society has taken an "indifferent" perspective of nature? Validate your response by giving examples in the media, industry, technology, education, and so forth.
5. Describe your worldview. Discuss the origin of that view and how it has changed since you were a child.

FURTHER READING

Colson, Charles and Nancey Pearcey. *How Now Shall We Live?* Wheaton, IL: Tyndale, 1999.

Halverson, William H. *A Concise Introduction to Philosophy.* 4th ed. New York: Random House, 1981. See especially Part XIII, "World Views," pp. 411-42.

Kraft, Charles H. *Christianity in Culture.* Maryknoll, NY: Orbis, 1979.

Naugle, David K. *Worldview: the History of a Concept.* Grand Rapids, MI: Eerdmans, 2002.

Orr, James. *The Christian View of God and the World.* 7th ed. New York: Scribner's, 1904.

Pearcey, Nancy. *Total Truth: Liberating Christianity from Its Cultural Captivity.* Wheaton, IL: Crossway, 2004.

Redfield, Robert. *The Primitive World and Its Transformations.* Ithaca, NY: Cornell U., 1953.

Sire, James W. *Naming the Elephant: Worldview as a Concept.* Downers Grove, IL: InterVarsity, 2004.

2
THE WORLD OF WORLDVIEWS

Getting a Handle on Worldviews
    Thinking "Worldviewishly"
    Organizing the Worldviews
Exploring the Worldviews
    Naturalism: The World as We See It
        Confronting God
        Confronting Humanity
        Confronting Nature
        Expressions of Naturalism
    Transcendentalism: The World as We Want It
        Confronting God
        Confronting Humanity
        Confronting Nature
        Expressions of Transcendentalism
    Theism: The World from God's Hands
        Confronting God
        Confronting Humanity
        Confronting Nature
        Expressions of Theism
    Postmodernism: The World as We Experience It
        Historical Perspective: How We Lost Our Minds
        Confronting Reality: How the Rules Changed
        Confronting Humanity: The Death of Self
Where Do We Go from Here?

Getting a Handle on Worldviews

Thinking Worldviewishly

There is crisis in worldview thinking. On the personal level there is great *neglect*. The average person forges ahead in life giving little thought to worldviews, philosophies of life, or any other such "intellectual" endeavors. The compartmentalization of life and thought have resulted in the fragmentation of everything from education to entertainment.

Those who do not consciously evaluate their worldview beliefs end up "catching" their worldview the same way they might "catch" a cold—they absorb it from the culture around them. While a worldview like this may not be thought out at all, it remains and functions as a worldview nonetheless.

Unfortunately, it is a life lived backwards. Rather than wrestling with the big questions of life and allowing these beliefs to shape values and behavior, this is a life that merely absorbs values and behaviors that are considered culturally normal and allowing them to shape ultimate beliefs (see Diagram 2.1: Living Backwards). A worldview of this sort is quite *volatile*, susceptible to great inconsistency. It is also *vulnerable*, subject to deep confusion in the face of the dissonance caused by life's deepest existential experiences (e.g. pain, suffering, abandonment, the fear of death, and death itself).

Diagram 2.1
Living Backwards:
The Worldview Triangle Reversed

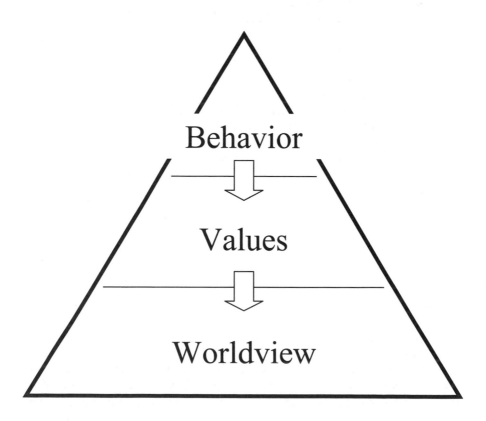

On the public level, there is a growing illusion that worldviews and religions should be considered equally valid for whoever holds them. In this postmodern view, worldviews are nothing more than communal beliefs that we inherit; we are ourselves victims of worldviews and therefore unable to evaluate them or to understand those that others hold. It matters little whether a worldview is *true*, as long as it *true for someone somewhere*. (The authors believe that postmodernism may be accused at times of intellectual cowardice, and at other times of intellectual bullying).

The invitation of this book is to call all people, especially Christians, to think deeply about their worldview and to live consistently by its tenets. As we do this, the important issues will become clearer and the challenges better defined.

Organizing the Worldviews

In chapter one we described a worldview as *a framework of basic beliefs that forms a view of and a view for the world.* There are several ways worldviews could be organized.

Worldviews could be sorted into geographical families, such as a Western worldview, an Eastern worldview, an African worldview, and so on. Worldviews may also be arranged by ethnic group, as is usually the case with anthropological studies. Such a grouping would yield a Cherokee or a Hopi worldview, a Hispanic or a Slavic worldview, etc. Worldviews have also been classified in broad historical terms, which tends to highlight the changes in the prevalent cultural moods throughout the history of western civilization. Typically, this approach distinguishes the pre-modern worldview from the modern and postmodern worldviews.

Books discussing current worldviews catalog a number of diverse views and explain their beliefs. For example, in James Sire's *The Universe Next Door: A Basic World View Catalog,* he lists and discusses eight major worldviews, but admits that there are other views that could have been included also.[1] David Noebel has expanded his list of influential worldviews from four to six in the latest edition of his

---

[1]   James W. Sire, *The Universe Next Door: A Basic World View Catalog*, 4th ed. (Downers Grove, IL: InterVarsity, 2004). Sire discusses Christian theism, deism, naturalism, nihilism, existentialism, Eastern pantheistic monism, the New Age, and postmodernism.

Understanding the Times.[2] Geisler and Watkins in their *Worlds Apart: A Handbook on World Views,* also discuss seven worldviews but group them into three categories, according to the view of God.

While each approach is helpful, a more comprehensive arrangement of worldviews is necessary for our purposes. The crucial feature of any worldview is what it says about ultimate reality; that is, how does it answer the ultimate questions of origin, meaning, morality, destiny and identity?

Using ultimate reality as our starting point, we may divide most worldviews into three major groups: naturalism, transcendentalism, and theism. Briefly stated, *naturalism* includes those worldviews that suggest ultimate reality is limited to the physical matter of the universe; *transcendentalism* includes those that see ultimate reality as being only spiritual or psychic (mental energy); and *theism* refers to those worldviews that posit a personal God as ultimate reality who created the material and spiritual universe.[3] Similar threefold perspectives of worldviews have been given by C. S. Lewis,[4] William Halverson,[5] and Arthur Holmes.[6]

Another "worldview" that will be discussed in this chapter does not fit so easily into one of these three categories. There are two reasons for dealing with *postmodernism* separately. First, postmodernism differs from naturalism, transcendentalism and theism by suggesting that it is impossible to have the sort of knowledge about ultimate reality claimed by the worldviews. Second, the recent emergence of postmodernism is striking, and the current influence it holds over western culture demands that we give it due attention as an influential worldview.

---

[2] David A. Noebel, *Understanding the Times: The Collision of Today's Competing Worldviews.* 2d ed. (Eugene, OR: Harvest House Publishers), 2005.

[3] These are working definitions to explain how we are using the terms.

[4] C. S. Lewis, *Mere Christianity*, reprint ed. (Westwood, NJ: Barbour and Co., 1952), pp. 18-23. Lewis called the three worldviews the materialist view, the life-force view, and the religious view.

[5] William Halverson, *A Concise Introduction to Philosophy*, 4th ed. (New York: Random House, 1981), pp. 411-41. Halverson's views are: *ethical theism, naturalism,* and *transcendentalism.* He also includes *humanism,* which he claims is not a worldview but "a group of insights that must be incorporated into any world view if that world view is to be regarded as adequate" (p. 436)

[6] Arthur Holmes, ed., *The Making of a Christian Mind* (Downers Grove, IL: InterVarsity, 1985), p. 12.

While these are not the *only* worldviews, most of the major ones can be placed into one of these categories. Below is a chart showing several major worldviews grouped into these categories. The perceptive reader should be able to see where other views not listed in the chart would fit as well.

Diagram 2.2
Classifying the Major Worldviews

Ideas	Expressions	Ideas	Expressions	Ideas	Expressions	Ideas	Expressions
Materialism	Secular Humanism	Pantheism	Buddhism	Deism	Islam	Pragmatism	Dada (art)
Positivism	Marxism/Leninism	Panentheism	Hinduism	Traditional	Judaism	Anti-realism	Deconstruction
Secularism	Existentialism	Polytheism	Taoism	Theism	Biblical	Perspectivalism	
Scientism	Nihilism	Animism	Scientology		Christianity	Anti-essentialism	
Atheism	Hedonism	Panpsychism	Wicca				
Agnosticism		New Age					

A biblical worldview falls under the chart's category of theism. In part two of this book, we shall explore the essentials of a biblical worldview and address common challenges to it. First, we must set the stage by exploring and evaluating the major worldview alternatives: naturalism, transcendentalism, theism, and postmodernism.

Exploring the Worldviews

Naturalism: The World as We See It

"When I became convinced that the universe is natural—that all the ghosts and gods are myths, there entered into my brain, into my soul, into every drop of my blood, the sense, the feeling, the joy of freedom. . . . There was for me no master in all the world—not even in infinite space. I was free . . . free from all ignorant and cruel creeds, all the 'inspired' books that savages have produced, and all the barbarous legends of the past . . . I stood erect and fearlessly, joyously, faced all worlds."[7] Such was the manifesto of Robert Green Ingersoll (1833-1899), one of the leading statesmen and orators of the nineteenth century. His bold proclamation of freedom arises from his worldview, which we define as a popularist expression of naturalism.

Naturalism[8] projects the view that ultimate reality is material. The physical universe is all there is. There is nothing beyond or separate from that which we can see, touch, and measure. Matter and energy are the basic "stuff" from which all existence is derived. Such a view of reality implies that all obtainable answers for the questions relating to the universe and mankind can be found by the investigation of physical phenomena. Most naturalists would not deny the real existence of such things as thoughts, plans, language, and so on, but would claim that these things are explainable as a form or function of some material entity.

In order to more fully understand the implications of naturalism as a total philosophy of the world and life, we shall now examine the major tenets from the perspective of its confrontation with God, the self, and nature.

Confronting God

THE GOD WHO IS NOT THERE. A university biology professor traditionally began his semester with the quip, "Christians say, 'In the beginning, God'; I say, 'In the beginning, hydrogen.'" His remark was more than a joke. It revealed the starting point of his worldview: the cosmos. In naturalism, the supernatural God is replaced by natural elements.

---

[7] Quoted by Philip Mass, "Robert Green Ingersoll," in *The Humanist* (November/December 1988):29.

[8] We are using *naturalism* to denote the philosophy that denies real existence beyond the physical world. This definition also includes the views commonly called *materialism* and *physicalism*.

Ernest Nagel, in his essay "Naturalism Reconsidered," defends a materialistic view of reality. In naturalism, he states, "there is no place for the operation of disembodied forces, no place for an immaterial spirit directing the course of events, no place for the survival of personality after the corruption of the body which exhibits it."[9] If there are no spiritual realities, then it is impossible for God to exist.

However, one may challenge the naturalistic assertion that the existence of God is impossible. If God does not exist, then from where does the idea of God originate? Why is it that belief in God is almost a universal characteristic of man?

Most naturalists respond by asserting that man created God in his own image to satisfy his dreams and hopes for purpose in life and immortality. Humanist Paul Kurtz claims "the theist's world is only a dream world; it is a feeble escape into a future that will never come."[10] Sigmund Freud described belief in God as "the fulfillment of the oldest, strongest, and most urgent wishes of mankind."[11] Bertrand Russell disparaged Christians as "timid seekers after the childish comforts of a less adult age."[12]

For the naturalist, reality is understood only by the careful use of the scientific method, not wishful thinking. This perspective borders on scientism, which is "the belief that all truth is scientific truth and that the sciences give us our best shot at knowing 'how things really are.'"[13]

Such a scientific view of the world seems strange when we remember that so many of the earliest scientists were strong Christians. But we can gain an insight into this scientism by analyzing the development of naturalism.

THE GROWTH OF NATURALISM. Naturalism, as a full-blown atheistic worldview, is a relatively new perspective. The modern roots of naturalism are found in the scientific revolution of the eighteenth century. James Turner points out that atheists were practically unheard of before 1800. Even the skeptic David Hume once noted that he never laid

---

[9] Ernest Nagel, "Naturalism Reconsidered," in *Essays in Philosophy*, ed. Houston Peterson (New York: Washington Square, 1959), p. 487.

[10] Paul Kurtz, *Forbidden Fruit: The Ethics of Humanism* (Buffalo, NY: Prometheus, 1988), p. 243.

[11] Sigmund Freud, *The Future of an Illusion* (London: Hogarth, 1961), p. 30.

[12] Bertrand Russell, *The Scientific Outlook* (London: Unwin, 1931), p. 30.

[13] C. Stephen Evans, *Preserving the Person: A Look at the Human Sciences* (Downers Grove, IL: InterVarsity, 1977), p. 18.

eyes on an atheist.[14] The scientific enterprise continued to view God as part of the universal scheme of things for two reasons.

The first was the "God-habit," that is, the fact that humanity had persistently held to a belief in God. Such an ingrained tradition was hard to extract from any area of thinking, in public or private life. Atheist Max Otto admitted, "For those who have reasoned themselves into a naturalistic position, there still remains a substratum of allegiance to the supernatural."[15]

The second reason science held so tenaciously to a belief in God was the conclusion that the orderly Newtonian universe served as a constant proof for an orderly God. All truth was God's truth, and the starry heavens above blinked down God's favor. As late as the nineteenth century, most scientists gave the purpose of scientific investigation, in the words of John Herschel, "to shore up religious belief."[16]

However, such a perspective began to change. The Marquis de Laplace spent the better part of thirty years investigating the effect of gravitational force in the world. The result of his labors was a five-volume work entitled *Celestial Mechanics*, published in 1827. When he presented an early volume to Napoleon, he was surprised the monarch studied it so carefully. Calling for Laplace, Napoleon remarked, "You have written a large work on the universe without once mentioning its author." Laplace replied, "I have no need for that hypothesis."[17] A practical atheism slowly began to be a part of a scientific worldview that no longer found the "God-hypothesis" necessary.

One question lingered: atheistic scientists in the nineteenth century had no genuine explanation for the design of the universe. In 1859, Charles Darwin gave skeptical thinkers the mechanism they had been looking for. The design of the universe was not the handiwork of an intelligent and purposeful God, but the result of natural selection, the "blind, unconscious, automatic process which Darwin discovered, and which we now know is the explanation for the existence and apparently

---

[14] James Turner, *Without God, Without Creed: The Origins of Unbelief in America* (Baltimore: Johns Hopkins, 1985), p. 44.

[15] Max Otto, "A Humanist Questioned by Youth," *The Humanist* (Spring 1941; reprinted May/June 1988):27.

[16] John F. W. Herschel, *A Preliminary Discourse on the Study of Natural Philosophy* (London, 1830; reprint edition, Chicago: U. of Chicago, 1987), p. 7.

[17] Eric Temple Bell, *Men of Mathematics* (New York: Simon and Schuster, 1937), p. 181.

purposeful form of all life."[18] Now the order of the universe could be described as the result of mechanical laws. Darwin did not prove God's nonexistence; he merely left God out of the picture.

A new sense of urgency and excitement about the natural world developed. Science was taking a turn and began to uncover the "secrets" of the universe. Metaphysical questions paled in the brilliant light of scientific discovery. However, for several years after the 1859 publication of Darwin's *The Origin of Species* the term *atheist* was still negative and unpopular. It took Thomas Huxley in 1869 to articulate a new viewpoint that freed naturalistic thinking from the impediments of the "God-question." Huxley coined the term *agnosticism* to describe a tentative, uncertain attitude toward any question about God and the meaning of life.

Huxley stated, "Agnosticism is not properly described as a 'negative' creed, not indeed as a creed of any kind, except in so far as it expresses absolute faith in the validity of a principle. . . . This principle may be stated in various ways, but they all amount to this: that it is wrong for a man to say that he is certain of the objective truth of any proposition unless he can produce evidence which logically justifies that certainty."[19] Agnosticism revitalized science and philosophy with a spirit of adventure and freedom. "Truth" became synonymous with "scientific fact," and the great sin became holding to certainty in metaphysical questions.

Whether atheistic or agnostic, naturalism sets forth a worldview in which God is unnecessary. Although most naturalists consider themselves agnostic about questions of ultimate concern, such questions actually do not matter in their worldview. The naturalist's approach to God is no approach to God. The implications of this attitude are seen in the naturalist's confrontation with the self.

Confronting Humanity

Life from the dust. For the naturalist, man originated from the dust of the earth . . . without the breath of God. Humanity is solely a part of the mechanistic universe. Even the most abstract facets of man's behavior are reduced to component natural processes. For example,

---

[18] Richard Dawkins, *The Blind Watchmaker: Why the Evidence of Evolution Reveals a Universe Without Design* (New York: W. W. Norton, 1986), p. 5.

[19] Thomas H. Huxley, *Science and Christian Tradition* (London: Macmillan, 1894), p. 310.

Herbert Spencer concluded that the human mind was the end product of the evolution of the nervous system.[20] Thoughts and personality were described as electrical impulses in the brain. Birth is the absolute beginning and death is the absolute end. Man is merely a machine that works for a while and then eventually runs down and quits.

Christians believe that man's ethical nature is the result of God's moral standards impressed into his soul. The naturalist responds by claiming that morality is the result of social convention. The sense of right and wrong within each person does not indicate the existence of moral absolutes but rather reflects conditioning of acceptable behavior by authority figures. Like a dog whose behavior is shaped by his master, human behavior is shaped to society's norms by reward and punishment.

The ethical system of naturalism is utilitarian for either individual-istic or societal ends. For example, in his book *Ethics Without God*, Kai Nelson concludes that the individual is the center of moral decision, "happiness, self-consciousness and self-identity are essential to give significance to human living."[21] Whatever promotes happiness, self-consciousness and self-identity in my life and in the lives of others is "good"; whatever hinders them is "bad."

The result, of course, is ethical relativism, the belief that morality depends upon the individual or situation. This is reflected in the response by Dr. Tal Biron-Shental, a lead researcher in harvesting eggs from aborted fetuses and fertilizing them with sperm to create embryos in the laboratory. When asked about the moral justification for creating embryos from children who themselves were not allowed to live, he replied: "I'm fully aware of the controversy about this—but probably, in some place, it will be ethically acceptable."[22]

LIFE WITHOUT MEANING. Naturalists, because of their view of ultimate reality, see no overarching meaning for the universe or humanity. Human destiny, according to Nagel, is "an episode between two oblivions."[23] Natural history and human history are the same thing. By a series of random and chance events, humanity has evolved and possesses the capability to reflect on the past and project his thoughts to

---

[20] Herbert Spencer, *Principles of Psychology*, 3d ed. (New York: D. Appleton, 1898), 3 vols., 1:145ff. Spencer described mental processes as a series of "nervous shocks."

[21] Kai Nelson, *Ethics Without God* (London: Pemberton Books, 1973), p. 65.

[22] Quoted in Eric Cohen, "Orphans by Design," *First Things* 158 (December 2005), p. 14.

[23] Nagel, "Naturalism," in *Essays in Philosophy*, p. 496.

the future. These abilities give man the illusion of uniqueness and superiority.

At the personal level, the consequences of existence without God are disturbing. Naturalists do not consider their view one of despair, yet they admit there is no consolation for the injustice in life or hope beyond the grave.

Confronting Nature

As its name implies, naturalism defines every existence and every event by natural causes. Nothing is "super"natural. Therefore it is up to mankind to understand how nature works so that he will be able to harness its power for the improvement of human life.

This view of nature, however, does not absolve the naturalist from grappling with the two basic questions concerning the physical universe: From where did the universe come? (the question of origins); and, Why is the universe organized as it is? (the question of design).

The naturalist will answer the question of design, as discussed above, by appealing to natural selection. The laws of nature have caused the resulting appearance of design and purpose within the universe. Whatever design is present is the result of completely natural processes, many of which we do not presently understand.

But the nagging question, "From where does the universe originate?" causes the naturalist to search for credible answers. Something cannot come from nothing, and the evidence seems to indicate that the universe had a definite beginning. Christians appeal to this evidence as proof that the universe was set in motion by God, a claim the naturalist must reject. How, then, does he respond to the question of origins?

One response by certain writers is to attempt to prove that something can come from nothing. For example, Paul Davies applies the theories of subatomic physics to the universe (an application known as quantum cosmology) to conclude that creation can be explained as a completely natural, impersonal process. He concludes, "It is no longer entirely absurd to imagine that the universe came into existence spontaneously from nothing as a result of a quantum process."[24] Davies sees the universe as self-creative and self-organizing.

From another perspective, elaborate theories have been generated to explain the existence of the universe without the need of a creator. Cambridge University physicist Stephen Hawking believes the universe

---

[24] Paul Davies, *The Cosmic Blueprint* (New York: Simon and Schuster, 1988), p. 5.

is not infinite and eternal but rather finite and temporal with no boundary and no beginning. He concludes, "If the universe is really completely self-contained, having no boundary or edge, it would have neither beginning nor end; it would simply be. What place then, for a creator?"[25]

Naturalistic explanations for the origin and design of the universe do not account for the origin of life in the universe. But, in naturalism, the cosmos is the beginning and end of all questions; matter is all that matters. Hopes and beliefs that go beyond the physical realm are illusory. The best man can do is live his life to the fullest and not concern himself with questions for which there are no answers.

Expressions of Naturalism

Some naturalists believe their worldview ultimately makes life absurd. Such an approach is called *nihilism*, from the Latin word *nihil*, which means "nothing." Because life is meaningless, man's existence and quest for purpose amount to nothing. Novelist Albert Camus summed up a nihilist point of view when he wrote, "There is but one truly serious philosophical problem, and that is suicide."[26]

By its very nature, naturalism excludes the quest for meaning in life. For example, Sigmund Freud admitted that his naturalistic worldview would not allow him to accept any purpose for his existence. Such ultimate concerns, he claimed, could be raised only by religion.[27] But this does not stop naturalists from asserting that life can be lived with some purpose. Atheist John Mackie bravely concludes that man gets all the purpose he needs from within himself.[28]

---

[25] Stephen W. Hawking, *A Brief History of Time* (New York: Bantam, 1988), p. 141.

[26] Quoted in Louis P. Pojman, *Philosophy: The Quest for Truth* (Belmont, CA: Wadsworth, 1989), p. 453. (This statement was originally in Albert Camus, *The Myth of Sisyphus and Other Essays*, trans. Justin O'Brien [New York: Alfred A. Knopf, 1955].)

[27] Freud states, "So again, only religion is able to answer the question of purpose in life. One can hardly go wrong in concluding that the idea of a purpose in life stands and falls with the religious system" (*Civilization and Its Discontents*, The Great Books [Chicago: U. of Chicago, 1952], 54:772).

[28] John Leslie Mackie, *The Miracle of Theism* (Oxford: Oxford U., 1982), pp. 250-51. Mackie states, "Still less do we need anything like a god to counter the supposed threat of aimlessness. Men are themselves purposive beings. In their own nature they unavoidably pursue aims and goals, they do not need these to be given from the outside."

The despair of nihilism is a logical consequence of naturalism, yet man cannot live with such emptiness. This gives rise to several approaches to life that attempt to surmount this despair. One of these is *existentialism*, an approach to life that ventures to overcome the hopelessness of naturalism by creating one's own meaning for life. In a world of emptiness, each person must fill life with experiences, love and joy, making the most of the time he has. Each person must find his own meaning. There are no rules except those which he chooses to follow, there are no truths except those which he chooses to believe. He is justified in pursuing anything that will give meaning to his life.[29] Thus existentialism attempts to overcome the terrifying consequences of a naturalistic worldview by locating man's purpose within himself.[30]

Another approach is *hedonism*, which views the goal of life as pleasure. Hedonism makes a great deal of sense if naturalism is true. Because this life is all there is, we should make the most of it and enjoy it to the fullest. Therefore, whatever brings pleasure in life is good, whatever brings pain is bad.

Certain naturalists choose to focus their energies on making the world a better place to live. Overcoming poverty, disease, handicaps and other natural limitations of this life is their agenda. Peace and love for all people is their goal. This approach, known as *humanism*, discards any ultimate meaning for life and places the needs of humanity as a whole at the center of all universal concerns. This focus is seen clearly in the three Humanist Manifestos (presented in 1933, 1973, 2000) that proclaim "the quest for the good life is still the central task for mankind."[31]

The naturalist's desire to find purpose in life in a purposeless universe is noble, but it is small comfort in light of a meaningless existence. Sartre honestly evaluated the plight of man from a naturalistic perspective when he stated, "Man is a useless passion, condemned to freedom."[32] How can the average person live with such a perspective on

---

[29] Jean-Paul Sartre, *Existentialism and Human Emotions*, trans. Hazel E. Barnes (Secaucus, NJ: Castle, n.d.), p. 51.

[30] Here we have described what is commonly known as pessimistic or atheistic existentialism. There are many streams of Christian thought that embrace a more positive form of existentialism, especially in the thought of Soren Kierkegaard and Karl Barth.

[31] "Humanist Manifesto I," in *Humanist Manifesto I and II*, ed. Paul Kurtz (Buffalo, NY: Prometheus Books, 1973), p. 10.

[32] Jean-Paul Sartre, *Being and Nothingness*, trans. Hazel Barnes (Secaucus, NJ: Citadel Press, 1957), pp. 755ff.

life? Cab driver Jose Martinez summarizes it best. When asked about the meaning of life, he replied bluntly, "We're here to die, just live and die. I drive a cab, I do some fishing, take my girl out, pay taxes, do a little reading, then get ready to drop dead. Life is a big fake."[33]

Transcendentalism: The World as We Want It

> The currents of the Universal Being circulate through me;
> I am part or parcel of God.[34]

These words may sound familiar to one who is acquainted with Eastern religions or the contemporary New Age thinking; but Ralph Waldo Emerson made this statement more than 150 years ago. He represents a line of thinking that came to be known as New England Transcendentalism.

Unhappy with what they considered the stale and rational theology of Christianity and the spiritual bankruptcy of deism, the transcendentalists sought to return God to the experience of everyday life. They perceived a godlike character for man and proclaimed that nature was not a vast machine but a living organism. God was not "out there," He was "right here," all around us, in everything we see and do. God could not be known by finely figured syllogisms but was experienced as a part of everything we feel. God was active in me, around me, and through me. Imagination triumphed over reason; creativity over theory.

New England Transcendentalism of the nineteenth century reflects a mood present in Western society today. Reacting against the authoritarian nature of some religions and the distressing implications of naturalism, many have tried to find a middle ground. Such an approach is what C. S. Lewis called the "Life-Force" philosophy, a view that imparts a spiritual nature to all of reality.[35]

This perspective of ultimate reality is a second worldview that we are labeling transcendentalism. A number of religions and movements reflect this worldview. Among them are Hinduism, Buddhism, Taoism, Confucianism, Hare Krishna, Baha'ism, Christian Science, Scientology, Unity School of Christianity, and the many New Age organizations and

---

[33] Quoted in "The Meaning of Life," *Life*, December 1988, p. 80.

[34] Ralph Waldo Emerson, "Nature," in *Collected Works of Ralph Waldo Emerson*, ed. Robert E. Spiller and Alfred R. Ferguson (Cambridge: Cambridge U., 1971), 1:10.

[35] C. S. Lewis, *Mere Christianity*, pp. 18-23.

groups. We are viewing transcendentalism as a melting-pot of mystical and psychic movements.

A great deal of variation can be found among those who take a transcendental approach to reality. For example, most Buddhist thought concludes that ultimate reality is impersonal, whereas Hare Krishna believe that it is personal. Some believe that the physical world is unreal whereas others believe it is merely an illusion. A transcendental world-view can take so many avenues that it will be impossible to explore all the current expressions. In fact, squeezing a transcendental worldview into a Western mindset is tenuous. Our discussion here shall focus on some of the general areas of agreement that such a worldview demands [36]

Confronting God

Much transcendental thought is based on the fundamental idea that all things are a unified whole, a concept known as *monism*. Everything that exists comes from the same stuff; there is no essential difference between a rock, a tree, a cow, and a man.[37] All "objects" are separate manifestations in different forms of the one reality. This ultimate reality is spiritual or psychic in nature. In this way transcendentalism denies naturalism's basic tenet that all reality is material.

Two major characteristics of the transcendental "God" differ from the God of Christian theism. First, the transcendental God and the universe are inseparable. This does not necessarily mean that God and

---

[36] Among the many religious expressions of transcendentalism, the most important are: *animism*, the primitive belief that nature is filled with spirits; *panpsychism*, a "modernized" view of animism, which claims that all objects in the universe are animated and possess a soul; *panentheism*, the "progressive" view that the universe is God's "body"; and most if not all of the mystical and occultic movements and religions. *Polytheism*, the belief that the universe is populated with many gods, is difficult to categorize. However, it shares more affinities with animism and pantheism than with theism. (See Alasdair MacIntyre, who concludes that pantheism grew out of primitive polytheism; *The Encyclopedia of Philosophy*, 8 vols. [New York: Macmillan, 1967], 6:32.)

[37] There is no easy way accurately to depict the variations of monistic thought. What we are describing here is generally referred to as classical pantheism or a form of absolute monism. Modified views of pantheism and monism view God as the energizing force or "soul" of the material universe. However, even in these views God is still not a personal being nor is He separate from the material universe.

the universe are equal (although pantheistic monism believes this is true) but that the two are inextricably intertwined in one fabric of reality. This leads to the second difference: the transcendental God is not a personal being. The concept of personality is a construct of human thought and therefore not an essential feature of reality. God is thus beyond personality and possesses none of the qualities necessary for personal interaction. For the transcendentalist, God is the impersonal force, principle, or spirit behind the created world.

Confronting Humanity

According to transcendental thought, man's nature is an extension of the divine oneness. Therefore, it is readily claimed that each person is divine. Why is it, then, that each of us is not conscious of his divinity? Transcendentalism answers that awareness of this divine nature is muddled behind the encumbrances of the physical life and individual distinctiveness. According to early Buddhism, a person could be separated into five elements or parts. What we call an individual ego is no more than a temporary combination of form, feeling, perceptions, impulses, and consciousness.[38]

If such a view of the self is true, how is the internal struggle with right and wrong explained? In transcendental thought, man's moral nature is a product of his physical limitations and not an indication of a moral Lawgiver. The Hindu *Upanishads* state, "The immortal man overcomes both the thoughts, 'I did evil' and 'I did good.' Good and evil, done or not done, cause him no pain."[39] Much of transcendentalism has little to do with ethics, at least as far as the Western mind perceives moral systems.[40] However, this does not mean that an ethical lifestyle is ignored by transcendental religions and movements. Moral behavior, although not based upon absolute norms given from heaven, still allows a person to attain oneness. A life of wanton behavior, because it is usually a quest for individual sensual fulfillment, is a hindrance to the recognition of the individual's divine unity with all things.

Man's problem is manifested by the rampant suffering and injustice in the world. Two characteristics of man's nature are the cause for these

---

[38] See Edward Conze, *Buddhism: Its Essence and Development* (Oxford: Bruno Cassirer, 1951; reprint, New York: Harper & Row, 1975), p. 107.

[39] *The Upanishads*, trans. F. Max Muller. *Sacred Books of the East* (Oxford: Clarendon, 1900), Brhadaranyake 3.4.

[40] Albert Schweitzer, *The Quest for the Historical Jesus* (New York: Macmillan, 1964), p. 43. Schweitzer refers to Hinduism as "supra-ethical."

deficiencies. First, mankind possesses a fragmented vision of the oneness of all things. Because of man's incarnation his perspective is impaired by the limitations of human thought and reasoning. He sees life in fragments. For instance, I can choose to focus attention on my unique self and ignore my connection with the universe. I can crave things that are impermanent (such as sex, power, or possessions) and make them symbols and goals of my individual pleasures or accomplishments.

Such a perspective is what Alan Watts called our "ego illusion."[41] As long as a person sees himself as a separate reality he will never escape the prison of incarnation since "we are not human beings having a spiritual experience, we are spiritual beings having a human experience."[42] He is doomed to the cycle of birth and death until he breaks free from the bondage of selfish living. Thus, reincarnation is a fundamental feature of transcendental philosophy. Successive rebirths form the links in the chain of the individual soul's journey back to the One.[43]

The second cause of suffering and injustice is man's ignorance of his own divine nature. He has a fundamental ignorance of truth, which results in selfish pursuits. Man looks too often for answers to his problems outside himself, in the world of shadows and illusions. As a result, the spark of the divine nature within is ignored and overwhelmed by the false perceptions of the world.

Man's solution to his problems is not to be found outside himself. Truth, salvation, peace, and enlightenment are all found within. The transcendentalist view of salvation is one of overcoming the fragmented vision of his incarnation. A person's ideal goal should be some form of enlightenment by which he moves beyond his individualness and "becomes one" with ultimate reality. Many different paths are proposed to overcome man's ego illusion. Some find it in meditation, others through good works and a denial of desires, still others through intellectual achievement. All approaches have two common elements: (1)

---

[41] Alan Watts, *Spirit of Zen* (New York: Dutton, 1936), p. 23.

[42] Pierre Teilhard de Chardin; quoted in Laura Nash and Scotty McLennan, *Church on Sunday, Work on Monday: The Challenge of Fusing Christian Values with Business Life* (Ontario: John Wiley & Sons, 2001), p. 3.

[43] For an explanation of the purpose and nature of reincarnation from a transcendental perspective, see *Coming Back: The Science of Reincarnation, based on the teachings of A. C. Bhaktivedanta Swami Prabhupada* (Sydney, Australia: The Bhaktivedanta Book Trust, 1982).

the need to see the unity of all things; (2) the need to actualize the divinity within each person.

At the emotional level transcendentalism becomes an appealing alternative to naturalism. The drive toward intellectualism and scientific discovery, and the meaninglessness of a life lived only for the here and now with no afterlife, seems cold and lifeless to many who desire a view of reality that surges with warmth, love, and hope for a future. The cycle of births, deaths and rebirths as the move toward final unity with ultimate reality is the shared eternity of everything. For the transcendentalist, even nature possesses the emotional characteristics of life and joins with man in the quest for universal peace and unity.

Confronting Nature

The world, at least the material aspect of creation, is viewed differently among transcendentalists. Even among the Eastern religions there is much disagreement as to the exact nature of the physical world. Hindu thought, for example, holds to the doctrine of *maya*, that is, that the physical world as perceived by human senses is not true reality. Certain Buddhist groups view the material world as unreal, an illusion. Jainism, on the other hand, considers the material world to be real. In general, the physical realm is at best a part of reality and at worst a bad dream. The focus of transcendentalism is upon the fabric of reality that underlies the physical world. "What we take to be real self-subsisting entities in the phenomenal world are in reality interdependent structures existing only momentarily."[44]

Transcendentalism commonly sees the physical realm as a profound manifestation of the divine nature; however, the divine is not dependent upon the physical realm. Still, there is the sense that the universe emanates from God necessarily. Radhakrishnan states, "Creation is a necessary part of God's being. God needs it for the fullness of His being."[45] The distinctions between ultimate reality and the physical world are clear.

Transcendentalism accuses both naturalism and theism of focusing too much attention on the physical realm. The diversity and change of the physical realm is deceptive, according to transcendentalism. As a result, the alternate worldviews have applied human reason and

---

[44] Mark R. Mullins, "The Worldview of Zen," *Update* 7:4 (December 1983):48.

[45] S. Radhakrishnan, *Eastern Religions and Western Thought*, 2d ed. (New York: Oxford U., 1940), p. 92.

personality to ultimate reality and/or the material world. In seeking reasonable answers for the meaning of life, they ask temporal questions of a nontemporal order.

The transcendental perspective rejects the subject/object dichotomy that is a major part of naturalism and theism. To the transcendentalist, all is subject. The world is not indifferent or hostile to man, it is a part of the organic fabric of all reality. We are one. We are the world.

Expressions of Transcendentalism

The transcendental view of nature has practical outworkings in several areas. For example, there has been little emphasis on scientific inquiry in cultures where a transcendental worldview is dominant. This makes a great deal of sense if the physical world is viewed as deceptive and illusory. For this reason a lack of interest in science and technology and their advancements is pervasive in many Eastern countries.

On the positive side, if the world is seen as an organic whole, then care for all aspects of the environment and life is important. Only a crass form of selfishness causes a person to view humanity as more important than other aspects of the world. The ecological gospel of saving the whales, rescuing seals, preserving redwoods, and so forth, promises our own salvation from mutual destruction and the achievement of universal harmony.

"All animals have the same rights as humans" is the rationale of many behind the animal-rights movement. Organizations such as the Animal Liberation Front and the Guardian Apes have taken a vigilante approach to protecting animals from human exploitation. Demonstrations and marches by the "Transcendental Right" seek protection for animals from fur-traders and medical researchers. Although many animal rights activists do not resort to extreme tactics, the transcendental foundation of their rhetoric is clear.

From a broader perspective there are two elements of transcendentalism that make it a popular worldview. The first is that transcendentalism promises a progression toward unity. Modern society is enamored with the concept of progression. The belief that the world is ultimately moving toward global unity is a promising alternative to predictions of Armageddon.

Albert Einstein saw man's religious feelings developing over history in three progressions. First, man held to a religion of fear in which his superstitious beliefs resulted in rituals and prayers. Second, mankind developed the religion of morality in which social feelings were dominant. The final stage is what Einstein called the "cosmic religious feeling." Here the individual is overwhelmed by his own nothingness compared to the marvelous order in nature and human thought. At this stage man will "look upon individual existence as a sort of prison and want to experience the universe as a single significant whole."[46]

Einstein's view is part of an interesting phenomenon whereby scientists and the scientific fields are being used to promote a transcendental worldview. Some are using the tentative results of quantum physics to prove a universal pantheism.[47] Still others, by claiming that the universe has a "free will" to create new things,[48] view the cosmos as not only self-creative but also self-organizing and possessing a "personality." This coming together of science and religion is viewed as a positive step toward the unity of human thought and experience. The most positive aspect of transcendentalism is the promise of a "New Age" of global harmony and peace. As mankind progresses toward this unity, the shackles of theistic religions and atheistic naturalism must be removed.

A second element resulting in its popularity is that transcendentalism presents a positive view of the human situation. It replaces the theistic view of man's depravity with a positive acclamation of man's divinity. Such a view fits in well with an American culture that prides itself on individual determination and accomplishment. Actualizing one's divine nature results in breakthrough experiences for individuals in their careers, health, and relationships.

For example, one introductory nursing class suggested that medical professionals recognize "the presence of an intelligent life force" in their patients that is "self-correcting," and that "illness is a result of a disturbance" in that force. It also recommended therapies such as therapeutic touch (the transferring of positive energy from a well person to a sick person), meditation (the use of imagination to alter one's "inner space consciousness"), hypnosis, and the repetition of affirmations such as, "I

---

[46] Albert Einstein, *The World as I See It*, trans. Alen Harris (New York: Citadel Press, n.d.), p. 26.

[47] For example, see Gary Zukav, *The Dancing Wu Li Masters* (New York: Morrow, 1979); Fred A. Wolf, *Taking the Quantum Leap* (San Francisco: Harper & Row, 1981); and Fritjof Capra, *The Tao of Physics* (Boulder, CO: Shambala Publications, 1975).

[48] See for example, Eric Jantsch, *The Self-Organizing Universe* (Oxford: Pergamon, 1980), pp. 96ff.

am a radiant being, filled with light and love. I am the Master of my life. Everything I need is already within me."[49]

Using teachings based on Eastern mysticism, pantheism, and "self-actualization" philosophies, New Age-related firms provide employee training for various businesses. These sessions often include hypnosis, chanting, meditation, channeling, and even tarot cards and fire walking. These "training seminars" are not limited to the voluntary participation by adventurous self-seekers but are sometimes mandated by major employers, such as Pacific Bell, California's largest utility company.[50] Other corporate giants officially enlisted the aid of New Age consultants. A 1987 *Newsweek* article estimated that corporations spent four billion dollars a year to finance New Age programs.[51]

New Age thinking influences every area of life in America. A survey of the abundance of New Age-related writings makes this clear. There is a *New Age Bible*, a *New Age Politics*, a *New Age Medicine*, a *New Age Handbook on Death and Dying*, a *New Age Yellow Pages*, and a *New Age Community Guide Book*. There is even a book on *New Age Tennis*, a *New Age Brown Rice Cookbook*, and the *New Age Baby Name Book*. If there is a New Age coming soon, the book publishers will certainly have prophesied (and profited from) the event.

Theism: The World from God's Hands

Three-fifths of the world's population hold to a belief in some form of personal deity.[52] However, truth cannot be determined by opinion polls. Either God exists or He does not. Theism must wrestle with the same questions and cover the same territory as any other worldview.

Naturalism builds its system on the assumption that the material universe is all that exists. Transcendentalism assumes that all reality is one great mind or spirit. Theism begins with the assumption that God exists. Each of these worldviews interact with the ultimate questions based on their assumptions (see Diagram 2.3: Comparing the Worldviews).

---

[49] Kate Freeman, "Holism," Personal e-mail (4 Oct. 2005). See also Barbara Dossey, Lynn Keegan, and Cathie Guzzetta, eds., *Holistic Nursing: A Hand-book for Practice* (Gaithersburg, MD: Aspen, 2000).

[50] See Steve Rabey, "Karma for Cash: A 'New Age' for Workers?" *Christianity Today*, 17 June 1988, pp. 69, 71, 74.

[51] Annetta Miller and Pamela Abramson, "Corporate Mind Control," *Newsweek*, 4 May 1987, pp. 38-39.

[52] Information taken from David Barrett, ed., *World Christian Encyclopedia*, 2d ed. (New York: Oxford, 2001), pp. 1-21.

Diagram 2.3
Comparing the Worldviews

	ORIGIN	IDENTITY	MEANING	MORALITY	DESTINY
NATURALISM	Natural causes and processes	Self-conscious animals	No source for ultimate meaning	Human-centered (relative)	No afterlife, no ultimate direction to history
TRANSCENDENTALISM	Fragmentation of divine oneness	Expression of divine oneness	Seek unity with all things	Human-centered (relative)	All people and things return to divine oneness
THEISM	Created by God	Special creation of God	Determined by God for His creation	God-centered (absolute)	Eternal life with or apart from God

Acknowledging the existence of God is not merely a sentimental belief in a kindly "Father in the sky"; it is a bold and powerful declaration concerning the origin and meaning of the universe. Unlike naturalism, theism holds that real things do exist beyond the physical realm: God, angels, the human soul, immortality, and the like. Christians can speak of eternal things not seen (Gen. 1:1; 2 Cor. 4:17; Heb. 11:1)—there is more than meets the eye. Unlike transcendentalism, theism sees the created world as a work of art from the hand of the Creator. Theism also delivers an indictment against man because of his personal rebellion against the truth revealed by God (see Diagram 2.4: Theistic Distinctives).

While biblical Christianity is a theistic worldview, there are many other variations of theism that depart drastically from the essentials of biblical teaching. Before we discuss these variations, we will outline the essential beliefs of a theistic worldview as it confronts God, humanity, and nature. In chapter four, we shall fill in the specific teachings of a biblical worldview as it also faces this threefold division.

Diagram 2.4
Theistic Distinctives

COMMON THEISTIC BELIEFS…	CONTRARY TO…
God Exists	Naturalism
God Is Personal	Transcendentalism
God Has Revealed Truth about Himself and the World	Postmodernism

Confronting God

Whereas transcendentalism views the term *God* as a reference to the impersonal life-force of all reality, theism sees God as a personal being who is separate from the natural world. Therefore, God exists in a different way than does the creation He brought into existence. Douglas Groothuis explains, "God differs from His creation not in degree (of being) but in kind. He is uncreated, unchanging and self-sufficient; creation is created, subject to decay, and dependent on its Creator."[53]

Theism agrees that God's nature is beyond the world He has created, but does not agree that He is removed from it. Most theists hold that God is also active within the physical realm. Such an understanding of God opens up the possibility of His interceding in the affairs of His creation. This involves both revelation (God communicating with man) and miracles (God "interfering" with nature or the course of events).

THE NATURE OF GOD. God's general revelation of Himself through nature gives us scant specific or reliable information about Him. For example, "Nature can teach one about divine wrath, for the universe can be a terrible and savage place, but nature will teach nothing of mercy. Nature suggests both the omnipotent and the omniscient, for the universe is vast, intricate, and well-ordered; yet it knows of no God who would be a friend of man."[54]

Much like reading the résumé of a person we do not know, we are left wondering about the personality of the individual, as well as his plans and goals. We can derive from the evidence around us that God is a powerful, orderly, moral being, but little about His character traits and His plan for the world and humanity.

For this reason, the theistic religions do not rely solely upon God's revelation in nature for the foundation for their beliefs. Much is derived from their own scriptures and teachings of "holy men." A good description of the theistic understanding of the nature of God is given by Richard Swinburne: God is "a person without a body (i.e., a spirit), present everywhere, the creator and sustainer of the universe, a free agent, able to do everything (i.e., omnipotent), knowing all things, perfectly good, a source of moral obligation, immutable, eternal, a necessary being, holy, and worthy of worship."[55] While one may quibble about the exact meaning of some of these terms, this represents a basic description of God which almost all theists accept.

---

[53] Douglas Groothuis, "The Christian Mind," *CSSH Quarterly* V11:2 (Winter 1984):13.

[54] Alan J. Birkey, Fred Van Dyke, and Ted D. Nickel, "Integration and the Christian College: Reflection on the Nineteenth Psalm," *Faculty Dialogue* (Fall 1987), p. 92.

[55] Richard Swinburne, *The Coherence of Theism* (Oxford: Oxford U., 1977), p. 2.

Confronting Humanity

In light of God's existence, when I try to understand my place in the world I am able to look beyond myself for answers. I am not the product of transcendental emanation or of naturalistic evolution. I have been brought into existence by an intelligent being—God. My existence is not by chance, but the result of a purposeful choice. My existence as a human can be summarized by three major themes: dependence, dignity, and dominion.

To claim that man is *dependent* means that he is not autonomous. Even his life is not merely a biological event, but an intelligent choice by God to bring that individual into existence. Practically, I recognize that I am dependent on God for my existence and continuance. I am not the captain of my own fate. Further, if God is a moral being, then I must admit that I am dependent on Him as the moral judge of my life. Theism teaches that each person will be evaluated for how he lives and either be rewarded or punished by the supreme authority, God.

To claim that man has *dignity* is to make a strong assertion about the nature of man's being. Unlike naturalism, which centers the essence of the individual in physical matter, theism sees each individual as a special creation by God. In some way, man shares in the nature of God. However, unlike transcendentalism, man is not "part or parcel" of God. He is separate from God and shares in the divine nature only as a direct act of God's will.

Such a share in God's nature causes man to ask the ultimate questions of life. Thus all human life has dignity—not because of the inherent worth of the person, but because God ascribes worth to humanity created in His image. Our abilities to seek that which is true, good, and beautiful are profound indicators of God's imprint in the soul of each person.[56]

Man's dignity is further highlighted by his immortality. Our birth is the beginning of our personal history, but through God's will and power all people continue eternally. There is no cycle of continued incarnation as in transcendentalism. In theism there is one life, one death, one judgment.

---

[56] The three categories of human reason, human volition, and aesthetic sensitivity are celebrated faculties that are distinctly human. The classical philosophers expounded man's exploration of these capabilities. Immanuel Kant devoted his major works to them in *Critique of Pure Reason*, *Critique of Practical Reason* and *Critique of Judgment*.

Each person is unique. The individual ego is not evil or an illusion as in transcendentalism, but another mark of God's special creation. Biologically, psychologically, and spiritually, each person bears a unique imprint from the Creator.

The fact of man's dignity leads to the paradox of humanity. Humanity is capable of the greatest acts of kindness and selflessness, the greatest discoveries of the universe, the greatest thoughts of creativity, and the greatest acts of courage; yet he is also capable of the grossest acts of decadence and violence against himself and others. This paradox is often understood by the theistic religions as the result of the conflict between God's image in man and man's rebellion by sin, which has resulted in an alienation from God. The only remedy is deliverance from this sinful state. How this is accomplished constitutes the various salvation schemes of the theistic religions.

The concept of *dominion* is difficult to articulate, yet there is a compelling notion that mankind is, in a small way, ruler over his environment. In one sense we are a part of nature. We are born through natural processes and our activities are governed by natural laws. But our essential qualities go beyond the natural world. By our free will we may act contrary to nature, and with our imaginations we are able to transcend our own existence. Man's dominion over nature is, of course, not a blank check to exploit the earth to benefit his own desires. Rather, theism calls for man to nurture his world as a steward.

While reflecting some of the most positive features of naturalism and transcendentalism, theism solves the mysteries concerning man's purpose and meaning, his individual personality and destiny. From a personal point of view, the naturalist would claim, "There is no God"; the transcendentalist would affirm, "I am god"; but the theist would insist, "I am God's."

Confronting Nature

Theists believe that God created the universe *ex nihilo* ("out of nothing"). He did not form the universe out of eternal pre-existing material, as was thought by the early Greek cosmologies, but instead He brought matter and energy into existence. The world exists as the result of God's free decision to create. This is a crucial point in the understanding of theism. God alone is the ultimate reality and everything else is derived from Him.

The first verse of the Bible declares, "In the beginning God created the heavens and the earth" (Gen. 1:1). This is a bold proclamation of God's existence, His transcendence over the universe, His creative power, and His authority. Unlike naturalism, nature is not autonomous and purposeless, but is dependent and purposeful. Unlike transcendental-ism, nature is not divine but designed.

The natural world is not only created by God but is also sustained by Him. The natural laws that describe physical events are God's design to maintain an orderly universe. The created world is not eternal; even physicists point out that the universe is "running down." Whatever future the natural world has is held in the hands of the One who brought it into existence.

Expressions of Theism

Most of the major theistic religions would generally agree with the descriptions of God, humanity and nature given in the paragraphs above. However, it is clear that merely acknowledging the existence of God does not set a single agenda for a worldview.

Within the realm of a theistic worldview, there are several worldviews that run counter to Christian theism. We will look briefly at four of them here. The first two are derived from, though depart from, Christianity: deism and finitism. Both of these views alter the traditional view of God as an all-powerful, all-good Being who is active within His creation.

DEISM. Deism claims that God is beyond the world, not within it. The deistic God created the physical universe and instilled within it natural laws to ensure its orderly operation. Now the world runs accord-ing to God's precise initial design without any need for His intrusion. A watchmaker or engine designer is no longer needed after the instrument is constructed. Because deism rejects divine intervention in the affairs of the created world, the only means available for man to know God is through what has been made—creation itself. Verbal revelation in the Bible, the deity of Christ, and miracles are all discarded as impos-sibilities. Deism flourished in Europe and later in America in the latter days of the Renaissance until the early part of the nineteenth century. Well-known American deists of that era were Thomas Jefferson, Benjamin Franklin, and Thomas Paine.

FINITISM. Another alternate form of theism is known as *finitism*, the belief that God is limited in certain aspects of His nature and power. Finitism attempts to solve the dilemma of evil that plagues traditional theism. This is more fully explored in chapter 5; however, we can summarize at this point. How can an all-good, all-powerful God allow evil to persist in a universe He created? Finitism attempts to solve the problem by claiming that God is limited and incapable of destroying evil by Himself.

Such a perspective of God has been popularized by Rabbi Harold Kushner in his best-selling *When Bad Things Happen to Good People* and *When All You've Ever Wanted Isn't Enough.*[57] Kushner notes, "God has a hard time keeping chaos in check and limiting the damage that evil can do."[58]

Both deism and finitism unnecessarily limit God. Deism implies that God supernaturally created the world but does not supernaturally work within it. Finitism renders the future uncertain: if God cannot control evil, then there can be no assurance that He will ever overcome it. In both cases God must be redefined and the biblical evidence rejected.

Two other variations of theism arise from the two world religions— Judaism and Islam—that compete with Christianity (see Diagram 2.5: Comparing the Three Great Theistic Religions). While all three of these religions, known as "the Great Religions," agree that God *exists* and that God has taken steps to *reveal Himself,* they differ about *who God has revealed Himself to be.* These disagreements concern the nature of God and His plan for the world (see chart comparing the theistic religions). Is He the God of Abraham and/or Jesus and/or Muhammad? Is He active in the world today? Is He limited in His ability to control world events or the influence of evil?

JUDAISM. Judaism is perhaps the religion that is most similar to Christianity in its history and views about God. The various sects of Judaism, for example, view God as the single, supreme ruler of the universe. Judaism locates the authoritative source of its theism in the Torah (Old Testament) and the Talmud.[59] The God of Judaism is the God Who specially chose Israel as His people and Who is working out His covenant with them through history. While Judaism and Christianity share a belief in the authority of the Old Testament as the Word of God, they disagree on whether Jesus Christ fulfills the promises of God found in the Old Testament to send Messiah.

---

[57] Harold Kushner, *When Bad Things Happen to Good People* (New York: Avon, 1981); *When All You've Ever Wanted Isn't Enough* (New York: Summit, 1986).

[58] Kushner, *When Bad Things Happen,* p. 43.

[59] Although Judaism relies upon the Torah as the authoritative Word of God, the Talmud serves as the official interpretation and application of the Torah to life. The Talmud is made up of the *Mishnah* (early teachings and discussions of the Rabbis dating until A.D. 210) and the *Gemara* (a rabbinical commentary on the Mishnah).

Diagram 2.5
Comparing the Three Great Theistic Religions

	Judaism	Christianity	Islam
Inception	ca. 2,000 B.C.	ca. A.D. 30	ca. A.D. 600
Founder	Abraham, Moses	Jesus	Muhammad
Scripture	Old Testament	Old Testament, New Testament	Torah, Psalms, Gospels, Quran
View of God	Unitarian and relational	Trinitarian and relational	Unitarian and non-relational
State of Humanity	Morally obliged to Mosaic law	Morally fallen and incapable	Morally capable of obedience
View of Salvation	Restoration of Israel	Redemption via work of Christ	Submission to Islamic belief and practice

ISLAM. Islam (the Arabic term for "surrender") was founded by Muhammad (A.D. 570-632) and is generally touted as Christianity's greatest challenge for the future.[60] The strict legalistic lifestyle of the *Muslim* ("one who surrenders") is a result of the Islamic view of God as

---

[60] See George Fry, "Christianity's Greatest Challenge," *Christianity Today*, 7 November 1969, pp. 9-12.

one who exacts justice according to a stern ethical and ritual code.[61] The Islamic view of God is a mixture of Jewish, Christian, and Arabic religious concepts derived from four sacred books: the Torah (delivered through Moses), the Psalms (through David), the Gospel (through Jesus) and, most important, the Koran (through Muhammad).

In spite of their differences, Judaism and Islam share a common understanding of God as a single, personal Being. Christianity, on the other hand, views God as "tri-personal," a view that is expressed by the doctrine of the Trinity. More specifically, Christianity is unique in its view on Jesus Christ and His role in God's plan for the creation. We shall return to these distinctions later in our discussion of the biblical worldview (chapter four).

The most important point of theism is that God exists. He is the final reality. Everything that exists is ultimately dependent upon Him. To acknowledge God is to cast all of human history and all personal destiny upon the will and character of the Creator and Judge.

Postmodernism: The World as We Experience It

It's a unique building to say the least: stairs that go nowhere; support beams that do not extend to the floor and others that do not extend to the ceiling; permanent scaffolding by the front entrance; and broken glass (not manicured grass) as landscaping. The Wexner Center for Performing Arts on the campus of Ohio State University, which opened in 1989, was primarily designed by Peter Eisenman. A pioneer of postmodern architecture, Eisenmen suggests that the Wexner Center is "… a building that is waiting to be a building."[62]

Postmodernism, according to David Wells, "comes in all kinds of shapes and expressions."[63] This sort of variety can make it difficult to understand. Further, postmodernism resists categories and distinctions, and this makes it more difficult to nail down as a worldview. As we have

---

[61] The Islamic system of works is described by the "Five Pillars": (1) recitation of the Islamic creed ("There is no god but Allah and Muhammad is his prophet"); (2) prayer (five times daily facing Mecca); (3) pilgrimage to Mecca once during a lifetime; (4) observance of the Fast of Ramadan (abstaining from food, drink, and sexual relations from sunrise to sunset during one month of the year); and (5) charity (giving alms to the poor).

[62] Quoted on "Linking the Past and the Future." Online at http://www. wexarts.org/kiosk.php? swf=/about/architecture/arch.swf.

[63] David F. Wells, *Above All Earthly Pow'rs: Christ in a Postmodern World* (Grand Rapids, MI: Eerdman's, 2005).

seen, naturalism, transcendentalism and theism each offer distinct views of the nature of ultimate reality, and this makes categorizing them somewhat straightforward. Postmodernism is different.

> Postmodernity is more of a condition than a distinct position, a mood rather than a metaphysic; it nonetheless communicates something about human being-in-the-world. It is a world and life view, not in the sense that it yields a system of propositions, but in the sense that it creates an ethos. Postmodernity may be more than a philosophy, but it is not less; it is a world and life view that is in a relationship of codependency with modernity.[64]

Postmodernism can resemble the more pessimistic expressions of naturalism: there are no transcendent categories of truth or morality; life is largely meaningless; there is no overarching design or direction to history. Frederick Nietzsche, the "godfather" of postmodernism, suggested near the end of the nineteenth century that God (and he meant the idea of God) was dead; and a universe without God is a universe where meaning, truth, and knowledge are impossible. These Nietzscheian ideas were picked up by prominent postmodern theorists like Jacque Derrida, Michel Foucault, Richard Rorty, and Stanley Fish.

Despite its similarity with naturalism, postmodernism requires a separate look for two primary reasons: First, while early postmodernists were almost all atheists, current expressions of postmodernism extend well beyond naturalism. Second, since its emergence during the latter half of the twentieth century, postmodernism has infiltrated many key areas of thought including philosophy, the arts, literature, history, sociology, psychology, inter-cultural studies, and increasingly, technology. Its influence, especially in academia, is strong and continues to grow. Therefore, it demands our attention.

Historical Perspective: How We Lost Our Minds

There is a larger intellectual history that must be understood in order to grasp the uniqueness and significance of postmodernism as a worldview. While dividing history into distinct time periods is not an exact science, there are two major historical transitions that can help us clarify the emergence of postmodernism: (1) the transition towards

---

[64] Kevin Vanhoozer, "Pilgrim's Digress: Christian Thinking on and about the Post/Modern Way," in *Christianity and the Postmodern Turn: Six Views,* ed. Myron B. Penner (Grand Rapids, MI: Brazos, 2005), p. 77.

modernism, typically dated around the 1700s and (2) the transition away from modernism which began in the late twentieth century (see Diagram 2.6: Postmodernism: An Historical Perspective).

The transition from what is often called the pre-modern period into the modern period corresponds with the influence of Enlightenment thinking and the scientific revolution. Prior to the Enlightenment, there was a dominant cultural belief in the existence of the supernatural. This was due in large part to the rise of Christianity and specifically the Roman Catholic Church as the most powerful cultural presence in medieval times. This was a world of *authority,* and authority rested in the hands of traditional institutions, especially the church, since it was entrusted with interpreting and communicating this truth to the common person.

With a belief in God came a strong belief in the concept of *revelation*, that God not only existed but had revealed Himself and His will in the Bible. This revelation was considered the primary source of truth, and could be trusted to unlock God's metanarrative (or, "Big Story") for the world. Believing was the starting point of real knowledge. St. Anselm typifies a pre-modern perspective on truth: "For I seek not to understand in order that I may believe; but I believe in order that I may understand, for I believe for this reason: that unless I believe, I cannot understand." This view of revelation and authority did not fare well during the Enlightenment.

The Enlightenment was a movement among European intellectuals in the seventeenth and eighteenth centuries. In the decades leading up to this time, the church's authority had been successfully challenged politically (reactions against corruption), theologically (Luther, Calvin and the Protestant Reformation), philosophically (downfall of scholasticism), and scientifically (Galileo, Copernicus, and Baconian method). There was a growing disillusionment with the traditional educational, political and religious institutions, as well as their authoritative sources.

During the Enlightenment, authority shifted from traditional institutions to human reason. A scientific approach to the world yielded tremendous advances in medicine, technology, and communications and challenged the centrality of theology and religious belief as the paradigm for learning. Free from the restrictive shackles of traditional beliefs (thus, *modern*ism), progress seemed inevitable. Immanuel Kant described this

Diagram 2.6
Postmodernism: An Historical Perspective

	Pre-Modernity Prior to...	Modernity 1500 AD until...	Post-Modernity Late 1900s
		Key transitions...	
Ideas	Greek philosophy	Scientific method	Death of truth
Events	Birth of western civilization	The Enlightenment (age of reason)	Events of twentieth century
		Key beliefs about...	
God	Belief in supernatural and revelation	Skepticism of supernatural and revelation	Certainty about God is impossible
Authority	Trust oral and written traditions	Trust human abilities of reason and investigation	Authorities tend to be oppressive (distrust)
History	Faith in divine governance over history	Inevitability of progress under human control	Disbelief in progress and coherence of history
Humanity	Created, fixed nature (body and soul)	Self-determined, biological machine (body)	Socially constructed, no fixed nature
Truth	Objective, revealed by God	Objective, discovered by scientific investigation	Subjective, determined by communal experience

period of time in this way: "*Sapere aude!* 'Have the courage to make use of your own mind!' is thus the slogan of the Enlightenment."[65]

The *modern period* had begun. The growing skepticism in regards to anything supernatural was matched by growing faith in human ability to know the world, control it, and reap the inevitable benefits. The "Big Story" of the world was not *given* by revelation; rather, it was to be *discovered* and perhaps even *determined* by science, reason and technology. This major transition was at the heart of the modern period.

However, from our twenty-first century perspective, it is clear that the predictions of utopia guaranteed in the modern period never materialized. Instead, modernists became disillusioned as military increase brought world wars; failed development policies led to class oppression and colonialism; economic idealism resulted in communism and the Cold War; and our best science created nuclear weapons and the threat of global devastation.

Postmodern writers, beginning with Nietzsche, began to question the integrity of modernism's metanarrative of progress. In fact, the main casualty of a postmodern perspective is the very idea of a metanarrative. Postmoderns are skeptical of any and all claims to an authoritative comprehensive worldview, absolute truth about reality, and an over-arching purpose to the human story.[66] Postmoderns embrace local narratives, not metanarratives; a multitude of stories, not a "Big Story."

In short, it could be said that religious metanarratives were dismissed by modernism. Man-made ones are dismissed by post-modernism. This is what Myron Penner and others have referred to as "the postmodern turn":[67] postmodernism is a turn away from the certain-ty and optimism of modernism. As Jean Francios Lyotard wrote: "Simplifying to the extreme, I define *postmodern* as incredulity toward metanarratives." [68]

---

[65] Kant, "An Answer to the Question 'What is Enlightenment?'" [online] (1784; accessed 10 January 2006); available from http://www.personal.ksu.edu/ ~lyman/ english233/Kant-WIE.htm; Internet.

[66] Wells, *Above All Earthly Pow'rs*, pp. 74-90.

[67] Myron Penner, "Introduction" in Penner, *Christianity and the Postmodern Turn: Six Views*, pp. 19-28.

[68] Jean Francois Lyotard, *The Postmodern Condition: A Report on Knowledge* trans. Geoff Bennington and Brian Massumi, in *Theory and History of Literature*, vol. 10 (Minneapolis: Univ. of Minnesota Press, 1984).

Confronting Reality: How the Rules Changed

There are vast disagreements among postmodernists in several areas: some are optimistic, some are not; some preach hope, others preach despair. Still, there is a key belief that characterizes all forms of post-modernism: an acute awareness of our "situatedness" as humans. Or, to put it another way, we all come from a perspective, or bias, that is shaped by the culture we inhabit. According to postmodernism, we cannot claim objectivity for our views. As Kevin Vanhoozer states, "Postmoderns are so preoccupied with the situated self that they cannot get beyond it."[69]

This is the clearest difference between postmodernism and the other worldviews we have studied so far. Whereas the central concern of naturalism, transcendentalism and theism is on what the real world actually is, the focus of postmodernism is on *how we perceive* and *how we describe* what the world is. In this view, everything is contingent; nothing is fixed. There are several implications of confronting reality this way.

First, *reality is ultimately unknowable.* Our *situatedness* prevents us from directly accessing the real world. This is not to say that it is not there (though some would suggest this), only that we can never shed our perspectives to access it. No one has a "god's eye view" of reality; therefore no one can claim to have *the* truth about it. Stanley Fish describes this dilemma this way:

> Moreover, not only is there no one who could spot a transcendent truth if it happened to pass through the neighborhood, but it is difficult even to say what one would be like. Of course one would know what it would *not* be like; it would not speak to any particular condition, or be identified with any historical production, or be formulated in the terms of any national, ethnic, racial, economic, or class traditions.[70]

We are trapped in our situatedness. There are no foundations that are not themselves contingent from which to build a certain and agreed-upon body of knowledge. Knowledge really comes down to one's perspective: we never really have the *facts;* there is only *interpretation.*

Second, *truth and knowledge are constructions of language.* They reflect the perspective of the one who is claiming, but should not be

---

[69] Vanhoozer, "Pilgrim's Digress," p. 76.
[70] Stanley Fish, *There's No Such Thing as Free Speech: And It's a Good Thing, Too* (New York: Oxford, 1994), p. 8.

confused as a statement of fact about actual reality. Of course, if truth merely reflects one's perspective and does not actually represent anything about objective reality, it cannot be absolute. This is an inescapable conclusion of the postmodern worldview: there is no absolute truth; there are only "truths."

It is important to note that postmodernism does not argue that each person has their own truth, but that our perspectives on what is true are shaped largely by the communities, or cultures, in which we find ourselves. Each community constructs, through language, its own story of the world. No story is more true than another (since all stories are valid); but, in fact, truth is produced by the narrative of a community. "Truths," then, are not propositional statements about reality, but rather narrative realities for a particular group; and every group is distinguished by their particular use of language.

In a sense, the postmodern turn can be considered a *linguistic* turn. Richard Rorty puts it this way, "We need to make a distinction between the claim that the world is out there and the claim that truth is out there... To say that truth is not out there is simply to say that where there are no sentences there is no truth, that sentences are elements of human languages, and that human languages are human creations. . . . The world does not speak. Only we do."[71] In other words, since we simply cannot escape language in our attempts to describe reality, all objectivity is jettisoned.

This view of language is at the root of the practice of "deconstruction" in literature, which was first espoused by Jacque Derrida. He suggested that there is no fixed meaning of any text, since it is only the perspective of the author. But, each reader has his perspective too. Therefore, meaning is *imposed* on the text by the reader; this meaning is not fixed either, of course. Therefore, every text can have a multitude of meanings, despite the original intention of the author.

A third implication of postmodernism is that *progress is an illusion.* The optimism of the modern project, which was based on a false confidence in human objectivity and certainty, has been chastened. Like the stairs that go nowhere in the Wenxer Center, we really don't get anywhere. Advancement and achievement are socially constructed concepts; they are leftover baggage that only come from a world that can

---

[71] Richard Rorty, *Contingency, Irony, and Solidarity* (New York: Cambridge, 1989), pp. 4-5.

be explained by a metanarrative; they are expressions of our situatedness that cannot be used to evaluate another culture or another time.

Without the concept of progress, then what does it mean for a society to move forward (and what does "forward" mean)? There are two main options. Richard Rorty suggests *pragmatism*. As ideas, expressions, and concepts in a clash, one will emerge as a better working option; and something that works in a particular culture (like monogamy) or situation (like an appropriate age of sexual consent) may not in another culture or situation.

Contemporary sitcoms clearly illustrate this view. Sitcoms from a former time (basically, most of the ones prior to *Seinfeld*) tended to follow a pretty standard formula: a character (usually in the context of a family) would be faced with a crisis; through the course of the show, the character would wrestle with and resolve that crisis, and by facing consequences a moral lesson was learned in a humorous way. This is not usually the case today. The crisis remains, but real resolution is rare, consequences can be avoided, and morality disappears if the character can get away with it.

Another option was posited by Michel Foucault. Foucault, a Frenchman who was heavily influenced by Nietzsche and Marx, suggested that every society was made up of the powerful and the oppressed. The powerful decided what was normal in terms of social behavior, laws, and sexuality and imposed these views on the oppressed. By showing how standards of normalcy changed from one society to another, Foucault concluded all cultural standards were arbitrary and only a way for one group to exert its power over another. Thus is it important to reveal power structures and recognize the oppressed (although such exposure is not to be regarded as moving forward).

The influence of Foucault can hardly be overstated. His views have especially influenced studies in an area with which Foucault himself was fascinated: human sexuality. It is not unusual to find major universities offering classes on pornography, or to hear homosexual rights groups refer to themselves as "oppressed" and equate their plight with that of nineteenth century African-Americans. Foucault's own sexual exploits are well-documented, especially his immersion in the very promiscuous homosexual lifestyle of San Francisco later in his life. He died in 1984 from an AIDS-related illness. Foucault is one of the most frequently cited sources in Western academia, especially in the social sciences.[72]

Confronting Humanity: The Death of Self

The implications of postmodernism are significant and have led to drastic changes in philosophy, the study of literature, and the study and practice of the arts. Still, the most drastic shift initiated by postmodernism has to do with its view on humanity, especially the concept of personal identity. From a postmodern perspective, our sense of personal identity is as much a social construct as any other claim about reality.

This is a very different idea about humanness than what was assumed in the pre-modern and modern periods. The pre-modern perspective viewed human nature as fixed and centered on the soul. This only made sense if everything in the world had been designed by a personal deity.

The view of modernism moved the determining of human nature from God to man himself. The result was a radical individualism that continues to infect Western culture: self-made, self-sufficient, and self-defined. The closing stanza of William Ernest Henley's *Invictus* (1875) states this defiantly:

> It matters not how straight the gate,
> How charged with punishments the scroll,
> I am the master of my fate:
> I am the captain of my soul.[73]

However confident this sounds, modern autonomy proved to be overrated. Scientific reductionism simply could not sustain the dignity of the human self. Henry Grunwald explains it well in his article, "The Year 2000: Is It the End, or Just the Beginning?"

> The ultimate irony, or perhaps tragedy, is that secularism has not led to humanism. We have gradually dissolved—deconstructed—the human being into a bundle of reflexes, impulses, neuroses, nerve endings. The great religious heresy

---

[72] Roger Dale, "Positive Poststructuralism? A Response to Ninnes and Burnett" in *Comparative Education,* vol. 39, no. 3 (Aug. 2003), p. 308. Also, Lynne E. Angus and John McLeod, *The Handbook of Narrative and Psychotherapy: Practice, Theory, and Research* (Sage, 2004), p. 64.

[73] William Ernest Henley, *Invictus* in Untermeyer, Louis. *Modern British Poetry.* New York, Harcourt, Brace and Howe, 1920; Bartleby.com, 1999. Online at www.bartleby.com/103/.

used to be making man the measure of all things; but we have
come close to making man the measure of nothing.[74]

Like its reaction to certainty and progress, postmodernism denies
autonomy. "God is dead," Nietzsche thundered; a few decades later,
thinkers like Foucault would say, essentially, "humanness is dead."
Postmodernism boldly declares the demise of a fixed self (the "I"), and
embraces a new concept of the self:

> Today, it is the speaking subject who declared God dead one
> hundred years ago whose very existence is being called into
> question. No longer is the speaking subject unquestionably
> assumed to be the source of language and speech, existence
> and truth, autonomy and freedom, unity and wholeness,
> identity and individualism. . . . The speaking subject appears
> to be not a referent beyond the first person pronoun, but,
> rather, a fragmented entity produced by the act of speaking.[75]

What then is left of man, if not intrinsically valuable by design or
self-made dignity? According to postmodernism, only our relationships.
We are social constructs situated in groups. We are identified by our
networks, not our souls.

Two key factors reinforce this postmodern view of identity. First, the
pluralism of Western societies increases our tendency to see ourselves
and others as part of groups. This is most clearly seen today in "identity
politics," or the tendency of many to claim victim status by way of their
identification with a particular race, group, or sexual orientation. As
Walter Truett Anderson observes, "Issues of identity frequently become
issues of rights."[76]

Second, there is a great *fluidity* to contemporary life. Traditional
lines that defined family, work, and neighborhoods are no longer as fixed
as they once were, especially as the internet makes more and more
experiences virtually accessible. Careers change, long distance moves are
common, and the ease of travel has made the world smaller than ever

---

[74] Henry Grunwald, "The Year 2000: Is It the End, or Just the Beginning," *Time*
30 March 1992. Available online at http://www.time.com/time/magazine/
article/0,9171,975194,00 .html.

[75] Paul Kugler, "The 'Subject' of Dreams," *Dreaming* 3, no. 2 (1993):125;
quoted in Walt Truett Anderson, *The Future of the Self: Exploring the Post-
Identity Society* (New York: Tarcher/Putnam, 1997), p. 43.

[76] Walt Truett Anderson, *The Future of the Self: Exploring the Post-Identity
Society* (New York: Tarcher/Putnam, 1997), p. 213.

before. Genetic engineering, cybernetics, new reproductive options, and innovations in medical technology stretch and change previously fixed boundaries of parenting, appearance, and human capacity.

All of this means that a great amount of flexibility is required of people today. Lines are constantly being drawn and re-drawn, and we are constantly moving in and out of different groups and relationships. According to Kenneth Gergen, "These relationships pull us in myriad directions, inviting us to play such a variety of roles that the very concept of an 'authentic self' with knowable characteristics recedes from view."[77]

How then are we to understand humanness in a postmodern context? Not as a stable sense of identity: the concept of identity dies and is replaced with a self that is flexible, multi-faceted, and always changing.

As we have seen, as a worldview, postmodernism is different than naturalism, transcendentalism, and theism. Still, as a worldview it provides a unique approach to truth, knowledge, reality, and humanity; and it continues to exert astounding influence on the Western world.

Where Do We Go from Here?

Naturalism prevails in Western culture. Charles Malik, former president of the General Assembly of the United Nations, concludes, "Because scientific naturalism is deeply entrenched in the university, the university has become a principal disseminator of atheism."[78] In government, employing the separation of church and state doctrine has resulted in the attempt to be "God-neutral." The secularization of legislation and public school education has rendered God a *persona non grata* in the public square.

While transcendentalism has traditionally been the embedded worldview of much of the Eastern world, it now also dominates the spheres of popular religious expression in the west. All forms of media and art are influenced by transcendental thinking, especially under the guise of New Age thought. The open-minded character of transcendentalism, accompanied by the shining promises of a new age of hope, is an offer too good to pass up.

---

[77] Kenneth Gergen, *The Saturated Self: Dilemmas of Identity in Contemporary Life* (New York: Basic Books, 1991), p. 69.

[78] Charles H. Malik, *A Christian Critique of the University* (Downers Grove, IL: InterVarsity, 1982), p. 44.

No religion has changed the face of the globe over the last several decades as much as Islam. The fastest growing religion in the world, it is the first legitimate contender to displace Christianity as the largest religion in the world. Also, it figures prominently in many of the international conflicts on the world scene. By any measure, this theistic worldview is a force to be reckoned with.

The influence of postmodernism has created a context where significant debate over worldviews is inevitable, but progress in the debate is difficult. Claiming a position of neutrality or anticipating a future of consensus is simply no longer feasible in a postmodern context. Conflict is inevitable and any hope for resolution seems naïve.

In the face of all of these competing ideas about life and the world, clear thinking about worldviews is essential. What then is a Christian to do? Is it possible to evaluate worldviews? If so, then how? We turn our attention to these questions in chapter three.

DISCUSSION QUESTIONS

1. The average person forges ahead in life giving little thought to worldviews, philosophies of life, or any other such "intellectual" endeavors. Why is this true? If every person has a worldview, then why are so many fragmented in their thinking and living?
2. Describe the starting points of naturalism, transcendentalism, theism, and postmodernism. How are they similar? How do they differ?
3. How was reference to God excised from science? In what ways did Darwin's theory help to change the philosophical base of science and set the stage for modern agnosticism?
4. Describe how existentialism, hedonism, and humanism are practical responses to a naturalistic worldview.
5. What elements of a transcendental worldview contribute to its popularity? What are manifestations of this worldview with which you are familiar?
6. Why is reincarnation such an important aspect of transcendental thought? In what ways is reincarnation contrary to biblical teachings?
7. In what ways are naturalism and postmodernism similar? How do these similarities make both worldviews particularly appealing to the American way of thinking and living?
8. How does modern western society (internet, technology, diversity, etc.) contribute to the popularity of postmodern thought?"

Further Reading

Grenz, Stanley. *A Primer on Postmodernism*. Grand Rapids: Eerdmans, 1996.

Middleton, J. Richard, and Brian Walsh. *The Transforming Vision: Shaping a Christian Worldview*. Downers Grove, IL: InterVarsity Press, 1984.

Noebel, David A. *Understanding the Times: The Collision of Today's Competing Worldviews*, 2d ed. Eugene, OR: Harvest House Publishers, 2006.

Pearcey, Nancy. *Total Truth: Liberating Christianity from its Cultural Captivity*. Wheaton, IL: Crossway, 2004.

Sire, James. *The Universe Next Door: A Basic Worldview Catalog,* 4th ed. Downers Grove, IL: InterVarsity Press, 2004.

Sookhdeo, Patrick. *A Christian's Pocket Guide to Islam*. London: Christian Focus, 2006.

White, Heath. *Postmodernism 101: A First Course for the Curious Christian*. Grand Rapids: Brazos, 2006.

3
PUTTING WORLDVIEWS TO THE TEST

Can Worldviews Be Evaluated?
    The Test of Reason
    The Test of the Outer World
    The Test of the Inner World
    The Test of the Real World
Evaluating Naturalism: A Limited Perspective
Evaluating Transcendentalism: An Unreal Perspective
Evaluating Theism: A Narrow Perspective
Evaluating Postmodernism: A Self-Refuting Perspective

Can Worldviews Be Evaluated?

"Where are you going?" I asked the lady sitting beside me, as we settled in for the long international flight. I was returning from an overseas trip.

"I am going to Orlando," she replied.

"What's going on in Orlando?" I asked.

"I am going to an Avatar conference."

"What's an Avatar conference?"

"It's a conference that teaches people how to find the truth that resides deep inside them. Rather than looking for answers from others, or from religions, or from holy books, we need to just realize that we all have the truth we need inside our own hearts."

My attempt to be polite to the person who would be sitting beside me for the next twelve hours had quickly turned into a deep conversation about life and truth and God and meaning. It took only three questions to become obvious that we were operating from two different worldviews, and our differences in perspective only became more obvious as the conversation continued.

Throughout our three-hour discussion, my conversation partner assured me that I had all of the truth I needed within me, that voices other than my own would only confuse me, and that no one had a right to assert their view was right and another wrong. About an hour or so into the conversation she revealed why she thought this: "Because I really believe that you are God, and I am God, and that flight attendant is God."

I have been called many things during my life, but God was a new one.

She continued, "Since you are God, you have the truth inside you. You should not let anyone other than yourself tell you what is right and wrong."

It is not popular today to even suggest that beliefs *can* or *should* be evaluated. In fact, attempts to do so often earn the accusation of intolerance. However, we test ideas and beliefs every day. In fact, when we encounter new ideas in a book or from a traveling companion, it is our natural response to test them. We will often think things like, "That doesn't sound quite right." Or, "That seems very compelling." Or, "If *this* is true, then *that* certainly cannot be true."

I was doing this throughout my conversation with the woman on the airplane, and several things made her beliefs unacceptable to me. First, I found it strange that she would pay thousands of dollars and travel thousands of miles only to have someone assure her that she needed only to look inside of herself to find truth. Didn't that show that she really didn't believe *all* truth could be found inside of her?

Second, it occurred to me that despite not believing in right and wrong, she was trying hard to convince me that her views about right and wrong were in fact right! So, I asked her, "Are you saying that I am wrong if I listen to someone else tell me what is right and wrong?" Her reply? "Well, I didn't mean that you were wrong."

Third, I wondered if she really, really believed that whatever I discovered inside myself would be acceptable, regardless of what it actually was that I discovered. So, I asked her about this too: "What if I look deep inside myself and I determine that what is right for me is to torture babies for fun? Would that be wrong?" After thinking for a moment she replied, "Why do you have to talk in such extremes?" When I inquired further, she wasn't clear on what made it so extreme based upon what she had already said.

In this chapter, we offer four tests that should be used in evaluating worldviews and worldview beliefs. We did not create these tests ourselves; rather, we are attempting to identify the tests we tend to employ in situations like the one described above. Of course, by endorsing these tests, we recognize that we are still operating from within the Christian theistic worldview. We readily admit that we are not able to be purely objective here. Still, we believe these tests to be legitimate since a) they cohere with a Biblical worldview and b) they are really just formal expressions of tests that people, even those from worldviews different than ours, employ in the everyday world of competing ideas.[1]

The Test of Reason

The test of reason evaluates the *reasonableness* of a worldview. In other words, can the worldview be logically stated and defended? Worldviews that violate primary laws of logic may be believed by some people but, in reality, they are nonsensical. They simply cannot be true. Several key questions flow from this test.

First, does the worldview affirm views that are self-contradictory? If so, it should be strongly questioned, as it violates a fundamental rule of logic. The law of non contradiction was first suggested by Aristotle and states, "A cannot be both B and non-B in the same time and in the same sense." If I were to say, "I am a married bachelor," that would be nonsensical, for one cannot be both married and a bachelor at the same time. Another example would be the declaration, "There is no absolute

---

[1] One cannot escape some measure of circularity in evaluating worldviews. Christian Theism flows from God's revelatory claim, "God has spoken" (Heb. 1:1-2). Hebrews 6 refers to God's self-validation, "I swear by myself." God is *sui generis,* a set of one. No other being may make this claim but God alone. To what higher source of authority could God appeal to than Himself? Otherwise, *that* someone would carry higher credibility for purposes of epistemic justification than God Himself, which would be a patent absurdity. This reasoning may be circular, but it is the fate of all worldviews. However, for theism this is not a vicious circle but a *necessary* circle. No source but a personal God who exists independent of reality can claim this sort of authority. Naturalism and transcendentalism do not allow for anything to exist independently of reality that could reasonably be considered authoritative in this way; theism does. This epistemic challenge has been rightly recognized by postmodernists like Stanley Fish and Richard Rorty and is the basis for their claim that worldviews cannot truly be evaluated. Fish notes that a "god's eye view" would be required for authoritative pronouncements. Rorty states it even more directly: "I came to realize that the search of the philosophers for a grand scheme that would encompass everything was illusory. Only a theism that combined a God with equal measures of truth, love, and justice, could do the trick. But since I could not imagine myself being religious, and had indeed become more raucously secular, I did not consider that an option for me." "Trotsky and the Wild Orchids" in *Wild Orchids and Trotsky: Messages from American Universities,* ed. Mark Edmundson (New York: Penguin, 1993), pp. 41-42. The God that Rorty describes and admits that he cannot believe in is, of course, what Christian theism affirms.

truth." If the statement is true, then the statement is false. If a worldview demands views that are self-contradictory, it should be dismissed.

The Test of the Outer World

This test evaluates the *evidence* for a particular worldview. If a worldview is true, we can expect to find at least some external corroborating evidence to support it. This does not mean that something is true because there is evidence for it, but rather evidence will be available because something is true.

We should hesitate to embrace a belief that is directly contradicted by evidence. Of course, people hold to views all the time that fly in the face of the evidence. Sports fans are notorious for believing that their teams still have a chance despite being badly beaten and highly outmatched by their opponents the last time they met. Devotees of particular religions hold on to hope of deliverance, despite all the evidence to the contrary in the midst of their suffering. Sometimes believing in spite of the evidence is wise; other times it is naïve, silly or even dangerous.

Still, evidence, or the explanation of its absence, remains worthy of our consideration. This can be seen in the use of evidence by attorneys in a courtroom. It is never expected that the evidence will provide a conclusion that is beyond a shadow of a doubt. This would be impossible since the judge, jury, and attorneys are not omniscient. What is expected is that the evidence is presented that makes the case beyond *reasonable* doubt. This standard helps us to make reasonable decisions.

A striking example of the power of evidence was the announcement of an Associated Press article on December 9, 2004 that renowned atheist philosopher Anthony Flew had changed his mind about the existence of God. One of the most outspoken and significant minds of twentieth century atheism, Flew has attributed his conversion to deism to "following where the evidence leads," especially noting recent discoveries about the complexities of DNA.[2]

The challenge in dealing with evidence is to keep several things in mind. First, how one defines "evidence" may be reflective of a worldview. For example, for the naturalist, only physical data qualifies as legitimate evidence. Therefore, anything that appears to be a miracle (an occurrence of divine intervention) simply can*not* be a miracle by

---

[2]   See "Where the Evidence Leads" in Anthony Flew, *There Is a God: How the World's Most Notorious Atheist Changed His Mind.* (New York: HarperOne, 2007), pp. 31-64, 74-75. It is important to note that Flew also points to philosophical reasons for his change of mind.

naturalist terms. The Harvard population biologist Richard Lewontin admitted as much when he conceded that his commitment to materialism was prior to—and not a result of—his scientific investigation, and that "materialism is absolute for we cannot allow a divine foot in the door."[3] Clearly, this is a commitment that is prior to defining or evaluating the evidence.

It is more accurate to recognize that different kinds of evidence exist, depending on the subject matter that is being examined, as well as for what purpose we are using the evidence. For example, mathematical evidence may apply to a physics problem, but may not be appropriate for proving your love to your spouse. It is important, as we evaluate ideas, to be careful not to limit evidence due to preconceived notions.

Second, evidence is always subject to interpretation, and interpretation also can be subject to bias. Thus, creationists and evolutionists, despite using the same physical evidence, deduce very different conclusions about questions of origins. Often, to each their conclusions are so *obvious*, it is difficult for them to believe any thinking person could possibly see it another way. To a hammer, everything looks like a nail.

Third, evidence can be manipulated, hidden, or arranged in ways that do not always accurately represent that to which the evidence actually points. In 2002, a group known as the Raelians claimed that their research organization CloneAid had successfully birthed the first human clone and featured a picture of the child on their website as evidence of their claim. However, their unwillingness to allow any outside medical scientists to directly evaluate the child led most of the world to quickly dismiss the claim (and not much has been heard from the group since).[4]

Finally, just because evidence has not been found yet does not imply that it does not exist. More evidence may be forthcoming. A hundred years ago, the lack of historical evidence for King David led many scholars to doubt that he even existed. Since then, enough evidence has been found to demonstrate that he was, in fact, an historical person, and was, in fact, king of Israel.

---

[3] Richard Lewontin, "Billions and Billions of Demons," *The New York Review of Books*, 9 January 1997, p. 28.

[4] For more on this group, see "Raelians" by The Religious Movements Homepage Project at the University of Virginia. Available online at http://religiousmovements.lib.virginia.edu/nrms/rael.html. Also a more critical look is found at "Raelians" by the Rick A. Ross Institute for the Study of Destructive Cults, Controversial Groups and Movements. Online at http://rickross.com/groups/raelians.html.

The Test of the Inner World

Blaise Pascal wrote, "The heart has reasons that reason cannot know."[5] This is the realm where "the test of the inner world" operates. A worldview may be reasonable and supportable, but it is not much use if it cannot adequately address the victories, disappointments, blessings, crises, and relationships of our everyday world. In fact, many people walk away from or embrace a particular worldview because of the dissonance caused by personal experience: the parent who gives up on God after the death of a child; the young lady who embraces Buddhism because her heart has been won by a pursuing devotee; the hardened atheist who re-thinks whether God exists or not when confronted with his own mortality late in life.

Of all the tests we offer in this chapter, this is certainly the most subjective. Still, it remains valid if for no other reason than we are human *beings*, not just human doings or human thinkers. Human life is not experienced in the same way as plant or animal life. We live it, we feel it, we wrestle with it, and we cannot escape it. We tend to live as though life had meaning.

Our challenge here is not to allow mere feelings to shape our interpretations of the existential dilemmas of life. If we are merely reactive to our life experiences, we may settle for a worldview that cannot satisfy our deepest longings. For example, evil and suffering may seem sufficient cause for a wounded person to dismiss the existence of God, without realizing that a world that has no God is a world that has no purpose. This leaves our wounded friend with no direction or resolution for their hurt or suffering. (See chapter seven for a further explanation of this specific issue).

Instead, the experiences we have should force us toward intentional reflection and evaluation of our worldview. We will not, of course, satisfy all the skeptics. We can, however, reach a level of knowledge by which we can manage our experiences and the personal dissonances they create.

The Test of the Real World

While the test of the inner world focuses more on the perspective of the individual, the test of the real world evaluates what a worldview looks like in its *application*. A worldview may look compelling as an explanation of the evidence, but when the assumptions of that worldview are actually applied in a particular cultural setting its shortcomings are

---

[5]   Blaise Pascal, *Pensées* (New York: Dutton, 1958).

revealed. Simply put, ideas are not isolated cognitive concepts. They have consequences: good ideas have good consequences and bad ideas have bad ones.

The twentieth century was replete with examples of bad ideas and their bad consequences, especially in two aspects. First, it was a century of *utopian* ideas. For example, economic philosophies promised to rid the world of poverty while scientific arrogance promised to make the world convenient, productive, and free of disease. Yet, each set of utopian ideas was based on a faulty worldview, and the story of the twentieth century is a story of bloodshed and aggression. By looking at the results these faulty worldviews spawned, we can more accurately assess the worldviews themselves. (Of course, a distinction must always be made between ideas that emerge from a worldview and ideas that emerge from a misrepresentation of that worldview.)

Second, it was a century of *marginalizing* ideas. The eugenics movement in America at the beginning of the century, the attempt by the Nazis to exterminate the Jews in the middle of the century, and the millions of aborted children at the end of the century each reflects ideas in which some people are not considered valuable persons. Worldviews exert their greatest influence in offering definitions, and faulty worldviews define words—and consequently ideas and persons—in destructive ways. G. K. Chesterton is reputed to have said, "If words aren't worth fighting for, what on earth would be?"

Having examined the tests, we will now apply them to the world-views of naturalism, transcendentalism, theism, and postmodernism.

Evaluating Naturalism: A Limited Perspective

To the Western mind, naturalism is an appealing worldview because it seems so closely tied to the scientific enterprise. In regards to our tests, naturalism seems to have the evidence (test of the outer world) stacked on its side. Science has the aura of objectivity and progress, which generates confidence. Further, naturalism is personally satisfying (test of the inner world) by teaching that each individual chooses his or her own goals and morality. Ethical relativism and freedom from ultimate judgment are enticing ideas.

Positively, naturalism affirms the importance of the physical world. Naturalism affirms the uniformity of the universe, which is necessary for science to be possible. In addition, science has removed the superstitions associated with primitive views of nature. Demons do not cause lightning, and spirits do not make crops grow. Barrenness can be reversed. Science also illustrates that truth can be derived by our senses as we investigate the world. Practically, some streams of naturalism remind us of our responsibility to care for the world's human needs.[6]

However, there are many ways in which naturalism miserably fails when put to the tests listed above.

THE TEST OF REASON. A major problem for naturalism is that it cannot offer proper foundations for its conclusions. A world which is the result of natural causes and processes is the product of a cosmic accident. According to naturalist Richard Dawkins in his book *River Out of Eden: A Darwinian View of Life*, "The universe we observe has precisely the properties we should expect if there is, at bottom, no design, no purpose, no evil and no good, nothing but blind, pitiless indifference."[7]

However, if this is the case, then the minds that we use to develop theories are also accidental and purposeless as well. Whence, then, would real knowledge come from? The answer is not clear in a naturalistic view. Says theistic philosopher Alvin Plantinga, in a scathing critique of naturalism:

> From this point of view, our beliefs would be dependent on neurophysiology, and a belief would just be a neurological structure of some complex kind . . . but why think for a moment that the beliefs dependent on or caused by that neurophysiology will be mostly true? . . . from a naturalist point of view the thought that our cognitive faculties are reliable would be at best naive hope. . . . In fact, he'd (the naturalist) have to hold that it is unlikely, given unguided evolution, that our cognitive faculties are reliable. . . . If this is so, the naturalist has a *defeater* for the natural assumption that his cognitive faculties are reliable—a reason for rejecting that belief, for no longer holding it. And if he has a defeater for that belief, he also has a defeater for any belief that is a product of his cognitive faculties. But of course that would be *all* of his beliefs—including naturalism itself. So the naturalist has a defeater for naturalism; naturalism, therefore, is self-defeating and cannot be rationally believed.[8]

---

[6] However, Arthur Brooks suggests that people who are religious give, on the average, far more than their secularist counterparts. See *Who Really Cares: The Surprising Truth about Compassionate Conservatism* (New York: Basic Books, 2006).

[7] Richard Dawkins, *River Out of Eden: A Darwinian View of Life* (New York: Basic Books, 1995), p. 133.

[8] Alvin Plantinga, "The Dawkins Confusion: Naturalism *ad absurdum*" in *Books & Culture,* vol. 13, no. 2, March/April 2007, p. 21.

THE TEST OF THE OUTER WORLD. In spite of its contributions to understanding the world around us, there are major hesitations about the interpretive scope of naturalism as a full-blown worldview. The first hesitation is the *limitation of science*. Naturalism is often proved to be true by an appeal to the scientific nature of knowledge. Even though it claims great objectivity and certainty, science begins with presuppositions about knowledge, about the objective existence of the universe, about the orderliness of natural law, and so forth. Carl Henry points out, "No historian and no scientist approaches historical or physical events without presuppositions. He may not wear his view of total reality on his lapel, but he nonetheless interprets the particularities of his life by it."[9]

By its very nature, science is limited to observable and repeatable events in the physical realm. But to reduce all knowledge to this realm excludes the possibility of real things existing beyond the physical. Therefore, even though science does give us true knowledge it does not give us full knowledge. Robert Jastrow, professor of astronomy and geology at Columbia University, acknowledges that science "is one avenue of truth. But it is clear to me that it is not the only one."[10]

Paul de Vries notes that the scientific method "cannot pretend to provide answers to the ultimate questions. At some point in every explanation of phenomena, the question 'Why?' can no longer be answerable within science."[11] Science cannot even give final truth about matters of science, let alone about matters of morals or religion.[12]

Such an admission of science's limitations is also acknowledged by nontheistic scientists. For example, as we pointed out above, Stephen Hawking attempts to prove that if there is no "edge" of the universe there is no God. But Hawking's theory, while it appears to explain away the need for a creator, still fails to answer the fundamental question, "Why is there something rather than nothing?" Simply saying, "The universe just *is*," does not advance our understanding beyond that of the ancient Greeks who believed the universe was eternal. Even Hawking himself admits this limitation. He notes, "When I was eleven, I wanted to know how and why the universe works. Now I know how, but I still do not

---

[9] Carl F. H. Henry, *God Who Speaks and Shows*, vol. 1 of *God, Revelation and Authority* (Waco, TX: Word, 1976), p. 261.

[10] Quoted in an interview with Bill Durbin in "A Scientist Caught Between Two Faiths," *Christianity Today*, 6 August 1982, p. 15.

[11] Paul de Vries, "Naturalism in the Natural Sciences: A Christian Perspective," *Christian Scholar's Review* 15:4 (1984):394.

[12] See Carl F. H. Henry, *God Who Speaks and Shows*, pp. 165-80.

know why."[13] Even if scientists were to explain all causes for every effect in the universe, such knowledge of the mechanics of the physical world will not answer the question why the world is as it is.

There is a Latin phrase *ex nihilo, nihil fit,* or "from nothing, nothing comes." In other words, if there was ever a time when nothing existed, then nothing would ever exist. However, this is precisely what is implied by naturalism. The speculations of the so-called quantum cosmology are questionable. Davies' claim that quantum physics "routinely produces something from nothing"[14] is unfounded and misleading. Quantum physics has never discovered "something being created from nothing," because even it adheres to basic laws. The experiments to which Davies refers require pre-existing energy in a system for there to be any conversion of energy into matter.[15]

To believe that science is valid does not mean that one must adopt a naturalistic worldview. Christianity affirms that science is a valid means of uncovering truth about the physical world, but Christianity goes further and affirms the existence of real things beyond the reach of scientific investigation.[16] Science gives a view that embraces the material realm but is not a comprehensive view of all reality. Naturalism does not have a corner on the scientific enterprise.

The choice is not between science and faith. Princeton physicist Freeman Dyson acknowledges, "Scientific materialism and [religion] are neither incompatible nor mutually exclusive. We have learned that matter is weird stuff. It is weird enough, so that it does not limit God's freedom to make and do what he pleases."[17] Science and religion are better seen as partners in the quest for truth. Philosopher Richard Westfall notes, "If

---

[13] Stephen Hawking, quoted in "The Creation of the Universe," special edition of "Nova," Public Broadcasting Service, 1985.

[14] P. C. W. Davies, *God and the New Physics* (London: J. M. Dent, 1983), p. 216. Davies more fully develops this statement in his later book *The Cosmic Blueprint*, referred to earlier in this chapter.

[15] William Lane Craig, "God, Creation and Mr. Davies," *British Journal for the Philosophy of Science* (1986):165-69.

[16] For example, the Bible affirms the existence of God and angels, the existence of a human soul and life after death, the existence of "things not seen" (2 Cor. 4:18; Heb. 11:1), and so forth.

[17] Freeman Dyson, *Infinite in All Directions* (New York: Harper & Row, 1988), p. 8.

Christianity is true, the valid conclusions of science can never be in conflict with it."[18]

THE TEST OF THE INNER WORLD. Another hesitation in accepting naturalism as an adequate worldview is the *problem of human thought and meaning*. Seeing the universe as a closed system of physical events appears fine when we consider rocks, mountains, planets, and stars; but when humanity is brought into the picture, naturalism falters. How is it that man has the ability to reason abstractly and transcend his own existence? The very fact that the human mind can apprehend objects outside itself goes beyond physical explanation. How did unconscious forces give rise to minds and sound reasoning? Pascal noted, "Thought constitutes the greatness of man. Man is a reed, the most feeble thing in nature, but he is a thinking reed."[19]

Naturalists have consistently struggled with the implications of their worldview as applied to certain facets of man's nature. That human beings possess such powers of reasoning, art, and morality calls into question the premise of purely materialistic explanations. Darwin was mystified by the human eye, and Freud was baffled by human creativity.

Naturalism assumes that reality is completely physical and there is no ultimate purpose or meaning to be found. But if the universe is meaningless, then so is the statement "The universe is meaningless." How can such an evaluative statement be made if indeed there is no meaning in the universe? By what criterion is meaning being judged? If the universe is meaningless, how would we know? C. S. Lewis observed this about his own conversion from atheism to theism, and eventually, to Christianity. "Atheism turns out to be too simple. If the whole universe has no meaning, we should never have found out that it has no meaning."[20]

THE TEST OF THE REAL WORLD. There is no question that religion and religious belief have a sketchy history when it comes to war, intolerance, and human rights abuses. However, *unbelief* was at the heart of most of the devastating philosophies of the twentieth century. Nazism, communism, and other various forms of fascism that were responsible for hundreds of millions of deaths in the twentieth century were aggressively atheistic philosophies. Further, the "might makes right" mentality that characterized these views is *consistent* with a naturalistic

---

[18] Richard S. Westfall, "The Trial of Galileo: Bellarmino, Galileo, and the Clash of the Two Worlds," 1988 Gross Memorial Lecture (Valparaiso, IN: Valparaiso U., 1988), p. 17.

[19] Pascal, *Pensées.*

[20] C. S. Lewis, *Mere Christianity* (New York: Macmillan, 1943), p. 46.

view of the world in which any progress is the result of natural selection. Indeed, from a naturalistic worldview, it is difficult to see how these views can be considered wrong.

Frederick Nietzsche (1844-1900) was one of a few atheistic writers who foresaw, and embraced, where the naturalistic ideas of the nineteenth century would lead civilization in the twentieth. In his "Parable of the Madman," Nietzsche talked about the death of God as the ends of modern science and philosophy: "Where has God gone? I will tell you. We have killed him, you and I. All of us are his murderers." Where does this leave us? He tells us: "Must we ourselves not become gods simply to appear worthy of it."[21]

In another of his parables "Thus Spake Zarathrustra" Nietzsche clarifies what he means: "Lo, I teach you the Superman. The Superman is the meaning of the earth!"[22] For Nietzsche, the Superman was the person willing to transcend categories of good and evil in the name of power. Looking ahead to the coming century, he predicted, "The concept of politics will have merged entirely with a war of spirits; all power structures of the old society will have been exploded—all of them are based on lies. There will be wars the like of which have never yet been seen on earth."[23] It is no secret that the writings of Nietzsche influenced Adolf Hitler and Benito Mussolini.

As a means of understanding the world around us, naturalism provides tools necessary to explore and discover truth. As a full-blown worldview, however, naturalism fails to explain far too many aspects of the world and life as we see them. Also, it fails to offer any moral guidelines either for the individual or for society.

---

[21] Friedrich Nietzsche, "The Parable of the Madman" in *The Gay Science* sec. 125 [online] (accessed 3 January 2006); available from http://www.historyguide.org/europe/madman.html; Internet.

[22] Friedrich Nietzsche, *Thus Spake Zarathustra*, trans. by Thomas Common (Hertfordshire: Wordsworth Editions, 1997), p. 3.

[23] Friedrich Nietzsche, *Ecco Homo: How One Becomes What One Is*, trans. by R. J. Hollingdale; rev. ed. (Suffolk: Penguin Books, 1992), p. 96.

Evaluating Transcendentalism:
An Unreal Perspective

Transcendentalism has a tremendous appeal at the emotional level. It promises everything a person could desire: divinity, self-reliance, moral freedom, and a second chance. C. S. Lewis concluded that such a worldview was "the permanent natural bent of the human mind."[24]

From a Christian perspective, transcendentalism makes several positive *contributions*.

First, transcendentalism recognizes that ultimate reality is beyond the human categories of thought and language. Whereas naturalism teaches that all truth potentially can be uncovered by the scientific method, transcendentalism holds that a complete understanding of the physical universe does not begin to exhaust the knowledge of truth.

Second, transcendentalism recognizes that ultimate reality is not only beyond human understanding but is also spiritual in nature. There is a bond between our own spiritual makeup and that which is the final reality of the universe.

Third, transcendentalism sees the unity of all creation. All things are one in spite of the diversity present in the world.

However, there are several major *hesitations* one should have regarding a transcendental worldview, in light of our tests.

THE TEST OF REASON. The most glaring difficulty is the inability to evaluate transcendentalism. It appeals more to the emotions than the mind. Since, in the view of transcendentalism, ultimate reality goes beyond human thinking, then there no doubt will be logical inconsistencies and contradictions. For example, the Bhagwan Shree Rajneesh suggests, "It is not that the intellect sometimes misunderstands. Rather then intellect always misunderstands. It is not that the intellect sometimes errs, it is that the intellect is the error."[25]

In this view, transcendentalism is not only beyond proof, it is also beyond disproof. This aspect of transcendentalism is often no problem for its proponents, many of whom enjoy the logical absurdities of their view. But does such a perspective of reality actually fit the world in which we live? Can we survive without reliance on the intellect? In fact, this view is self-contradictory, for one cannot reach the conclusion that

---

[24] C. S. Lewis, *Miracles* (London: Geoffrey Bles, 1959), p. 100.
[25] Rajneesh, *I Am the Gate* (New York: Harper and Row, 1977), p. 18.

the intellect should be dismissed without using the intellect in the process of dismissing it.

Another problem, from a biblical and reasonable perspective, is the promise of reincarnation. The Bible clearly excludes any possibility for "other lives" when the writer of Hebrews states, "And inasmuch as it is appointed for men to *die once* and after this comes judgment" (Heb. 9:27, italics added). It is popular among New Agers to discuss the influences of past lives (and even future lives!)[26] on their personalities. This romantic sense of history makes the whole idea of reincarnation an exciting future hope. However, popular views of reincarnation are typically distortions of common pantheistic view of reincarnation. To the Eastern mind, reincarnation is a *curse,* not a romantic cycle of interesting, exciting lives.[27]

THE TEST OF THE OUTER WORLD. Another difficulty is the problem of origins. It is not clear how a perfect "oneness" could produce the diverse physical universe, including individual personalities. Also, if all things are one, why are so many persons not aware of this oneness?

Transcendentalism also fails to adequately address the reality of evil. If all is one, how can evil be such a real and powerful part of the physical universe? Is ultimate reality also evil? The only recourse is to claim that the physical realm is totally an illusion, thus evil is not real. Shirley Maclaine suggests, "Until mankind realizes that there is, in truth, no good and there is, in truth, no evil—there will be no peace."[28] However easy this may be to say and believe in times of relative peace and pleasant circumstances, this does not square with our experience in the real world where significant evil and suffering do exist.

THE TEST OF THE INNER WORLD. The view that evil is an illusion is small consolation for those who suffer. Denying the reality of evil does not make it go away. "Illusory" pain ends up hurting just as much as real pain.

Further, transcendentalism leaves us no place to find healing, direction, or peace but inside ourselves. For example Nancy Wilson Ross suggests, "Zen does not go along with the Judaic-Christian belief in a

---

[26] See Bruce Goldberg, *Past Lives, Future Lives: Accounts of Regression and Progression Thru Hypnosis* (New York: Ballantine, 1988).

[27] Some New Age teachers refer to biblical passages to support reincarnation. For examples and a brief analysis of this usage of Scripture, see Norman Geisler and J. Yutaka Amano, *The Reincarnation Sensation* (Wheaton, IL: Tyndale, 1984), pp. 133-54. See also Doug Groothuis, *Confronting the New Age* (Downers Grove, IL: InterVarsity, 1988), pp. 94-103.

[28] Shirley Maclaine, *Dancing in the Light* (New York: Bantam, 1986), p. 357.

personal savior or a God—outside the Universe—who has created the cosmos and the human race. To the Zen view, the Universe is one indissoluble substance, one total whole, of which humanity is a part."[29] If this is so, then we must necessarily have the answers we need within. Accordingly, Shirley Maclaine posits, "...one individual is his or her own best teacher, and no other idol or false image should be worshipped or adored because the God we are all seeking lies inside oneself, not outside."[30]

If it is true that the source of our healing is inside, then two issues must be resolved. First, looking inside often leads to confusion, not clarity. Pascal's statement on that seems to match our experience: "It is in vain, oh man, that you look within yourself for the answers for all of your miseries. All of your searching has only led you to the knowledge that it is not in yourself that you discover the true and the good."[31]

Second, if truth is found only in looking within ourselves, we have no basis from which to condemn the actions of anyone else. What if looking inside leads us to conclude that what is good and right is to torture babies for personal pleasure? The transcendentalist would respond, "But someone really seeking truth would never say that." Still, the reality is that our newspapers are filled daily with stories of those who do reach this conclusion and live accordingly. The transcendentalist lacks any legitimate grounds upon which to say that this is not an authentic expression of one's inner truth.

THE TEST OF THE REAL WORLD. Transcendentalism is a religious step backward. Rather than giving humanity the hope of a maturing new age, transcendentalism actually forges a retreat to an earlier period of human development when man attempted to appease "the spirits" for his own benefit. Rabbi Harold Kushner concurs: "For me, New Age religion infantalizes our relationship with God. It would take us back to the premoral stage of religion, asking for something, trying to manipulate God to get what we want, without our having to meet any standards at our end of the relationship."[32]

---

[29] Nancy Wilson Ross, *Three Ways of Asian Wisdom* (New York: Simon and Shuster, 1966), p. 145.
[30] Shirley Maclaine, *It's All in the Playing,* (New York: Bantam, 1988).
[31] Pascal, *Pensées*.
[32] Harold Kushner, *Who Needs God?* (New York: Summit Books, 1989), p. 80.

Evaluating Theism: A Narrow Perspective

Because theism is built squarely upon belief in God's existence, we must look at it first. Can the existence of God be proven? If it can be shown that the belief in God is either unreasonable or lacks proper evidence, than this would essentially be a deathblow to any theistic worldview from the outset.

Undoubtedly, many have claimed to have demonstrated that this is, in fact, the case. Dan Barker, former Christian minister turned atheist and now president of the Freedom from Religion Foundation makes this claim in an article responding to the events of September 11, 2001: "There is no evidence for a God, no good argument for a God, and no need for a God. . . . Besides, the attacks are proof that prayer has already failed us . . . it would not have been difficult for an all-powerful God to divert those jets. . . . I would call him something of an accomplice, if he truly existed."[33] In other words, the existence of God lacks evidence and the existence of evil makes the existence of God unreasonable to believe.

THE TEST OF REASON. Is it unreasonable to believe in God? From Dan Barker's point of view, the existence of evil indeed makes belief in God unreasonable. The argument is that if there were an all-good, all-powerful God, he would be unwilling to co-exist with evil and would be powerful enough to eliminate it. This challenge deserves our serious attention, and we have devoted an entire chapter to it. However, an important observation needs to be made from the outset. The very fact that we recognize evil as something that *ought not be* suggests that we know what *ought to be*. C. S. Lewis put it this way: "As an atheist my argument against God was that the universe seemed so cruel and unjust. But how had I got this idea of *just* and *unjust*? A man does not call a line crooked unless he has some idea of a straight line...."[34]

Second, it is often suggested that it is unreasonable to believe in something that cannot be proven. Can the existence of God be proven? Well, *proof* may not be an appropriate term to describe the evidence for the existence of God. The idea of proving that something exists usually refers either to reasoning deductively to a conclusion from true premises, or to the realm of science, where proof is limited to the physical world. For example, I can prove that I know how to make banana nut pancakes by cooking a stack for you, or I can prove that my car is brown by showing it to you. But the essential nature of God is not physical. As the

---

[33] "Interview with Atheist Dan Barker," *Bryan College Triangle*, vol. 24, no. 4 (28 September 2001), p. 2.

[34] Lewis, *Mere Christianity,* p. 45.

final reality, God is beyond the material world—the physical universe was created by Him, but He is not bound by what He created. Defining proof in this way reflects a naturalistic worldview that limits proof to something that exists in the physical realm. God is dismissed *a priori.*

This does not mean the physical universe provides no clues to God's existence. The Christian may point to evidence within the physical realm as "proof" for God's existence: the order of creation, human conscience, miracles, or religious experiences. To search scientifically for the presence of God in the physical universe is like searching for the artist in the canvas of a painting. All that can be found is evidence of the artist's handiwork. In the same way, by searching the physical realm we would expect to find evidence of God's handiwork in creation. Also, if the definition of proof is not limited by a naturalistic bias then other evidence emerges that merits consideration. This evidence is seen in several ways in what have traditionally been called the arguments for God's existence.

Because other works explore these arguments at length, we shall simply summarize three of them here: the cosmological argument, the teleological argument, and the moral argument. The focus of the cosmological and the teleological arguments is the existence and the nature of the cosmos, or the outer world. The moral argument argues from universal human experience, or the inner world. For consistency, we will examine the arguments in light of the respective tests with which they correspond.

THE TEST OF THE OUTER WORLD. The *cosmological argument* points to the existence of the cosmos as evidence of God's existence. The cosmological argument has been a part of Greek, Arabic, Jewish, and Christian thought. [35] The argument generally takes two forms.

The first is to claim that something outside the universe is required to explain its existence. The universe itself consists of a series of cause/ effect relationships: for everything that exists there is something that existed prior and caused its existence. Such relationships could not move infinitely into the past; there had to be a first cause. (It is true that some have argued that an infinite regression of cause/effect is not absurd.

---

[35] For a good explanation of the history and development of the cosmological argument, see William L. Craig, *The Cosmological Argument from Plato to Leilmiz* (New York: Macmillan, 1980). The classic exposition was given by Thomas Aquinas. See *Summa Theologica*, Part 1, Question 2, Article 3, in *Basic Writings of Saint Thomas Aquinas*, ed. Anton C. Pegis (New York: Random House, 1948).

Although this may be true philosophically, the actual evidence within the present form of the material universe points to a definite starting point.)

A second form of the cosmological argument focuses on the *necessary* existence of God. It is argued that God is the only existence that *must* exist, all other things are not necessary. For example, you can imagine many of the things around you not existing: your car, the pine tree in your front yard, your neighbor's house, even your neighbor. In fact, there is nothing in the universe that absolutely must exist. Things that do not have to exist are said to be contingent, that is, dependent on something else for their existence. Because the universe is made up of contingent things, it seems reasonable to assume the universe itself does not have to exist—it is contingent on some first cause for its existence.[36] This "something else" is God.

A second argument for the existence of God is the *teleological* argument, which looks beyond the mere existence of the cosmos and extends the scope of inquiry to the apparent design within the creation. If not the strongest, the argument for design is certainly the most popular approach to demonstrate the existence of God.[37] The argument is based on the analogy of human design and purpose. When we see evidence of intelligent design within the world (i.e., an automobile, a watch, a building, etc.) we naturally assume that an intelligent designer was responsible for constructing the object.

The classic explanation of the teleological argument was given by William Paley, who used the analogy of a watch discovered in a field. Because a watch is an instrument of intricate design, the natural conclusion, claimed Paley, is that the watch is the product of a watchmaker. The intricate design of the universe, therefore, leads us to conclude that it is the product of a "universe-maker," or God.[38] Richard Swinburne updated this argument by taking into account the philosophical and scientific objections.[39]

The teleological argument claims not only that the universe shows evidence of an intelligent scheme, but also that several aspects of the created world show evidence of conscious design: the laws of nature, the intricate and purposeful function of plant and animal life, the balance of

---

[36] Because the universe consists of contingent things, it does not necessarily follow that the universe itself is contingent. However, for the naturalist to claim otherwise is a bold statement of faith. How can a universe of contingent things be necessary?

[37] See J. L. Mackie, *The Miracle of Theism* (Oxford: Clarendon, 1982), p. 133.

[38] William Paley, *Natural Theology*, 2d ed. (Oxford: J. Vincent, 1828).

[39] See his *The Existence of God* (Oxford: Oxford U., 1979), p. 135.

nature, and the emerging discoveries in the field of molecular biology and genetics.

Not everyone is convinced by the argument for design. Philosophically, some believe that the analogy between human design and the apparent design within the universe is not so evident. Further, they argue, there is a great deal of disorder within the universe. If God is a God of order, they ask, why did He seem to fall short of a universe that is completely ordered?[40] Scientifically, as we mentioned in chapter 2, the natural selection theory of Charles Darwin, which has been expanded to include a host of other natural processes, supposedly takes away the mystery of design within the biological world. Darwin claimed, "The old argument of design in nature . . . which formerly seemed to me so conclusive, fails, now that the law of natural selection has been discovered."[41]

Neither of these arguments is sufficient to reject completely the teleological approach to God's existence. The concept of disorder implies an understanding of order. From where does this idea arise except from a divine orderer? The theory of natural selection, even if it is true, certainly does not rule out God.

Also, recent thinkers such as Phillip Johnson, William Dembski and Michael Behe, have used emerging discoveries in molecular biology and information theory to successfully challenge the Darwinian explanation of natural selection.[42] Their work has spawned an entire movement of "intelligent design" theorists, the founding of the Discovery Institute to promote and disseminate intelligent design research, and the drafting of a statement entitled "A Scientific Dissent from Darwinism" which reads: "We are skeptical of claims for the ability of random mutation and natural selection to account for the complexity of life. Careful examination of the evidence for Darwinian theory should be encouraged." The statement has been signed by over 600 scientists,

---

[40] See David Hume, *Dialogues Concerning Natural Religion*, ed. Nelson Pike (Indianapolis: Bobbs-Merrill, 1970) and Anthony Flew, *God and Philosophy* (New York: Dell, 1966).

[41] Quoted in John C. Greene, *Darwin and the Modern World View* (Baton Rouge, LA: Louisiana State U., 1961), p. 43.

[42] Phillip Johnson, *Darwin on Trial,* 2d ed. (Downers Grove, IL: InterVarsity, 1993) and *The Wedge of Truth: Splitting the Foundations of Naturalism* (Downers Grove: InterVarsity, 2002); William Dembski, *No Free Lunch: Why Specified Complexity Cannot Be Purchased without Intelligence* (Rowman and Littlefield, 2006); Michael Behe, *Darwin's Black Box: The Biochemical Challenge to Evolution,* 2d ed. (Free Press, 2006).

including professors from major universities and international research institutions, and members of the National Academies of Science. [43]

A final observation is that the teleological argument has great appeal because it fulfills the aesthetic longings *within* us as we view the beauty of the world *around* us. The argument may be summed up in a statement by Martin Luther, "All creation is the most beautiful book of the Bible; in it God has described and portrayed Himself."[44]

THE TEST OF THE INNER WORLD. A third argument for God's existence is the *moral argument*, which sees the reality of man's moral nature as evidence for a "moral Lawgiver." This argument focuses on the pervasive sense of right and wrong that is present in humanity. Morality may have different expressions in different cultures, but the fact of moral standards is a most striking feature. Among all people there is an approval of benevolent behavior and the tendency to act benevolently toward others. This of course does not mean that people always behave kindly toward others, but actions are consistently judged as being right or wrong; good or bad; fair or unfair.

By what standard are such judgments made? Why do we believe we are answerable to some moral standard for our behavior? Why do we expect others to play by the same rules? Who imposed the standards on us? Theists believe God has given mankind an obligation to meet certain behavioral standards that are a reflection of His character. Morality is an intensely personal matter and thus only a personality could have imposed such standards.

Not everyone agrees that human morality is evidence for the existence of God. Atheists argue that morality is the natural product of biological and social evolution. Further, many atheists consider the idea of a moral law to be an unlikely "miracle." For example, J. L. Mackie believed it was impossible for God to impose His will on mankind. He claimed, "Moral values, their objectivity and their supervenience, would be a continuing miracle . . . , a constant intrusion into the natural world. But then our post-Humean skepticism about miracles will tell against this whole view."[45] Mackie concluded that because David Hume proved that miracles are impossible, anything resembling a miracle (i.e., God imposing His will on mankind) is dismissed as impossible.

---

[43] See www.dissentfromdarwin.org. The statement and full list of signatures is available online.

[44] Quoted by Martin E. Marty, *Health and Medicine in the Lutheran Tradition* (New York: Crossroad, 1983), p. 27.

[45] Mackie, *Miracle*, p. 118.

The moral argument is best suited to complement the other arguments for the existence of God. Although it makes strong statements about the source of man's moral nature, the moral argument nevertheless interprets human behavior and cultural norms from a metaphysical perspective.

The moral argument, however, has been a formidable proof over the past few centuries. The German philosopher Immanuel Kant considered the moral argument to be the only compelling one for God's existence.[46] Later apologists, such as J. H. Newman[47] and C. S. Lewis,[48] used the moral argument as a powerful statement for the existence of God.

There are other "inner world" arguments that suggest God's existence. Among them are the argument from religious experience (If there is no God, how is it that millions of people have religious experiences?); the argument from consciousness (How can a material object give rise to conscious thought?); and the ontological argument (Is not the very idea of God proof of His existence?). Many theists would say that even though the individual arguments may be answered, the overwhelming impact of the arguments as a whole is not easily dismissed—they give reasonable evidence to believe that God does exist.

However, it is crucial to recognize that the theistic arguments alone are not irrefutable proof for God's existence. An atheist may point to evidence of a *lack* of design or of cruelty in nature's design as evidence that God does not exist. One's assumptions often determine the outcome of one's arguments.

The arguments, however, are not useless. They do point out that belief in the existence of God is not a foolhardy leap of faith. Further, they show that a monotheistic interpretation of the world can be a thinking man's view. Belief in God's existence does not violate a logical and rational approach to the particular evidences and experiences in the world.

THE TEST OF THE REAL WORLD. A final point to consider in our evaluation of theism is what faith looks like when applied to the real world of human circumstances and relationships. Unfortunately, theistic worldviews suffer from a bad reputation, and there have been times when that reputation is well deserved (instances of resistance to progress, justifications of racism and slavery, responsibilities for wars and

---

[46] Immanuel Kant, *Grounding for the Metaphysics of Morals*, trans. James W. Ellington (Indianapolis: Hackett Publishing, 1981).

[47] J. H. Newman, *A Grammar of Assent* (London: Longmans, 1870).

[48] C. S. Lewis, *Mere Christianity*, reprint ed. (Westwood, NJ: Barbour and Co., 1952).

terrorism, and expressions of violence against those that hold contrary views). However, the outworking of the theistic worldview has on balance been of great benefit to the world it penetrates.

First, as stated earlier, it is important that a worldview be judged at its best, and not at its worst. It is easy to caricature a religion or worldview by an expression of it that is actually incomplete or even contrary to the tenets that it actually teaches. For example, while much was done in the name of theism and Christian theism in particular, to justify racism and slavery in the British Empire and the American colonies, any justification of such a reprehensible behavior actually went against a fundamental teaching of Christian theism that all human beings are created valuable in the image of God.[49]

Second, it is equally easy to ignore examples in which that same religion and worldview was appropriately expressed in a way that significantly and positively contributed to history. To continue our example, it was this view of Christianity of the inherent value in all human life that was a main impetus behind the abolition of slavery across the British Empire under the leadership of William Wilberforce and many others.[50]

Third, we live in a real world where things are good, pleasant and enjoyable (waterfalls, good-tasting food, and romance), and where humans are capable of doing amazing things (feats of engineering, works of art, and self-sacrificing heroism). We also live in a world where other things are bad, unpleasant, and harmful (natural disasters, death, and disease), and where humans are capable of perpetuating great evil (genocide, abandonment, and incest). This is one of the great tensions of reality. In fact, sometimes good and evil mix in truly astounding ways; some of the greatest evils ever perpetuated in the history of the world

---

[49] Many of the popular stories about the evils of theism, and Christian theism in particular, have been grossly exaggerated. It is essential that we are honest as to what actually happened in history, for good and for bad. Thankfully, there are recent works which correct many of the myths surrounding the role Christianity played in, among others, the development of modern science, the slave trade, and the persecution of witches. See for example Rodney Stark's *For the Glory of God: How Monotheism Led to Reformations, Science, Witch-hunts, and the End of Slavery* (Princeton, NJ: Princeton University, 2003) and *The Victory of Reason: How Christianity Led to Freedom, Capitalism, and Western Success* (New York: Random House, 2006).

[50] See Eric Metaxas, *Amazing Grace: William Wilberforce and the Campaign to End Slavery* (New York: HarperCollins, 2007).

were done in extremely creative ways and by those with amazing gifts of leadership.

Theism, with its view of a divinely created world and the significance of humanity as responsible actors in history, helps make sense of one of the tensions of the real world. There is something profoundly good and profoundly twisted about our world and the people in it, and naturalism and transcendentalism fail to offer adequate explanations for this. Naturalism cannot account for feats of self-sacrifice and creativity that express something beyond the survival instinct. Transcendentalism, with its view of universal divinity, cannot account for the depths of human depravity we experience. The explanation offered by theism is that this world reflects the goodness of its creator, as well as the evil that human freedom can produce.

Of course, we have not answered all the questions that evil in the world poses for the theist and the Christian theist in particular. Another real world problem facing the theist is what to do with the vast amounts of competing views of God available within a theistic (and even a semi-theistic) framework. In other words, what becomes of those who disagree? What becomes of those who have never heard of the God who is there? The narrow perspective of theism is hard for many people to embrace, particularly in today's world where we are exposed to so many different religions. These problems, which are associated with *pluralism*, along with the problems associated with evil and suffering, are significant issues and will be dealt with extensively in later chapters.

Evaluating Postmodernism: A Self-Refuting Perspective

Postmodernism's impact on Western culture is hotly debated, and various thinkers and writers—including those coming from a Christian worldview—have offered diverging opinions of it. Some see it as a passing fad; others see it as long-lasting paradigm shift. Some decry it as dangerously destructive; others embrace its destruction of the oppressive structures of modernity.

An initial challenge in attempting to evaluate the postmodern worldview is that it resists the concept of evaluation. Postmodernism considers any claim to knowledge to be socially constructed; therefore, any statement critiquing postmodernism would be socially constructed also. (In fact, so would the idea that worldviews can be evaluated at all!) Of course, postmodernism does not play by its own rules (a point we shall return to shortly); but, before we offer a critique of postmodernism as a worldview, it is important to note its positive aspects.

The most helpful contribution of postmodernism is, first, that it has successfully challenged the reigning paradigm of the modern period, which was based largely on naturalistic humanism. As D. A. Carson notes, "Postmodernism is proving rather successful at undermining the hubris of modernism, and no thoughtful Christian can be entirely sad about that."[51] Modernism, in seeking to arrive at absolute knowledge through empirical investigation, separated matters of faith from matters of objective knowledge about the real world. Postmodernism confronts this dichotomy in ways that are helpful for the Christian worldview.

Second, postmodernism has cast a large shadow of skepticism (and has offered a strong dose of humility) on the modern belief in the efficacy and near inerrancy of human reason. As was seen during the modern period, human reason can be quite productive, especially in the arenas of science, medicine, and technology. However, human reason can also be manipulative and destructive, especially when it produces the totalizing ideologies (e.g. communism, Nazism, colonialism, etc) that characterized the modern period. Postmodernism offers "a radical protest against oppressive systems of thought."[52]

Third, postmodernism has demonstrated that objectivity and certainty are not exclusive to the realm of science as was claimed during the modern period. In fact, science is often quite biased and agenda-driven, and is therefore in no place to claim to be the final arbiter on all matters of knowledge. This is especially helpful for Christians, who often feel the burden to play by the rules of modernism and empirically demonstrate every aspect of Christian truth.

Fourth, postmodernism rightly reminds us of the power of our culture, and especially the language of our culture, in creating our frames of reference. The modern period demonstrated that this power can be used to marginalize and oppress others at the personal and the systemic level. For the Christian, then, care should be taken to distinguish Scriptural teaching from our cultural perceptions.

Finally, the emphasis of postmodernism on story and narrative fits (to a limited extent) with the way the Bible presents God's interaction with the world. The Bible is, on the whole, a narrative through which God gives us the Truth about Himself, humanity and the world. Of course, for the postmodernist, no story is to be considered true in this

---

[51] D. A. Carson, *The Gagging of God: Christianity Confronts Pluralism* (Grand Rapids, MI: Zondervan, 1996), p. 78.

[52] Vanhoozer, "Pilgrim's Digress: Christian Thinking on and about the Post/Modern Way" in Penner, *Christianity and the Postmodern Turn: Six Views*, p. 80.

absolute sense over and above any other story, and propositions from one interpretive community are irrelevant for others.

The Bible does not present a God whose story is one among many, but a God whose story is *the* story above all others. So, in dealing with the postmodern mind, evangelicals face a difficult situation. For the past several centuries, modernity has relegated Christianity to the category of an unscientific, unrealistic worldview that is simply not believable for thinking people. Some Christians are tempted to settle for having Christianity accepted as *a* truth rather than face the prospect of being dismissed due to dogmatically claiming to be *the* truth, and abandoning the concept of worldview seems to be a small price to pay for having at least some claim to truth.

This temptation is similar to the one that liberal churches yielded to during the early twentieth century fundamentalist/modernist controversy when faced with Darwinism, higher criticism and scientific dogmatism: remain credible with the larger culture at all costs and adjust Christianity to accommodate emerging science. Historically, when dealing with these temptations, few people reflected on how much could be conceded before one's identity as a Christian was no longer recognizable.

Although the dethroning of humanistic scientific reason is attractive to battle-weary Christian intellectuals, the postmodern denial of all objective truth is unacceptable. Further, it is important to note that none of the positive contributions of postmodernism originated with post-modernism! In fact, the Christian worldview has always attested to the limitations of unaided human reason, the effect of the fall on objectivity and certainty, the tendency of humans towards marginalizing others, and the role the concept of story plays in our experience.

Despite the popularity of postmodernism among many Christians, the Christian worldview and the postmodern worldview cannot co-exist without one capitulating to the other. One could argue that we are chronologically postmodern; but ideologically, we cannot become postmodernists. Therefore, let us see how postmodernism does in light of our four tests.

THE TEST OF REASON. Postmodernism is full of self-contradiction. It denies that any metanarrative can offer an all-encompassing story that applies to all people and all times. The basic suggestion here is that the only story that applies to all people and all times is that no story can encompass all people at all times. In other words, postmodernism offers a metanarrative that there are no metanarratives.

Postmodernists suggest that we ought to reject metanarratives because we are trapped within our cultural perspectives, and therefore are only able to express our interpretations. For the postmodern, there is nothing but interpretation. But, would not the statement, "There is only interpretation" also be an interpretation?

In the denial of metanarratives, postmodernism also denies the existence of objective, absolute truth (especially propositional truth), and instead embraces the existence of many truths held by different people. However, the statement "there is no absolute truth, there are only truths" is an objective, absolute propositional statement. Consider again the claim by Stanley Fish that we cited in chapter two:

> . . . not only is there no one who could spot a transcendent truth if it happened to pass through the neighborhood, but it is difficult even to say what one would be like. Of course [one] would know what it would *not* be like; it would not speak to any particular condition, or be identified with any historical production, or be formulated in the terms of any national, ethnic, racial, economic, or class traditions."[53]

While claiming transcendent truth is impossible, Fish suggests that *somehow* we know truthfully what truth would *not* be like. If all truth is socially contingent, would not *this* truth be socially contingent as well? Who was able to access *this* truth about reality?

As we stated earlier, postmodernists tend not to play by the rules they set. These contradictions do not often seem worrisome for postmodernists, however. Richard Rorty states this in his typical winsome way, "We must decry the notion of having a view while avoiding having a view about having views...."[54] In reality, this amounts to presenting "an argument which prove(s) that no arguments are sound- a proof that there is no such thing as proofs- which is nonsense."[55] By now the perceptive reader may have grasped that postmodernism is guilty at times of intellectual cowardice, at other times of intellectual bullying, and at other times of intellectual laziness.

THE TEST OF THE OUTER WORLD. While the biases of a community certainly shape the perspectives of the members of that community, it does not follow that reality itself is socially constructed and that we never have access to objective reality, as postmodernists also claim. In fact, reality is what reality is. Our view of reality is constantly being imposed upon, challenged, and even altered by reality itself. For example, transcendental groups whose social construction of reality is

[53] Rorty, *Contingency, Irony, and Solidarity,* pp. 4-5.
[54] Rorty, *Philosophy and the Mirror of Nature* (Princeton: Princeton University Press, 1979), p. 371.
[55] Lewis, *Miracles*, pp. 14-15.

that the physical world is illusory, still find themselves constrained by the physical reality of time and space.

THE TEST OF THE INNER WORLD. While modernism placed the hubris of authority with the autonomous self, postmodernism attempts to place it with the community. However, postmodernism ironically tends to *increase* our isolation from others. One reason for this is that most of us belong to many different communities: we grow up in one, settle to live in another, work in another, worship in another, and retire to another. With so many communal perspectives competing for our allegiance, the tendency is ultimately to belong to none of them. It is ironic that the generation that boasts better communication technology than any in the history of the world is often the most isolated.

Finally, if the only reality we can access is the one we essentially construct, that would necessarily mean that life is devoid of any larger morality or meaning. Postmodernism is, in its most despairing form, a rehash of classic nihilism. In its most positive form, it cannot elevate itself beyond a more corporate existentialism. In either case, all ultimate values are eliminated.

THE TEST OF THE REAL WORLD. Perhaps the ultimate proof that postmodernism cannot adequately explain reality is that it can never ultimately be lived out. People are made in the image of God, and being self-consciously aware of morality and meaning is a part of who we are. The postmodern ethicist essentially claims, "There is no such thing as good or evil," and then pauses and adds, "and that's a good thing." There is an intuitive and implacable place within us that insists that there is such a thing as good and evil, even when we disagree among ourselves what we place within those categories. Alister McGrath passes along a delightful story told about Kenneth Kirk, professor of moral theology at Oxford University. His wife was asked about her husband's work, and she replied, "Kenneth spends a lot of time thinking up very complicated and sophisticated reasons for doing things we all know perfectly well to be wrong."[56]

As a matter of perspective, it is important to note that post-modernism only exists as a viable worldview in certain contexts. The worldview that claims that all worldviews are historically and culturally contingent turns out to be historically and culturally contingent itself. In fact, in all of its rebellion against the evils of modernism and Western civilizations, postmodernism ironically exists only in the context of modernism and Western civilization! This is not accidental. The

---

[56] Cited in David Horton, ed. *The Portable Seminary: A Master's Level Overview in One Volume* (Bloomington, IL: Bethany House, 2006), p. 610.

productivity of Western civilization has created a culture that is mostly defined by its consumerism. Ours is a culture of unlimited choices, from cereal to philosophies, and the only absolute value is to value everyone's right to choose their own existence, even their own *meaning*. Life, experientially, seems to mimic the postmodern ethos, "presenting it as only one incident of choosing after another, none of which is related to the others."[57] This view of life, however, only works in cultures where this sort of choice and self-determinacy actually exists; and even then, only until this pattern of life gets disrupted by actual reality.

Rather than capitulate to postmodernism, the biblical Christian is wise to recognize it for what it fundamentally is: a cultural context in which Christianity exists, can survive and even thrive. Truth does not yield to popular opinion. Unlike the other worldviews we have evaluated, the biblical worldview can withstand all challenges and still speak to the dominant culture. We now focus our attention on the biblical worldview in Part Two.

DISCUSSION QUESTIONS

1. Name and describe the four tests offered in this chapter for evaluating worldviews.
2. How do these tests emerge from the way we interact with people and their ideas in everyday life?
3. What is the law of non-contradiction? How does the statement, "there is no absolute truth" violate this law?
4. In your opinion, which of the four tests offered in this chapter do naturalistic worldviews struggle with the most? Transcendental worldviews? Theistic worldviews? Postmodernism?
5. Read again the opening story of the chapter. If you have ever had a conversation like this one, describe what happened and how you responded. Would you respond differently now? How?

---

[57] Wells, *Above All Earthly Pow'rs,* pp. 75-79. Quote on p. 78.

FURTHER READING

Naturalism, Science, and the Christian Faith:

Clark, Gordon. *The Philosophy of Science and Belief in God*. Nutley, NJ: Craig, 1964.

Dooyeweerd, Herman. *The Secularization of Science*. Memphis: Christian Studies Center, 1954.

Flew, Anthony. *There is a God: How the World's Most Notorious Atheist Changed His Mind*. New York: HarperOne, 2007.

Greene, John C. *Science, Ideology and World View: Essays in the History of Evolutionary Ideas*. Berkeley, CA: U. of California, 1981.

Jaki, Stanley. *The Road to Science and the Ways to God*. Chicago: U. of Chicago, 1978.

Kekes, John. *The Nature of Philosophy*. Totowa, NJ: Rowman and Littlefield, 1980.

Lennox, John C. *God's Undertaker: Has Science Buried God?* Oxford: Lion Hudson, 2007.

Noebel, David A. *Understanding the Times: The Story of the Biblical Christian, Marxist/Leninist and Secular Humanist Worldviews*. Eugene, OR: Harvest House Publishers, 1991.

Novak, Michael. "Remembering the Secular Age" in *First Things*. June/July 2007, pp. 35-40.

Ratzsch, Del. *Philosophy of Science*. Downers Grove, IL: InterVarsity, 1986.

Rolston, Holmes. *Science and Religion: A Critical Survey*. New York: Random House, 1987.

Transcendentalism and the Christian Faith:

Albrecht, Mark. *Reincarnation: A Christian Appraisal*. Downers Grove, IL: InterVarsity, 1982.

Chandler, Russell. *Understanding the New Age*. Waco, TX: Word, 1989.

Clark, David, and Norman L. Geisler. *Apologetics in the New Age: A Christian Critique of Pantheism*. Grand Rapids: Baker, 1990.

Cox, Harvey. *Turning East*. New York: Simon and Schuster, 1977.

Groothuis, Douglas R. *Confronting the New Age*. Downers Grove, IL: InterVarsity, 1988.

_____. *Unmasking the New Age*. Downers Grove, IL: InterVarsity, 1986.

Sire, James W. *The Universe Next Door*. 4th ed. Downers Grove, IL:
    InterVarsity, 2004.
Tucker, Ruth A. *Another Gospel: Alternative Religions and the New Age
    Movement*. Grand Rapids: Zondervan, 2004.

Islam and the Christian Faith:

George, Timothy. *Is the Father of Jesus the God of Mohammad?* Grand
    Rapids: Zondervan, 2002.
Geisler, Norman L. and Abdul Saleeb. *Answering Islam: The Crescent in
    Light of the Cross,* 2d ed. Grand Rapids: Baker, 2002.
Lewis, Bernard. *The Crisis of Islam: Holy War and Unholy Terror*.
    Random House, 2004.

Postmodernism and the Christian Faith:

Carson, D. A. *The Gagging of God: Christianity Confronts Pluralism*.
    Grand Rapids, MI: Zondervan, 1996.
Gay, Craig M. *The Way of the (Modern) World: Or, Why It's Tempting
    to Live as If God Doesn't Exist*. Grand Rapids: Eerdmans, 1998.
Groothius, Douglas. *Truth Decay: Defending Christianity against the
    Challenges of Postmodernism*. Downers Grove: InterVarsity, 2000.
McCallum, Dennis, ed. *The Death of Truth: Responding to Multi-
    culturalism, the Rejection of Reason, and the New Postmodern
    Diversity*. Bethany House, 1996.
Penner, Myron B., ed. *Christianity and the Postmodern Turn: Six Views*.
    Grand Rapids, MI: Brazos, 2005.
Veith, Gene Edward. *Postmodern Times: A Christian's Guide to Con-
    temporary Thought and Culture*. Crossway, 1994.
Wells, David F. *Above All Earthly Pow'rs: Christ in a Postmodern
    World*. Grand Rapids: Eerdmans, 2005.

PART 2:
A *BIBLICAL* WORLDVIEW

The earth is crammed full of heaven and every bush is aflame
with the fire of God, but only those who have eyes to see take
off their shoes. The rest just pick the berries.

Elizabeth Barrett Browning

The central miracle asserted by Christians is the Incarnation.
They say that God became Man. . . . If the thing happened, it
was the central event in the history of the earth—the very thing
that the whole story has been about.

C.S. Lewis

According to pollster George Barna, fewer than 10% of adults who
identify themselves as born-again Christians hold to a biblical worldview.[1] What makes Barna's study so striking are the thin requirements of
what he suggests constitutes a biblical worldview. For the purposes of
this particular study, he identified a biblical worldview as holding to the
following: (1) Absolute moral truth exists, (2) The Bible is the source of
that truth, (3) Jesus lived a sinless life, (4) God created the universe and
continues to rule it, (5) Salvation is a gift from God, (6) Satan is a real
living entity, (7) Christians have a personal obligation to share the
Gospel, and (8) The Bible is accurate in all of its teaching. One wonders
what Barna's numbers would be if his survey included questions that
dealt with biblical perspectives on history, or anthropology, or law!

In Part One, we looked at the world of worldviews. While it is
crucial that Christians be able to identify other worldviews and evaluate
their claims, their greater responsibility is to personally develop a
biblical worldview by which to understand and engage the world in
which they live. The Christian who is not intentional in developing a

---

[1] Barna, George. "Only Half of Protestant Pastors Have a Biblical Worldview"
[online] (2002, accessed 30 December 2005); available from http://www.
barna.org/FlexPage.aspx?Page=BarnaUpdate&BarnaUpdateID=156; Internet. Of course, surveys can only evaluate one's stated beliefs and not the
very important "lived-out" part of one's worldview. This aspect of the
biblical worldview will be examined in Part 3.

biblical worldview will find himself with a worldview that is more culturally shaped than biblically shaped.

Unfortunately, adherents of other worldviews often tend to realize the worldview implications of Christianity more readily than Christians do. For example, Leslie Newbigin relays a stunning statement said to him by a Hindu leader and friend:

> As I read the Bible I find in it a quite unique interpretation of universal history and, therefore, a unique understanding of the human person as a responsible actor in history. You Christian missionaries have talked of the Bible as if it were simply another book of religion. We have plenty of these already in India and we do not need another to add to our supply. [2]

It is the responsibility, and the opportunity, of Christians to think and live in accordance with the view of life and world set out in the Scriptures. To do this, we must first be clear about what the Bible itself is clear about: who God is, what He wants, and who He has made us to be. This will be the goal of chapter four.

If we fail at this basic aspect of thinking biblically, then the next task of arriving at biblically consistent conclusions in areas where the Bible is *not* specific will be virtually impossible. The goal is to think in what T. S. Eliot referred to as "Christian categories."[3] This is the real indication of whether one holds to a biblical worldview.

Of course, if we are to be fair to how we dealt with the other worldviews in Part One, we must also acknowledge that there are significant challenges to the biblical worldview. So, after examining the basics of the biblical worldview, we will seek to respond adequately to the most serious challenges. These include: the trustworthiness of the Scriptures (chapter five), the existence of evil and suffering (chapter six), and the response of Christianity to other religions (chapter seven).

---

[2] Leslie Newbigin, *The Gospel in a Pluralist Society* (Grand Rapids: Eerdmans, 1989), p. 89.

[3] T. S. Eliot, *Christianity and Culture* (New York: Harcourt Brace, 1940), p. 22.

4

THE ESSENTIALS OF A BIBLICAL WORLDVIEW

The Source of the Biblical Worldview: Revelation
    A Description of Biblical Revelation
    An Explanation of Biblical Revelation
The Substance of the Biblical Worldview: What Scripture Reveals
    Confronting God
    Confronting Humanity
    Confronting Nature
The Development of the Biblical Worldview: Steps
    Comprehension
    Application

A theistic worldview and a biblical worldview are not synonymous. Theism refers to any worldview that holds to belief in a personal Supreme Being. However, we should not confuse a mere belief in God with a biblical worldview. Once the existence of God is established, the most important issue becomes the nature of God. In other words, who is this God, and what does He require of me?

Much has been written about a Christian worldview. Unfortunately the concept of Christian varies to such an extent that it often designates little more than theistic. It is for this reason that we are focusing our attention on the idea of a biblical worldview. Our preference in the wording of *biblical* over *Christian* in no way intends to replace Jesus Christ with the Bible as the center of the biblical worldview. Our usage of *biblical* follows the conservative, evangelical understanding of the Bible as the divinely inspired writings constituting the canonical Old and New Testaments, whose purpose is to point to Jesus Christ as the ultimate revelation of God (Hebrews 1:1).

Although the term *biblical* may be ambiguous also, it is at least more focused. In this chapter, we will describe the basics of the biblical worldview.

The Source of the Biblical Worldview: Revelation

A Description of Biblical Revelation

In chapter two, we surveyed the major expressions of theism, including the three major religions of Judaism, Christianity, and Islam. Each assume that God has spoken and that man can, and is expected to, understand and respond. Each claim, essentially, that "God has revealed himself in words to *minds*."[1] If God exists, then what He has revealed is of utmost importance, since it is our only means of discovering both *who God is* and *what God requires*. Where then do the theistic religions disagree? The primary disagreement is about *what God has said*. For theistic religions, everything comes back to revelation.

The biblical worldview assumes one basic presupposition: "the living and personal God is intelligibly known in his revelation."[2] A biblical worldview presents itself not as a metaphysical theory hammered out by the speculations of human thought, but as revelation.

The primary means by which God has revealed Himself is the Scriptures. There are other means of revelation, including the creation, which point us to God. Article 2 of the Belgic Confession describes the creation as being "before our eyes like a beautiful book in which all creatures, great and small, are as letters to make us ponder the invisible things of God."[3]

However, the Bible as the written and established Word of God remains primary. It is through God's *Word* that we may properly understand God's *world*. Also, biblical revelation points us to what is described as God's final revelation of who He is, Jesus Christ.

Is the belief in biblical revelation so irrational? Hardly. A biblical worldview does no violence to reason, science, or any of the intellectual endeavors of man. In fact, revelation provides a solid foundation for these endeavors, as well as certain boundaries that prevent them being misused in devastating ways.

---

[1] This proposition is the focal point of Carl Henry's six-volume series, *God, Revelation and Authority* (Waco, TX: Word, 1976-83). This particular reference is found in volume one, page 212.

[2] John R. W. Stott, *Your Mind Matters* (Downers Grove, IL: InterVarsity, 1973), p. 17.

[3] "Article 2: The Means By Which We Know God" in *The Belgic Confession*. Available online at http://www.reformed.org/documents/index.html?main frame=http://www.reformed.org/documents/BelgicConfession.html.

An Explanation of Biblical Revelation

What is the biblical worldview? Ronald Nash gives the "touchstone proposition" that defines it: "Human beings and the universe in which they reside are the creation of God who has revealed himself in Scripture."[4] If this proposition is not true, then a biblical worldview is false.

Can this touchstone proposition be proved true? No, it is the assumption upon which the worldview is worked out. Indeed, *all* worldviews begin with certain assumptions and metaphysical claims that cannot be proved. Naturalism, for example, assumes that the universe is orderly, operated by fixed physical laws that can be understood in terms of rational thought. Can these assumptions be *proved?* No, but they can be demonstrated to work when they are applied to practical experience.

The assumption of a biblical worldview also may be demonstrated to work when it is applied to practical experience. In fact, Christians accept the scientific assumptions of naturalism and go a step further: the source of the orderliness of the universe and of man's rational abilities is God. At this point, naturalism counters with the claim: God and all other non-material entities do not exist. But how can such a claim be proved? Certainly not in the observable realm of science. It is an assumption naturalists make in order to justify their system. To deny the existence of God is an announcement of the naturalist's disbelief, not a pronouncement of his belief.

The biblical worldview rests solely on the revelation of God to His creation. This revelation is made alive by the Holy Spirit to those who embrace it. Let others attack a biblical worldview, but they must not feel they have destroyed it simply because it fails to match their own assumptions.

The Substance of the Biblical Worldview: What Scripture Reveals

Now we come to the central task of the Christian: to explore, explain, and obey the revelation of God. Is it rational? Is it credible? What are its demands? Christians must proclaim to the world that "this earth has been indeed invaded—from outside its own being, outside its

---

[4] Ronald Nash, *Faith and Reason: Searching for a Rational Faith* (Grand Rapids: Zondervan, 1988), p. 47. Nash calls this the touchstone proposition of a Christian worldview and notes that by the term Scriptures he is referring to the canonical Old and New Testaments.

own resources, outside its own possibilities; it has been and, moreover, continues to be invaded by the transcendent Logos made known in divine revelation."[5]

Confronting God

The Bible gives us great insight into *who* God is and *what* God does. Whereas theistic arguments may point to the existence of an "Unmoved Mover" or "Moral First Cause," a biblical worldview fills in many of the gaps that tell us of God's nature and plans. In addition to the general evidence describing God from a theistic worldview, the Bible adds the following crucial truths about God.

The Self-Revelation of God to His Creation

The transcendental view of God negates any possibility of God as a *personality*. God is rather the sum of all reality; human personality is an embarrassing fragmentation of that unity. Many Western thinkers, especially George Hegel, viewed God as a great thinking mind that permeates the physical realm and causes the progression of nature, history, and humanity.[6] However, such an impersonal view of God seems unnecessarily reductionistic. The presence of individual personalities in the world who are created in "His image and likeness" is a strong indication that God is also personal, while not denying that He is all-powerful and everywhere-present.

From the biblical perspective, God is seen as an individual Being with all the attributes of personality. As a person, God expresses emotions such as anger (Ps. 30:5), love (1 John 4:8-10), and sorrow (Gen. 9:6; Isa. 63:10). The most profound implication of God's person-ality is that He can personally relate to man. The relationship between God and man is a two-way street. The social aspect of personality allows for mutual communication and shared emotions. God also "speaks" to man. Verbal communication from God to man is possible. We shall explore the nature of this communication as it relates to the Bible in chapter five. Essentially we will see that the Bible can serve as an authoritative source for truth, if indeed it is the record of God speaking to man.

---

[5] Henry, *God, Revelation and Authority*, 1:30.

[6] See George Hegel, *Lectures on the Philosophy of Religion* (New York: Humanities, 1962), 1:90105.

The Sovereignty of God in All History

Human history is not a series of random, unplanned events, neither is it a repetitive cycle of incarnations. History is ordained by God—there is a purpose and a goal for the course of human and natural events. God has made man's days (Ps. 139:13-16) and He knows the future. He "carries everything" (Heb. 1:3, Beck) for the fulfillment of His plans. Nothing escapes God's concern or His purpose, because He works "all things after the counsel of His will" (Eph. 1:11). History is not an inward private matter nor is it a personal interpretation of historical events; rather a biblical worldview is an all-embracing scheme of universal history.

The Triunity of God in His Personhood

Traditional theism holds that there is only one God. As we mentioned earlier in this chapter, the major theistic religions—Judaism, Christianity, and Islam—have always put forth the contention that a single, personal God exists. However, a biblical worldview adds the dimension of triunity to God's nature. He is three in personality yet one in essence; the Father, Son, and Holy Spirit are each God. Both Judaism and Islam argue strongly against the historic Christian view of the Trinity. Such a view of God has led to the charge of tritheism by Judaism, and particularly by Islam.

The Bible is clear that there is only one God (Deut. 6:4; 1 Cor. 8:4), yet this unity does not preclude statements that allow three persons—the Father, the Son, and the Holy Spirit—to be called "God" or "Lord" (Matt. 11:25; Rom. 9:5; 2 Cor. 3:17). Jesus told His disciples to baptize new converts in the "name" (singular) of "the Father and the Son and the Holy Spirit" (Matt. 28:19). The equality among the members of the Trinity is seen in many passages (i.e., Acts 2:32–33; 1 Cor. 6:11; 12:4–6; 2 Cor. 13:14; 2 Thess. 2:13–14; etc.).

Natural analogies will not suffice to portray the Trinity adequately. Because of man's limited understanding and language, the doctrine of the Trinity is impossible to comprehend.[7] This does not mean the

---

[7] This does not mean that belief in the Trinity is absurd or that Christians have not attempted to understand the nature of the Trinity. The historic quest to comprehend the Trinity and its implications is a monument to man's desire and ability to think at levels beyond his own limited perspective. The quest continues. For example, Linda Zagzebski argues that the Persons of the Trinity do not differ in essential, external relations but do differ in accidental, external relations. Thus, the Persons of the Trinity can be

doctrine is impossible to describe, only that the nature of God is beyond human understanding. C. S. Lewis illustrates the differences between the human and divine perspective: "On the human level one person is one being, and any two persons are two separate beings—just as, in two dimensions (say a flat sheet of paper) one square is one figure, and any two squares are two separate figures. On the Divine level you still find personalities; but up there you find them combined in new ways which we, who do not live on that level, cannot understand."[8] He continues the analogy by pointing out that in three dimensions, several squares can be combined to form one figure (as a cube). In a similar way, in the divine dimension several personalities can be combined to exist as one Person.

Many books discuss the tri-personal nature of God[9] and the student of theology would do well to explore the biblical evidence and philosophical issues involved with the doctrine. The most practical implication of the biblical view of the Trinity is the insight we achieve into the nature of God. The respective roles and relationships within the Trinity present God as a dynamic fellowship rather than a static unity. God has exercised an eternal relationship of love and communication within His own nature. This relationship is the source of all actions directed toward His creation.

The Incarnation of God in the Savior

Here we come to the most important focus of a biblical worldview: the Person of Jesus Christ. A biblical worldview is essentially *Christus Nexus*, Christ at the center. His life and teachings are the central core of truth. For example, Christians consider the Bible to be the authoritative Word of God because Jesus did. We shall discuss this at length in chapter five, but it is necessary at this point to emphasize that a biblical worldview is Bible-centered because it is also Christ-centered.

Transcendentalism views Jesus Christ as one of many enlightened masters (in the tradition of Buddha, Mohammad, Confucius) who has revealed mystical truth to the world. Naturalism feels that Jesus was at

---

numerically identical yet differ in some sense of identity. Linda Zagzebski, "Christian Monotheism," *Faith and Philosophy* 6:1 (January 1989): 3-16.

[8] C. S. Lewis, *Mere Christianity*, pp. 138-39.

[9] See for example, Arthur Wainwright, *The Trinity in the New Testament* (London: S. P C. K., 1962); G. A. F. Knight, *A Biblical Approach to the Doctrine of the Trinity* (Edinburgh: Oliver and Boyd, 1953); and the more recent Alistair E. McGrath, *Understanding the Trinity* (Grand Rapids: Zondervan, 1988). Also see the standard systematic theologies that usually give extended treatment to the doctrine of the Trinity.

best a Jewish social reformer and at worst a deranged cult leader.[10] Neither approach is close to the biblical teaching of Jesus as the focal point of all creation and history. In fact, "all things have been created by Him and for Him" and "in Him all things hold together" (Col. 1:16-17). Paul states that history is moving toward "the summing up of all things in Christ, things in the heavens and things upon the earth" (Eph. 1:10). These are not references to some principle or ideal, but to the historic Person of Jesus Christ.

The earliest confession of the Christian church, "Jesus is Lord" (Rom. 10:9), will one day be the acclamation of all creation, "that at the name of Jesus every knee should bow, . . . and that every tongue should confess that Jesus Christ is Lord, to the glory of God the Father" (Phil. 2:10-11).

Who is Jesus? The Bible describes Him as a real man. He passed through normal human processes: He was born (Matt. 1:18-2:11), He grew up (Luke 2:40, 52), and He died (Luke 23:46). The Bible also points to the normal human functions and emotions displayed by Jesus: hunger (Matt. 4:2), thirst (John 19:28), weariness (John 4:6), sorrow (Matt. 26:37), joy (Luke 10:21), anger (Mark 3:5), and love (John 11:35-36).

But Jesus was not a man who became a god, He was God who became a man. His deity is affirmed by the direct references to Jesus as God (Rom. 9:5; Titus 2:13; John 1:1; etc.). Jesus claimed to exist with God, the Father, before the world was created (John 17:5; cf. 8:58). His actions while on earth (working miracles, forgiving sins, etc.) and expressed future intentions (coming in power, judging the earth, etc.) are clear indications that He claimed to be God.

The biblical writers are no less hesitant to ascribe deity to Jesus. Because God alone is the creator of all things (Isa. 44:24), the New Testament authors unequivocally designate Jesus Christ as God when they call Him the creator of all things (John 1:3; Col. 1:16; Heb. 1:2). Although the disciples may not have fully *understood* the implications of the eternal God living in human flesh, they were clear that such an event had taken place and that Jesus was God-incarnate (Phil. 2:5-11; Col. 2:9).

---

[10] For a brief description of some contemporary views of Jesus compared to the biblical view, see "Why Believe in Jesus?" in William E. Brown, *Making Sense of Your Faith* (Wheaton, IL: Victor, 1989), pp. 86-89. Also see Michael J. Wilkins and J. P. Moreland, *Jesus Under Fire: Modern Scholarship Reinvents Jesus* (Grand Rapids: Zondervan, 1996) and N. T. Wright, *The Resurrection of the Son of God* (Augsburg Fortress, 2003).

Jesus is the *unique* incarnation of deity; He is not one among many as the New Agers claim. He is the only mediator between God and man (1 Tim. 2:5) and the only name by which men can be saved (Acts 4:12). Thus, a biblical worldview gives a very narrow explanation of the means of redemption.

In Christ the sum of God's plan for all creation is worked out: by His life, God is revealed; by His sacrifice, man is redeemed; by His return, the universe is restored to its original holiness.

The Indwelling of God Through the Spirit

God is active in the person of the Holy Spirit. The role of the third Person of the Trinity can be summed up in the phrase "relating God to man."[11] Imagine traveling in a country in which you do not understand the language. Conversations are impossible; road signs are unreadable; restaurant menus are cryptic. How valuable a translator would be—a constant companion to make sense out of what you could not understand otherwise. You could then relate to the people and events around you.

The Bible presents the work of the Holy Spirit in a similar capacity: to translate to man the spiritual dimension of reality. The apostle Paul states, "Now we have received, not the spirit of the world, but the Spirit who is from God, that we might know the things freely given to us by God" (1 Cor. 2:12). Everything man can know about God is accomplished through the work of the Holy Spirit. He takes the raw evidence of creation and conscience and frames it in the understanding of general revelation (Rom. 1:19-21; 2:14-15; Ps. 19). His oversight in the recording of special revelation resulted in the product known as Scripture (2 Pet. 1:19-21).

The Holy Spirit draws mankind to God by convincing him of his need for repentance (John 16:7-11) and spiritually "recreates" him when he responds to God's offer of salvation through grace (Titus 3:5; 2 Cor. 5:17). The Holy Spirit enters the life of every believer, an event that marks the beginning of a new relationship with God as Father (Rom. 8:15; Gal. 4:6; John 1:12-13). In a mysterious way, the Holy Spirit

---

[11] The nature of the Holy Spirit has been the subject of debate for centuries. Is the Holy Spirit merely the spiritual presence of the omnipresent God or an impersonal divine force? Biblically, it seems clear that the Holy Spirit is a separate person from the Father and the Son and is, by nature, full deity. For a discussion of the various views concerning the nature and work of the Holy Spirit, see Millard Erickson, *Christian Theology*, one-vol. ed. (Grand Rapids: Baker, 1983-85), pp. 865-886; and Michael Green, *I Believe in the Holy Spirit* (Grand Rapids: Eerdmans, 1975).

remains present within the life of the believer to guide, empower, and convict (Rom. 8:14-17). The Holy Spirit provides the dynamic present witness of God in the world today. God is not just out there, He is also right here.

A biblical worldview presents a picture of God as the transcendent, sovereign, omnipotent Creator; the immanent, suffering, and redeeming God-man; and as the speaking, indwelling, empowering presence.

Confronting Humanity

Once we understand the nature and extent of God's working in the world, the place of the self in creation comes into sharper focus. We shall devote chapter seven to a discussion of a biblical view *for* the self. So let us summarize here briefly a biblical view *of* the self.

Mankind is the special creation of God. Man is "creaturely" in that he shares in the creation of the physical world. But each person is more than a physical being, because the Bible claims that the human race in total is created in the image of God. Even though the *imago Dei* of man is difficult to specify,[12] it is important to note that man was created in God's image (Gen. 1:26-27, 31; 5:1; 9:6). Thus, God's image involves man's essence, not his function; that is, it is part of what man is, not what he does. God's image in man seems to be his capacity to relate to God, which involves man's higher intellectual abilities, morality, spiritual sensitivity.

Every person shares in God's image by virtue of his creation by God. God has specially designed man to reflect His glory. For this reason, the Bible commands respect for the individual, specifically in the prohibitions against murder (Gen. 9:6) and cursing (James 3:9-10). Even the most physically fragile or mentally impaired person deserves respect because God has "crowned him with glory and majesty" (Ps. 8:3-6).

Mankind is separated from God by sin. Every person, without regard to his spiritual status (1 Cor. 11:7; James 3:9), bears the image of God.

---

[12] For different perspectives on the many views concerning the imago Dei, see the various contributions in Richard Lints, Michael S. Horton, and Mark R. Talbot, eds., *Personal Identity in Theological Perspective* (Grand Rapids: Eerdmans, 2006). Also, Philip Edgcumbe Hughes, *The True Image: The Origin and Destiny of Man in Christ* (Grand Rapids: Eerdmans, 1989), pp. 1-69; Reinhold Niebuhr, *The Nature and Destiny of Man: A Christian Interpretation* (New York: Scribner's, 1943); G. C. Berkouwer, *Man: The Image of God* (Grand Rapids: Eerdmans, 1962); Ray S. Anderson, *On Being Human: Essays in Theological Anthropology* (Grand Rapids: Eerdmans, 1982); and Richard J. Middleton, *The Liberating Image: the Imago Dei in Genesis 3* (Grand Rapids: Brazos, 2005).

However, this image has been damaged by sin. The *imago Dei* has not been eradicated but skewed and distorted. When mankind fell into sin, he began seeking to love created things rather than the Creator (Rom. 1:25). He became self-serving rather than God-serving, and his ability to know God and His will was altered.

Man's rebellion against God is seen initially as his desire to be autonomous, self-reliant, and independent (Gen. 3:5-6), which resulted in an alienation from God (Rom. 3:23). But the Fall is more than a spiritual problem. As a result of man's rebellion, he finds he is alienated from himself. Francis Schaeffer noted, "The most striking part of this [self-alienation] is our coming physical death when the body will be separated from our spiritual portion. But also in the present we are each separated from ourselves psychologically. Each of us is to some extent 'schizophrenic.' There are degrees, but this present psychological separation is true of each of us."[13]

The Fall has affected man morally, physically, and intellectually. Morally, he is born in sin and by nature seeks the fulfillment of selfish desires apart from God (Eph. 2:1-3; Rom. 3:8ff.). Physically, man is dying (Rom. 5:12-21; 1 Cor. 15:21-22) and doomed to death. Intellectually, man's thoughts are darkened and hostile toward God (Col. 1:21; Eph. 4:17-24; Rom. 1:18-32), and the center of his being is couched in self-deceit (Jer. 17:9). However, certain aspects of man's reason are still intact. The Fall seems to have more impact on his will than on his reasoning powers.

The overall effect of man's situation is a terrifying sense of anxiety, alienation, and apprehension. Such feelings are not merely psychological phenomena, but the outgrowth of a real separation of man from his Creator, a condition that can be remedied only by the Creator Himself.

Mankind is redeemable through the initiation of God. Salvation is the restoration of the fullness of the divine image in man and the divine relationship with man. Many of the English terms related to salvation highlight that the act is a restitution of the relationship God intended: *re*conciliation, *re*demption, *re*turn, *re*pentance. This restoration, of course, does not happen all at once, because the initial stages of salvation are effected within mortal bodies in a corruptible world. The terrible effects of sin upon man physically are taken away through the impartation of eternal life (Luke 18:30; John 3:16ff.; Rom. 6:23). The redeemed will not suffer eternal death but will live with the Lord forever (1 Thess. 4:17).

---

[13] Francis Schaeffer, "The Dust of Life," *Eternity*, March 1981, p. 37.

Morally, each of the redeemed receives the righteousness of Christ. Each is considered positionally holy through the removal of the penalty for sin and the imputation of Christ's righteousness (Rom. 3:21; 4:5). Intellectually, the redeemed has a mind that is made holy. Even though the full effects of this sanctified mind are still future (Rom. 7:18-24; 1 Cor. 13:12), each redeemed person has the potential for a "renewed mind" through the power of Christ (Rom. 12:1-2; Eph. 4:22-24).

Salvation is initiated solely by God's grace on behalf of a sinful humanity that is incapable of restoring its own relationship with God (Eph. 2:1-8; Rom. 3:9-24; Titus 3:3-7). But bringing about the possibility of salvation was not just a discretionary decision by God. God could not deny His own holiness and justice and therefore had to remove the penalty of sin by an act of earned judgment. This was accomplished through the atoning death and glorious resurrection of Jesus Christ (Rom. 3:21-26; 4:25). That single event in history makes it possible for mankind to be free from the penalty of sin, since God, "having canceled out the certificate of debt consisting of decrees against us and which was hostile to us; and He has taken it out of the way, having nailed it to the cross" (Col. 2:14).

The *provision* of salvation is God's grace through the atonement of Christ, but the *personal possession* of salvation is accomplished by an act of trust: "But as many as received Him, to them He gave the right to become children of God, even to those who believe in His name" (John 1:12). The acquisition of salvation is a response to God's offer of forgiveness and restoration, not a result of human effort or achievement (Rom. 3:21-24; Eph. 2:8-10; Titus 3:3-5).

Mankind is destined for an eternal future existence. Man was created to live forever. However, this everlasting life is more than a long life, it is a specific destiny. Carl Henry notes, "Man's destiny is therefore not simply an endless existence, but is moral—either a life redeemed and fit for eternity, or a life under perpetual divine judgment."[14]

For the child of God, the promises of Scripture are very clear. C. S. Lewis summarizes the future for the Christian in five areas: "It is promised, firstly, that we shall be with Christ; secondly, that we shall be like Him; thirdly, with an enormous wealth of imagery, that we shall have 'glory'; fourthly, that we shall, in some sense, be fed or feasted or entertained; and, finally, that we shall have some sort of official position

---

[14] Carl F. H. Henry, "Man," in *Baker's Dictionary of Theology*, ed. Everett F. Harrison (Grand Rapids: Baker, 1960), p. 341.

in the universe—ruling cities, judging angels, being pillars of God's temple."[15]

Naturalism promises only the grave; transcendentalism promises another incarnation; but a biblical worldview promises resurrection, "the transformation of a person's once mortal body to an immortal one."[16]

Confronting Nature

Throughout the Scriptures there is a consistent reference to nature as the product of God's creative will and power. The act of creation is thus the basis for the biblical view of nature. All things are not engaged in some impersonal, cosmic ebb and flow, but rather are controlled by the personal hand of the Creator.

The created world is distinct from the Creator. A biblical worldview presents the universe as created at the initiation of God. There was a time when only God existed. The creation account in Genesis 1-2 is recorded to show Israel the transcendence of God over His creation. Unlike the Canaanite religions, which saw their gods within nature (and dependent upon it), the Bible affirms clearly that God is prior to, above, and beyond the universe.

The created world reflects the person and character of God. The universe God created was initially "good" (Gen. 1:31), no doubt a reflection of the character of God, as Paul notes, "Everything created by God is good" (1 Tim. 4:4). The seasons and regular harvests of the earth are also a testimony to God's goodness to man (Acts 14:17). This is unlike transcendentalism and ancient Greek cosmologies, which saw the physical world as evil.

The created order testifies of God's invisible attributes, eternal power, and divine nature (Rom. 1:20). The general statement by the psalmist, "The heavens are telling of the glory of God" (Ps. 19:1), sums up the biblical view of nature's revelation of God.

The created world is ordered and purposeful. The prophet Jeremiah records the words of God:

> Thus says the Lord,
> Who gives the sun for light by day,
> And the fixed order of the moon and the stars for light by night.
> Who stirs up the sea so that its waves roar;

---

[15] C. S. Lewis, *The Weight of Glory and Other Addresses* (Grand Rapids: Eerdmans, 1949), p. 7.

[16] James Sire, *Scripture Twisting* (Downers Grove, IL: InterVarsity, 1980), p. 92.

The Lord of hosts is His name:
"If this fixed order departs from before Me," declares the Lord,
"Then the offspring of Israel also shall cease
From being a nation before Me forever." (Jer. 31:35)

The prophet points to God's control over nature as well as the fixed order of certain natural events. The natural random events (roaring waves) and the natural regular events (sun, moon, and stars) are the results of God's personal, creative control.

All things were created *for* God (Col. 1:16-17) and are the objects of His possession, thus there is a purpose in their existence and in the events that occur. The psalmist remarks, "O Lord, how many are Thy works! In wisdom Thou hast made them all; the earth is full of Thy possessions" (Ps. 104:24).

This biblical view of creation paves the way for the scientific enterprise. In fact, it was the Judeo-Christian perspective that led observers to see the diversity in creation as a unified whole. Such a view correlates with three basic aspects of science. Physicist Joseph Spradley enumerates these:

> First, the reality and goodness of creation provide a basis and motivation for experimental science. Second, the order and intelligibility of nature are essential for theoretical science. Third, the purpose and meaning of creation encourage the development of applied science. Each of these principles can be contrasted with Greek attitudes to show how a Christian view transcends the limitations of Greek science, as well as similar limitations in Oriental science.[17]

The created world is dependent upon God for its continuance. Not only did the Lord bring the universe into existence, but He continuously sustains it: "And He is before all things, and in Him all things hold together" (Col. 1:17). The writer of Hebrews claims, in a similar way, that the Lord "upholds all things by the word of His power" (Heb. 1:3). The repetition of the inclusive "all things" shows that the biblical writers were referring to *all* creation.

In spite of the power and expanse of creation, it is not eternal, at least not in its present form (Heb. 1:10-12). As a direct result of man's sin, the earth was cursed and subjected to decay (Gen. 3:17-18; Rom. 8:20). The Scriptures speak of a time in the future when the universe will

---

[17] Joseph Spradley, "A Christian View of the Physical World," in *The Making of a Christian Mind*, ed. Arthur Holmes (Downers Grove, IL: InterVarsity, 1985), p. 60.

be made new. The creation "will be set free from its slavery to corruption" (Rom. 8:21) and a "new heaven and new earth" will replace the old (Isa. 65:17; 2 Pet. 3:12-13; Rev. 21:1).

The created world is to be cared for by man. The declaration that the natural world was "good" (Gen. 1:31) expressed both God's pleasure in what He had made and its intrinsic value. God tends His "garden" and cares for His creatures (Ps. 104:15-18). Man must also care for that which God created. Clearly man was granted dominion over nature (Gen. 1:28; 9:1-7; Ps. 8:3-8), but if "the earth is the Lord's and everything in it" (Ps. 24:1, NIV) man's rulership over nature is delegated and must reflect God's attitude.[18] The key concept is stewardship—we are managers but not owners.[19]

The biblical view concerning the natural world is all-encompassing: it describes the past origin and development of the universe; it prescribes man's involvement with the created world in which he lives; and it predicts the ultimate end of all things and the reconstitution of the present world into a new world where "righteousness dwells" (2 Pet. 3:13).

The Development of a Biblical Worldview: Steps

We must remember that embracing a biblical worldview commits us to a view of reality that is greater than our ability to explain everything that it contains. The preceding discussion has only provided a brief sketch of the basic tenets of a biblical worldview. The implications and applications of such a view are inexhaustible. So now we ask the question, What does it mean to develop a biblical worldview?

The idea of developing involves more than merely accepting, believing, or even knowing the teachings of a biblical worldview. It is a

---

[18] Many claim that the Christian worldview is at the root of the modern ecological crisis. The belief that man was "special" and detached from nature allegedly allowed him to exploit the natural realm for his own pleasure. See, for example, Lynn White, Jr., "The Historical Roots of Our Ecological Crisis," *Science* 155 (1967):1203-6. However, the case is not convincing. A misunderstanding of biblical teaching in this area certainly could have resulted in a misuse of natural resources, but because a Christian worldview has dominated Western culture for centuries, it could conceivably be seen as the "root" of all current social and ecological problems.

[19] Richard T. Wright, *Biology Through the Eyes of Faith* (San Francisco: Harper & Row, 1988), p. 173.

dynamic two-step process that is constantly being refined. It involves both a mindset and a willset.

Comprehension

The first step is to *comprehend the biblical worldview.* Although there are unchangeable truths at the foundation (truth often has a way of being narrow), a biblical worldview is not a procrustean bed upon which every question or issue must be made to fit. When answers are inconclusive and options are many, a biblical worldview is better seen as a light to illuminate the darkness.

Therefore, it is imperative for every Christian to learn to think biblically. First, Christians must know what is in the Bible. Australian theologian Rod Thompson states this bluntly: "The most important single factor in the formation of Christian worldview is our immersion in the Scriptures."[20]

Unfortunately, many Christians simply do not know have a good understanding of what is in the Bible. Christians often tend to read books *about* the Bible, but not the Bible itself. Others tend to read certain parts of the Bible (like the Gospels and the Psalms), while ignoring other parts (like the Old Testament historical books and the Prophets).

Second, thinking biblically involves having an ability to think in a way that is *consistent with* what is in the Bible. T. S. Eliot described this as thinking in "biblical categories,"[21] and it involves an understanding of the theological, philosophical, and practical implications of biblical truth. Many contemporary issues (for example, how to think about Islam, or about cloning) are not specifically mentioned in the Bible, but the Bible establishes our framework for approaching these, and all, issues. For the Christian, the Bible is not merely a book to be looked *at*, it is also a lens to be looked *through*.

Application

The second step is to *apply a biblical worldview consistently.* If the biblical worldview is true, then we should seek to conform our lives to that truth. A biblical worldview cannot be developed in a vacuum but must be active in changing the individual and society. Both in our personal lives and in public issues, the biblical worldview should

---

[20] Rod Thompson, *A Biblical Introduction to Worldview* (Auckland, New Zealand: Compass Foundation, 2004).

[21] T. S. Eliot, *Christianity and Culture* (New York: Harcourt Brace, 1940), p. 22.

determine the course of decision and action. This is the view *for* the world that we shall explore in the third part of this book.

However, before we turn our attention to the application of a biblical worldview to life, we must address three major concerns or challenges to this worldview. The first is, Why a biblical worldview? Why should the Bible serve as the authority for determining a worldview? We shall discuss this challenge in chapter five.

The second challenge concerns the problem of evil and suffering in the world. How can the all-powerful and all-good God of the Bible allow evil to persist in His creation? We shall confront this issue in chapter six. The third challenge is the dilemma of pluralism. With so many conflicting worldviews, how can any one of them be the correct view? What about those who never hear the truth? Are they held accountable? This challenge shall be the subject of chapter seven.

DISCUSSION QUESTIONS

1. How does theism as a worldview differ from a biblical worldview?
2. What is the value of the proofs for God's existence?
3. Ronald Nash gives the "touchstone proposition" that defines a biblical worldview: "Human beings and the universe in which they reside are the creation of God who has revealed Himself in Scripture." What are the basic elements of this proposition? Do you agree that this proposition gives the essential elements of a biblical worldview? Why or why not?
4. "A biblical worldview is essentially *Christus Nexus*, Christ at the center." Why is this true?
5. How do the major points of confrontation (God, humanity, and nature) of a biblical worldview differ from those of naturalism and transcendentalism?

FURTHER READING

Anderson, J. N. D. *The World's Religions*. Grand Rapids: Eerdmans, 1955.

Beckwith, Francis A., William Lane Craig, eds. *To Everyone an Answer: A Case for the Christian Worldview.* Downers Grove, IL: InterVarsity Press, 2004.

Blamires, Harry. *The Christian Mind: How Should a Christian Think.* Vancouver: Regent Publishing, 2005.

Davis, John Jefferson. *Foundations of Evangelical Theology.* Grand Rapids: Baker, 1984.

Eliot, T. S. "The Aims of Education." In *To Criticize a Critic.* New York: Farrar, Straus, and Giroux, 1965.

Evans, C. Stephen. *The Quest for Faith.* Downers Grove, IL: InterVarsity, 1986.

Frame, John M. *The Doctrine of the Knowledge of God.* Phillipsburg, NJ: Presby. & Ref., 1987.

Garber, Steven. *The Fabric of Faithfulness: Weaving Together Belief and Behavior During the University Years.* Downers Grove, IL: InterVarsity Press, 1996.

Henry, Carl F. H. *God, Revelation and Authority.* 6 vols. Waco, TX: Word, 1976-83.

Mavrodes, George. *Belief in God: A Study in the Epistemology of Religion.* Rev. ed. New York: University Press of America, 1983.

Neill, Stephen. *Christian Faith and Other Faiths.* Downers Grove, IL: InterVarsity, 1984.

Noebel, David A. *Understanding the Times: The Collision of Today's Competing Worldviews*, 2d ed. Eugene, OR: Harvest House Publishers, 2006.

Noll, Mark, and David Wells, eds. *Christian Faith and Practice in the Modern World.* Grand Rapids: Eerdmans, 1987.

Palmer, Michael D., and Stanley M. Horton, eds. *Elements of a Christian Worldview.* Springfield, MO: Logion Press, 1998.

Pearcey, Nancy. *Total Truth: Liberating Christianity from Its Cultural Captivity.* Wheaton, IL: Crossway, 2004.

5
WHY A BIBLICAL WORLDVIEW?

Is the Bible God's Word?
    From God to Us
    Jesus' Biblical Worldview
Is the Bible *All* of Written Revelation?
    The Meaning of Canon
    The Old Testament Canon of Jesus and the Apostles
    The New Testament Canon of Jesus and the Apostles
Is the Bible Text Historically Reliable?
    The Tests for Textual Historicity
    The Old Testament Text
    The New Testament Text
Are the Words of the Bible Dependable?
    Jesus' Explicit Teaching
    Jesus' Implicit Teaching
    Arguments against Inerrancy
Conclusion

It's a rainy afternoon, and you are sitting at a coffee shop trying to witness to some friends about Jesus Christ. We will call them Reuben, Thomas, Hakeem, Caleb, Ralph, and Heather. You care about your friends, and are concerned that they understand the Gospel.

But the very minute you begin to say anything at all about the Bible, Reuben, who is Jewish, says, "Wait a minute. When you say 'Bible' we aren't talking about the same book. What I call the Bible you call the Old Testament. And not only that, where do you get 39 books for what you call the Old Testament? My Bible stops with Second Chronicles and has only 24 books!" What would you say?

Then Thomas, the Roman Catholic, chimes in: "Wait a minute. Reuben's Bible has less than yours does, but my Bible has *more* than yours does. Your Bible has only sixty-six books, but mine has seventy-nine! Why doesn't your Bible include the Apocrypha between Malachi and Matthew like mine does? And my church has decreed that these books—books like Tobit, Judith, and the Maccabees—are all Scripture, just like the Old Testament and the New Testament! Besides, even the first editions of the 1611 King James Bible contained the Apocrypha!" What would you say?

Then Hakeem, your Muslim friend, chimes in: "The Bible you use has been distorted. Yes, Abraham is our Father, but Jesus was a *prophet* of Allah—your Bible was changed to make Jesus the prophet into Jesus the Messiah! Jesus was not crucified on the cross, Judas was. The final revelation was not through Jesus or in the Bible; the final revelation came through the greatest of all prophets, Mohammad, in the divine and inerrant word of the Qu'ran, written from 610-632 A.D."

Then Caleb, your Mormon friend, says, "No, wait, in the early 1800s the angel Moroni enabled Joseph Smith to translate with divine aid *The Book of Mormon.*"

Ralph is a Christian who goes to a "progressive" non-traditional church. Even so, he also surprises you by undercutting the authority for your case and taking the other side: "Many people have different views of the Bible, and while it's an important book, the main thing is Jesus, not what the Bible says about Jesus."

Another friend, Heather, is a member of the Fresh Wind Holiness Worship Center. She says, "Well, I believe we are continuing the New Testament—we are Acts 29! Or Revelation 23! And God continues to give us new revelation all the time. It is possible that sometimes the Spirit may tell me to do something different than what the Bible says."

So you sit there, look at your friends, they look at you, and, well, what *would* you say? As we said in the last chapter, a biblical worldview appeals to the Bible as its authority. The Bible tells me that God exists, that the world is His creation, and that I am accountable to my Creator. God's Word tells me how to view my unsaved neighbor, how to treat my spouse, how to raise my children, how to use my money—in short, my view *of* and *for* the world. But why should Christians submit themselves to the authority of an ancient book for both mundane and momentous decisions?

Is the Bible God's Word?

Many Christian young people have been reared in "the Christian ghetto" and have never been outside its walls. Their families have attended church faithfully; many have gone to Christian schools or have been schooled at home. For some, their faith is not their own, but is *faith in others' faith*, whether parents, pastors, or professors. They have been told what to believe, and this has been enough—until their faith is challenged.

When they are asked *what* they believe, whether they have answers or not, they know their answers should come from the Bible. But when they are asked *why* they believe in the Bible itself, where do they go for answers? How can they give a reasonable defense and at the same time avoid reasoning in a circle?

From God to Us

Is it possible for a "book of God" to exist? Think carefully. If God is our Creator, we may assume we have been created for a purpose that He has determined. Because man forms relationships, God may have created us for some kind of relationship with Him. "Indeed, would a patently wise, intelligent creator leave his creatures to grope in the dark for some clue to his existence without making himself known? The thought is palpably absurd."[1] Our relationship with God would begin at the point of revelation, in which God communicates Himself to us

If God's Person is such that He can function with human language (certainly being greater than man!), then God *could* condescend to communicate verbally to man. If God's character is such that He is both a truthful and loving Creator who is concerned about His creatures, then God *would* condescend to communicate verbally to man. No loving God would play cosmic hide-and-seek with His beloved ones.

What would we expect of this communication from God? It might take different forms, according to the needs of His creatures. Some oral revelation might be through dreams, visions, or words spoken through prophets. But if God wanted His revelation to be used by His followers throughout the centuries He would have His truth permanently written down. Because human writings are often mixtures of truth and error, we would expect a divine book to be absolutely true (inspired), reflecting the character of its Author. Thus the idea of a book such as the Bible becomes not only possible, but probable.

The Bible claims to be God's absolutely true Word. Of course, simply making that claim does not mean it is true. But surely it would be folly for Christians to make these claims about the Bible if the Bible did not make these claims about itself. Building a case for Scripture's trust-worthiness is an enjoyable task; the problem is deciding where to start. Consider the following valid deductive argument:

A. God is true (= without any mixture of falsehood).
B. Whatever God says is true.
C. Scripture is God's Word.
Therefore: Scripture is true (= without any mixture of falsehood).

"Aha!" some would say, "you have ignored the fact that the Bible did not drop from the sky, but is the product of human beings. The fact

---

[1]   Bruce Milne, *Know the Truth* (Downers Grove, IL: InterVarsity, 1982), p. 20.

that fallible men wrote the Bible shows it is no more reliable or authoritative than the frailties of those men." Therefore, when premise C (above) is changed to read "Scripture is God's Word *through human agents*," the whole argument is thrown off.

But this objection ignores first the *process* of inspiration: the Holy Spirit guided human authors ("borne along" 2 Pet. 1:21) to produce Scripture. Second, it ignores the *purpose* for inspiration: the Holy Spirit guaranteed that the (potential) limitations of human finiteness would be overcome to protect Scripture from untruth.

But did God *actually* overcome human limitations so that Scripture was written without error? Some argue strongly that the Bible is filled with mistakes and therefore is not a reliable source for a coherent and consistent worldview. In 1859 William Henry Burr published *Self-Contradictions of the Bible*. In the preface to the 1987 edition, Joseph Hoffman charges, "The fact is that fundamentalism—the belief that the Bible is the inspired, inerrant, and literally true word of God—thrives on ignorance, not just of a general sort, but an ignorance of the Bible."[2]

If true, Hoffman's challenge undercuts the sole foundation of a biblical worldview—the Bible. We say without apology that the Bible is the sole authority, but not without an *apologetic* (a reasoned defense of this belief). The Bible speaks for itself (with intrinsic authority); but we must not ignore what it says *about* itself as our source of authority.

If we accept claims about the Bible that come from within the Bible, is this not circular reasoning? Actually, all worldviews operate with no provable assumptions. The alternatives are not objective proof on the one hand and subjective circularity on the other, but rather competing sets of assumptions. The thinking person will make sure his assumptions are *reasonable*, able to explain *evidence*, personally *satisfactory*, and *livable* in the real world.[3] We believe a biblical worldview can be established that will meet all these criteria. C. S. Lewis said, "I believe in Christianity as I believe the sun has risen, not only because I see it, but because by it I see everything else."[4]

---

[2] R. Joseph Hoffman, Introduction to William Henry Burr, *Self-Contradictions of the Bible* (reprint; New York: Prometheus, 1987), p. 7.

[3] Or in other words, they are coherent (they pass the test of internal *logical fit*), consistent with reality (they pass the test of external *factual fit*), and satisfying (they pass the test of existential *psychological fit*). See chapter 3.

[4] C. S. Lewis, *The Weight of Glory and Other Addresses* (New York: Macmillan, 1980), p. 92. See also Greg L. Behnsen, "Inductivism, Inerrancy, and Presuppositionalism," *Journal of the Evangelical Theological Society*, 20 (December 1977), pp. 289-305, and James M.

In our society science is worshiped. People say, "Seeing is believing!" or, "I'm from Missouri—show me!" In our empirically-oriented world we tend to trust *most* what we see, hear, touch, and experience personally. But the worldview of the Bible is broader.

First, as we discussed in chapter two, the scientific method offers a limited view of reality and limited options for knowing. The Bible speaks of realities that cannot be reduced to empirical testing. The scientific method cannot adequately encompass subjective realms of human knowledge: "I feel depressed," "I love you," or "Murder is wrong." Second, we may misinterpret what we perceive through the senses. The New Testament records sensory *mis*-interpretation even of direct communication from God (John 12:28-30; Acts 22:9). In contrast to sources of knowledge that may be limited—or distorted—Peter regarded the written "prophetic word" *more certain* than his empirical experience of seeing and hearing the Transfiguration (2 Pet. 1:16-21). Thus a biblical worldview can reasonably ask the believer to trust the authority of God's Word in areas that cannot be objectively verified.

In this chapter, however, we do not intend to *prove* the inspiration of the Bible, but rather to show that belief in an inspired book from God is a serious option that any thinking person must consider. The purpose of this chapter is fourfold: first, to discuss the source of a biblical worldview (the question of *authority*); second, to discuss the extent of Scripture (the question of *canon*); third, to ask if it has come to us in reliable historical form (the question of *textual reliability*); and finally, to probe just how trustworthy Scripture is (the question of *inerrancy*).

Jesus' Biblical Worldview

In chapter four we maintained that Jesus is who He claimed to be: the second Person of the Trinity, God incarnate. He also claimed to be truth incarnate (John 14:6). Jesus regularly confronted error with truth. He never hesitated to confront His disciples—and even the religious leaders—with their inconsistent behavior or with their bad theology. At one point He told His disciples, "if it were not so, I would have told you" (John 14:2). Jesus would not allow error to remain in the minds of His disciples for long.

The authority of Jesus is the final word that settles all issues for Christians, including questions raised about Scripture. His Bible should be our Bible and His view of Scripture—its authority, its extent, its authenticity, and its integrity—should be our view. As we shall see,

Grier, "The Apologetic Value of the Self-Witness of Scripture, *Grace Theological Journal*, 1:1 (Spring 1980), pp. 71-76.

Jesus' view of Scripture was embraced by the apostles and by the early Christians.

Is the Bible *All* of Written Revelation?

The Meaning of Canon

One subject about which Christians know very little is the *canon* of Scripture—why these sixty-six books?[5] But first, what does the word canon mean? The original Greek word meant "reed" or "measure" and came to refer to the standard by which things were measured. Biblically, it referred to the standard of inspiration by which books of the Bible were measured, and then came to refer to the list of books that met that standard. So now when we refer to the canon of Scripture we are talking about the list of books that were inspired by God, as opposed to other books that were not.

The Old Testament Canon of Jesus and the Apostles

Is there any way for Christians to settle the dispute between Reuben and Thomas? What did Jesus consider to be the canon of the Old Testament? Jesus affirmed the exact Old Testament we have today in our Protestant canon as being the very Word of God. This is implied when He stated that the blood of all the prophets, "*from the blood of Abel to the blood of Zechariah* . . . shall be charged against this generation" (Luke 11:51, italics added). Jesus was alluding to the first martyrdom in the Bible (Gen. 4:8) and to the last martyrdom (2 Chron. 24:19-22).

The Hebrew canon was ordered into three sections (the Law, the Prophets, and the Writings), although it included *exactly the same books* found in the Protestant Old Testament canon. Significantly, 2 Chronicles was the last book in the Writings. Thus "Abel's martyrdom is the first, and comes near the beginning of the first book of the canon; Zechariah's martyrdom is the last, and comes near the end of the last book. All the martyrdoms from Abel to Zechariah are therefore equivalent to all the

---

[5] The term *canon* has as its root meaning the Hebrew word for "reed." F. F. Bruce observes "the Greek word was probably borrowed from the Semitic word which appears in Hebrew as *qaneh*, 'reed, rod.' From the same origin come Latin *canna* and Eng. *cane*" (F. F. Bruce, *The Canon of Scripture* [Downers Grove, IL: InterVarsity, 1988], p. 17n.). Because the reed was a handy instrument for measurement (like our yardstick), other usages derived from the root word, such as "rule" (a literal measuring rod) and "standard" (the figurative usage). This latter usage is the idea behind biblical *canon*—the standard of faith. Another related (and valid) derivation usage is the idea of a list—e.g., of authoritative books.

martyrdoms from one end of the Jewish Bible to the other."[6] Thus Jesus implicitly affirmed as His Bible the exact same thirty-nine books that make up our present Old Testament.

Past Authority

There are few subjects clearer than Jesus' attitude toward the authority of the thirty-nine Old Testament books. Jesus always assumed that both the ordinary and the miraculous events of the Old Testament took place historically—exactly as they were written—and used them as true illustrations to support His teaching.[7] Furthermore, He always assumed that all Old Testament prophecy must be fulfilled (in the present or the future) as it was written (in the past).

Present Authority

Jesus never corrected the Scriptures, nor did He rebuke His disciples or even His enemies for their adherence to Scripture. For Jesus, Scripture was not only true, but was a source of authority for faith and practice in the present. Indeed, He leaned on the Scriptures (Matt. 4). Further, He indicted the Jews (who prided themselves on their adherence to the letter of the law) because they were not loyal enough to the Scriptures or sufficiently biblical in their thinking (Matt. 22:23-28, John 5:45-47). He also rebuked them for adding their traditions to God's Word[8] and placing them on the same level of authority as the truth of God.

It is important to notice how Jesus quoted from Scripture. He labeled Moses' editorial comments as words from the Creator (Gen. 2:24; Matt. 19:4-5), because for Jesus, what Scripture says, God says. Jesus' vivid use of the present tense ("it says," "is saying") and the perfect tense ("it

---

6   Roger Beckwith, *The Old Testament Canon of the New Testament Church* (Grand Rapids: Eerdmans, 1985), p. 215. For a brief but thorough study of possible interpretations of this passage, see pp. 212-22.

7   E.g., creation, Adam and Eve, Noah and the Flood, the judgment of Sodom, the burning bush, manna in the wilderness, the bronze serpent, and even the embarrassing episode of Jonah's fish story. See Matt. 12:39-41; 16:4; 19:4; 24:37-39; Luke 11:32; 17:28-32; John 3:14; 6:31-51; and so forth.

8   For the objection that Jesus denied the Old Testament on occasion (e.g., Matt. 5: "it was said . . . but I say unto you . . . "), see John W. Wenham, "Christ's View of Scripture," in Norman L. Geisler, ed., *Inerrancy* (Grand Rapids: Zondervan, 1979), pp. 23-30. Jesus was actually stripping Old Testament commands of current misinterpretations and reinforcing greater reverence for Scripture.

stands written")[9] reinforced the living and present authority of Scripture. By contrast, when men distorted Scripture by adding their traditions, Jesus did not use the introductory formulas above, but began, "You have heard it has been said."[10] This distinction is important because Jesus regarded Scripture, even though written down by human beings, as being the very Word of God—because the human writers were under the Spirit's control—whereas additions by other human beings distorted God's message.

Future Authority

After Jesus' resurrection, He did not do away with the need for Scripture, but instead strongly reinforced it. For example, Jesus did not chide the two disciples on the road to Emmaus because they were slow to believe in the compelling circumstantial evidence regarding the resurrection, but rather because they were slow "to believe in all that the prophets have spoken" (Luke 24:25). After this, He "explained to them the things concerning Himself in all the Scriptures." When He appeared to the twelve, He "opened their minds to understand the Scriptures" (24:44-46). Rather than eliminating the need for the Old Testament, Jesus tethered their minds to the very words of Scripture—to equip them for the task ahead.

Did the apostles follow their Master in His dependency on the written Word of God? Yes, they did. After cataloging an extensive list of minor historical details found in the Old Testament, which are affirmed as authoritative in the New Testament, Grudem summarizes, "No detail is too insignificant to be used for the instruction of New Testament Christians."[11] A sampling of the two most prominent leaders in the early church will illustrate that the apostles did indeed assert the supreme authority of the Old Testament Scriptures.

---

[9] *Legei, gegraptai*, and the perfect participle *gegrammenon* in the Greek. See Matt. 4:4, 6, 10; 11:10; 21:13; 26:24, 31; Mark 9:12, 13; 11:17; 14:21, 27; Luke 7:27; 19:46.

[10] Matt. 5:21 (Ex. 20:13; Deut. 5:17); Matt. 5:27 (Ex. 20:14; Deut. 5:18); Matt. 5:33 (Ps. 50:14); Matt. 5:38 (Ex. 21:24; Lev. 24:20); Matt. 5:43 (Lev. 19:18). See Richard Longenecker, *Biblical Exegesis and the Apostolic Period* (Grand Rapids: Eerdmans, 1975), p. 60.

[11] Wayne A. Grudem, "Scripture's Self-Attestation and the Problem of Formulating a Doctrine of Scripture," in D. A. Carson and John D. Woodbridge, eds., *Scripture and Truth* (Grand Rapids: Zondervan, 1983), p. 43.

Peter

Peter's "last will and testament" (2 Pet. 1:13-14) records the priority he placed on Scripture. According to Peter, the clearest apprehension of God's revelation is through His written Word. On the Mount of Transfiguration, Peter had been an eyewitness (1:16) of Jesus' majesty, and an eyewitness (1:18) of the Father's voice. Peter's attitude toward this amazing and unique revelation is instructive: the written Scripture is more sure even than men's perception of God's immediate revelation.[12]

The clearest description of the process of "inscripturation" is found in verse 21: the prophetic spokesmen were "borne along" or "driven" (see the same term in Acts 27:15, 17) by the Holy Spirit. Michael Green observes, "The prophets raised their sails, so to speak (they were obedient and receptive), and the Holy Spirit filled them and carried their craft along in the direction He wished."[13] They did not only speak *about* God or *with* God, but *from* God. In other words, as they spoke, God spoke.

Paul

Although he came to Christ years after the ascension, Paul followed his Master in affirming that what Scripture says, God says (Rom. 9:17; Gal. 3:8). His "last will and testament" (2 Tim. 4:6-8) reveals the priority he placed on Scripture. Paul urged Timothy to be a diligent student of Scripture, "handling accurately the word of truth" (2:15). In the same epistle Paul states that all Scripture is *inspired* by God (3:16).[14] Whatever writings may be called "Scripture" are to be placed in this category.[15] Paul ends this section with the exhortation "Preach the Word" (4:2).

Both Peter and Paul placed the highest priority on the written Word of God. This was no innovative posture, but demonstrates their

---

[12] The NASB incorrectly reverses the sense of the passage by inserting the italicized words "and so we have the prophetic word made more sure." But see Michael Green, *The Second Epistle of Peter and the Epistle of Jude* (Grand Rapids: Eerdmans, 1968), pp. 86-87.

[13] Ibid., p. 91.

[14] Greek, *theopneustos*. For a complete discussion of this term, see B. B. Warfield, *The Inspiration and Authority of the Bible* (reprint; Philadelphia: Presby. & Ref., 1948), pp. 245-96.

[15] This is the simplest form of logical relationship (the A-form categorical proposition), which means that "inspiration" is predicated to everything in the class "Scripture." If the class "Scripture" contains more than just the Old Testament, then inspiration would also be predicated to those writings.

commitment to their Master who set their example by His reverence of God's authoritative Word.

Let's return to our coffee shop: Reuben needs to understand that even though the Christian "Old Testament" may be arranged differently, it contains exactly the same books as does Reuben's Hebrew Bible—no more, and no less.

But what about Thomas, our Catholic friend? Yes, some early translations included the Apocrypha, but even at the time these books were not considered inspired Scripture. First, the prophetic formula "Thus says the LORD" (used over two thousand times in the OT) is entirely absent from the apocryphal books. In other words, the writers themselves did not claim specifically that they were recording the words of God. That is, the writers themselves were not claiming they were from God's prophetic revelatory circle. Second, neither Jesus nor the apostles quoted from the books of the Apocrypha as authoritative. Third, Jesus' actual canon (Luke 11:51; 24:44) demonstrably excludes these books. Fourth, the Jews themselves never regarded the books as divinely given scripture.[16] Fifth, the Apocrypha was not universally decreed to be scripture until the Council of Trent (A.D. 1546), in an attempt to bolster Roman Catholic teachings that were being challenged by the protestant Reformation.

The New Testament Canon of Jesus and the Apostles

What of the claims made by Caleb and Heather about the canon of the New Testament? Why these 27 books? The New Testament canon grew very differently from the Old Testament. First, there was no central repository for New Testament Scripture, like the Ark of the Covenant was for the Old Testament. Second, most of these books were letters (epistles) written to different people in different parts of the Mediterranean world, extending from Jerusalem to Rome. These letters were not mass emails; each had its own primary destination. Some were to churches, some were to individuals, extending from Jerusalem to Rome. If someone planned to collect these books together into one volume, the challenge would be enormous. So it is to be expected that a communications problem like this would result in greater controversy over which books could be recognized as scripture.

Does the view of Jesus offer any help in establishing the New Testament canon? Whereas Jesus' view of the Old Testament is a matter of affirmation of what all Jews believed at the time, His view of the New Testament is a matter of anticipation of future revelation. Although we

---

[16] Harris, *Inspiration and Canonicity*, pp. 180-185.

would expect the evidence would be scanty (because the New Testament source document itself was not begun during Jesus' incarnation), some helpful indicators are present.

The Canon Jesus Anticipated

The Upper Room Discourse (John 13-17) records Jesus' "last will and testament" to His disciples prior to His crucifixion. Three facts are noteworthy. First, the things Jesus said were emphasized even more than usual by the refrain "these things I have spoken to you."[17] Second, Jesus is not addressing all Christians in this discourse, but the narrow group of the twelve. Third, Jesus promised another Comforter, who was to perform a future ministry in them.

Jesus told His disciples they were to keep His commandments (John 14:15-24). He then specified the future ministry of the Holy Spirit (John 14:26). Jesus promised that, although He had spoken many things to them while abiding with them (for more than three years), the Spirit would "bring to your remembrance all that I said to you." Most probably this refers to the Spirit's doing a work of enhanced memory and protection from errors of memory as the four gospels were penned.

Later in the discourse Jesus takes this promise further (John 16:12-15). Although He had more revelation to give the disciples, they did not have the spiritual capacity to receive it at that time. However, after the Holy Spirit came and indwelt them, "the Spirit of Truth will guide you into all the truth." In other words, there was more revelation to be received, but not until after the Spirit came (Acts 2).[18] This would refer to the revelation given in the chronicles of the apostolic church (Acts) and its apostolic teaching (the epistles and Revelation).[19]

Two further statements Jesus made are relevant. First, the disciples were promised that their words would be directly related to Jesus' words in authority (John 15:20). Those who keep Jesus' words will keep the

---

[17] Greek, *Tauta lelaleka*—John 14:25; 15:11; 16:1, 4, 6, 25, 33. The use of the perfect tense may indicate the permanence of the things spoken of (cf. also 15:17).

[18] The passage does not simply say that the Spirit "will guide into truth," but it refers to a specified agent ("the spirit of truth"), with specified objects ("you"), specified task ("show you . . . show you . . . show you . . ." -vv. 13, 14, 15), specified content ("the truth"), for a specified time ("all"—if all revelation was to be through these men [and their associates, as we shall see] then there must necessarily be a time limit)—all resulting in a specified purpose ("glorify me"-cf. v. 14; 17:3).

[19] It is clear that this authority applied not only to oral teaching, but included written precepts (2 Thess. 2:15).

disciples' words. Second, Jesus prayed to the Father not only for the disciples, but "for those also who believe in Me through their word" (John 17:20). This includes modern readers if they have believed in Jesus through the Spirit-prompted and Spirit-protected apostolic testimony.

Jesus' remarks invite us to assign the same degree of reliability and canonical authority to the New Testament (which Jesus anticipated) as He assigned to the Old Testament Scriptures: absolute trust and authority. This is indeed the practice found throughout the New Testament. The apostles were given the authority to speak and write God's words (2 Pet. 3:2).

The Authority of the New Testament

Several pertinent observations may be made regarding the authority of the New Testament.

First, Jesus gave His associates authority to perform miracles (Matt. 10:1-2, 40), which power authenticated both the messenger and his message (e.g., Acts 2:22). Later Scripture refers to this ability as a "sign of an apostle" (2 Cor. 12:12; see Heb. 2:1-4).

Second, the authority of the apostles was recognized by the early church as unique among all believers (Acts 2:42-43; 5:1-13; 10:44; 14:3; 19:6).[20] "To lie to the apostles (Acts 5:2) is equivalent to lying to the Holy Spirit (Acts 5:3) and lying to God (Acts 5:4).[21]

Third, we have said that Jesus specified a task the Holy Spirit would perform through the apostles: "inscripturation" (John 14:16, 25-26; 16:12-15; 17:17, 20).

Fourth, the apostles claimed divine authority for their own writings (1 Cor. 2:13; 4:14-21; 14:37-38; 1 Thess. 4:15; 2 Thess. 2:15; 3:14; 2 Pet. 3:2).

Fifth, not only did the apostles write authoritatively to specific churches, they expected their written words to be authoritative and applicable to all Christians in general.[22] It is clear that the intended

---

[20] See Walter Chantry, *Signs of the Apostles*, 2d ed. (Carlisle, PA: Banner of Truth, 1976).

[21] Wayne Grudem, *The Gift of Prophecy in the New Testament and Today* (Westchester, IL: Crossway, 1988), p. 284.

[22] Although the epistles were "to" specific audiences (specified by either the address or the contents of the books), they were "for" the entire church. In Colossians 4:16 the Colossians were told to switch letters with the Laodicean church (though there is no evidence the church at Laodicea was troubled by "the Colossian heresy"). First Timothy 3:14-15 informs a general audience (all readers of all ages)—though specifically written to Timothy—that this book serves as a conduct manual for all churches. First

readership of any given New Testament Scripture is broader than the immediate occasion and setting; whether or not a passage of Scripture is written to us, it is certainly written for us.

Sixth, apparently the apostles also claimed this authority for the writings of other apostles. Peter identified Paul's collected writings as "Scripture" (2 Pet. 3:15-16).

But what about non-apostolic authorship? Five New Testament books were written by associates of the apostles, and—even though it is true that they were within the apostolic circle—they were not a part of the twelve, nor were they specifically called apostles. These books are Mark, Luke, Acts, Hebrews, and Jude.[23] There is strong indication that the apostles extended their authority to their associates (see Acts 6:6 with 8:6-16), and even to the writings of their associates. For example, Paul classified Luke's writing as "Scripture"[24] (1 Tim. 5:18). This assumption about non-apostolic authorship has been the consensus of the church throughout history.

Thus the extent of the canon of Scripture is directly tied to the apostles and the apostolic circle. (Whether or not this argument would be accepted by our friends Caleb and Heather will depend upon their willingness to accept the testimony from Jesus and the apostles, as well as the converging arguments from church history and those cited in the addendum at the end of the chapter. What our friends *could not* argue is that this is an unbiblical, incoherent, or self-contradictory position, and

---

Timothy 6:21 closes with "grace be with you [plural]." Likewise, 2 Timothy 4:22 ends with "The Lord be with your [singular] spirit. Grace be with you [plural]." Titus 3:15 closes, "Grace be with you all [plural]." The epistle to Philemon dealt with a personal matter between Paul and Philemon, but was also addressed to "the church in your house" (Philem. 2). After each of the seven specific addresses to single churches in Revelation 2-3, each "mini-epistle" closes with "He who has an ear, let him hear what the Spirit says to the churches [plural]."

[23] Grudem remarks concerning James, "James seems to be considered an apostle in Galatians 1:19 and 1 Corinthians 15:7. He also fulfills functions appropriate to an apostle in Acts 12:17; 15:13; 21:18; Galatians 2:9, 12; and perhaps Jude 1" (*The Gift of Prophecy*, p. 329n).

[24] Because in fifty out of fifty New Testament occurrences "scripture" is used of the divine Old Testament, Paul is putting Luke's writing (Luke-Acts) in the same category as the inspired Old Testament. (See Grudem, "Self-Attestation," p. 49.) We should add that, as Luke was Paul's associate, so Mark was the associate of Peter. Jude was the brother of James and Jesus. The authorship of Hebrews remains uncertain, but has long been deemed of apostolic authority.

what we *could* argue is that they own the burden of proof for further revelatory claims.)

F. F. Bruce observed, "There is a distinction between the canonicity of the Bible and its authority. Its canonicity is dependent upon its authority."[25] Historically the books were not deemed authoritative because they were included within the canon, but rather that they were included within the canon because they were authoritative.[26] God's own people recognize the extent and authority of God's own Word ("my sheep hear my voice"), provided there are not personal distractions that hinder the process. However, the church does not ultimately stand over the canon; the canon stands over the church. We do not have an authoritative collection of books, but a collection of authoritative books. The authority of the Bible is not some ad hoc external doctrine imposed upon the canon from without, but is a position affirmed within both the Old and New Testaments and ultimately anchored in the authority of Jesus.

Is the Bible Text Historically Reliable?

Our Muslim friend Hakeem asserted that we have a Bible that was historically distorted. Abraham was God's chosen, yes, and was the father of Ishmael; but from there the story skewed into an untrue extended pro-Jewish blog. And the New Testament entirely distorts the truth of the story of the prophet Jesus (which was later corrected in the Qu'ran).

Is he correct? While his objection relates to the intentional distortion of historical facts, the truth is that the closer we are to the original writings describing those events, the closer we are to the most accurate record of those events.

The Tests for Textual Historicity

Are the actual texts of the Bible, which have gone through centuries of transmission, accurate to the original writings? Doesn't the simple fact of the age of the Old Testament writings and the writing materials available raise questions regarding the authenticity of the texts that we do have, which are hundreds of years older than the claimed time of writing? And since we do not actually have the writings of Paul, Peter,

---

[25] F. F. Bruce, *The Books and the Parchments*, 3d ed. (Westwood, NJ: Revell, 1963), pp. 95-96.
[26] Ibid.

and John, could someone not argue that they have been altered through centuries of transmission?

This is an historical question, and may be approached by historical standards. There are three criteria by which the authenticity and integrity of ancient texts may be judged:

Quantity	How many ancient manuscripts are there? Sheer volume helps, provided the second criterion is added.
Quality	How good are the manuscripts we do have? If they are few in number, are they of good quality?
Time Interval	How much time elapsed between the original writing and the manuscript(s) we have? (Generally, the shorter the interval, the higher the reliability.)

We shall apply these three tests first to the Old Testament text, and then to the New Testament text. We shall also draw analogies with texts from other ancient literature.

The Old Testament Text[27]

As far as *quantity* is concerned, there arc relatively few entire ancient manuscripts of the Hebrew Old Testament.[28] There are several reasons for this lack of manuscripts. First, the Jews wrote the Old Testament on animal skins, which did not last as long as clay tablets. Second, they were a migrant people who were also under political subjugation for a large portion of their history.[29] Certainly conditions were not friendly to the survival of manuscripts over a period of two or three thousand years. A third factor is not a negative but a positive one.

---

[27] See F. F. Bruce, "Transmission and Translation of the Bible" and Bruce K. Waltke, "The Textual Criticism of the Old Testament," both in Frank E. Gaebelein, ed., *The Expositor's Bible Commentary*, vol. 1 (Grand Rapids: Zondervan, 1979).

[28] Rudolf Kittel's *Biblia Hebraica* was based on four manuscripts. Later notable manuscript finds include the Cairo Genizeh and the Dead Sea Scrolls.

[29] Norman L. Geisler and William E. Nix, *A General Introduction to the Bible* (Chicago: Moody, 1968), p. 251, comment, "The city of Jerusalem was conquered forty-seven times between 1800 B.C. and A.D. 1948."

Because of their very reverence for the Old Testament text, worn or flawed manuscripts were destroyed or buried by Hebrew scribes. Thus fewer manuscripts would be available for discovery.

The *quality* of the Old Testament manuscripts, however, should silence critical historians. This quality is the result of work done by a group called the Masoretes—Jewish scribal scholars of the fifth through the ninth centuries A.D., whose main work was copying and standardizing the text of the Old Testament. Geisler and Nix describe the care taken by the Masoretes in copying:

> According to the Talmud, there were specifications not only for the kind of skins to be used and the size of the columns, but there was even a religious ritual necessary for the scribe to perform before writing the name of God. Rules governed the kind of ink they were to use, the spacing of words, and also forbade their writing anything from memory. The lines, and even the letters, were counted methodically. If a manuscript was found to contain even one mistake, it was discarded and destroyed. This scribal formalism was responsible, at least in part, for the extreme care exercised in copying the Scriptures.[30]

As far as *time interval* is concerned, the scene has changed rapidly because of a landmark archaeological discovery. The Dead Sea Scrolls, discovered beginning in 1947, closed the time interval between the manuscripts we had and our earliest copies by a thousand years. More than one hundred copies of books of the Old Testament were found,[31] which have been dated from 200 B.C. to A.D. 68. Did the scrolls confirm the previous faith the scholarly community had placed in the Masoretes? Millar Burrows, textual scholar at Yale University, wrote, "It is a matter of wonder that through something like a thousand years the text underwent so little alteration. . . . [The chief importance of the find is in] supporting the fidelity of the Masoretic tradition."[32] Kenneth Boa's and

---

[30] Geisler and Nix, *General Introduction*, rev. ed. (Chicago: Moody, 1986), p. 380. See also F. F. Bruce, *The Books and the Parchments*, p. 117ff. For comparisons of Old Testament Masoretic Text vs. Septuagintal quotes within the New Testament, see Gleason Archer and G. C. Chirichigno, *Old Testament Quotations in the New Testament: A Complete Survey* (Chicago: Moody, 1983).

[31] Some books were repeated, and others were in various stages of completeness due to decomposition. They are now still being catalogued.

[32] Millar Burrows, *The Dead Sea Scrolls* (New York: Viking, 1955), p. 304, cited by Geisler and Nix, rev. ed., p. 367. For additional details on textual

Larry Moody's conclusion is certainly warranted: "the quality of manuscripts of the Hebrew Bible surpasses all other ancient manuscripts."[33]

Before considering the New Testament manuscripts, one final observation should be noted. The authority of Jesus Christ is paramount for the believer's reliance on the text of the Old Testament. Jesus assumed that the Old Testament text was reliable enough for Him to base arguments on the very words of a *translation of a copy* of the Hebrew Old Testament. He assumed that copies, and a translation of a copy, were tethered to the original autographs accurately enough for them to bear the arguments He put forth.

The New Testament Text

There is just as much cause for confidence in the textual reliability of the New Testament as there is for the Old Testament. As far as *quantity* of manuscripts, there are more than five thousand Greek manuscripts and fragments. To this can be added about eight thousand Latin manuscripts and more than one thousand early translations (from Coptic, Syriac, etc.). The church Fathers offer the converging evidence of tens of thousands of citations from the New Testament.[34]

It is true, however, that the *quality* of New Testament manuscripts is less than that of the Old Testament ones. More variant readings do exist, although these are usually matters of spelling or word order, not matters of doctrine. However, because there are so many manuscripts of the New Testament available, by comparing the readings the original can be reconstructed. The result of the science of textual criticism is an almost pure text, and most of the remaining textual problems have reasonably sure answers.

The *time interval* for the New Testament manuscripts is unusually short for an ancient document. Some manuscripts are from the third and fourth centuries.[35] We have other manuscripts of the New Testament that

---

comparisons see F. F. Bruce, *Second Thoughts on the Dead Sea Scrolls*, 2d ed. (Grand Rapids: Eerdmans, 1961).

[33] Kenneth Boa and Larry Moody, *I'm Glad You Asked* (Wheaton, IL: Victor, 1982), p. 77.

[34] See F. F. Bruce, *The New Testament Documents: Are They Reliable?*, 5th rev. ed. (Grand Rapids: Eerdmans, 1960); Josh McDowell, *Evidence That Demands a Verdict* (San Bernardino, CA: Campus Crusade, 1972), pp. 53-54.

[35] Some fragments are earlier still, which offers further proof of first-century authorship. For details on all the major Greek manuscripts, their condition, and their dates, see Bruce M. Metzger, *The Text of the New Testament*, 2d ed. (New York: Oxford, 1968).

date from within one hundred fifty years of their originals, and papyri that are within twenty-five years. Sir Fredric Kenyon, late director of the British Museum, stated,

> The interval, then, between the dates of original composition and the earliest extant evidence becomes so small as to be in fact negligible, and the last foundation for any doubt that the Scriptures have come down to us substantially as they were written has now been removed. Both the authenticity and the general integrity of the books of the New Testament may be regarded as finally established.[36]

For a broader perspective, we can compare the manuscript evidence for the New Testament with similar manuscript evidence from other ancient documents, which the scholarly community does *not* question. First, consider the criterion of *quantity* of manuscripts:

> It is sufficient to remember that while there are only 643 manuscripts by which the *Iliad* is reconstructed, nine or ten good ones for Caesar's *Gallic War*, twenty manuscripts of note for Livy's *History of Rome*, and only twenty by which Tacitus is known, yet there are more than fifty-three hundred Greek manuscripts to attest the New Testament.[37]

When considering the *quality* of manuscripts, there are far fewer variants in the New Testament documents (taken in proportion) than there are among those ancient secular writings. This is reasonable because New Testament copyists revered Scripture—an attitude that would motivate accurate transmission.[38]

Finally, the *time interval* between the actual writing and our earliest copies of *Gallic Wars* is nine hundred years; for the two manuscripts of Tacitus, eight hundred and a thousand years respectively; for Thucydides and Herodotus, thirteen hundred years; for Sophocles, Aeschylus, and Aristophanes, fourteen hundred years; for Plato, thirteen hundred years; for Demosthenes, twelve hundred years; for Euripides, sixteen hundred

---

[36] Sir Fredric Kenyon, *The Bible and Archaeology* (New York: Harper & Row, 1940), pp. 288-89, cited in John W. Montgomery, *History and Christianity* (Downers Grove, IL: InterVarsity, 1964), p. 28.

[37] Geisler and Nix, rev. ed., p. 408. To the many Greek manuscripts we may add the church Fathers (from which the New Testament can be reconstructed) and the thousands of early translations.

[38] Clark Pinnock, *Set Forth Your Case* (Chicago: Moody, 1971), pp. 78-79.

years; and so forth.[39] Clearly, the relatively short time interval between Greek manuscripts and the original Scripture writings further enhances our appreciation for the New Testament text by comparison.

Montgomery's verdict is well-founded: "To be skeptical of the resultant text of the New Testament books is to allow all of classical antiquity to slip into obscurity, for no documents of the ancient period are as well attested bibliographically as the New Testament."[40] In conclusion, the reliability of the historical documents that constitute the Bible is not a matter of subjective faith, but of public, objective fact.[41]

Are the Words of the Bible Dependable?

What about the objection of your friend Ralph, who seems to be unconcerned about the truthfulness of *all* of the Bible? Not only unbelievers, but also many liberal Christians wonder about the historical truthfulness of the Bible. They are faced with the challenge, however, of where to draw the line between truth and falsehood. As one non-believer pointed out: "To preserve their intellectual integrity, biblical liberals deny inerrancy. In doing so, however, they merely ignore the problem . . . truth must generally be seamless."[42]

We have considered the dependability of the manuscripts of both the Old and New Testaments, which deals with what Scripture actually *is*, and concluded that we may be confident that we have *Scripture* in our hands. But what about the reliability of its message? Just how trustworthy is what Scripture *says*? *Inerrancy* is a term that describes the degree to which Scripture is trustworthy, and it is commonly used by most Bible believers today. The Evangelical Theological Society requires its members to sign annually a doctrinal statement, which reads in part: "the Bible alone, and the Bible in its entirety, is the Word of God written and is therefore *inerrant in the autographs*" (italics added).[43]

---

[39] Cited by Geisler and Nix, rev. ed., p. 408, and Montgomery, p. 27. Actual details for further comparison may be found in "Ms. Authorities for the Text of the Chief Classical Writers," in F. W. Hall, Companion to Classical Texts (Oxford: Clarendon, 1913).

[40] Montgomery, p. 29.

[41] See the discussion in chapter two of Mark D. Roberts, *Can We Trust the Gospels* (Wheaton: Crossway Books, 2007).

[42] C. Dennis McKinsey, *The Encyclopedia of Biblical Errancy* (Prometheus, 1995), p. 350.

[43] This statement is printed inside each issue of *The Journal of the Evangelical Theological Society*. The restriction of inerrancy to the original manuscripts

Is inerrancy simply a matter of placement past a certain inerrancy cut-off point on a spectrum of trustworthiness, with those writings below the point being error-ridden and those fortunate writings above the point being error-free? Not at all. As Kathleen Boone rightly observes, "Inerrancy is . . . a non-relative term. Like *unique* or *black*, it ought not to admit of modification."[44] Having said this, however, it ought to admit of careful definition.

Inerrancy describes the *product* of inspiration: Scripture. It means that "Scripture is without error or fault in all its teaching."[45] If the Bible were not inerrant, then it would be like most other books: a mixture of truth and error. The *purpose* for inspiration includes (1) directing the thoughts of the human authors (the assertive purpose; 2 Pet. 1:21), and (2) rendering them incapable of error (the protective purpose).

Mathematics textbooks may be without error, but no one derives theological significance from this fact because no mathematics textbook is inspired by God. The inerrancy of the Bible would not be significant apart from inspiration, which lends authority to the inerrant words of Scripture.

As we have said before, the authority of the Bible is rooted in the claims of Jesus Christ. Jesus believed that Scripture was not only authoritative, but inerrant. Inerrancy was stated both explicitly and implicitly by Him.

Jesus' Explicit Teachings[46]

Matthew 4:4

When Jesus was tempted by Satan, He had the perfect opportunity to ignore Scripture if it were simply a psychological crutch human beings leaned on in times of weakness. However, in response to every challenge

---

(autographs) is itself a biblical distinction; see Greg L. Bahnsen, "The Inerrancy of the Autographa," in Geisler, *Inerrancy*, pp. 151-93.

[44] Kathleen C. Boone, *The Bible Tells Them So: The Discourse of Protestant Fundamentalism* (Albany, NY: State U. of New York, 1989), p. 26.

[45] For the most complete recent definition of inerrancy (from which the above-quoted statement is taken), see *The Chicago Statement on Biblical Inerrancy*, reprinted in various theological journals in late 1978. Its nineteen articles of "Affirmation and Denial" and an "Exposition" section are reproduced in Geisler, *Inerrancy*, pp. 493-502.

[46] Many fine books include discussions of Jesus' view of Scripture. Three excellent treatments are John Wenham, *Christ and the Bible* (Downers Grove, IL: InterVarsity, 1972); R. T. France, *Jesus and the Old Testament* (London: Tyndale, 1971); and Robert P. Lightner, *The Savior and the Scriptures* (Philadelphia: Presby. & Ref., 1966).

of Satan, Jesus cited Scripture as a source of common authority by which both He and Satan were bound.

In the beginning of His temptation, Jesus offered a statement of principle: "man shall not live by bread alone, but by every word that proceeds from the mouth of God." Not only did Jesus rest His defense upon Scripture, but He reinforced the *verbal* nature of inspiration: the individual words of Scripture, not just the message or ideas, are trustworthy. Furthermore, this reliability is *plenary*, because it extends to every word of Scripture.

Matthew 5:17-20

In the midst of the Sermon on the Mount, Jesus made a graphic and sweeping statement about Scripture's trustworthiness. Scripture is accurate down to the very "jot" and "tittle" (KJV), "iota" and "dot" (RSV).[47] The jot refers to the smallest letter of the Hebrew alphabet, about the size of our apostrophe. The very letters of Scripture are inerrant. The tittle refers to the slight stroke of a pen, which could make a difference between two letters; this refers to something even more minute than single letters. For example, in English add one tittle to the word *fun* and you get *pun*. Add another and you get *run*; still another will give you *bun*.[48] Jesus is solemnly claiming that Scripture is reliable even to the most minute detail.

John 10:35

Jesus made the startling claim that He is God incarnate. In answer to His opposition, He supported His claim by pointing to two prongs of evidence: His words and His works (miracles).[49] In the midst of His defense of His deity, Jesus quoted from Psalm 82 and reinforced His quotation with the comment "And the scripture cannot be broken."

---

[47] This is well illustrated in the second temptation, where Satan distorts the meaning of Psalm 91. The psalm teaches that God will keep the righteous on their journeys, not that He will preserve them when they take needless risks, which was exactly what Satan had proposed to Christ. The Lord replied that to rely on part of a verse is to distort the verse; it would be to tempt God. Instead "Jesus would rely on every word that came from God, including every word of Psalm 91:11-12" (Charles C. Ryrie, *What You Should Know About Inerrancy* [Chicago: Moody, 1981], p. 77).

[48] Ryrie, p. 60.

[49] For a detailed analysis of the logic of the argument, see W. Gary Phillips, "John 10:34-36: An Apologetic Study," *Bibliotheca Sacra* (September-December 1989).

Jesus based His claim to be God on the reliability of a single word ("gods") found in an obscure psalm; it is not even a Davidic or a messianic psalm. His rationale for such dependence is that "the Scripture" (even *this* Scripture) partakes of the quality of all Scripture: it cannot be broken. "He rightly assumed that He could count on any part of the Bible and any word in any part."[50] On this word He was basing (immediately) His defense of His life, and (eternally) His claim to be God incarnate. Although His critics objected violently to His divine claim, they did *not* criticize His use of, or appeal to, Scripture.

John 17:17

Jesus' declaration in John 17:17 is one of the Bible's most unique statements about God's Word, yet is one of the most neglected. At first glance, the statement "Thy Word is truth" seems rather innocuous, or at least so general as to be bland. Actually, it is contained within Jesus' "High Priestly Prayer." We are eavesdropping on a unique conversation between God the Son and God the Father in which the subject of God's own Word is addressed. Two of the most important words in John's gospel—*word* and *truth*—are placed in the simplest of logical relations to each other.

Truth is a crucial theme in John's writings—more than half the New Testament usages of the words for truth occur in his books. Here in John 17 Jesus asks the Father, in a private moment, to sanctify those who belong to Jesus by means of God's Word, which is truth. The grammatical emphasis in the sentence is on the attribute of truth.[51] God's Word is that which corresponds to reality, which is the biblical meaning of truth in John.[52] In other words, the Bible corresponds with facts, whether scientific and historical (verifiable) facts, or spiritual (unverifiable) facts. Only truth corresponds with facts; error does not.

---

[50] Ryrie, p. 62.

[51] The predicate nominative (Greek, *alethia*, "truth") precedes the verb, a practice that lays stress on *truth*. John does the same in 1:14 ("the word *flesh* became"), 5:30 ("my judgment *righteous* is"), and in 1 John 4:16 ("God *love* is"). See F. Blass and A. Debrunner, *A Greek Grammar of the New Testament and Other Early Christian Literature*, trans. R. W. Funk (Chicago: U. of Chicago, 1961), p. 428.

[52] For a study on the biblical meaning of "truth" see Roger Nicole, "The Biblical Concept of Truth," in D. A. Carson and John D. Woodbridge, eds., *Scripture and Truth* (Grand Rapids: Zondervan, 1983); for a philosophical study, see Norman L. Geisler, "The Concept of Truth in the Inerrancy Debate," *The Evangelical Review of Theology* 5:2 (October 1981), pp. 185-97. Both Nicole and Geisler support the "correspondence" view of truth.

Jesus' Implicit Teaching

Jesus rests His case at times on a word,[53] a tense,[54] and even a suffix.[55] These arguments assume that such things as words, forms of words (tense, number), and parts of words (suffixes) are reliable enough to bear the arguments they support. This degree of reliability is an important element in the definition of inerrancy.

Arguments against Inerrancy[56]

Adequate treatments of phenomena that diverge from inerrancy are found in many places, including Gleason Archer, *The Encyclopedia of Bible Difficulties* (Grand Rapids: Zondervan, 1982); Charles Ryrie, *What You Should Know About Inerrancy* (Chicago: Moody, 1981), pp. 81-100; John W. Haley, *Alleged Discrepancies of the Bible* (Nashville: Gospel Advocate Co., 1974 reprint); Everett F. Harrison, "The Phenomena of Scripture," in Carl F. H. Henry, ed., *Revelation and the Bible* (Grand Rapids: Baker, 1959), pp. 235-50; and Norman Geisler and Thomas Howe, *When Critics Ask: A Popular Handbook on Bible Difficulties* (Wheaton: Victor Books, 1992).

Counter arguments certainly can challenge any faith position. If the Bible were error-ridden, then the above discussion would be worthless. That both detractors from and advocates for inerrancy exist indicates that the discussion may well depend less on the evidence analyzed and more on the worldview of the analyst.

---

[53] John 10:34-35: "God." For an argument dependent upon singular vs. plural, see Galatians 3:16.

[54] Matthew 22:32: present tense, "I am."

[55] Matthew 22:43-45. This argument hinges on David's calling the Messiah "my Lord." In Hebrew, possessives ("my") are expressed in suffixes. Wayne Grudem comments, "The word my is signified by only one letter [very much like our apostrophe] in the consonantal Hebrew text. . . . A slight lengthening of the final consonant [to the length of our letter 'I'] would make 'his Lord'; a bit more lengthening. . . would make 'your lord,' in either case the argument would no longer work. Here Jesus' argument depends on the reliability of one letter of the written Old Testament" (Grudem, "Scripture's Self-Attestation," in Scripture and Truth, pp. 40-41).

[56] Errantists find errors; inerrantists do not. Theological experience has shown that interpretation of these details reflects whether or not the interpreter has committed a priori to inerrancy (see Norman L. Geisler, "Philosophical Presupposition of Biblical Errancy," in *Inerrancy*, pp. 307-34). Other inductive data includes the *phenomena* of Scripture, or the myriad details of the biblical text that converge with or diverge from inerrancy.

However, three common theoretical objections have been raised against the idea of inerrancy. First, with such a large number of human authors (more than forty) who had different writing styles, in what sense can the Bible truly be God's Word? Second, by what reasoning should the rare claims for infallibility, made by particular Scriptures, be extended to include the whole of Scripture? Third, why make such a point of arguing for this teaching when inerrancy is not even a prominent theme within the Bible itself?

Question 1: What about Human Authorship?

Many have argued that divine and human authorship working together would necessarily pollute the process of inspiration. It is true that careful students of the Bible notice different styles and vocabularies. Paul tended to employ long sentences with involved grammar (and was fond of illustrations from the world of sports), whereas John used short, simple sentences. Luke the physician occasionally employed medical terminology. But certain perspectives help us understand what inspiration does and does not mean.

First, inspiration does not mean dictation. There was still room for individual personalities not only to remain but to be used to write God's truth while the Holy Spirit superintended the process (2 Pet. 1:21).

Second, it is true that to err is human. But this cliché is not a tautology that can be reversed to read "to be human is (necessarily) to err." Error is not a defining characteristic of humanity, or else Jesus Christ was not fully human and glorified man will not be fully human in heaven.

Third, God is sovereign. Scripture says He providentially worked in the lives of the human authors, controlling genetics, education, and circumstances (Gal. 1:15; Jer. 1:4, 5, 7, 9) so that the resulting personalities were precisely who God wanted to use. Thus we have a man like Paul, with his precise legal mind, writing the book of Romans, and we have David, the shepherd-king who spent his youth among God's creation, writing psalms of nature. Thus the fact of human authorship is not in itself a valid objection to inerrancy.

Fourth, although human authorship is discernible throughout the biblical writings, it is a non sequitur to assume that the Spirit could not overcome human limitations in knowledge to communicate His truth to mankind. Such work of the Spirit is precisely what inspiration means.

Fifth, the authority with which the Bible speaks assumes that human personalities do not pollute the integrity of the message. It was Jesus who claimed that what David said was actually spoken by David "in the Spirit" (Matt. 22:43).

Question 2: Is the Entire Bible Inspired?

A critic might object, "By what logic do you claim inspiration for the entire Bible, when only a few passages even claim it themselves?" However, when Jesus said, "Scripture cannot be broken," He did not mean just that Scripture but "Scripture as a whole." That Scripture in particular cannot be broken because it partakes of the characteristics of the whole, which cannot be broken. When Paul claimed inspiration for Scripture, it was explicitly inclusive: "all Scripture is inspired."

We have already seen that Scripture was considered authoritative in all its parts. The evidence supporting the doctrine of inerrancy is representative and may be enlarged to include all of Scripture. In other words, Scriptures that are not explicitly given Jesus' imprimatur also partake implicitly of the same characteristic of authority. A scientist checking a pond for purity does not have to test every drop; a sample is sufficient because what is true of the parts reflects what is true of the whole.

Question 3: Isn't This Just Majoring on Minors?

Obviously, the attribute of inerrancy does not guarantee that a book bears the imprimatur of God. A railway schedule can be free from error. The Bible is not the Word of God because it is inerrant; rather, the Bible is inerrant because it is the Word of God. That is, not all inerrant books are God's Word, but any book that is inspired by God will be inerrant.

One primary reason for affirming inerrancy is that it is a crucial theme of Scripture. It was not asserted more often because all biblical writers assumed this degree of integrity (I have never read in any book a formal argument for the proposition that "paper exists"). The burden of proof would rest squarely on anyone who would assert otherwise.

The contention for the factual, historical inerrancy of Scripture is motivated beyond the concern for the specific details under review. There would be no point in having mere inspired history. Inerrancy is intended to assure the authority also of the spiritual claims of the Bible, which make us "wise unto salvation."

Conversely, if the factual accuracy of Scripture is not absolutely trustworthy—even if it were established as "generally reliable" rather than absolutely reliable—then we have a problem of knowing just what is or is not God's Word,[57] and we have no reason to trust the Bible's spiritual truth. If the Bible proves unreliable in those areas we can verify, by what logic should we ask people to take a leap of faith to trust the

---

[57] It is a dangerous thing to edit God. There is no higher authority by which Scripture can be authenticated than by Scripture itself (cf. Heb. 6:13).

Bible in areas they cannot verify-the spiritual claims on which they base their eternal destinies?[58]

Question 4: Doesn't the Bible Contradict Itself?

The year 1859 saw significant attacks against the Christian faith. Not only did Charles Darwin publish *On the Origin of Species*, but the infamous *Self-Contradictions of the Bible* was published anonymously. The author was William Henry Burr, a newspaper reporter who was also an enthusiastic follower of Darwin.

The book simply listed 144 opposing propositions (contradictions), printed with the King James Version of the Bible texts that were said to be in tension. One review of the period described it as "a vilely composed and wretchedly printed attempt to destroy the faith of the civilized world in the Christian Religion."[59]

Recently Burr's book has been reissued by Prometheus Press, publishers of *Humanist Manifestos I and II*. R. Joseph Hoffman begins the new edition with this statement: "Sometimes old diseases demand old cures."[60] Thus the book was published to counter "the resurgence of fundamentalism."[61]

In his preface Hoffman makes a fascinating statement—or admission—about Burr's first edition: "[Burr's] failure to invoke context or linguistic usage to explain away any of the contradictions is precisely what made [the work] the threat that it was."[62] Thus, as long as one ignores context and the meanings of words, it is easy to challenge the Bible with falsehood. Of course, as long as one ignores context and meanings of words it is easy to challenge any document! A modern (and more sophisticated) challenge from Prometheus Press was published in 1995, *The Encyclopedia of Biblical Errancy*, by C. Dennis McKinsey.

Because of the authority of the Bible and its teachings on inerrancy, we conclude that anyone who is tempted to embrace an "errant" Bible should consider the following:

First, when confronted by a skeptic with an "error" in Scripture, we should make sure that a problem truly exists. Often problems disappear when the details of a passage are studied carefully and in context. For example, when McKinsey insists that the teaching of Proverbs lauding

---

[58] Francis Schaeffer, *No Final Conflict* (Downers Grove, IL: InterVarsity, 1972), pp. 33-34. See 1 Corinthians 11:8.

[59] Cited by R. Joseph Hoffman in William Henry Burr, *Self-Contradictions of the Bible* (reprint; New York: Prometheus, 1987), pp. 9-10.

[60] Ibid., p. 7.

[61] Ibid.

[62] Ibid., p. 10.

wisdom contradicts the teaching of Ecclesiastes which despairs of wisdom[63], he does so without regard for the larger context of Ecclesiastes (which serves as a first-millennium B.C. tract to skeptics), in which the writer is on a skeptical journey on his way through pleasure and destructive philosophy to find true happiness in the fear of the Lord. The contrived contradiction is the same as claiming that the Bible contradicts itself when it claims both that Saul of Tarsus was anti-Christian, and that Paul the apostle was an ardent follower of Jesus. Which is it? Of course both are true; one doesn't isolate a verse from the whole of the story in order to force a problem.

Second, we should determine whether the problem we are wrestling with is a conflict between the Bible and some external authority (e.g., archaeology), or if it is a problem internal to the Bible. If external, then we may give the Bible the benefit of the doubt. This procedure has been vindicated repeatedly throughout history. [David, the Hittites, etc.] If internal, it is wise to analyze the conflict logically. We may, for example, distinguish between a *contradictory* (error) and a *contrary* (problem of harmonization). A contrary would be a problem wherein two propositions require harmonization (e.g., this page contains the color white, this page contains the color black; in reality both propositions are true). A contradictory is a problem wherein two propositions seem to be irreconcilable (e.g., this is a book, this is not a book). For example, it is clear that Paul teaches one is justified (redeemed) by faith alone (Romans 1-5, Titus 3:5, Ephesians 2:8-9). McKinsey sets James in direct contradiction to Paul: "the book of James is the death knell to those who contend that you are saved by faith alone."[64] After all, doesn't James use the same illustration that Paul uses (Abraham) and say, "You see that a man is justified by works, and not by faith alone" (James 2:24)? This seems a clear candidate for a contradictory, does it not?

However, one must look more closely to word meanings and context. First, the word justify has two meanings: declare righteous and prove genuine.[65] Paul speaks of the first, but James is speaking of the second. Second, when examining the contexts, both Paul and James use Abraham as an illustration, but focus on two different episodes in his life: Paul speaks of the time when Abraham "believed God" and was redeemed (Genesis 15:6; Romans 4:1-9; Galatians 3:6), but James refers to the time when his existing faith was manifested as he was willing to offer Isaac (Genesis 22; James 2:21), and concludes, "thus the Scripture

---

[63] McKinsey, p. 78.

[64] McKinsey, *Encyclopedia of Errancy*, p. 318.

[65] *New Bible Dictionary*, s.v. "justification" by J. I. Packer.

was fulfilled which says, 'And Abraham believed God, and it was reckoned to him as righteousness'" (James 2:23a). In other words, Abraham's action of obedience in Genesis 22 validated that faith he already possessed. One could ignore grammar, word meanings, and context in order to insist that James and Paul contradict each other, but such mental gyrations are not intellectually honest.

Most specific internal objections to inerrancy are contraries and await further study. But before leaving any problem unresolved—as a contradictory—we should make sure that all terms have the same definitions in both propositions (for example, "this is a table; this is not a table" may not be contradictory propositions if one is making a statement about a piece of furniture, while the other is referring to the water level).

Third, in this world we see reality in limited perspective; we do not have all the answers (1 Cor. 13:9-12). In fact, there is no doctrine of our faith that does not confront us with problems at some level. We recognize that God is infinite and man is finite, and therefore we should not be upset if we cannot work out all troublesome details immediately.

Conclusion

In contrast to the common slogan "seeing is believing," Jesus said "believing is seeing" (John 11:40; 20:24-29). The Bible presents a view of reality that includes the empirical world, but its view extends beyond the limitations of scientific method (2 Cor. 4:18; 2 Kings 6:15-17). Therefore for believers to know things truly, they must view them through God's eyes. We believe that the lens of God's written Word gives the clearest vista of reality.

The most crucial consideration for the Christian is whether or not to accept the authority of Jesus Christ. The historical gospels present Jesus' claims accurately enough to induce belief in Him as the incarnate Son. These are the same records in which Jesus makes statements and implications about the absolute authority of the Bible, the extent of the Bible, and the dependability of the Bible. Surely it is inconsistent to accept Jesus' words about the one and reject His words about the other. Our convictions about the written Word are anchored in the incarnate Word.

But does belief in the Bible yield a coherent and consistent world-view? Two challenges face any worldview: the problem of evil and the problem of pluralism. How does a biblical worldview answer these challenges? This question shall be addressed in the next two chapters.

Addendum: Additional Criteria for the Canon of Scripture

In this chapter we have suggested that the primary "test" for canonicity is Christological—what Bible Jesus Christ *affirmed* (the Old Testament), and what Bible Jesus *anticipated* (the New Testament). Further tests for canonicity can be added to this Christological test. By putting the following approaches together we maximize the strengths of all and minimize the shortcomings of each. An attorney building his case step by step before a jury will certainly depend most heavily on his star witness, but he would be foolish to ignore other evidence that supports and strengthens his case.

The Subjective Test

The question of canon may be approached subjectively, in which the intrinsic authority of the Bible is sufficient to validate itself and adequate to refute challenges.[66] There is a measure of truth to this approach. The canon of Scripture as it stands is majestic literature, and at the spiritual level the Bible does certainly "read me." Historically, however, Christians have differed on the canonical status of some books. This fact reveals that the subjective test is not adequate by itself to handle all the questions that arise. Therefore adding more objective tests is helpful.

The Test of Authoritative Spokesmen[67]

An extremely important test for canonical status of books in both testaments was whether or not the writer was an "authenticated spokesman" for God. This test could be applied progressively throughout Scripture.

Those who spoke for God in the Old Testament are simply called prophets. In the Old Testament the authority of the prophet was not his own, but was the authority of the one who sent him. God placed His words in the mouth of the prophet, who often spoke for God in the first person. When God told His prophets to write down the words of their prophecy,[68] their written words were regarded as authoritative as their

---

[66] Isaiah 55:11; this seems to be the approach of M. R. James, ed. and trans., *The Apocryphal New Testament* (Oxford: Clarendon, 1924), pp. xi-xiii.

[67] For full development of this important argument, see R. Laird Harris, *Inspiration and Canonicity of the Bible* (Grand Rapids: Zondervan, 1957), pp. 154-79, 219-35.

[68] E.g., Ex. 17:14; 24:4; 34:27; Num. 33:2; Deut. 31:22, 24 (see Josh. 24:26; 1 Sam. 10:25; 1 Chron. 29:29; 2 Chron. 9:29; 12:15; 13:22; 20:34; 26:22; 32:32).

spoken words.[69] Prophetic spokesmen continued in Israel from Abraham (Gen. 20:7) to Malachi.[70]

This criterion was clearly recognized and applied by the Jews. For example, "Thus says the LORD," which occurs more than two thousand times in the Old Testament, is totally absent from the Apocrypha.[71] Further, the writer of the Apocryphal book of 1 Maccabees (written between 140-104 B.C.) states that prophets had ceased in Israel (9:27), and 1 Maccabees 4:46 implies that no revelation was being given because there were no more prophets. The Dead Sea Scrolls, the Talmud, Josephus, and the Jewish philosopher Philo agree.[72]

This is precisely the position adopted by the New Testament.[73] At one point the entire Old Testament is alluded to as "the Scriptures of the prophets" (Matt. 26:56). God's speech through the prophets is regarded in the same way as God's speech through Christ (Heb. 1:1-2).[74]

Whereas God's spokesmen in the Old Testament were prophets, those who spoke for God in the New Testament were called apostles. Malachi 4:5 seems to be "an indication that the prophetic witness would

---

[69] When Moses read the book of the covenant, the people responded, "all that the Lord has spoken we will do" (Ex. 24:7). See Grudem, "Self-Attestation," in *Scripture and Truth*, p. 27, and 2 Kings 14:6; 2 Chron. 25:4; Neh. 8:14; Mal. 4:4.

[70] Because anyone could claim to speak for God as His prophet, there were certain tests of prophetic message, whether oral or written. See Norman L. Geisler, *Signs and Wonders* (Wheaton, IL: Tyndale House, 1988), pp. 133-36.

[71] Bruce M. Metzger, "Introduction to the Apocrypha," in *The Oxford Annotated Apocrypha*, rev. ed. (New York: Oxford, 1977), p. xiv. Metzger continues, "From first to last the apocryphal books bear testimony to the assertion of the Jewish historian Josephus, that 'the exact succession of the prophets' had been broken after the close of the Hebrew canon of the Old Testament. . . . When a writer imitates the prophet character, as in the book of Baruch, he repeats with slight modifications the language of the older prophets." But he does not use the formula "Thus says the Lord."

[72] See citations in Harris, *Canonicity*, pp. 169, 171-72, and Grudem, "Self-Attestation," in Scripture and Truth, p. 37.

[73] That which prophets wrote is referred to as what God said (Matt. 1:22; Mark 7:9-13; Luke 1:70; 24:25-27; Acts 1:16; 2:16-17; 3:18, 21; 4:25; 13:47; 28:25; Rom. 1:2 [cf. 3:2]; 2 Pet. 1:21).

[74] Harris calls prophetic authorship "a practical and reasonable test of canonicity that could have been applied by all the generations of the Jews and, except for a few places where evidence now is more slender, can be readily applied even today. What was prophetic was regarded as the Word of God. What was not prophetic was . . . not regarded as the Word of God" (*Canonicity*, p. 174).

end with Malachi and not begin again until the coming of an Elijah-type prophet in the person of John the Baptist (Matt. 17:11-12)."[75] We have maintained that the *authority* of Jesus was passed to the apostolic circle. The miracles the apostles performed were called "signs of an apostle."[76] The authority of the apostles was recognized as unique by all believers in the early church[77] and (as with the Old Testament prophets) their authority extended to their writings.[78] External evidence that such a criterion was in force comes from Ignatius (martyred before A.D. 117), who said, "I do not, as Paul and Peter, issue commandments unto you. They were apostles; I am but a condemned man."[79]

A "thumbnail sketch" of the canon of Scripture, which assumes the criterion of authoritative spokesmen, may be found in 2 Peter 3:2. Peter stresses that in both his epistles he desires to arouse the minds of his readers "that you should remember the words spoken beforehand *by the holy prophets* and the commandment of the Lord and Savior spoken *by your apostles*" (italics added).

The Exclusion Tests

Two tests that would exclude material from Scripture (and thus would be negative tests) are the tests of *convergence* and *coherence*. Both assume that God is a God of consistent truth. Any document that does not cohere (internally) with itself, but rather has internal contradictions, would not qualify as Scripture.

Similarly, any document that does not converge (externally) with previously revealed and recognized canon, would not qualify as Scripture. In Galatians 1:8-9, Paul insists that any message contrary to what the Galatians had received is false, even if it were to come from Paul himself. The previous revelation (the accepted canon) was the standard and authority for judging the reliability of subsequent revelation—even when the human author was the same person (see 2 Thess. 2:5, 15; 3:4, 6). In any court of law, testimony that contradicts firmly established testimony is suspect (e.g., a thief protests he didn't steal the necklace, while his fingerprints were on the jewelry case, the hidden security camera clearly records him as the thief, and the person who provided his alibi has just admitted she was lying).

---

[75] Charles Ryrie, *Basic Theology* (Wheaton, IL: Victor, 1987), p. 106.

[76] See Walter J. Chantry, *Signs of the Apostles*, 2d ed. (Carlisle, PA: Banner of Truth, 1976), and 2 Cor. 12:12; Matt. 10:1-2, 40; Acts 2:22; Heb. 2:1-4.

[77] Acts 2:42-43; 5:1-10; 5:11; 8:6,13-16; 10:44; 14:3; 19:6.

[78] 1 Cor. 2:13; 4:14-21; 14:37-38; 1 Thess. 4:15; 2 Thess. 3:14; 2 Pet. 3:2 (see also 1 Tim. 5:18 and 2 Pet. 3:15-16).

[79] Cited by Harris, *Canonicity*, p. 237.

The Signature Test

Certain tests for apostolic genuineness had to be applied early because of false teachers within the church. Some false doctrine was difficult to detect because it went beyond current Scripture so that the other tests, such as convergence, could not be clearly invoked. Furthermore, some false teachers were actually signing Paul's name to letters as though they had his authority (2 Thess. 2:2).

Because samples of Paul's writings were available, Paul could give them an immediate test of his own (primary) testimony: his distinctive signature. Thus Paul writes in 2 Thessalonians, "I, Paul, write this greeting with my own hand, and this is a distinguishing mark in every letter; this is the way I write" (3:17). Because it was unlikely that the false teachers had firsthand samples of Paul's signature to forge, this would serve as a certain test for the Thessalonian Christians.[80]

Of course, the test of "immediate testimony" was capable of being used only on a limited basis. However, after the original autographs of Paul's letters were lost, the test was usable in a secondary sense: it gave further confidence in the discernment of the early church, which preserved the apostolic Scriptures.

The Test of Historical Providence

Finally, it is important to note that no book *became* canonical by decree of any council. Councils recognized formally, in a historical context of controversy, the sources of theology that were already historically in practice among Jews and within the church. The books of the Old Testament and New Testament were not *made* canonical (any more than Sir Isaac Newton *invented* gravity), they were *recognized as* canonical.

This is where a biblical worldview recognizes the providence of God in history. In about A.D. 90 a rabbinical council was held at Jamnia (Jabneh, north of Ashdod near the Mediterranean). A common misconception is that the Hebrew canon was set at Jamnia. Actually, the canonical discussions were limited to Ecclesiastes and the Song of Songs, and the verdict was to confirm what the Jews had practiced all along: that these books remained *with their companions* in a canon that came from God.

---

[80] See also 1 Cor. 16:21 ("The greeting is in my own hand-Paul"), Gal. 6:11 ("See with what large letters I am writing to you with my own hand"), Col. 4:18 ("I, Paul, write this greeting with my own hand"), and (perhaps less so) Philem. 19 ("I, Paul, am writing this with my own hand, I will repay it").

As far as the New Testament is concerned, the church Fathers recognized all the books which we now have as "Scripture." The Council of Carthage (A.D. 397) served the same function as did Jamnia for the Old Testament: it confirmed the twenty-seven New Testament books that were *already recognized* as from God and *were already in use*.

DISCUSSION QUESTIONS

1. Can you *prove* to a skeptic that the Bible is inerrant? Why or why not?
2. Your best friend comes home from college, and the two of you get together. She begins by saying, "I don't believe the Bible anymore. It's full of contradictions. Besides, it was written too long ago to have any meaning for today." Dissect the objection, and describe how you would respond to each point.
3. A new Christian comes to you with a question: "I grew up in the Catholic church. My priest says that the Apocrypha is supposed to be in the Bible, but you don't have it in yours. Why do you say the Apocrypha is *not* God's Word?" How would you respond?
4. Summarize Jesus' view on the following topics, with two Scriptures supporting each point:
    The *authority* of the Bible
    The *dependability* (inerrancy) of the Bible
    The *extent* (canon) of the Bible.
5. You are a university student in 1930. Your professor has just told the class that Moses could not have written the first five books of the Bible, because writing had not yet been invented. This is in obvious contradiction with the Bible. What kind of contradiction is it? How would you answer it?

FURTHER READING

Archer, Gleason. *The Encyclopedia of Bible Difficulties*. Grand Rapids: Zondervan, 1982.

Beckwith, Roger. *The Old Testament Canon of the New Testament Church*. Grand Rapids: Eerdmans, 1985.

Bruce, F. F. *The New Testament Documents: Are They Reliable?* 5th rev. ed. Grand Rapids: Eerdmans, 1972.

Geisler, Norman L., and William E. Nix. *A General Introduction to the Bible*. Rev. ed. Chicago: Moody, 1986.

Geisler, Norman L. *Systematic Theology, Vol. 1: Introduction, Bible.* Minneapolis, MN: Bethany House, 2002.

Harris, R. Laird. *Inspiration and Canonicity of the Bible*. Grand Rapids: Zondervan, 1957.

Henry, Carl F. H. *God, Revelation and Authority*. 4 vol. Waco, TX: Word, 1976-79.

Kitchens, K. A., *On the Reliability of the Old Testament.* Grand Rapids: Eerdman's, 2006.

Metzger, Bruce M. *The Canon of the New Testament: Its Origin, Development and Significance*. Oxford: Oxford U., 1987.

Warfield, B. B. *The Inspiration and Authority of the Bible*. Philadelphia: Presby. & Ref., 1948.

Wenham, John. *Christ and the Bible*. Downers Grove, IL: InterVarsity, 1972.

6
WHAT'S WRONG?
THE PROBLEM OF EVIL AND SUFFERING

What Problem?
> Clarifying the Problem: What Evil?
> Defining the Problem: God Is Great, God Is Good?
> Approaching the Problem: When Bad Things Happen . . . to Me!

Whose Problem?
> Naturalism: Evil as Bad Luck
> Transcendentalism: Evil as Illusion or Evil as Karma
> Postmodernism: Evil as Social Oppression
> Islam: Evil as God's Doing

What We Cannot Say...
> What Problem? (Fideism)
> Is God "Great"? (Finitism)
> Is God "Good"? (Transmoralism)

What We Can Say...
> A View of the Past: Free Will and Possible Worlds
> A View of the Future: The Factor of Time
> A View for the Present: The God Who Suffers with Us

We were praying with the family in the emergency waiting room, desperately beseeching God that their lovely eighteen-year-old daughter would live through the night. The wreck had left all the other teenagers unharmed. The vigil was over when the doctor announced that their daughter would survive. After a few moments, joy slowly dissolved as the parents grimly wondered what life would be like as they cared for their daughter who was now severely brain-damaged. The father asked, *Why, Lord, did this happen to my daughter?*

It was Sunday morning in Lisbon, Portugal. The devout were dutifully worshiping in their churches when the earthquake struck. Thousands were killed. The European world of the Enlightenment noted that the pious who were going to church were more likely to be killed than the atheists who were still in their beds, many sleeping off their drunkenness. *Why would God allow a tragedy that punished the pious, but spared the guilty?*[1]

Elie Wiesel catalogs the horrors of the Holocaust in his book *Night*. Weisel observed small children and women humiliated and babies pitchforked, as well as the other horrors of Auschwitz. A child was hanged for taking bread, and Wiesel overheard someone groan, "Where is God? Where is He? Where can He be now?"[2]

The problem of evil is the shadow that falls across the biblical teaching about God's character. Why does an all-good and all-powerful God allow evil in His creation? How do we reconcile the pain in the world, and the pain in our own lives, with the character of the God we see in the Bible? The question simply will not be reduced by the admission that we are dealing with incomplete evidence. Something more must be said, for we are also dealing with God's goodness and His love—qualities foundational to Christian theology. Philosopher Ronald Nash summarized the impact of the dilemma in this way:

> Objections to theism come and go. Arguments many philosophers thought cogent twenty-five years ago have disappeared from view. A few other problems continue to get a sympathetic hearing from one constituency or another. But every philosopher I know believes that the most serious challenge to theism was, is, and will continue to be the problem of evil. I share the view that the most serious intellectual obstacle that stands between many people and faith is uncertainty about the existence of evil.[3]

Stephen Davis concurs: "The problem of evil, in my opinion and in the opinion of many others, is the most serious intellectual difficulty that Christians and other theists face."[4] Jaroslav Pelikan observes, "Every answer to that question [of evil] has been fraught with danger to one or another central affirmation of the Christian faith—or to several of them at the same time."[5]

---

[1] Robert C. Solomon, *Introducing Philosophy*, 4th ed. (New York: Harcourt Brace Jovanovich, 1989), p. 318.

[2] Elie Wiesel, *Night* (New York: Avon Books, 1969), p. 9.

[3] Ronald Nash, *Faith and Reason* (Grand Rapids: Zondervan, 1988), p. 177.

[4] Stephen Davis, *Logic and the Nature of God* (Grand Rapids: Eerdmans, 1983), p. 93.

[5] Jaroslav Pelikan, *The Melody of Theology* (Cambridge, MA: Harvard U., 1988), p. 84.

The problem of evil is universal. The problem does not arise only because some people have been victims of evil, but because all people may conclude that things can be better. Even people whose lives have been untouched by personal tragedies can envision a better world with less suffering.

How are we to approach the problem of evil from a biblical worldview? The problem is not merely a philosophical one to be analyzed by the test of coherence (whether or not the existence of evil fits with my theistic worldview). My answer must also correspond to what I know the world to be. Further, my answer should pass the test of experience: Can my worldview provide a response (beyond the answers of armchair philosophers) to the emotional turmoil that senseless evil evokes?

What Problem?

Clarifying the Problem: What Evil?

Often problems can be resolved simply by clarifying the terms used by opposing sides. Although the dilemma of evil is not so easily settled, much excess baggage can be jettisoned when we clearly understand what we do and do not mean by the term *evil*. Some things we call evil are simply things that displease us because they hinder the fulfillment of our inflated desires. For example, it may be that "we desire to do something—to play tennis, let us say—and we count it an evil that the weather does not cooperate. Much of our muttering about evil is nothing more than the tantrum behavior of God's spoiled children."[6] Clearly, however, deprivation of desire and/or fulfillment is not what is normally meant by evil.

By evil we mean both moral evil and natural evil. The term *moral evil* refers to the evil choices made by free human agents.[7] If I choose to be a terrorist, or to overeat, or to beat my dog, I am making a free moral choice. Rape, the 9/11 attack on the World Trade Center, genocide in its various expressions, and the lynching of Emmett Till in a 1955 Mississippi Delta community are each examples of moral evil.

Natural evil does not involve human willing or acting, nor does it necessarily reflect any observable, intelligent purpose. The tragedies of

---

[6] William H. Halverson, *A Concise Introduction to Philosophy*, 3d ed. (New York: Random House, 1967), p. 164.

[7] Other personal, moral agents, such as angels, are not in view in this discussion.

Mt. St. Helens, of the 2004 tsunami, or of famine and drought are examples of natural evil. Some see the occurrence of natural evil as the greater problem for theists to explain. When moral evil occurs there is an intermediate agent between God and the evil so that the blame is in some sense diffused. But with natural evil God is more immediately involved. No human being caused the earthquake in Portugal. In a case such as that, some argue, God may not delegate the blame so easily.

At times when a free choice results in natural evil, the two categories overlap into what some call *mixed evil*. My friend's free decision (moral choice) to smoke may result in the ravages of cancer (natural evil). If lightning destroys a building, the contractor who bribed the fire-safety inspector to certify that standards had been met is not exonerated from blame simply because he did not cause the lightning.[8]

A further distinction is important. Some expressions of evil, whether moral or natural, are so dark and senseless that they seem to demand another category. Sometimes, the *quality* of a particular evil, such as involves the suffering of the seemingly innocent or that seems to be drawn out senselessly, make attempts at explanation all the more difficult. Does God have morally sufficient reasons for permitting senseless evil, such as the slow, painful death of a child? This is sometimes called *gratuitous evil* and is the most difficult kind of evil for theists to resolve on the personal (and particularly emotional) level.

Some have tried to narrow the problem by pointing out that good results occur from pain, results that presumably would not otherwise occur and that justify the amount of evil suffered to produce the good. An athlete might say, "No pain, no gain." The pain of bodily surgery or dental drilling may be necessary for a healthy body. At the spiritual level, for example, patience can be seen as a good that comes through enduring hardship.

While some evil may certainly be understood in this way, we are still left with two important questions. First, isn't the problem of evil compounded when we consider the sheer *quantity* of evil in the world? If God uses pain to make some kind of point, does the quantity of suffering (such as took place in the Nazi holocaust) justify the point He is making? The problem of evil remains, because at times the quantity of evil far exceeds the quantity of good that may result.

Second, why did God create a world in which these good results could have come about *in no other way*? Couldn't God think of a better way? (Couldn't God create a world in which doctors and dentists were not even necessary?) Good results do not necessarily mean that evil is no

---

[8]   Halverson, p. 171.

longer bad. In fact, Scripture never attempts to trivialize that evil is, in fact, evil.

In seeking to understand more clearly the overall problem of evil we shall first discuss the *logical problem* of evil. We shall then turn to the personal and *emotional problem* of suffering.

Defining the Problem: God Is Great, God Is Good?

A common prayer a child would utter begins, "God is great, God is good." This juxtaposition of two of God's attributes creates a problem when those attributes are viewed through the lens of evil in this world. If God is all good (omnibenevolent) and all powerful (omnipotent), why did He make a world with so much suffering? If He is all knowing (omniscient), then certainly He knew who would suffer as the victims of senseless evil. Why did He even allow them to be born? If He created all things that exist, and evil exists, does it not follow that He created evil? The very character of God is at stake. J. L. Mackie states the case with flair: "If you are prepared to say that God is not wholly good, or not quite omnipotent, or that evil does not exist, or that good is not opposed to the kind of evil that exists, or that there are limits to what an omnipotent Being can do, then the problem of evil will not arise for you."[9]

The problem of evil is complex and needs to be carefully unraveled before we give in to the temptation to offer simplistic answers. David Hume, H. G. Wells, and Bertrand Russell formulated the problem into a dilemma similar to this one:[10]

1. Both God and evil are realities that truly exist.

2. If God were all-powerful, He could destroy evil.

3. If God were all-good, He would destroy evil.

4. Evil has not been destroyed.

5. Therefore, there is no all-good, all-powerful God.

---

[9] J. L. Mackie, "Evil and Omnipotence," in *Philosophy of Religion: Selected Readings*, ed. William Rowe and William Wainwright (New York: Harcourt Brace Jovanovich, 1989), p. 224.

[10] D. Hume, *Dialogues Concerning Natural Religion*, pt. 10; see also *The Encyclopedia of Philosophy*, vol. 3 (New York: Macmillan, 1967), s.v. "Evil, The Problem of," by John Hick (included is a valuable chronological bibliography).

The three great theistic worldviews of Christianity, Judaism, and Islam traditionally affirm propositions 1-4 and therefore are faced with the dilemma of the problem of evil. For many insightful people, the problem of evil does not *necessarily* disprove logically that there is a God.[11] However, they would argue that the presence of unexplained evil offers a good reason for not believing in such a God. In other words, although the problem of evil may no longer be a logical reason for *disproving* God, it does offer a personal reason for *disbelieving* in Him.

Approaching the Problem: When Bad Things Happen . . . to Me!

My relatives were numb. Everyone around them was silent. The tiny casket made no sense at all. Cancer and car wrecks at least are somewhat understandable. But their toddler was not the victim of cancer or a drunk driver. The baby had simply climbed out of the crib in the middle of the night—on the wrong side. Strangulation. Between the wall and the crib railing. *Why would God allow such a senseless evil?*

The death of a child is, understandably, often cited as a test case for proposed resolutions to the problem of evil, both in Western and Eastern cultures. Hindu texts cite the death of a young child as an illustration of the problem of extraordinary evil.[12] Dostoyevsky used it to draw out the agony of the problem of evil as a reason for disbelief in God in *The Brothers Karamazov*.[13] Job lost all of his children through divinely permitted tragedy. Job believed in the sovereignty of God. But Job's faith in God's sovereignty did not relieve his anguish; it *caused* it. Job was not tempted to disbelieve the *sovereignty of God*, but to disbelieve the *goodness of God*.

This story gets at the heart of why evil is such a problem for human beings. It isn't just a fact of reality that we can point to and describe, it is a fact of reality that we experience. It hurts. It break us. While the logical formulation of the problem above is a significant challenge, the personal problem of suffering is more significant still. The logical problem asks the question: "Why does God allow evil and suffering?" The personal problem asks, "Why did God allow *that* evil?" And, "Why does He allow *me* to suffer like this?"

---

[11] This includes most current philosophers of religion, according to Rowe and Wainwright, *Philosophy of Religion*, p. 193.

[12] D. Carmody and J. Carmody, *Ways to the Center* (Belmont, CA: Wadsworth, 1989), p. 109.

[13] Fyodor Dostoyevsky, *The Brothers Karamazov*, trans. C. Garnett (New York: Macmillan, 1923), chapter on "Rebellion."

A coherent worldview must provide a consistent and realistic framework from which to manage the pain of personal suffering. It is one thing to deal with suffering in the abstract and discuss philosophical issues relating to the problem of evil. It is quite another thing to try to offer yourself or people you love carefully reasoned solutions to the logical problem of evil, when what is needed is comfort.

Whose Problem?

While evil is a problem which is rightfully posed to the theist, it is not exclusively his to explain. Every worldview purports to offer an explanation as to why the world is the way that it is. Therefore, every worldview has to explain the existence of evil and suffering in the world. If we were to abandon theism because of evil and suffering, to which worldview could we turn to provide us with an adequate, and personally satisfying, explanation? Although we have already spent significant time evaluating the worldviews, the explanatory power of each worldview in light of evil and suffering is worth considering as well.

Naturalism: Evil as Bad Luck

All naturalistic worldviews suggest that we live in a universe governed by purely natural causes and processes, without any supernatural intervention or oversight. In this sort of a world, "some people are going to get hurt, other people are going to get lucky, and you won't find any rhyme or reason it, nor any justice . . . nothing but blind, pitiless, indifference. . . ."[14] For the naturalist, there is no deeper meaning to evil and suffering to be found. We have no control, nor does anyone else, over the hand that we have been dealt. If we must suffer, it is only because we have been unlucky, and there is no hope whatsoever that anything redeeming will come of our suffering.

Another perspective is important. While theists must wrestle with the problem of evil, naturalists have twice the problem. Not only must they account for evil, they must account for good (and why they define it as such). Prager and Telushkin aptly note, "The believer in God must explain one thing, the existence of sufferings; the nonbeliever, however, must explain the existence of everything else."[15] Harry Emerson Fosdick said it well, "The mystery of evil is very difficult when we believe in a

---

[14] Richard Dawkins, *River Out of Eden,* p. 113.
[15] Dennis Prager and Joseph Talushkin, *The Nine Questions People Ask about Judaism*, quoted in *Reader's Digest*, October 1988, p. 158.

good God, but the problem of goodness seems to us impossible when we do not."[16]

Transcendentalism: Evil as Illusion or Evil as Karma

There are two possible explanations for evil according to transcendental worldviews. First, those transcendental worldviews that consider the physical world to be illusory, suggest that any evil that occurs in the natural world to be illusory as well. "Evil is an illusion of the human mind. It is just an emotional reaction to events that are otherwise without objective value."[17] For example, advocates of Vedanta Hinduism teach that this world, including the appearance of evil, is *maya*, or illusion. Western philosopher Benedict Spinoza's pantheistic approach affirms that whatever exists, exists eternally as one substance. Therefore when people refer to "evil," the term is a mere convention that obscures the fact that evil is a part of the one (neutral) substance which is called "God."

The attractiveness of this view is that evil becomes redefined in such a way as to relieve the problem of its "existence." Because reality is not material and the senses are a source of error, then suffering and even death are simply phases in the process of the total illusion.

Problems with the illusory view far outweigh its single advantage. On one hand, this view does not fit with actual experience of the world, or of evil. Although my experience is not necessarily the final criterion for determining whether or not a physical view of reality is true, the burden of proof would certainly rest on those who would deny material reality. I may argue verbosely that words do not convey meaning, or shout at the top of my lungs, "Vocal chords do not exist!" but neither is convincing. An illusionist suffers no less from the illusion of a toothache than he or she would from a real toothache. This explanation is especially difficult to accept in cases of extreme, gratuitous evil.

Also, the problem of evil is not answered by identifying it as illusion. It has simply been shifted to a different level. The origin of the illusion of evil requires just as cogent an explanation as real evil does. Instead of asking, "Whence evil?" we ask, "Whence the illusion of evil?" The second question is just as significant a challenge as the first one. Further, whenever evil seems to be properly dealt with, is the satisfaction of seeing justice triumph over evil not also an illusion?

---

[16] Harry Emerson Fosdick, quoted in Clendenin, "Security But No Certainty," p. 325.

[17] Peter Facione, *A Student's Guide to Philosophy* (Mountain View, CA: Mayfield, 1988), p. 142.

A second transcendental explanation for evil and suffering is karma. In this view, any evil that one experiences in this life is the result of negative energy from former incarnations. Thus, the suffering of a child, the destruction of a village by earthquake or tsunami, or the victimization of one person by another is actually deserved in light of previous lives and decisions. Actor Richard Gere illustrated this view in his response to the terror attacks of 9/11: "In a situation like this, of course you identify with everyone who's suffering. (But we must also think about) the terrorists who are creating such horrible future lives for themselves because of the negativity of this karma. It's all of our jobs to keep our minds as expansive as possible. If you can see (the terrorists) as a relative who's dangerously sick and we have to give them medicine, and the medicine is love and compassion. There's nothing better."[18]

Several problems emerge from this view. First, are the victims of evil that is perpetuated by others—including the thousands who died in the World Trade Center attacks—not victims at all, but really deserving recipients of the suffering they experience? Second, if people deserve what happens to them, why should we be obligated to provide any relief? Viewing evil in this way discourages acts which would help to alleviate the suffering of others. Third, would not this view also demand that we regard those who escape a tragedy as morally upright?

Postmodernism: Evil as Social Oppression

One strength of postmodernism is its unqualified acknowledgement that evil is a reality. Reacting with incredulity towards the modern era's promise of progress that will eventually eliminate the things which make us suffer, postmodernism recognizes that evil cannot be overcome with more scientific knowledge. In fact, scientific knowledge can, and often is, used to perpetuate great evil and suffering in the world. Progress for one individual or people group often means more trouble for other individuals or people groups. There is no truth; there is no progress; there are no fixed foundations; therefore, evil is here to stay.

Unfortunately, postmodernism's strong stance on evil leaves us without the possibility that anything can be done about it. First, in this view there is *no one* responsible for evil. Because humans and human identity are social constructs, they cannot be blamed for their evil deeds. Social structures of oppression are responsible, and everyone is shaped by them. Who then can be held responsible? As N. T. Wright argues,

---

[18] "Interview with Richard Gere," ABC News Radio, 10 October 2001.

"You can't escape evil within postmodernity, but you can't find anybody to take the blame either."[19]

Second, postmodernism offers *no way* to deal with evil. Social oppression is just the way the world is. There is no truth, only power being exerted over others. Wright continues, "There is no way out, no chance of repentance or restoration, no way back to the solid ground of truth from the quicksands of deconstruction. Postmodernity may be correct to say that evil is real, powerful and important, but it gives us no real clue as to what we should do about it."[20]

Islam: Evil as God's Doing

Clearly, any theistic view of the world suggests that God has allowed evil in the world for His own purposes. However, theistic views differ on the extent of God's involvement in the world in general, and with evil in particular; and on what may be God's purposes in allowing evil. Space will not permit a full analysis of the Islamic perspective on evil and suffering, but two things are worth considering for the purposes of this chapter.

First, Islam allows nothing to happen outside of God's specific decree. God does not merely oversee human decisions and natural happenings, He ultimately decides them. Islamic theologian Al-Ghazali writes: "Good and evil are foreordained. What is foreordained comes necessarily to be after a prior act of divine volition. No one can rebel against God's judgment; no one can appeal His decree and command. Rather, everything small and large is written and comes to be in a known and expected measure."[21]

Second, there is no fall of man or of the creation in Islam. While the events of the Garden of Eden were historical and teach man's responsibility to obey God's decrees, it did not result in any essential consequences to man (i.e. original sin) or nature (the curse). What this implies in an Islamic view, then, is that *nothing has gone wrong with the world.* In Islam, the world is as it was given by God. This provides a very different picture of "natural evil" than that given in Christianity and will

---

[19] N. T. Wright, *Evil and the Justice of God* (Downers Grove, IL: InterVarsity, 2006), p. 32. This two-fold analysis of postmodernism on evil belongs to Wright (pp. 30-34), and he develops it more fully than I have here.

[20] Ibid., p. 33.

[21] Abu Hamid al-Ghazali, "There Is No Evil in Allah's Perfect World" in Amelie Rorty, ed. *The Many Faces of Evil: Historical Perspectives* (Oxford: Routledge, 2001), p. 55.

be an important part of the biblical response we offer to evil and suffering later in this chapter.

What We Cannot Say...

Henri Blocher, in his book on the problem of evil[22], reminds us that there are three things that are non-negotiable if one is to hold a biblical view of evil and suffering. First, evil is evil, and it is unacceptable. Blocher writes, "Scripture never tires of denouncing the reality and the danger of evil; it is evil totally, radically, and absolutely." Evil is to be hated (Rom. 12:9); evil is to be clearly distinguished from what is good (Is. 5:20; Rev. 22:11); and throughout Scripture, evil incites the wrath of God.

Second, the Bible is clear that God is completely sovereign over His creation. There is nothing that happens outside of His oversight and control; nothing takes God by surprise. God does what He pleases (Ps. 115:3); God exercises absolute dominion (Ps. 103:19); God determines the flow of history as regards individuals and nations (Acts 17:26); God watches over the sparrow (Matt. 10:29).

Finally, God is ultimately, and completely, good. In no sense is He an accomplice of evil. God's justice and goodness are perfect (Deut. 32:4); His eyes are "too pure to behold evil" (Hab. 1:12ff.); He is not tempted by evil (Jas. 1:13); in Him there is no darkness (1 Jn. 3:4).

"The evil of evil, the lordship of the Lord, the goodness of God: these three immovable propositions stand together as the basis of biblical doctrine." Due to the logical difficulty and the personal intensity of evil and suffering, it is not surprising that responses have appeared which compromise one or more of these.[23] Such views either ignore evil, redefine evil, or even redefine God. We shall now briefly evaluate them.

---

[22] Henri Blocher, *Evil and the Cross: An Analytical Look at the Problem of Pain* (Grand Rapids: Kregel, 1994).

[23] Many helpful insights for this chapter were found in Millard Erickson, *Christian Theology* (Grand Rapids: Baker, 1983), 1:411-32, and in Ronald Nash, *Faith and Reason* (Grand Rapids: Zondervan, 1988), ch. 13-19.

What Problem? (Fideism)[24]

The first approach considers the problem of evil a dilemma that human beings will never resolve. Some have argued that "God works in mysterious ways, and therefore we cannot understand His purposes in allowing evil." This view is not simply saying that we *cannot* understand God's ways but that we should not even try to understand them. Whenever we try to resolve the logical problem of evil, our closely reasoned arguments seem to backfire and actually compound our problem—we then have both the problem of suffering and the problem of doubt. Therefore, victims of evil should simply do their best to manage their pain (most would add: with God's help) and not probe too deeply into mysteries that are not their ultimate concern.

Certainly it is difficult for thoughtful people to maintain such a position in the face of admitted paradoxes. We may admire the faith that prompts this response to the problem.[25] Rather than giving up on God's goodness, or God's power, or denying the reality of evil, persons who believe this way have given up any personal claim to grasp a solution to the problem—they have given up on themselves.

However, we believe that this solution to the problem is too costly. It seems more an indictment of God than a defense. biblical belief in God's all-good and all-powerful nature and in the reality of evil is established and maintained as a matter of *rational* belief. To retreat at the point of tension into nonrationality (or anti-rationality) while still holding to the other beliefs is inconsistent. Further, once fideism is adopted as an operating principle, it cannot be invoked merely for difficult problems. Assurance of understanding *anything* rationally about our faith has then been abandoned.

Biblically, God has made us as image-bearers who have self-consciousness and who engage in thought processes. Further, He has made Himself known to us. It is through the reasoned apprehension of revelation that we know that God is good. "God's goodness implies He would provide us with at least some understanding of His purposes. These considerations suggest that the theist should be able to provide fairly plausible accounts of at least some significant kinds of evil even if

---

[24] Given propositions A and B (teachings of my faith), there is a difference between saying that I do not understand how proposition A and B fit together and saying that proposition A and B are logically contradictory (i.e., B = non-A). The latter is what is proposed by the fideistic position.

[25] E.g., the eighteenth-century philosopher Pierre Bayle, "Paulicians," in *Introducing Philosophy*, 4th ed., Robert C. Solomon, ed. (New York: Harcourt Brace Jovanovich, 1989), pp. 318-22.

he or she cannot adequately explain all kinds (animal suffering, for example) or account for the quantity of evil."[26]

Further, revelation assumes that man's reason is the filter through which all thought about God should occur. Whenever special revelation took place, God assumed that the recipients were to follow His reasoning, which at times was quite detailed and logical. Christians are told to love God with their *minds* (Matt. 22:37). Jesus regularly presented arguments, all the while assuming the validity, ability, and necessity of man's reason as one component used in knowing Him. Paul rebuked the Corinthian Christians because they were adopting a form of worship that excluded their minds (1 Cor. 14:12-19).

Some cite Isaiah 55:8-9 as support for emphasizing the gap between God's thoughts and our thoughts, and God's ways and our ways. In its context, however, the statement is not emphasizing a finite/infinite cognitive gap in which we may take comfort, but is an indictment that the Israelites *should be* thinking God's thoughts and following God's ways.

This does not mean that believers know all truth exhaustively, but it does mean that we may know certain things truly, and that our true understanding is broad enough to embrace the problem of evil sufficiently without resorting to fideism.

Is God "Great"? (Finitism)

Another way to deal with evil is to redefine God's sovereignty: God is attempting to overcome evil, but He is unable to do so by Himself.[27] Many claim that God is somehow finite, subject to "laws" higher than Himself. These laws may be considered coeternal with God. Because God is not all powerful, there is no certainty of the final result; man must work *with* God to overcome evil. Thus this view maintains God's goodness at the expense of God's power.

Finitism is not new. It existed in various forms of ancient *dualism* (such as Zoroastrianism and Platonism). In more modern times it has been embraced by John Stuart Mill, Edgar S. Brightman,[28] and has

---

[26] Rowe and Wainwright, p. 195.

[27] Edgar S. Brightman, *A Philosophy of Religion* (New York: Prentice-Hall, 1940), pp. 285-303.

[28] Ibid., pp. 240-340. For a critique of Brightman's position, see Gordon Clark, *A Christian View of Men and Things* (Grand Rapids: Eerdmans, 1952), pp. 267-81.

become quite well known through Rabbi Harold S. Kushner's best seller *When Bad Things Happen to Good People*.[29]

In some ways, this approach solves the problem of evil. God is not at all responsible for evil, because He is unable to overcome it by Himself. In a sense God is also a victim of evil—His plan is victimized to the extent that it is contingent.

But again, finitism must be embraced at too high a price. If an exterminator tells you, "I got rid of your termites—I burned down your house!" you may feel that the solution is of little real help, because it creates even greater problems. This view relieves God from the moral responsibility for evil, but the origin of evil remains a mystery. In other words, this view solves *the problem of the problem of evil*, but not *the problem of evil*.

Finitism must redefine God's omnipotence by claiming that God is not sovereign over all creation. However, because God's attributes are being redefined, it follows that the term *God* itself is being redefined. God now becomes understood as a finite being. But because finite beings are conditioned by forces beyond their control, should those forces now be called God?

When we turn to the Bible, however, there is no doubt that God's power is total, including His power over evil (Ps. 147:4; Matt. 10:29-30; John 19:11; Eph. 1:11). There are no accidents in the universe outside God's knowledge or control. Job 1-2 clearly illustrates the control God exercises over moral and natural evil; God holds the reins of Satan, who can engage in evil only by God's permission.

Is God "Good"? (Transmoralism)

Whereas the previous view affirms God's goodness at the expense of His omnipotence, transmoralism affirms God's omnipotence at the expense of His goodness. God is not really good in the way man usually understands goodness. That is, the traditional definitions of God's goodness must be reconsidered, primarily by placing God's "goodness" into different theological perspectives in which God transcends morality. In the Hindu *Upanishads* the gods are either inadequate (finitism) or actively malevolent (transmoralism).[30]

The first theological perspective that may be used to redefine God's goodness is His absolute sovereignty. God is beneath no law or standard

---

[29] Harold S. Kushner, *When Bad Things Happen to Good People* (New York: Avon, 1981). See especially the chapter entitled "God Can't Do Everything, But He Can Do Some Important Things."

[30] Carmody and Carmody, *Ways to the Center*, p. 110.

(even of "goodness") to which He must conform. After all, does not the Bible quote God saying, "I . . . create evil" (Isa. 45:7, KJV)? Accountability determines morality. Because He is accountable to no one, God's character defines what is meant by "good." The view can be stated simply:

> Major Premise: Whatever happens is caused by God.
>
> Minor Premise: Whatever is caused by God is good.
>
> Conclusion: Whatever happens (including evil) is good.

Gordon Clark cites specific examples of apparent evils that are also "good." "The crucifixion of Christ—was it good or evil? To Judas and the Pharisees it was a crime productive only of evil and of the greatest of evils. To the disciples on the other hand it was productive of the greatest of goods."[31] Clark also maintains that Saul's persecution of Christians was "both good and evil, in different respects and to different persons; yet Christ met him on the road to Damascus and eliminated that evil."[32]

Many problems attend transmoralism. In a sense, it is *psychologically* difficult to accept, because labeling evil "good" does not make it so. What is at issue is not whether or not specific events may have mixed value to different people, but whether as an explanation transmoralism can account for *all* specific cases of evil. The explanation wears thin when trying to account for the occultic flaying of a baby or the horrors of a Nazi extermination camp.

Biblically, it does not follow from its supposed scriptural support. When the Bible quotes God as saying "I . . . create evil" (Isa. 45:7, KJV), the Hebrew parallelism makes it clear that God visits with calamity when He acts in judgment, not that He originates evil.[33]

Theologically, it is troublesome because in essence God can do with moral impunity what men are sent to jail for doing. But this view is also difficult to live with *practically*, because any words describing God's character lose their meaning and we are plunged into a sea of theological equivocation. "God does good" and "man does good" become so dissimilar that we no longer have a guarantee that a clear idea exists of what they mean. Yet God has given some of His attributes as models for His children to live by. Because He is holy, we are to be holy (1 Pet.

---

[31] Clark, *Christian View*, p. 272.

[32] Ibid., p. 273.

[33] R. C. Sproul, *Knowing Scripture* (Downers Grove, IL: InterVarsity, 1977), pp. 86-87.

1:16); because He is truth, we are to speak truth (Eph. 4:21-25). In other words, we are to "be imitators of God" (Eph. 5:1). God assumes that we are able to understand these qualities enough to reproduce them in our own lives.

What We Can Say . . .

We have dealt with several inadequate solutions to the problem of evil. Their inadequacies arise because they are unbiblical, and often inconsistent and/or emotionally unsatisfactory. Answers to tough problems are rarely simple. Not all of the evidence is in yet. Further, we are interpreting our world (which is affected by sin) with our minds (also affected by sin). Consequently, we may expect to wrestle deeply with questions for which we do not, at present, have all the information. Still, a biblical worldview contributes scriptural perspectives that not only explain the presence of evil but offer realistic hope for the future.

Suffering is easiest to understand when it comes as the direct result of a moral choice to sin. When David sinned by committing both adultery and murder, the judgment that befell him did not cause him theological anguish. He knew that God is both just and loving. However, not all suffering can be described as having an immediate cause/effect relationship with sin. Jesus' disciples were wide of the mark when they made this assumption, as were Job's friends centuries earlier (Job 42:7; John 9:1-2).

Suffering is also understandable when it can be seen to promote greater good. James 1 offers encouragement to believers who endure trials because James knew of the spiritual fruit that results from suffering. Paul's chronic suffering from his "thorn" was for a similar purpose (2 Cor. 12:7-9). When Joseph was enslaved, he certainly did not view what happened as good, yet later in his life comforted his brothers, "You meant evil against me, but God meant it for good in order to bring about this present result, to preserve many people alive" (Gen. 50:20).

It is always possible that God may view as ultimately good what we view as immediately evil. His perspective is eternal, His knowledge is infinite, and His judgments include all variables. Our judgments, by contrast, are based on incomplete data.

At times we try to superimpose a rationale for present suffering by positing some future "greater good"—from "God must be teaching me patience" to "God must want me to counsel others who also have lost a child." Even so, we know there is more to the matter and feel uneasy that we have simply accepted a contrived solution in order to make the pain more manageable; we have not been honest with our own minds. Further, in many cases the victim of evil would just as soon have done without the greater good and therefore without the accompanying pain. Rabbi Kushner admits,

> I am a more sensitive person, a more effective pastor, a more sympathetic counselor because of Aaron's life and death than I would ever have been without it. And I would give up all of those gains in a second if I could have my son back. If I could choose, I would forgo all the spiritual growth and depth which has come my way because of our experiences, and be what I was fifteen years ago, an average rabbi, an indifferent counselor, helping some people and unable to help others, and the father of a bright, happy boy. But I cannot choose."[34]

I appreciate Kushner's honesty and candor. Christians wrestle with similar problems. What should Christians think about those cases where there is *no observable good reason* for their suffering? Three components of the dilemma, which have so far been ignored, are *free will*, *time*, and *the suffering of Jesus*. Each of these has something to contribute to the biblical perspective on evil.

A View of the Past: Free Will and Possible Worlds

When creating man, God could have made him morally perfect, either with choice or without choice. However, man without free choice would not be man. God chose to make *man*, not an android.[35] Man's will, like other aspects of God's creation (e.g., water, fire), has the capacity to be used for good or evil. "God did not create sin. He merely provided the options necessary for human freedom."[36] In the biblical account, man plays a pivotal role in creation, and the fall of man had devastating implications for the rest of creation as well.

The "Free Will Defense" was originally put forth by Augustine and more recently has been meticulously defended by Alvin Plantinga.[37] It answers many of the questions of moral evil: free human agents decide whether or not to sin. It also reminds us that the problem is not external to us: *we are part of the problem*. Reportedly, a British newspaper once issued an open call to responses to the question: "What's wrong with the world?" G. K. Chesterton's short but poignant response is worthy of our reflection: "Dear Sir: I am."

---

[34] Kushner, pp. 133-34. Aaron Kushner died of progeria at the age of fifteen.
[35] Wenham, *Enigma of Evil*, p. 54.
[36] Erickson, *Christian Theology*, p. 429.
[37] Alvin Plantinga, *God, Freedom, and Evil* (Grand Rapids: Eerdmans, 1974).

The fall of man makes the biblical picture on evil and suffering fundamentally different than that of the worldviews we evaluated earlier in this chapter. In a biblical worldview, as noted by Cornelius Plantinga, the world is "Not the Way It's Supposed to Be."[38] In a world created "very good," something has gone very wrong. On the contrary, if man has not fallen (as is claimed by each of the other worldviews), there is no reason to expect the world to be any different than it is. A world that is the product of natural causes and processes (naturalism) or that continues as was created from the hand of God (Islam) is what it is.

But could God not have done it differently? Have we not simply redefined the problem on a different level so that we must now ask, Why did God make a plan like this? Consider the following propositions.

We know only *this* (actual) world.

We can conceive of other *possible* worlds (including one with less evil) but not all possible worlds, because we are finite.

God (who is infinite) knows *all* possible worlds.[39]

This world is not (at this time) the best of all possible worlds (even that we can think of).

When we stand in our Lord's presence and enter eternity, the Bible says we will be in the best of all possible worlds (John 14:1-6; 1 Thess. 4:13-18; Rev. 21-22; etc.).

Therefore, although this is not (now) the best of all possible worlds, a world of man's free choice (even to do evil) is the best way to achieve the best of all possible worlds.

Stephen Davis summarizes this approach: "What the Free Will Defense must insist on is, first, that the amount of evil that in the end will exist will be outweighed by the great goods that will then exist; and second, that this favourable balance of good over evil was obtainable by

---

[38] Cornelius Plantinga, *Not the Way It's Supposed to Be: A Breviary of Sin* (Grand Rapids: Eerdmans, 1995).

[39] For example, in Matthew 11:20-24 Jesus indicates that if He had performed certain miracles in Tyre and Sidon, they would have repented. See William Lane Craig, *The Only Wise God* (Grand Rapids: Baker, 1987), p. 132.

God in no other way that was within his control."[40] This position includes faith commitments arising from a biblical worldview. Knowing all possible worlds, God knew this was the best possible way to result in the best possible world. Thus the defense becomes a "best way" instead of a "best world" position. In this way, God achieves the greatest good.[41]

Biblically, natural evil in the world is a consequence of the decision by man to do moral evil. When Adam sinned, this world became the domain of Satan and his minions (Gen. 3:17ff.; see also Rom. 8:19-22, where the creation awaits its restoration to a pristine state). Yet God's power maintains control over both moral and natural evil, as a study of Job 1-2 reveals. In this sense God may be considered the *ultimate* cause of evil (in that He is the *Author* of the *author* [Satan] of sin); this does not, however, require that He is the *blameworthy* cause of sin. Thus, "although not without its problems (such as the riddle of evil *ex nihilo*), this affirmation of the traditional notion of the Genesis 3 fall accounts for both natural and moral evil."[42]

A View of the Future: The Factor of Time

The component of time is crucial to a biblical worldview of evil (Rom. 8:18). One day, God will wipe away all tears from our eyes (Rev. 21:4). Until then, even saints in the Lord's presence wail "How long, O Lord?" as they anticipate cosmic restoration (Rev. 6:10).

Let us reconsider our original propositions:

> Both God and evil are realities that truly exist.
>
> If God were all-powerful, He could destroy evil.
>
> If God were all-good, He would destroy evil.
>
> Evil has not been destroyed.

Before drawing the conclusion, the last proposition should be reworded to fit with our biblical worldview. This is how it should read:

---

[40] Davis, *Logic and the Nature of God*, p. 100.

[41] See Norman Geisler, *Philosphy of Religion* (Grand Rapids: Zondervan, 1974), pp. 349-79. For counter-arguments see Davis, p. 99.

[42] Daniel Clendenin, "Security but No Certainty: Toward a Christian Theodicy," *Journal of the Evangelical Theological Society* 31:3 (September 1988), p. 326.

Evil has not *yet* been destroyed.

Thus we may draw a new conclusion:

Evil *will be* destroyed by an all-good, all-powerful God.

This is logically coherent and is precisely what the Bible claims. Further, the Bible presents that this final eradication of evil is the final realization of the active stance God has been taking against evil since the minute it entered the creation. N. T. Wright observes, ". . . the entire canon (of Scripture) . . . tells a story which, from a bewildering variety of angles, is all about what God (the Creator God, please note) is doing about evil.[43] Although we do not yet have enough data to answer why each individual act of suffering takes place, we have a reasonable perspective within which to deal with our pain. Is our biblical worldview large enough to trust God with our remaining uncertainties?

In the realm of science, for example, physicists cannot logically harmonize the wave and particle nature of light. Lack of certainty in this area, however, does not render modern physics impossible. The assumption is made that the answer will be forthcoming, and in the meantime scientists go on about their work. Thus, the presence of unsolved dilemmas does not falsify a worldview. We assume God knows all possible worlds, and that we do not. We also assume He is good, loving, and just. May we not trust His judgment and know that His reasons are compelling and sufficient?

There is a startling biblical symmetry between sin's entrance into the world (Gen. 1-3) and its exit from the world (Rev. 20-22). A brief perusal is enough to convince us that the tragedy that was inaugurated in the beginning will be completely dealt with before we enter the eternal state (see Diagram 6.1: The Beginning and End).[44]

Further, Scripture indicates that the end product of redemption will be better than the original product of creation, and that this redemption was part of the eternal plan of God from the beginning. The biblical story begins in a garden that needs to be cultivated and ends in a city that will never end. There will be no need for a sun, as in the original creation, since God will be the light of that city. Christ is the "lamb, slain before the foundation of the world;" and it is this slain lamb that distracts the praise of the heavenly beings from their previous perpetual songs for the God "who created all things." (see Rev. 4-5). The question in biblical

---

[43] Wright, *Evil and the Justice of God,* p. 76.

[44] Adapted from Kenneth Boa, *Talk Thru the New Testament* (Wheaton, IL: Tyndale House, 1981), p. 225.

terms shifts from "Why did God create a world where evil would exist?" to "Why did God create a world that He was planning to redeem?"

In the meantime, however, those who belong to Jesus have been told to anticipate that they will follow their Lord in suffering (John 15:20-27; Rom. 8:17), realizing that Jesus has overcome the world (John 16:33). Therefore, we can take comfort in the fact "that the sufferings of this present time are not worthy to be compared with the glory that is to be revealed in us" (Rom. 8:18).

Diagram 6.1
The Beginning and the End

Genesis 1-3	*Revelation 20-22*
"In the day you eat from it, you shall surely die" (2:17)	"There shall no longer be any death" (21:4)
Satan appears as deceiver (3:1)	Satan removed forever (20:10)
"I will greatly multiply your pain" (3:16)	"There shall no longer be any mourning, or crying, or pain" (21:4)
"Cursed is the ground because of you" (3:17)	"There shall no longer be any curse" (22:3)
First paradise closed (3:23)	New paradise opened (21:25)
They were driven from God's presence (3:24)	"They shall see His face" (22:4)

A View for the Present: The God Who Suffers with Us

This "best world" apologetic may not, however, resolve our personal dilemma in dealing with private suffering. It is one thing to say in the abstract that this is a logical and biblically consistent solution. It is quite another thing to comfort yourself that this is the best of all possible worlds when you are facing terminal cancer. As one philosopher put it, "the happy phrase 'best of all possible worlds' may warm our hearts in the comfort of a church or a seminar room, but it quickly becomes cold when confronting real tragedy."[45]

On the other hand, this world in which we live, and in which evil seems to flourish, serves as an object lesson of need: "The existence of suffering on this earth is, I believe, a scream to all of us that something is wrong."[46] The presence of evil and our lack of acceptance of injustice or pain is an indication to believer and unbeliever alike that this world is not as it should be—or as it came from the hand of God.

Suffering and Jesus' Ministry

Although others may offer no hope, false hope, or illusory hope, the Bible offers realistic hope because of the work of our compassionate Savior. In Jesus' high priestly role God became man and thus understands experientially what our sufferings are like. We are exhorted to remember that "we do not have a high priest who cannot sympathize with our weakness" (Heb. 4:15). Isaiah reminds us that in the life of the Messiah He would become "acquainted with grief" (Isa. 53:3). He is now the head of His Body, and when members of His Body hurt, He hurts (Acts 9:4-5).

Our Lord does not ask His own to ignore pain. Jesus wept in the presence of death (John 11:35), despite the fact He knew Lazarus would be raised shortly thereafter. Even though Paul referred to his own death as "gain" (entrance into the immediate presence of Christ—Phil. 1:21), he referred to the potential death of one of his friends as "sorrow upon sorrow" (Phil. 2:27). Believers should expect suffering if they follow Christ (Mark 8:34; John 15:20) and thus can in a sense rejoice in those sufferings, which are for Christ's sake (2 Cor. 4:17-18; 7:4; Phil. 3:10; 1 Pet. 4:13).

---

[45] Solomon, *Introducing Philosophy*, p. 323.

[46] Philip Yancey, "Pain: The Tool of the Wounded Surgeon," *Christianity Today*, 24 March 1978, p. 14.

Suffering and Jesus' Death

From a biblical worldview, the ultimate apologetic for the problem of evil is God's action (through Christ) in becoming the victim of maximum evil. God took the punishment of sin upon Himself. He became man, and in that form He—and He alone—suffered the entire composite of human evil and misery. Not only did He bear our sins, He bore our emotional pain (Isa. 53:4).

Although components of the problem of evil may remain a present mystery, a more amazing mystery is that God allowed sin to occur at all, knowing that He would become its ultimate victim. Furthermore, the worst of all possible evils (the death of Christ—history's only absolutely sinless man) was not only permitted, but decreed from eternity past (Acts 2:23). "By taking it on Himself, Jesus in a sense dignified pain. Of all the lives He could have lived, He chose a suffering one."[47]

Edward Shillito was a British minister who witnessed the devastation of World War I. In his attempts to reconcile what he had seen with his faith, he penned these words:

> If we have never sought, we seek Thee now;
> Thine eyes burn through the dark, out only stars;
> We must have sight of thorn-pricks on Thy brow;
> We must have Thee, O Jesus of the Scars.
>
> The heavens frighten us; they are too calm;
> In all the universe we have no place;
> Our wounds are hurting us; where is the balm?
> Lord Jesus, by Thy Scars, we claim Thy grace.
>
> If, when the doors are shut, Thou drawest near;
> Only reveal those hands, that side of Thine;
> We know to-day what wounds are, have no fear;
> Show us Thy Scars, we know the countersign.
>
> The other gods were strong; but Thou wast weak;
> They rode, but Thou didst stumble to a throne;
> But to our wounds only God's wounds can speak;
> And not a god has wounds, but Thou alone.[48]

---

[47] Ibid., p. 15.

[48] Edward Shillito, "Jesus of the Scars" in Thomas C. Clark, ed. *The Master of Men: Quotable Poems about Jesus* (Manchester, NH: Ayer, 1970), pp. 113-114.

We are not claiming here to completely satisfy all of the dilemmas resulting from every evil and each instance of personal suffering. However, we do believe to have offered a resolution that explains the presence of evil in light of God's ultimate plan of redeeming the world He created. The Bible does not ignore the reality of evil. It describes its origins, its power, and its ultimate demise; and it offers a God who, in Christ, meets evil squarely and ultimately defeats it.

This is the consistent approach the biblical worldview provides. The biblical story is centered around the person and work of the incarnated Son of God. We might call it the "Christological Resolution." This perspective is unique among the religions of the world, and we will bring this important idea to bear on the next issue we will look at: the problem of pluralism.

DISCUSSION QUESTIONS

1. In what ways is the presence of evil in the world a problem for an atheist? For a materialist? For a pantheist? For an agnostic? For a Christian?
2. A friend to whom you are witnessing says to you, "My mom has had a hard life since Dad left us, and last week she just found out she has cancer. I wish I could believe what you say about God loving me and Jesus dying for me and all that, but I just can't believe in a God of love anymore." What could you say?
3. Your neighbor is a member of the Christian Science movement and has told you that his or her family does not believe that physical pain exists. What would you say?
4. Your marriage engagement has just been broken because your sweetheart has decided he or she does not love you. Your roommate pats you on the back and says, "Well, Romans 8:28—all things work together for good!" What should your attitude be toward your fiancé? Toward your roommate?
5. Read Lamentations 3. What was going on when Jeremiah penned these words? Can you detect a change within Jeremiah's attitude as the chapter progresses? If so, why? (Do the same for Habakkuk 3.)
6. How can the suffering of Jesus be used to evangelize people who are struggling with the problem of evil? How can the suffering of Jesus be used in counseling the bereaved?

FURTHER READING

Blocher, Henri. *Evil and the Cross:An Analytical Look at the Problem of Pain.* Grand Rapids: Kregel, 1994.

Clark, Ralph W. *Introduction to Philosophical Thinking: Readings and Commentary.* New York: West, 1987, ch. 4.

Feinberg, John S. *The Many Faces of Evil: Theological Systems and the Problems of Evil.* Wheaton: Crossway, 2004.

Lewis, C. S. *The Problem of Pain.* London: Geoffrey Bles, 1940.

Plantinga, Alvin C. *God, Freedom, and Evil.* Grand Rapids: Eerdmans, 1974.

Plantinga, Cornelius, *Not the Way It's Supposed to Be: A Breviary of Sin.* Grand Rapids: Eerdmans, 1995.

Solomon, Robert C. *Introducing Philosophy: A Text with Integrated Readings.* 4th ed. New York: Harcourt Brace Jovanovich, 1989, pp. 312-27.

Wenham, John W. *The Enigma of Evil.* Grand Rapids: Zondervan, 1985.

Wright, N. T. *Evil and the Justice of God.* Downers Grove, IL: InterVarsity, 2006.

Yancey, Philip. *Where Is God When It Hurts?* Grand Rapids: Zondervan, 1977.

_____. *Disappointment with God: Questions Nobody Asks Aloud.* Grand Rapids: Zondervan, 1988.

7
WHO'S RIGHT?
THE PROBLEM OF PLURALISM

Pluralism Described
Pluralism Defended
Pluralism Disputed
    Jesus Claimed to Be the Only Way of Salvation
    Jesus' Followers Claimed that He Is the Only Way of Salvation
    Jesus Claimed that Other Ways of Salvation Are False
    Jesus' Followers Claimed that Other Ways of Salvation Are False
    Conclusion: Jesus Is the Only Way of Salvation
Pluralism Disarmed
    Those Who Have Heard: The Question of Truth
        The Problem Described
        A Biblical Response
    Those Who Haven't Heard: The Question of Justice
        The Problem Described
        Some Biblical Responses
Conclusion: The Christological Resolution

James kept probing. The conversation had occurred many times before, but with different people.

"How can you believe in a God who would condemn anybody to hell? Many people have lived moral lives and been faithful in their religion! Are they damned simply because that religion was not Christianity?!"

"And furthermore," he continued, "what about those who have never heard about Christ? Are they condemned too?" He warmed to the topic, sensing the weakness of an Achilles' heel.

"And how do you explain the fact that in a Christian country, most people are Christians, in a Muslim country, most people follow Islam, and in a Buddhist country, most people are Buddhists? That doesn't sound like any God is at work, it sounds more like sociology to me!"

His face showed that he believed his triumph was complete.

Pluralism Described

Edward Gibbon, in *The Decline and Fall of the Roman Empire*, stated that during the decline of the Empire all religions were regarded by the people as equally true, by the philosophers as equally false, and by the politicians as equally useful![1] People react in different ways when the subject of other religions (the question of pluralism) is raised. For some, the topic is an interesting intellectual question; for many, pluralism is a deeply emotional issue.

Although discussions of pluralism are not new, all the relevant questions need to be carefully considered. What is God like? Is God a personal being or an impersonal force? Is man's destiny one of continued self-conscious existence, or reabsorption into the matrix of the cosmos? What is heaven—a real place or simply a state of consciousness? Is salvation heightened awareness of other beings, or redemption from sin? Is salvation attained by works, by meditation, or by faith? If Christianity is true, does it necessarily follow that all other religions are wrong? Can so many be wrong, or are all religions equally valid? Could it be that some are more valid than others, while those that fall short may be at least adequate for God's purpose of salvation?

The fact of a pluralistic world has required religious thinkers to adopt positions regarding believers in other religions. Several different approaches have been adopted.[2]

Selectivism says that other religions have elements of truth, but only one (the religion of the selectivist) is totally true. A selectivist enjoys the religious cafeteria approach: even though there is one main course, he may take what he likes and discard what he dislikes from each religion. The resulting religious fare will be acceptable to God.

Inclusivism says there is only one true religion through which salvation may be obtained (the religion of the inclusivist). But God may impute salvation to the sincere worshiper of false gods. Although those

---

[1] Cited in James Montgomery Boice, *The Minor Prophets* (Grand Rapids: Zondervan, 1986), 2:124.

[2] Different worldviews give different answers to these basic questions. Consequently, *religious pluralism* is difficult to define because one must assume a common understanding of such concepts as salvation, heaven, and even God. Furthermore, not all worldviews are explicitly religious, and of those that *are* religious, not all mean the same things by these terms. The definitions given here are *stipulative*—that is, this is what we mean by these terms.

in other religions may refuse to partake from (or not know about) the proper religious diet, God will not let them starve.

Exclusivism maintains that there is one true God, and that other truth-claims that conflict with the religion of the exclusivist are therefore false. All other positions lead to spiritual anorexia.

Universalism says (positively) all worldviews can be valid avenues of salvation and (negatively) exclusivism is wrong. Because all religions are equally true, we should toss all religious truth claims into one huge melting pot and enjoy religious stew. The undergirding assumption of universalism is that we have no access to ultimate reality for deciding which worldview is true. We are left with diversity but no unity; particulars but no universals; relatives but no absolutes.[3]

Pluralism Defended

I was shocked when I looked closely at the newspaper. There, with saffron robe and shaved head, sat one of my old friends—in lotus position, no less. The picture and its story told of my high school classmate who had gone on to Princeton and, earning a Rhodes scholarship, on to England for further study. There he encountered the teachings of Buddhism and became a Buddhist priest. He described himself now as a "Christian Buddhist." I would expect intense exposure to the worldview of Buddhism if he had gone to south Asia—but England?

Seventy-five percent of the world, though mostly theistic or pantheistic, is non-Christian. Hinduism claims 900 million followers (670 million are in India),[4] and there are now 376 million Buddhists worldwide. The growth of Islam is particularly significant, especially in light of its more aggressive expressions worldwide. There are an estimated 1.3 billion Muslims worldwide, with the Muslim population in the United States having almost tripled since 1990.[5] Some sources

---

[3] R. C. Sproul, *Lifeviews* (Old Tappan, NJ: Revell, 1986), p. 114. All the above positions (except universalism) affirm that at least some will not be saved. Universalism says that everyone will be saved; hell will be ultimately unpopulated.

[4] Some of the information to follow, particularly current statistics, is taken from www.adherents.com.

[5] There is disagreement among Muslim and non-Muslim sources about the growth and current state of Islam. Muslim sources tend to suggest higher numbers, especially regarding the number of Muslims in the United States.

suggest that Islam will surpass Christianity in total numbers sometime in the twenty-first century.[6]

Our global village is shrinking. Until recently, evangelizing a Muslim meant going across the ocean. Today, it means going across the driveway to have coffee with your next-door neighbor. Now more than ever, Christians need to be able to respond to the challenges of other worldviews (both religious and nonreligious). First, if Christianity is right, are all others wrong? Second, are those who do not believe in Christ, but warmly embrace another religion, bound for an eternity in hell? Third, what about the eternal destinies of those who have never had the chance even to hear of Jesus Christ?

Pluralism Disputed

"Christians are religious bigots. You think you are right and everybody else is wrong!" The lady's complaint could just as easily have been directed to a Muslim. Our survey of the options among theistic and nontheistic worldviews should make it clear that worldviews are mutually exclusive; they cannot all be right. If theism is true, then naturalism and transcendentalism are false. If Christian theism is true, then Islam and Judaism are wrong, and vice versa.

Christians do *not* think they are morally better than people in other religions. Because Christianity does not teach salvation by works but salvation by grace through faith, all boasting is excluded (Rom. 3:27). The central issue for a biblical worldview, however, is what the Bible claims about salvation through Jesus Christ. Is it exclusive? The following premises make a tight case.

Premise A:
Jesus Claimed to Be the Only Way of Salvation

He taught the multitudes that salvation was not by works but by believing in "Him whom He [God] has sent" (John 6:22-36, especially v. 29). This salvation to eternal life is a gift from Jesus (v. 27). In John 14:6 Jesus made both positive and negative statements. Positively, He claimed to be the way, the truth, and the life. Jesus did not simply claim to be a way of access to the Father.[7] The definite article preceding each noun

---

[6] See Samuel P. Huntingdon, *The Clash of Civilizations and the Remaking of World Order* (New York: Simon and Schuster, 1998). Also this is suggested on several websites including www.religioustolerance.org.

[7] Indeed, all Jesus needed to say to establish His point was that He was *the way*. By adding the other two terms, which emerge throughout the book as

emphasizes uniqueness. Negatively, Jesus claimed that *no one*[8] is able to come to the Father except through Him. It is difficult to imagine a clearer or more forceful statement of uniqueness.[9]

Premise B:
Jesus' Followers Claimed that He Is the Only Way of Salvation

The exclusive nature of Jesus' message became an integral part of the apostles' preaching. In Acts 4:12 Peter made two negative statements to his Jewish audience: first, there is salvation in no other *person* but Jesus; second, God has made no *provision* for salvation other than through Jesus. Here (as in premise A) salvation is linked with the *name* of Jesus—specific content his listeners needed to know so that they might be saved (see v. 10). Later, when speaking to a Gentile audience (Acts 10:43), Peter anchored their thoughts to the truth of the Old Testament and pointed out that (through His *name*) everyone who believes in Jesus the Nazarene (v. 38) receives forgiveness of sins.

Paul's claims were no less pointed. When asked by a pagan jailer in a pagan culture how to receive salvation, Paul did not encourage him to "be diligent in your religion, whatever it may be," or comfort him that his sincerity had already made him acceptable before God, but rather told him to fulfill a specific condition in order to be saved: "Believe on the Lord Jesus" (Acts 16:31).

In Romans 10:9-17 the condition for salvation is confession with the mouth that "Jesus is Lord" and belief that God raised him from the dead.[10] This message is to be taken to all people: both Jew and Greek (v. 12). Again, however, those who would be saved must call on the name of the Lord Jesus (v. 13—see v. 9 where "Lord" is specified).

---

significant themes, the argument is strengthened all the more. It is noteworthy that the first name by which the early Christians designated themselves was "the way" (e.g., Acts 19:9, 23; 22:4; 24:14, 22; see also 9:2; 16:17; 18:25-26).

[8] The fact that, in the Greek, *oudeis* is placed first in the sentence may indicate emphasis.

[9] The point at which Jesus stopped speaking to Nicodemus and John continued commenting (if indeed John commented at all) in John 3:18-21 is unclear. If Jesus uttered these words, we may add these verses to this premise; if the passage is John's comment, then this point fits under premise B.

[10] Paul is reflecting Moses' order (quoting Deut. 30:14 in Rom. 10:8); the presence of Hebrew synonymous parallelism indicates that no distinction should be made between "confessing" and "believing" (as there is no difference between the imputed "righteousness" and "salvation" in verse 10).

Therefore, there is great urgency in mission (vv. 14-15) so that the word of Christ (v. 17) will be proclaimed to all peoples.[11]

Premise C:
Jesus Claimed that Other Ways of Salvation Are False

In other words, Jesus was not claiming to be merely *a* way of salvation (premise A), but that all other ways were dead ends. John 3:18 indicates that people do not fall under the condemnation of God because they have actively rejected Christ, but because they have not accepted Him ("because he has not believed in the name of the only Son of God").

John 8 is filled with statements regarding the spiritual condition of the most religious men of the day: the Jewish leaders. In verse 19 Jesus said that because they had no relationship with Jesus, they had no relationship at all with the Father. In verse 24 Jesus applied to Himself one of the Old Testament self-designations of God, and told His audience that they would die in their sins (*not* in their ignorance) "unless you believe that I AM." In 8:41-42 Jesus corrected the misconception of the Jewish leaders. They claimed to be children of God, and Jesus rebuked them. If God were truly their Father, He said, then they would love Jesus. Because they did not love Jesus, then they had no relationship with God the Father. Indeed, their true "father" was the devil (v. 44). The reason they did not believe in Jesus (hear the words of God) is because they were "not of God" (v. 47).

Premise D:
Jesus' Followers Claimed that Other Ways of Salvation Are False

As before (premise B), the apostles continued to claim the restrictive nature of God's plan of salvation. On the first missionary journey, Paul addressed the Jews and the Gentile converts to Judaism in the synagogue at Pisidian Antioch. He declared that the means of salvation embraced by the Jews—the keeping of the law—did not bring about forgiveness of sins (Acts 13:38-39).

When speaking to a sophisticated Gentile audience in Athens, Paul told the philosophers of the Areopagus that they must repent (Acts 17:30). Previously, they had been worshiping deity in images of "gold, or silver, or stone" (v. 29)—which Paul referred to as "ignorance" (v. 30). Although it is true that God is "not far from each of us" (v. 27), the condition of repentance must be met to avoid judgment (v. 31). The significance of this confrontation is that Paul had an ideal opportunity to express the unity of all religions as legitimate means of salvation, but

---

[11] See also Rom. 6:23; Gal. 1:8; 1 Tim. 2:5.

instead told his audience that their religious systems did not bring salvation.

In Acts 26:17-18 Paul described to King Agrippa his commission from the mouth of God as "opening their eyes." Furthermore, those who were not Christians were described as being in darkness (not light), in the power of Satan (not God), and without forgiveness. First Corinthians 8:4-6 clearly denied that the polytheistic practices of the Corinthians led to salvation—indeed, Paul claimed that sacrifices offered to such idols were in reality offered "to demons and not to God" (10:20; 12:2; 1 Thess. 1:9). Other passages abound.

Conclusion:
Jesus Is the Only Way of Salvation

The conclusion of these premises can be stated both positively and negatively: Jesus is the only way of salvation (positive); other ways of salvation are false (negative). Salvation consistently is linked with Jesus' *name, person,* and *lordship.* Jesus is both the ontological basis and the epistemological basis for salvation.

Christian mission is not to supplement, complement, or add to other faiths, but to *displace* them. We may either accept or reject what the Bible says on this point. One option we do not have is to deny that this is indeed what the Bible says.

Pluralism Disarmed

Those Who Have Heard: The Question of Truth

There are indeed similarities between the world religions. First, most believe in God or gods and in the unseen but real world. This is in contrast with a materialistic or naturalistic worldview. Second, most religions have an ecclesiastical hierarchy and a fellowship of faithful believers. Third, most religions have a code of ethical conduct that devotees are to follow. [12]

The point is, however, that all religions cannot be true. There are significant differences between them, which include crucial foundational issues. The natures of God, of matter, and of man are all defined differently by various religious systems. Therefore, when man confronts God, nature, and self, the worldviews that arise will be different. Is life after death a new sphere or level of personal existence, or are we simply

---

[12] J. N. D. Anderson, "Do All Religions Lead to God?" *Radix* (May-June 1983):4.

absorbed into transcendental impersonal force? How do we come to know God? Is it through asceticism (purposely living a life of discomfort), through mysticism (meditation and focus on paradoxes), through the works of self-discipline, or by grace through faith?

What about Jesus Christ? Is Jesus an eternal being, or was He a created being? Was He truly God and truly man, or was He exclusively human? Did He die for the sins of mankind (Christianity), did He die a disillusioned and misunderstood itinerant rabbi (Judaism), or was He taken up into heaven without dying at all—and therefore is not a Savior (Islam)?

The Problem Described

The goal of every person is to discover truth about God, not to be found in error or to be self-deceived. The question of truth, however, is not how we might *want* things to be, but how things actually *are*. Truth and sincere faith are an ideal combination. However, it is possible to have sincere faith without truth. Those who work in coal mines may have sincere faith in the struts and bankments that protect them, but if the laws of geophysics are violated, their sincerity will not save them. It does not matter how sincerely a skater believes that the ice is two feet thick; if its thickness is really only a quarter of an inch, she is going to get wet. Those who embraced Adolph Hitler's doctrine of Aryan supremacy, or those who followed Jim Jones to Guyana, were sincere in their faith but were tragically wrong. In other words, faith has no intrinsic value; one may sincerely believe that which is false. The validity of faith depends not on the *sincerity* of the *subject* (who is believing) but rather derives from the *truth* of its *object*.

Truth is absolute; if not, then nothing is true. If truth were relative, the statement "truth is relative" would itself be relative. All guarantee of meaning and communication would disappear. In both the physical and spiritual realms truth is truth, no matter how narrow it may be perceived to be. "Christians believe this [teaching of salvation exclusively through Jesus Christ], not because they have made it their rule, but because Jesus Christ our Lord taught it. A Christian cannot be faithful to his Lord and affirm anything else. He is faced with the problem of truth."[13]

---

[13] Paul Little, *Know Why You Believe* (Wheaton, IL: Victor, 1967), p. 119.

A Biblical Response

The Christian exclusivist is classified by some as a bigot. Wilfred Cantwell Smith stated bluntly, "Religious diversity poses a general human problem, because it disrupts community."[14] He would be rid of all religious teachings in which one religion takes issue with the doctrines of another. Particularly abhorrent are evangelistic religions that seek converts out of other religious systems.

It is true that belief in Jesus Christ as God's exclusive way of salvation does motivate Christians to persuade those in other religions to abandon their religion and embrace Christ.[15] The exclusive claim of Christianity has always been challenged from the outside. Recently, however, Christian exclusivism has been challenged from within. For example, one of this century's best-known Christian writers, C. S. Lewis, stated that those who reject Christ can be finally saved when "divine Grace has guided them to concentrate solely on the true elements in their own religion."[16] Is this a position for a consistent Christian to embrace? This question concerns thoughtful believers, for there are many morally upright people who do not believe in Jesus but choose to serve another god instead—or no god at all.

The laws of reason affirm that two mutually exclusive propositions can both be false, but cannot both be true. If I say I am a husband, a father, a teacher, and a bank robber, these are not contradictory statements; they may not be true, but they are not necessarily contradictory. For example, if I say Jesus is God and Jesus is man, these are not necessarily two contradictory statements.[17] However, consider the following propositions:

---

[14] Wilfred Cantwell Smith, "The Christian in a Religiously Plural World" in *Christianity and Other Religions*, ed. John Hick and B. Hebblethaite (Philadelphia: Fortress, 1980), p. 94.

[15] *The Encyclopedia of Religion*, s.v. "Religious Pluralism," by John Hick (New York: Macmillan, 1987), p. 331.

[16] From a letter to Bede Griffiths, cited by Richard Purtill, *C. S. Lewis's Case for the Christian Faith* (New York: Harper & Row, 1981), p. 81. Although Lewis was not necessarily trying to promote this position, it is illustrated in Lewis's *The Last Battle* (New York: Macmillan, 1956), where Emeth, the virtuous soldier who has served the false god Tash (and consciously rejected Aslan), is accepted by Aslan because "all the service thou hast done to Tash, I account as service done to me" (p. 295). Lewis was not a universalist, however.

[17] Indeed their harmonization is the point of the words of both Jesus (Matt. 22) and Paul (Phil. 2). To show that these were mutually exclusive concepts, I

Jesus did die on the cross (Christianity).

Jesus did not die on the cross (Islam).

If I affirm both propositions (without equivocating terms), then I would be affirming that which would be contradictory. The Koran says Jesus did not die on the cross, but the Bible says He did. They cannot *both* be true.[18]

Consider two other basic Christian truths: (1) the Person of Jesus Christ, and (2) the way of salvation. The focus of Christianity includes both: the uniqueness of Jesus Christ as God's way of salvation. One may meditate on the great religious leaders of world history, but none of those claimed to be God, none of those claimed to make payment for the sins of the world, and none were resurrected.[19] Other religions may tip their hats to Jesus as a wonderful human being, but they all deny that He is God come in the flesh. If they are correct, Christianity is false; if Christianity is true, they are in error.

Furthermore, almost every religion has the ethical equivalent of the Golden Rule; but the Bible makes clear that because of sin, no one can fulfill even the Golden Rule (Rom. 3:10-23). Other religions offer means by which man earns his salvation. Biblically, the only thing man can earn is spiritual death (Rom. 6:23*a*). "In a sense, other religious systems are sets of swimming instructions for a drowning man. Christianity is a life preserver."[20] Christianity promises eternal life, provided through the work of Christ on the cross (Rom 6:23*b*; 10:9-10).

If Jesus is who He said He was, then we are bound by His words—including His claims to be the only way of salvation. They are not only

---

would have to demonstrate that deity and humanity cannot coexist in one person/Person. See S. Morris Engel, *With Good Reason*, 3d ed. (New York: St. Martin's, 1986), pp. 135-36, for the distinction between *contrary* and *contradictory*.

[18] J. N. D. Anderson, *Christianity & Comparative Religion* (Downers Grove, IL: InterVarsity, 1970), p. 93.

[19] See Romans 1:4. For information on the defense of the historical resurrection of Jesus, see Daniel Fuller, *Easter Faith and History* (Grand Rapids: Eerdmans, 1965); Gary Habermas, *The Resurrection of Jesus: An Apologetic* (Grand Rapids: Baker, 1980); Gary Habermas and Antony G. N. Flew, *Did Jesus Rise from the Dead? The Resurrection Debate*, ed. Terry L. Miethe (San Francisco: Harper & Row, 1987); Merrill Tenney, *The Reality of the Resurrection* (New York: Harper & Row, 1963). See also Pinchas Lapide, *The Resurrection of Jesus: A Jewish Perspective* (Minneapolis: Augsburg, 1983).

[20] Little, p. 121.

true, but also authoritative regarding how we are to think about other religions. In spite of the humanitarian appeal of nonexclusive positions, they will not work. The absolute nature of truth will not allow all religions to be true. To believe in everything is to believe in nothing.

Those Who Haven't Heard: The Question of Justice

What about those who have not heard about Jesus? Few questions are asked more often than this one. Some ask out of a motivation to be contentious, some to redirect an attempt to witness to them, but others ask because they have sensitive spirits and are concerned about how God's justice fits with God's mercy. Christians also are concerned and want to be both biblical and honest as they deal with the question of God's justice. Is salvation limited to those who live in a culture where the gospel is heard?

The Problem Described

Cultural pluralism has led to cultural and social tolerance. The Christian doctrine of exclusive salvation through Christ and eternal damnation of the lost is regarded as a maximal example of social intolerance. A pluralistic society will not tolerate intolerance. It seems grossly unfair that those with easy access to the message of Christ seem to have, in effect, "redemptive privilege" (this is a charge against all "exclusivist" religions that have content that must be believed or obeyed for salvation). As with the problem of evil, the question of God's justice in a pluralistic world results in a personal problem. It serves as a gauge of the believer's emotional comfort in God's character: His love, justice, and fairness.

Traditionally, an overwhelming evangelical consensus has affirmed Christian exclusivism.[21] However, a recent survey of evangelical college and seminary students showed that almost one-third no longer hold to the traditional view. James Davidson Hunter observes, "The existence of such a sizable minority of Evangelicals maintaining this [new] stance represents a noteworthy shift away from the historical interpretations. . . . If historical precedent is instructive, it becomes clear that these tendencies will probably escalate."[22]

For example, evangelical spokesman Clark Pinnock confidently asserts, "Of one thing we can be certain: God will not abandon in hell those who have not known and therefore have not declined His offer of

---

[21] James Davidson Hunter, *Evangelicalism: The Coming Generation* (Chicago: U. of Chicago, 1987), p. 34.

[22] Ibid., pp. 38, 49.

grace. Though He has not told us the nature of His arrangements, we cannot doubt the existence and goodness of them."[23] According to Pinnock and a growing number of evangelicals, ignorance does not disqualify grace.

Some Biblical Responses

THE RESPONSES DESCRIBED. Does the Bible offer the same clear comfort that Pinnock and others have offered? We shall describe and evaluate the following options held within Christian circles (these are regarded as more or less coherent and consistent with biblical theology). Even those who have no opinion have adopted attitudes that may fall into one of the following options:[24] universal light, designated light, existing light, greater light, and later light.

1. THE *UNIVERSAL LIGHT* VIEW. The view, sometimes called "univer-salism," teaches that ultimately all men will be saved. Jesus Christ is the light that "enlightens every man" (John 1:9), and He is present *incognito* in other religions. After all, did Jesus not say that he who is not against us is for us (Luke 9:50)?

Universalists support their position biblically by citing texts that they say: (1) teach that the cross ensured universal salvation (2 Cor. 5:19; Col. 1:20ff.; Titus 2:11; Heb. 2:9; 1 John 2:2); (2) teach that God intends universal salvation (1 Tim. 2:4; 2 Pet. 3:9); and (3) predict universal salvation explicitly (John 12:32; Acts 3:21; Romans 5:18-19; 1 Cor. 15:22-28; Phil. 2:9-11).[25]

The idea of an everlasting hell also motivates people toward universalism.[26] Many believe that biblical descriptions of God as just and loving would be contradicted by the existence of an eternal agony of punishment; in fact, because the redeemed would know about the ongoing torment of the damned, heaven would no longer be heaven for

---

[23] Clark Pinnock, "Why Is Jesus the Only Way?" *Eternity*, December 1976, p. 32.

[24] All taxonomies may be judged by the criterion of utility: Do they adequately and fairly portray the options? Some may be more complete than others, but the intent here is to be representative of logically possible views, whether or not they are widely held.

[25] J. I. Packer, "The Way of Salvation," *Bibliotheca Sacra* (January 1973), pp. 7-8. See Packer for critiques of these points.

[26] See Paul Helm, "Universalism and the Threat of Hell," *Trinity Journal* 4 (1983), pp. 35-43.

the redeemed. Universalists who claim a biblical basis for their positions affirm that, although hell is real, hell will be *finally* unpopulated.[27]

Even though all might wish this view were correct, we are again faced with the problem of truth. Scripture describes hell as a place not of annihilation, nor of emptiness, but of eternal destruction, conscious ruin, and endless pain (Matt. 25:46; Mark 9:43-48; Luke 16:24; 2 Thess. 1:9, 2:6-9).[28] Second, Christians who are embarrassed or offended by the biblical doctrine of hell lack a biblical perspective. "The thought of eternal judgment is the reverse of embarrassing to the Bible writers; on the contrary, it is fundamental to their theodicy, their gospel, and their knowledge of God."[29] Finally, universalism "condemns Christ Himself, who warned men to flee hell at all costs, as having been either *incompetent* (ignorant that all were finally going to be saved) or *immoral* (knowing but concealing it, so as to bluff people into the kingdom through fear)."[30]

2. THE *DESIGNATED LIGHT* VIEW. This view asserts that God has designated those who will have the light of the gospel, and therefore He has also designated those who will not. The rationale looks like this:

---

[27] For a discussion of this view, see John Wenham, *The Enigma of Evil* (Grand Rapids: Zondervan, 1985), pp. 34-41, and John Stott, *Evangelical Essentials* (Downers Grove, IL: InterVarsity, 1989), pp. 312-31. Standard critiques of universalism do not necessarily apply to "conditional immortality." Brunner spoke of this view as based on "evasion rather than exegesis" (Emil Brunner, *Eternal Hope*, trans. Harold Knight [London: 1954], p. 183, cited by Packer, "Way of Salvation," *Bibliotheca Sacra*, p. 7n.). For a critique of conditional immortality and annihilationism see Roger Nicole, "Universalism: Will Everyone Be Saved?" *Christianity Today*, 20 March 1987, pp. 32-39.

[28] Packer, "Good Pagans and God's Kingdom," *Christianity Today*, 17 January 1986, pp. 22-23. It is noteworthy that in Matthew 25:46 the exact Greek word describing the duration of both heaven and hell is *aionios*.

[29] Packer, "Way of Salvation," *Bibliotheca Sacra*, p. 6.

[30] Packer, "Good Pagans," *Christianity Today*, p. 25, italics his. Packer states elsewhere, "Now if universalism [= all faiths are ways of salvation] is true, and the founders of Christianity did not know it, their preaching stands revealed as ignorant and incompetent; and if universalism is true, and they did know it, their preaching stands revealed as bluff, frightening people in the kingdom by holding before them unreal terrors" ("Way of Salvation," p. 10).

Because God knew from eternity past who will/will not be saved, and

Because God knew from eternity past where the gospel will/will not be preached,

Conclusion: God has those people who will be saved born into circumstances (including geography) in which the designated light will be effective, and by extension those who *will not respond* are born into circumstances (including geography) in which He knows the light will not shine.

Some would say that God's motivation is *justice*. God in effect has nailed the lid on the spiritual coffin of the spiritually dead. "God's judgment settles all moral problems. Specifically, it addresses the question as to how God can still be powerful and just if there is evil in the world. It sees this present life as an interim period at the end of which God will publicly vindicate his character. This vindication (which cannot be *vindictive* . . .) will set truth forever on the throne and error forever on the scaffold."[31]

Others would add that God's motivation may also be *mercy*. Those who are in circumstances to be exposed to the gospel, but who reject it, are in worse shape than those who God knows will reject it but who do not specifically turn their backs on Christ. Although they are still under God's judgment, their judgment is not compounded by overt rejection of God's Son. In this sense God protects them from further judgment; He does not let the non-elect hear because of His compassion.

It is true that the Bible clearly states God's sovereignty over the affairs of men (Rom. 8:29-30; 9:6-24), including circumstances that begin from birth (Jer. 1:5; Gal. 1:15). God's intention (for at least some individuals) was in place even before they were born—before they made any rational decisions or were conditioned by any environmental circumstances. Furthermore, Jesus specifically said He would not pray for the non-elect (John 17:1-11, esp. v. 9); presumably they are irredeemable. Finally, Paul reminds the Ephesians that Christ loved and gave Himself for the *church* (Eph. 5:25).

This view leaves some questions dangling, however. It does not explain why God does let some hear the gospel who He knows will reject it. If part of His motivation is not to compound judgment of His

---

[31] David F. Wells, "Everlasting Punishment," *Christianity Today*, 20 March 1987, p. 42. Wells does not necessarily hold to the view described above.

creatures, why let them be exposed and thus become more accountable? Would it not make more sense for the gospel to be presented only to those who would accept it? In fact, why would God allow those who He knows will reject the gospel even to be born in the first place?

3. THE *EXISTING LIGHT* VIEW. This view suggests that those who respond positively to the light they have can be saved without further light. God's revelation in creation (Rom. 1:20) and conscience (1:19; 2:15) makes people aware that they are guilty before their Creator. No one can live up even to his own internal standard, and consequently a person may cast himself upon God's mercy without knowing upon what basis that mercy was provided. In fact, because almost all religions lack a concept of man's depravity being overcome by God's grace and mercy, the untold would be saved not *because of*, but rather *in spite of*, their own religious system.[32]

This does not mean the untold persons have "lived up to the light they have." A salvation founded on that basis would be a form of salvation by works. But proponents of the existing light view affirm that salvation is by means of grace on the basis of Christ's cross work, through faith, although the content of what is believed is a response to the light of general revelation: that I cannot save myself and need help. Thus the *form* of the gospel is there, without the *content*.

Some of the early church Fathers believed that "those who lived by the logos present in the whole world were in reality Christians if their attitude was right."[33] Similarly, since 1963, Roman Catholic teaching has affirmed that (1) Protestants, (2) those in non-Christian religions (Judaism, Hinduism, Buddhism, Islam), and (3) those who are unreached may be saved outside the visible Catholic church.[34]

Spokesmen for this view do not necessarily maintain that all people will be saved. Intensely religious people like the Pharisees were pronounced doomed by Jesus because they had faith in themselves and their own abilities to attain salvation. However, they do mean that God may sovereignly save some via His mercy, because (through

---

[32] J. N. D. Anderson, *Christianity and Comparative Religion* (Downers Grove, IL: InterVarsity, 1970), pp. 94, 109. For salvation, he contends, not knowledge but a right attitude toward God is essential; for *assurance*, however, knowledge is essential (p. 104).

[33] Clark Pinnock, *Why Is Jesus the Only Way?*, p. 15.

[34] See Walter M. Abbott, ed., *The Documents of Vatican II*, trans. Joseph Gallagher (New York: America Press, 1966), "The Church," ii.16; "Decree on Ecumenism," i.3; "Declaration on the Relationship of the Church to Non-Christian Religions," i.2-4.

circumstances only He can weigh) those persons have not otherwise been exposed to the gospel.

Biblical support for various parts of the existing light view comes from Scriptures such as *The New Berkeley Version* of Acts 10:35, where Peter says, "In every nation he who reveres Him and practices righteousness is acceptable to Him." Paul says much the same thing in Acts 14:17. It also comes from the analogy with Old Testament characters: Melchizedek, Jethro, Job, Abimelech, Baalam, Naaman, the sailors in Jonah's boat, Cyrus, and Nebuchadnezzar all worshiped God and were accepted by Him. We are reminded that John describes the preincarnate Word as "the true light which *enlightens every man*" (John 1:9, italics added).

The existing light view fits nicely with the idea of progressive revelation. Abraham was saved by faith, although the content of what was believed was God's promise about his offspring (Gen. 15:6). Some may object that because Abraham had no other special revelation available to him at that time, the analogy is imperfect. Apollos, however, may perhaps serve as a better example. Apollos had believed "accurately" regarding Jesus, but knew only John's baptism (Acts 18:24-26). Other revelation was available at the time, but Apollos did not know it.[35] Thus it is possible that God judges the individual not by the criterion of what revelation has been given to all of mankind up to that time, but by the criterion of what is available to the individual.[36]

A recent variation of this view has been put forth by evangelicals Evert D. Osburn[37] and John E. Sanders.[38] Osburn maintains that there is indeed redemptive hope for the untold through both general revelation and special revelation (oral tradition, dreams, visions, etc.). The analogy is drawn from the Old Testament: because many of the Old Testament

---

[35] The analogy is imperfect because Apollos did have special revelation, but the point may still hold.

[36] Further support comes from passages such as Matthew 25:34-40 where some who are redeemed do not seem to know they have served Christ. Robert H. Gundry disagrees; see "Salvation According to the Scripture: No Middle Ground," *Christianity Today*, 9 December 1977, p. 14, and William Banks, "They Are Without Excuse," *Eternity*, March 1977, p. 91.

[37] Evert D. Osburn, "Those Who Have Never Heard: Have They No Hope?" *Journal of the Evangelical Theological Society* 32:3 (September 1989):367-72.

[38] John E. Sanders, "Is Belief in Christ Necessary for Salvation?" *Evangelical Quarterly* 60 (1988):241-59.

redeemed did not believe directly in Jesus Christ, they fall into the same category as the untold.[39]

Also, suggests Osburn, some may be exposed by means of oral tradition to the basic themes of incarnation and salvation by grace through faith. At Pentecost "devout men from every nation under heaven" (Acts 2:5) may have taken the idea of the gospel back to their homelands.[40]

Five objections should be mentioned.

First, if oral tradition is invoked we must remember that any oral message becomes distorted through centuries of transmission by deletions and accretions. At some point a true message that is progressively distorted becomes untrue.

Second, although the theoretical possibility of coming to faith without special revelation should be considered, Paul's point in Romans 1-3 is that no one does (and from Romans 8:7-8, that no one *can*).[41]

Third, some have objected that this view could hinder missions efforts through lack of motivation. After all, if God were going to redeem His own anyway apart from specific knowledge of Christ, why fulfill the Great Commission?

Fourth, we have more warrant for believing that God gave direct special revelation in Old Testament times—particularly early in the progress of revelation—than we have for assuming that He does so today (Deut. 34:10; Heb. 1:1-2; 2:3-4).

Finally, the passages and illustrations that are used as support do not explicitly make the point they are supposed to sustain. We must be careful when declaring that Old Testament patterns for salvation (in which content varied due to the progress of revelation) are normative for the untold today.

4. THE *GREATER LIGHT* VIEW. The fourth view maintains that those who respond to the light they have will be given greater light. Cornelius's devotion to the Lord and seeking after the one true God was rewarded by the sending of a missionary (Peter) to share the good news for which Cornelius had been waiting. Modern illustrations from

---

[39] For a critique of Osburn's thesis, see W. Gary Phillips, "Evangelicals and Pluralism: Current Options," *Evangelical Quarterly* 64, (1992).

[40] Osburn, p. 370.

[41] Millard Erickson, *Christian Theology* (Grand Rapids: Baker, 1983), 1:173. Scripture describes the salvation of both Jews and pagans as the passage from *death* to *life*, not from less light to complete light.

contemporary missionaries abound, which reinforce this possibility.[42]
God rewards "those who diligently seek Him" (Heb. 11:6) with the
special revelation of the gospel. God will sovereignly intervene to make
the gospel available to His sheep, no matter where they are located.

The greater light view is not salvation by works, nor salvation apart
from the gospel content; salvation remains the same for all men. The
redeemed will have believed on the Lord Jesus Christ for their salvation.

Still, there are problems. It is difficult to fit this view with the
history of modern missions, which did not begin until the eighteenth and
nineteenth centuries. Does this view contend that no pagan was sincere
enough to receive greater light until recent history? Second, Cornelius is
not an illustration of God's sending special revelation to follow
acceptance of general revelation; he was a "God-fearer" (Acts 10:2),
which meant that he had believed in the God of Abraham, Isaac, and
Jacob (special revelation), and was sent more special revelation. Because
of the uniqueness of the Gentile situation in Acts,[43] the analogy is not
exact enough to validate the conclusions that are drawn.

5. THE *LATER LIGHT* VIEW. This view says God will allow those who
have never heard of Christ a chance to hear the gospel and respond for or
against Jesus at a future point—either after death, or at the second
advent. In addition, it may be that God will allow those who heard about
Christ the first time in adverse circumstances another chance to
respond.[44] The assumption is that because "God has not told us what His
arrangements with the unevangelized are,"[45] believers are free to specu-
late.

Again, this view is not advocating salvation by works. God's justice
requires that He must judge sin, and therefore He cannot allow those
without Christ's righteousness into heaven. Yet God's mercy requires
that all men have a chance to receive Christ's righteousness. Thus Peter

---

[42] Cf. Don Richardson, *Eternity in Their Hearts*, rev. ed. (Ventura, CA: Regal,
1984).

[43] Peter was exercising the authority Christ gave him to "unlock" the gospel
(Matt. 16:19) to all categories of people—to the Jews (Acts 2), to the
Samaritans (Acts 8), and to the Gentiles (Acts 10, the household of
Cornelius).

[44] Actually, though this is popularly called a "second chance," it is more
accurately a "*first* chance" in second mode of existence. For those who
heard in adverse circumstances (e.g., from those whose lives or mental
abilities did not commend the gospel), this would genuinely be a second
chance.

[45] Pinnock, "Jesus the Only Way?" *Eternity*, p. 15.

says Christ preached to those who had already vacated this life (1 Peter 3:18-20). To what purpose? Surely it was to evoke a decision for salvation, as was the rest of His preaching.[46]

Problems with this view abound. First, 1 Peter 3:18-20 does not clearly support the conclusions drawn from it.[47] Second, certain passages imply that choices made in this life are irrevocable (Luke 19:26; John 8:21, 24). Finally, the Bible states that "after death comes judgment" (Heb. 9:27), not second chances.

THE RESPONSES EVALUATED. Several biblical facts bring perspective to this problem of pluralism and exclusivism/inclusivism. First, the *basis* of man's condemnation is not that he has rejected Christ, but that he is a sinner. If the basis were simply that he had rejected Christ, then we should tell no one about Jesus, so they will not reject Him. All men are "in Adam" (Rom. 5:12-21). "People are not lost because they have not heard. They are lost because they are sinners. We die because of disease, not because of ignorance of the proper cure."[48]

Many people assume that because man is ignorant of special revelation, therefore he is innocent. Actually, man's ignorance is not absolute, but relative. Man is not ignorant of the existence and certain attributes of God the Father, nor is he unaware of his own sinful condition. In the first century, the Roman philosopher Seneca wrote, "We are all wicked; what we blame in another each will find in his own bosom."[49] Man has knowledge of external revelation in creation (Ps. 19; Rom. 1:18-25), as well as the internal revelation of both conscience (Ps. 19; Rom. 1:19; 2:15) and finite creaturehood (Eccles. 3:11).

---

[46] Ibid.

[47] First, the text does not say Christ preached to try to get persons in hell to respond, but merely that He proclaimed/announced something to them. Second, He preached to them *while* they were imprisoned—it does not say *"then* they were imprisoned"—their judgment seems already fixed. Third, verse 20 indicates these were individuals (possibly angels) from the days of Noah's pre-flood world, not people who had never heard, and not ones who were in environments that were unfavorable to belief. Fourth, these "spirits" were "disobedient" spirits and most likely not disobedient to general revelation alone, but also special revelation through the preaching of Noah. Fifth, the "preaching" may refer figuratively to Jesus' preaching through Noah prior to the Flood. (See R. Gundry, "Salvation According to Scripture," *Christianity Today*, p. 15.)

[48] Kenneth Boa and Larry Moody, *I'm Glad You Asked* (Wheaton, IL: Victor, 1982), p. 147.

[49] Cited by Boa and Moody, p. 152.

Paul's point is that mankind has rejected both external and internal revelation (Rom. 1:18-32; 2:1; 3:9-20). Thus, even though there may be relative ignorance, it is not to be considered excusable but inexcusable ignorance.

Second, the nature of man's condemnation is a real hell. It would be easier emotionally to accept that an unsaved person would simply be annihilated (which seems rather neutral by comparison) than it is to accept that my neighbor will spend an eternity in a conscious hell, especially if he never even heard of Jesus. If it were not for the doctrine of hell (anchored to the authority of the Scriptures) there would be much less concern with the problem of justices.[50]

Finally, the Bible clearly says that God does not want any to perish (2 Pet. 3:9), and that God's way of salvation is by believing in Jesus Christ (John 3:18, 5:23-24, 14:6; Acts 4:12; Rom. 1:16; 10:14). Those in non-Christian religions are described as "having no hope, and without God in the world" (Eph. 2:12).

It is important to gain a perspective on fairness in inequities. It is true, from our perspective, that life is not fair. But ignorance is not life's only inequity. Other inequities can be added to ignorance of the gospel. Some may have heard the gospel from a parent or a pastor who committed adultery. Others may have been told about Christ from someone whose intellectual abilities did not recommend Christianity as a faith for thoughtful people. Still others may have heard about Christ's being sent by His Father who "so loved the world," but themselves could not abide the thought of a "heavenly father" because they had been sexually abused by their earthly father. Some may have the unfortunate circumstance of being born into (or worse, having earned) great wealth, which is a hindrance from coming to Christ in self-abnegation (Matt. 19:24).

Robert Gundry has observed, "Do the suggestions of salvation through general revelation and of conversion after death in fact do the apologetical job they were intended to do? No. If we demand equal treatment for people who have never heard the Gospel, others cry out for equal treatment too. The attempt to justify God's ways cannot stop with the ignorant heathen. . . . Given the complexities, we might not be able to recognize perfect equality."[51] As finite and fallen beings we cannot evaluate all the variables that will constitute final, absolute justice.

---

[50] See the interesting discussion in Kathleen Boone, *The Bible Tells Them So: The Discourse of Protestant Fundamentalism* (Albany, NY: State U. of New York, 1989), ch. 7.

[51] Gundry, "Salvation According to Scripture," *Christianity Today*, p. 16.

Conclusion: The Christological Resolution

The problem of truth must be settled from within God's Word. If the way of salvation according to the Scriptures is true, then contradictory claims of other religions are false. Scripture is clear regarding the predicament of man and the requirements for salvation.

The problem of justice is more difficult for most Christians, because our emotions are torn as we attempt to harmonize God's justice with God's love. Scripture affirms that hell is a real state of eternal, destructive punishment, and that hell is a just state in which God inflicts punishment on man for sinful deeds. Scripture also indicates that there will be degrees of placement in eternity (both in heaven and in hell), according to the light we have received and our response to it.[52]

Certainly all Christians would love to be "hopeful agnostics" about any provisions God would make for people in other religions, and especially for those who have not heard of Christ. Scripture does not say, however, that God makes such provisions. Any suggestions that people can be saved apart from clear faith in Christ are not from explicit statements of Scripture, but are implicit. Wise interpretation does not jettison clear revelation for secondary, possible inferences. Packer observes, "It might be true [that God could save someone apart from their direct knowledge of Christ], as it may well have been true for at least some of the Old Testament characters. . . . But we have no warrant to expect that God will act thus in any single case where the gospel is not known or understood. Therefore our missionary obligation is not one whit diminished by our entertaining this possibility."[53] If forced to adopt a view, it is wisest to *assume* that all who are in other religions, including those who have not heard, are under God's eternal judgment. As Nicole observes, "It is dangerous to be more generous than God has revealed himself to be!"[54]

Throughout this discussion we have focused on the dark side of the way of salvation. The focus of the Bible, however, is that the gospel is *good* news—cause for joy, not cause for despair. We may rest confident in the judgment of God who is the epitome of fairness, love, wisdom, knowledge, and discernment. He alone is described as the "righteous judge." We may be assured that no one will be in hell crying out, "I

---

[52] Matt. 11:21-24; Mark 12:40; Luke 12:47-48; 20:47; 2 Cor. 11:15; Heb. 10:29; Rev. 20:12-15; see also Mark 14:21; Rom. 2:5; Jude 15; Rev. 22:12.

[53] Packer, "Good Pagans," *Christianity Today*, p. 25.

[54] Nicole, "Universalism," *Christianity Today*, p. 38.

wanted to be saved and would have believed, but God did not give me the chance."

We know that in a culture that embraces pluralism, the offense of the cross can only become increasingly offensive. But whereas we have limited knowledge, incomplete data, and possibly distorted perceptions of fairness, the One who will judge all men (John 5:22, 27) is the same One who loves us so much that He would rather die than live without us. He comforts us with the assurance that "my judgment is just" (John 5:30). We have confidence that "the judge of all the earth will do right" (Gen. 18:25).

DISCUSSION QUESTIONS

1. You befriend a young man from Pakistan who has just accepted Jesus as his Savior. He has received word this morning that his grandfather, a devout Muslim, has suddenly died. He asks you, "Is my grandfather in hell?" What will you say?
2. Which of the "light" views seems the *weakest* to you? Why? Which of the "light" views seems the *strongest* to you? Why?
3. Evaluate the case for Jesus Christ as the only way to God. How strong is it? Do you think a Muslim would accept your reasons?
4. Read Acts 13:14-41. Was the worldview of Paul's audience closest to naturalism, transcendentalism, or theism? How did Paul approach his audience? (What knowledge could he assume they shared? Did he challenge their worldview?, etc.)
5. Read Acts 17:16-34. Was the worldview of Paul's audience closest to naturalism, transcendentalism, or theism? How did Paul approach his audience? (What knowledge could he assume they shared? Did he challenge their worldview?, etc.)
6. Consider the various "light" views and answer this question for each one: How motivated would *you* be to evangelize if you believed in this "light" view?

FURTHER READING

Anderson, J. N. D. *Christianity and Comparative Religion.* Downers Grove, IL: InterVarsity, 1970.

Carmody, Denise L., and John T. *Ways to the Center: An Introduction to World Religions.* Belmont, CA: Wadsworth, 1989.

Carson, D. A. *The Gagging of God: Christianity Confronts Pluralism.* Grand Rapids, MI: Zondervan, 1996.

Hick, John. *God Has Many Names.* Philadelphia: Westminster, 1982 ed. *Truth and Dialogue in World Religions: Conflicting Truth-Claims.* Philadelphia: Westminster, 1974.

Huntingdon, Samuel P. *The Clash of Civilizations and the Remaking of World Order.* New York: Simon and Schuster, 1998.

Kantzer, Kenneth, ed. "Universalism: Will Everyone Be Saved?" in *Christianity Today.* Christianity Today Institute, 20 March 1987.

Livingston, James C. *Anatomy of the Sacred: An Introduction To Religion.* New York: Macmillan, 1989.

Neill, Stephen. *Christian Faith and Other Faiths.* Downers Grove, IL: InterVarsity, 1984.

Newbegin, Leslie. *The Gospel in a Pluralistic Society.* Grand Rapids: Eerdmans, 1989. (Published jointly with the World Council of Churches.)

Okholm, Dennis L. and Timothy R. Phillips, eds. *Four Views on Salvation in a Pluralistic World.* Grand Rapids: Zondervan, 1996. Includes contribution by W. Gary Phillips.

Packer, J. I. "The Way of Salvation." *Bibliotheca Sacra.* April-June 1972 to April-June 1973.

Tucker, Ruth. *Another Gospel,* 2d ed. Grand Rapids: Zondervan, 2004.

Wells, David F. *Above All Earthly Pow'rs.* Grand Rapids: Eerdmans, 2006.

PART 3:
SO WHAT? A VIEW *Of* AND A VIEW *For*

If Christianity should happen to be true—that is to say, if its God is the real God of the universe—then defending it may mean talking about anything and everything. Things can be irrelevant to the proposition that Christianity is false, but nothing can be irrelevant to the proposition that Christianity is true.

G. K. Chesterton

The Gospel is like a caged lion. It does not need to be defended; it just needs to be let out of its cage.

Charles Haddon Spurgeon

So what?

So we believe that the Bible gives a comprehensive and credible view of life and the world. So we can understand and articulate the essentials of a biblical worldview. So we have explored other world-views and are able to defend the biblical perspective against its detractors.

So what?

Just because we can explain the world from a biblical framework does not necessarily mean that we possess a biblical worldview. Unfortunately, merely assenting to a particular worldview does not always lead to a specific philosophy of life. Possessing a biblical worldview—*truly* possessing it so that we are convinced of its truth— compels us to action. A biblical worldview is more than a means of interpreting and explaining the world. If it is true we will be driven to conform our personal thoughts and actions, and even the world around us, to the guidelines revealed in Scripture.

The active side of a worldview comprises the second half of our definition of a worldview given in chapter one: "A worldview is *the framework of our most important and basic beliefs (whether we realize it or not) that shapes the view we have of the world and applies this view for the world*." Once we know the biblical perspective of life and the world, we must use it to forge a biblical agenda for how we can properly act in the world.

In light of our discussion of the different worldviews, it is important to explain that the enemy of a biblical worldview is *not* primarily naturalism or transcendentalism. Rather, the number one adversary is dualistic thinking. This mindset regards Christianity as something that is private and personal, limited to individual belief and piety; but having no real world impact on how we think and how we live.

David Gill locates this most devastating imposter of Christianity:

> The real problem with ideological secularism is not with some godless congress or faculty, but with intellectually secular (though personally, or churchly pious) *Christians*! [These are] Christians who read the Bible and pray at breakfast (good so far!) but then go to class or the office and think and work exactly in the pattern and style of the surrounding world. Secular Christianity, not secular paganism, is the great enemy of the Christian mind and the gospel.[1]

The crucial message to Christians is that a biblical worldview is more than believing the right things. The time has come for Christians to go beyond the "profession-of-faith" mentality. We may not live what we profess, but we will certainly live what we believe.

Secularization begins with the individual: with Westerners who think with their wallets; with teenagers who crave new experiences; or with professing Christians who live more like deists than theists. From the secular mindset of the individual comes the secularization of society. Os Guiness describes secularization as "the process through which, starting from the center and moving outward, successive sectors of society and culture have been freed from the decisive influence of religious ideas and institutions."[2]

The application of a biblical worldview is the exact opposite of secularization. It is also a process that must begin with me and then penetrate every area of my life—how I think and how I live (attitudes and actions, or *knowing* and *doing*)—with the truth of God. In Part 3 we will explore the implications of a biblical worldview that expand from that center through each successive circle of our world. We will begin with a biblical view for the self and then follow with the family, the church, and finally, the world.

---

[1] David Gill, *The Opening of the Christian Mind* (Downers Grove, IL: InterVarsity, 1989), p. 41. For an extensive study on secularization and its impact on the church, see Craig M. Gay, *The Way of the Modern World: Or, Why It's Tempting to Live as If God Doesn't Exist* (Grand Rapids, MI: Eerdman's, 1998).

[2] Os Guinness, *The Gravedigger File* (Downers Grove, IL: InterVarsity, 1983), p. 51.

8
A VIEW OF AND FOR THE SELF

A Biblical Self-View
    The View from Below
    The View from Above
        Man's Uniqueness: God's Special Creation
        Man's Sin: Diseased, Determined, or Depraved?
        Man's Redemption: God's Grace and Glory
A Biblical Response
    The Response toward God
    The Response toward Others
    The Response toward Self

A Biblical Self-View

Who am I?

The question seems simple enough. I would answer, "I am John," or, "I am Mary." But upon reflection, I must admit that I am not my name. My name, be it Bill Brown, Gary Phillips, or Jane Doe, is merely a label that designates me. My name is certainly not unique. Many others have the same name, but they are not me. I could change my name, yet I would still be me.

My physical body, which is typing these words, also changes constantly. The cells of my body are engaged in a ceaseless process of renewal. My name has remained the same, but my present physical body is not the same body I had seven years ago. Therefore, I cannot be my body. There must be something else that is "me."

Maybe I am my mind. Maybe my mental functions, including the memories of experiences and thoughts of the past, constitute the "real me." But I know that I cannot be *totally* my mind, because my physical body sets much of the agenda for my emotions and thinking. Illness, pain, or accident can radically change how I view myself, how I think, how I feel. On the other hand, my mind can also affect the way I feel physically. I can be mentally scarred, depressed or manic, and it influences me—the real me.[1] What if my brain is transplanted into the body of another person? Am I the same person? Does my mind accompany my brain?[2]

Now I am beginning to feel uncomfortable. My name, my body, my mind—it seems that not one of these is capable of being called "me." I have come full circle and am less knowledgeable for the trip. Who am I? What am I? Why am I?

The harder we think about who and what we are, the more confusing the quest seems to become. For this reason many do not even try to think about such matters and just get on with the rigors of daily living. After all, as Albert Camus reminds us, "We get into the habit of living before acquiring the habit of thinking."[3] It might be easy to conclude that how I think of myself must not be important.

But it is important. In fact, coming to grips with who and what we are is not optional. We all develop a self-concept—thoughts and feelings about ourselves as being a particular type of person. This image becomes the fundamental motivation for our choices, values, and behavior. Living up to our self-concept is the primary goal of every individual. Anthony Giddens suggests that to be a human being is "to know, virtually all of the time, in terms of some description or another, both what one is doing and why one is doing it."[4] This reflects the biblical truth "As he thinks within himself, so he is" (Proverbs 23:7).

Contemporary attempts to understand the self have unfortunately been limited to a horizontal search with no regard for God's revelation from above. The results have been a dismal commentary on man's inability to make sense of his world. G. K. Chesterton said, "The huge modern heresy is to alter the human soul to fit modern social conditions,

---

[1] Among the most cogent arguments for the non-identification of the "self" with the mind or the body is given by Richard Taylor in many of his works. See for example, "How to Bury the Mind-Body Problem," *American Philosophical Quarterly* 6 (April 1969):136-43.

[2] For a lively dialogue on this subject, see Derek Parfit and Godfrey Vesey, "Brain Transplants and Personal Identity: A Dialogue," in Louis P. Pojman, *Philosophy: The Quest for Truth* (Belmont, CA: Wadsworth, 1989), pp. 219-24.

[3] Albert Camus, *The Myth of Sisyphus and Other Essays* (New York: Alfred Knopf, 1969), p. 8.

[4] Giddens, *Modernity and Self-Identity: Self and Society in the Late Modern Age* (Stanford, CA: Stanford University Press, 1991), p. 35.

instead of altering modern social conditions to fit the human soul."[5] Peter Berger suggests that modern man is "afflicted with a permanent identity crisis."[6]

The question of identity is the key issue at the center of most of the important issues of Western culture. For example, issues of biotechnology center around this question, including deciding beginning- and end-of-human-life questions, establishing boundaries between human and non-human, exploring the limits of the human body through genetics and medical procedures, and integrating emerging biotechnologies in the free market.[7] Also illustrative of the cultural identity crises are issues of gender and sexuality, including the homosexual debate, the transgender emergence, and redefinitions of family. These, in turn, have wide application in areas of law and public policy, fashion, entertainment and the arts.

What this means is that we must think correctly about ourselves if we are to understand our place in the world. The proper application of a biblical worldview begins with a proper application of that view to myself and then to my relationships with the people around me. It does not matter what view of ourselves makes us feel comfortable or happy or fulfilled. Our goal must be truth. Unless we have an accurate self-concept we will be living a lie.

The View from Below

"I see the face of god, and I raise this god over the earth, this god whom men have sought since man came into being, this god who will grant them joy and peace and pride. This god, this one word: 'I.'"[8] Ayn Rand's statement is the thesis of her many novels and writings. Each person must be free, totally free, from any laws or restrictions that limit the full expression of the individual self.

---

[5] Quoted in Craig M. Gay, *The Way of the (Modern) World: Or, Why It's Tempting to Live as If God Doesn't Exist* (Grand Rapids, MI: Eerdman's, 1998), p. 237.

[6] Peter Berger, quoted in Kenneth J. Gergen, *The Saturated Self: Dilemmas of Identity in Contemporary Life* (New York: Basic Books, 1991), p. 73.

[7] See Leon R. Kass, *Life, Liberty and the Defense of Dignity* (San Francisco: Encounter Books, 2002).

[8] Ayn Rand, *For the New Intellectual* (New York: Random House, 1961), p. 65. The statement is made by a character in Rand's novelette, *Anthem.*

Ayn Rand's philosophy may seem extreme to many,[9] but she is boldly proclaiming the prevailing truth that the self has become the "god" of modern culture.[10] Self-enthronement has produced a society that cherishes the individual self above everything else. Charles Colson summarizes the societal results of this chilling truth as "a new dark age." He adds, "Having elevated the individual as the measure of all things, modern men and women are guided solely by their own dark passions; they have nothing above themselves to respect or obey, no principles to live or die for. Personal advancement, personal feeling, and personal autonomy are the only shrines at which they worship."[11]

Sociologist Robert Bellah's insightful evaluation of middle class Americans reveals a pervasive and growing trend toward blatant individualism.[12] Bellah found that most Americans place value only in the interests of individual pursuits. Some seek meaning through the attainment of money or things (utilitarian individualists) while others live for personal experiences or relationships (expressive individualism). In both cases, the ultimate focus is on me and "what I can get out of life."

Our sense of identity is intimately related to our worldviews. It is understandable that naturalism and transcendentalism focus on the self. In both of these worldviews there is no point of reference beyond the individual to provide a self-concept. Meaning and purpose must be self-derived because there is no hope except within the self in a society without a personal God. Stanford psychiatrist Irvin Yalom summarizes this view, "We can try very hard to put meaning into life, but we have to devise this meaning on our own."[13] This is life that is lived only at the horizontal level.

Naturalism locates the totality of the person in the physical processes of the body. For example, physicist and Nobel laureate I. I. Rabi stated simply, "The proper study of man is science."[14] The scientific study of

---

[9] To see the application of Rand's philosophy, see her *The Virtue of Selfishness: A New Concept of Egoism* (New York: Signet, 1961, 1964).

[10] For an analysis of the religious aspects of secular culture and the worship of the self, see Paul Vitz, *Psychology as Religion: The Cult of Self-Worship* (Grand Rapids: Eerdmans, 1977).

[11] Charles Colson, *Against the Night: Living in the New Dark Ages* (Ann Arbor, MI: Servant Books, 1989), pp. 107-8.

[12] Robert Bellah, *Habits of the Heart* (Berkeley, CA: U. of California, 1985).

[13] Irvin D. Yalom, "Exploring Psychic Interiors," *U.S. News and World Report* 107:17 (October 30, 1989):67.

[14] I. I. Rabi, interview with Jeremy Bernstein, *The New Yorker* (20 October 1975).

the human body, it is thought, will give us complete knowledge of the nature of humanity. Transcendentalism, on the other hand, views the individual personality as unnatural, almost an embarrassment to the oneness of all things. Yet transcendentalism still calls for the individual to "look within" for all the answers to life's questions because we are "god"—the ultimate self-worship. Both approaches are intensely religious and place the self in the position of the theistic God. Pop psychologist Wayne Dyer claims, "Using yourself as a guide and not needing the approval of an outside force is the most religious experience you can have."[15]

There are two reasons that this view of the self is particularly volatile in today's culture. First, our culture offers an almost *infinite level of distraction.* In other words, it is easy for people to go through life isolated without seriously considering things of ultimate importance. Anthony Giddens refers to this as *the sequestration of experience* or, "the separation of day to day life from contact with experiences which raise potentially disturbing existential questions."[16] It is through wrestling with the deeper questions (i.e. the ultimate questions) that we come to a sense of where we fit in this world. Ours is a culture where these ultimate questions often are not even being asked.

Second, we are faced with an *infinite number of choices* about what we can do, what we can look like, who we can communicate with, and where we can live. We can choose to change our physical appearance or to take on a particular look through the clothes and cars we buy; we can choose from an infinite number of religions and philosophies; on the internet, we can choose to be someone of a different age, race, or even gender; through emerging technologies, we will soon be able to fully choose what we want in our children. Descartes' "I think therefore I am" has been replaced with "I choose therefore I am."[17]

What is most disconcerting is the manner in which a large segment of professing Christians has bought into this view of identity also. The self has become the criterion by which all ministries are judged. If a particular ministry does not "meet my needs" then it is rendered unspiritual, unprofitable, or at least inappropriate for me; and I therefore have the right to choose another. Faith in God is seen as a means by

---

[15] Wayne Dyer, *Your Erroneous Zones* (New York: Avon, 1976), p. 68.

[16] Giddens, *Modernity and Self-Identity,* p. 244.

[17] See Brian J. Walsh and Sylvia C. Keesmaat, *Colossians Remixed: Aubverting the Empire* (Downers Grove: InterVarsity, 2004) and Wells, *Above All Earthly Pow'rs,* pp. 75-79. Quote is modified from Walsh and Keesmaat, *Colossians Remixed, p.* 32.

which I have my (financial, emotional, social, or family) needs met. Loving and accepting myself have become central parts of a message that is touted as "the new reformation."[18]

But self-centered and self-serving approaches are destined for self-delusion and despair.[19] All attempts to understand myself at the horizontal level are empty and tortuously tend toward despair. The Bible recognizes man's agonizing search to make sense of his life at the horizontal level. For example, Job acknowledges the difficulties present in man's attempt to understand himself (Job 14:1-6, NIV):

> Man born of woman
> is of few days and full of trouble.
> He springs up like a flower and withers away;
> like a fleeting shadow, he does not endure.
> Do you fix your eye on such a one?
> Will you bring him before you for judgment?
> Who can bring what is pure from the unpure?
> No one!
> Man's days are determined;
> you have decreed the number of his months
> and have set limits he cannot exceed.
> So look away from him and let him alone,
> till he has put in his time like a hired man.

Man's life appears meaningless and empty to the writer of Ecclesiastes (Eccl. 1:1), who moans that even hard work produces nothing significant for a man: "And this is also a grievous evil—exactly as a man is born, thus will he die. So, what is the advantage to him who toils for the wind? Throughout his life he also eats in darkness with great vexation, sickness and anger" (5:16-17). Such is life "under the sun." The horizontal search for personal identity and meaning produces only despair. Again, we need help from the outside. The Grand Artist must be allowed to explain His creation.

The View from Above

I remember the story of a fine arts professor who eloquently described the features of a classic painting to his class. The artist was Rembrandt, he explained, and this work of art poignantly revealed a

---

[18] Robert H. Schuller, *Self-Esteem: The New Reformation* (Waco, TX: Word, 1982) and Joel Olsteen, *Your Best Life Now: Seven Steps to Living at Your Full Potential* (Time Warner, 2005).

[19] For an analysis of how people form and sustain false beliefs about themselves, see David G. Myers, *The Inflated Self: Human Illusions and the Biblical Call to Hope* (New York: Seabury, 1981), pp. 43-111.

great deal of Rembrandt's character: the shadows illustrated the artist's dark moods, the brush strokes his vigor for life, the colors his ideal view of humanity. At the conclusion of his moving narrative, one of the students politely noted that the painting was not by Rembrandt but by Monet. "Oh, my," the professor cried, "that changes everything!" whereupon he began a new interpretation of the work.

By itself, an artistic creation has the potential of any number of interpretations, but the true meaning of the work must begin with the artist. In fact, the more one knows the artist, the more one will understand his creations. In the same way, since God is the creator of man, our view of the self must begin with God. His character and revelation must guide us to the true meaning of His "works of art."

A biblical view of the self may be summarized as follows. "We are originally good and special creatures (made in God's image); yet we are sinful and worthy of damnation; and in Christ we may become God's children."[20] We will take these three themes—creation, depravity, and redemption—as a springboard for our view for the self.

Man's Uniqueness: God's Special Creation

In light of the awesomeness of the created world, humanity seems an insignificant speck. Yet, there is an awareness that we are the special object of divine creation and concern. The psalmist lifts his eyes to God to ponder the unique place of man in creation (Psalm 8, NIV):

> When I consider your heavens,
> the work of your fingers,
> the moon and the stars,
> which you have set in place,
> what is man that you are mindful of him,
> the son of man that you care for him?
> You have made him a little lower than the heavenly beings
> and crowned him with glory and honor.
> You made him ruler over the works of your hands;
> you put everything under his feet:
> all flocks and herds,
> and the beasts of the field,
> the birds of the air,
> and the fish of the sea,
> all that swim the paths of the seas.
> O Lord, our Lord,
> how majestic is your name in all the earth!

---

[20] Eric Johnson, "Self-Esteem," p. 228.

The Bible is clear that man is the result of a special act of God's creation. The first man was made alive by the breath of God (Gen. 2:7). There is no human life (or any life for that matter) that is apart from the free creative act of God: "In Him was life" (John 1:4). Our being is thus rooted in the purpose and will of God.

Because of this special creation, man has a unique place in God's order. This is further amplified by the truth that man is created "in God's image" (see chapter 3). Three times in the Old Testament (Gen. 1:26; 5:1; 9:6) and twice in the New Testament (1 Cor. 11:7; James 3:9) the biblical writers affirm man's inherent nature as the "image of God." What this actually means is a matter of great discussion; however, it is certain that humanity's position in creation was intended by God to be unparalleled. Theologian John Gerstner summarizes the implications of this truth, "Man is a creature superior to all other creatures in this world—and therefore having rule over them—by virtue of his ability to know and love his Creator. This ability to know (mind) and love (will) is the *imago Dei* because in so knowing and loving God, man knows and does in finite measure what God does in infinite measure."[21]

Once I understand the nature of myself as God's special work of art I must also conclude that whatever value I have as a person is derived from God's purpose for the creation. I reflect His glory and His will. Therefore, self-actualization and self-realization are wrongly directed if they are not rooted in the utter dependency of the self to God. A biblical worldview affirms the significance of the individual but denies the misdirected focus of individualism.

Man's Sin: Diseased, Determined, or Depraved?

The fact that man was created originally good and holds a special place in God's creation is marred by the reality of man's sinfulness. Regardless of one's view of humanity, the evil present in our world cannot be ignored. Even a casual observer recognizes that sin in the world is not rooted in society but in the individual heart. Albert Einstein, in a 1948 lecture, remarked, "The true problem lies in the hearts and thoughts of men. It is not a physical one. . . . What terrifies us is not the explosive force of the atomic bomb, but the power of the wickedness of the human heart."[22]

---

[21] John H. Gerstner, "The Origin and Nature of Man: Imago Dei," in *Basic Christian Doctrines*, ed. Carl F. H. Henry (Grand Rapids: Baker, 1962), p. 89.

[22] Quoted in *Illustrations for Biblical Preaching*, ed. Michael P. Green (Grand Rapids: Baker, 1989), pp. 102-3.

Many naturalists, of course, believe that evil behavior is a *disease*, a condition that results from physical and environmental influences. Like a cold or the mumps, evil is hard to cure and takes the right prescription of counseling and behavior modification to overcome.

In light of the daily incidence of crime, such a diagnosis of the sin problem is difficult to accept. For example, in April of 1989, a group of boys between the ages of fourteen and seventeen raped, beat, and stabbed a young woman who had been jogging through New York's Central Park. The boys were not members of a gang but "normal," middle-class youths. Their attitude toward the victim and their crime was disdain. Even after their arrest, one of the assailants said of the victim, "She was nothing."

The overwhelming sense of revulsion at this incident is countered by a secular mindset that blames society for infecting these boys with the desire to commit such a horrible deed. Chuck Colson quotes experts who analyze the boys' behavior: "Forensic psychologist Shawn Johnston explained the boys are 'damaged . . . in pain inside . . . acting out their pain on innocent victims.' As Harvard educator Alvin Poussaint put it, 'They're letting out anger. There's a lot of free-floating anger and rage among a lot of youth.' And psychologist Richard Majors summed up, 'We have to be honest. Society has not been nice to these boys.'"[23]

The "disease" explanation for this terrible crime rings hollow. Such evil acts are the responsibility of those who perpetrate them. Yet the motivation arises not from societal influences but from within. The Bible is clear that every person, by nature, possesses a sinful disposition:

> There is none righteous, not even one;
> There is none who understands,
> There is none who seeks for God (Rom. 3:10-11)

> And you were dead in your trespasses and sins, . . .
> and were by nature children of wrath (Eph. 2:1, 3)

> The heart is more deceitful than all else
> And is desperately sick;
> Who can understand it? (Jer. 17:9)

> Furthermore, the hearts of the sons of men are full
> of evil, and insanity is in their hearts throughout
> their lives. Afterwards they go to the dead (Eccl. 9:3)

---

[23] Charles Colson, "You Can't Cure the Wilding Sickness," *Christianity Today*, 8 September 1989, p. 80.

But the Scripture has shut up all men under sin. . . . (Gal. 3:22)

For all have sinned and fall short of the glory of God (Rom. 3:23).

Others reject the biblical view of sin by concluding that all behavior is *determined*. Every action, from the most heinous crime to the slightest mistake, is predestined to occur. There is no free will, there is no choice. Therefore, we are not responsible for our actions no matter how despicable they may be.

The well-known atheist and attorney Clarence Darrow shared the following sentiments with the prisoners at the Cook County jail: "There is no such thing as a crime as the word is generally understood. . . . The people here can no more help being here than the people on the outside can avoid being outside. . . . There are a great many people here who have done some of these things (murder, theft, etc.) who really do not know themselves why they did them. It looked to you at the time as if you had a chance to do them or not, as you saw fit; but still, after all you had no choice."[24]

Biblically, such a deterministic view of behavior is in error. Our free will to choose our actions is not merely an illusion. God holds us accountable for our behavior (e.g., Rom. 2:6; 2 Cor. 5:10), and future judgment is based on the decisions we make in this life (John 5:22-29).

The "disease" and "determined" explanations for sin are an attempt to remove blame and guilt for a person's behavior. If this can be successfully accomplished, then an individual will sense no need to find forgiveness for sin. Anna Russell expresses this view in her humorous "Psychiatric Folksong":

> At three I had a feeling of
> Ambivalence toward my brothers,
> And so it follows naturally,
> I poisoned all my lovers.
>
> But now I'm happy; I have learned
> The lesson this has taught;
> That everything I do that's wrong
> Is someone else's fault.[25]

---

[24] Quoted in Ed L. Miller, *Questions that Matter: An Invitation to Philosophy*, 2d ed. (New York: McGraw-Hill, 1987), pp. 410-11.

[25] Anna Russell quoted by O. H. Mowrer in "Sin, the Lesser of Two Evils," *American Psychologist* 15 (1960):301.

Man's rebellious desire to be independent of God is rooted in the very fabric of his spiritual nature, an inheritance from the first man and woman (Gen. 3:1-7; Rom. 5:12-21). What person is there who does not harbor evil thoughts and intentions that no one ever sees? These hidden thoughts are internal evidences of man's sinfulness. Mark Twain once noted, "Every man is like the moon: he has a dark side that no one sees."

The external evidences of man's depravity are just as clear. Everywhere man's selfish exploitation of the people and things around him is even acknowledged by secularists as a reflection of human nature. For example, the widespread looting that often occurs in the aftermath of a natural disaster (like hurricane Katrina for example) is seen as an *expected* human reaction. University of South Carolina psychology professor Robert Heckel suggests, "It's human nature to take advantage of a situation like this."[26]

However, in spite of sin's pervasiveness, it is popular to deny personal depravity and its consequences. Television mogul Ted Turner boldly claimed, "Christianity is a religion for losers. I don't want anybody to die for me. I've had a few drinks and a few girlfriends, and if that's gonna put me in hell, then so be it."[27] Denying sin, giving it a different label, or limiting it to external influences do not change the destructive tendencies present in every heart. To deny that we are sinful is the ultimate self-deceit (1 John 1:8-10) because it takes away the possibility of ever truly dealing with that part of our nature which alienates us from ourselves, others, and God. Recognizing our sinfulness and accepting responsibility for it is the foundation for a truly biblical view of the self.

Man's Redemption: God's Grace and Glory

In spite of man's sin, the Scriptures are clear that God has purposed to rescue man from the consequences of his depravity. Jesus' mission was "to save His people from their sins" (Matt. 1:21); "to take away the sin of the world" (John 1:29); and "to seek and save that which was lost" (Luke 19:10). God's love and mercy directed toward man is the motivation to save (Eph. 2:4-5; Titus 3:4-5). The death of Jesus Christ is the means by which the judgment for every person's sin was accomplished. When any person responds in faith toward the offer of full forgiveness from sin, he becomes a child of God (John 1:12-13).

---

[26] Quoted by Steve Marshall, "Looting Spree: 'There's No Law and Order,'" *USA Today*, 21 September 1989, p. 5A.

[27] Quoted in *World* 4:24 (November 11, 1989):4.

The need for redemption is a universal need. Whereas cultures differ in what behavior is expected, man's sinfulness remains the same. Worldviews may explain life differently, but the outworking of man's sin is evident: evil, suffering, pain, and death are shared by all men. The anxiety caused by these elements of human life is the driving force behind man's quest to find peace and purpose. True salvation reverses the terrible consequences of sin.

When a person comes to Christ, he is not completely transformed; that is, there remains an element of his redemption that is yet to come. No Christian is guaranteed a preservation from sickness or suffering in this life, or deliverance from death (2 Tim. 3:12). There may be individual events of healing and deliverance (the Scriptures are full of these wonderful stories), but the reality that even the godly suffer cannot be ignored. Further, no Christian is promised total freedom from error. We see through a glass darkly in this present life (1 Cor. 13:12), and a clear vision of all reality is yet to be seen. The perfections secured by salvation are received in part in this life and more fully in the life to come.

There will come a day when all things will be made right, when truth will reign, when the final enemy, death, will be destroyed (1 Cor. 15:26). Man's future is an existence with God that stretches endlessly beyond the grave (Matt. 25:34, 46; 1 Thess. 4:17). This is the final solution to man's predicament in the world. We know our ultimate future, so we may have hope in this life.

A Biblical Response

The biblical view of the self contrasts radically with the perspectives of human nature given by naturalism or transcendentalism. I am a special creation of God, intended to reflect His image. Yet, I am sinful, and naturally tend toward independence of God. God has taken the initiative to reconcile me to Himself, and when I respond to His offer of forgiveness and redemption I become His eternal child.

In light of this view of myself, how should I live? What characteristic lifestyle should accompany my biblical self-view? Let's briefly explore the implications of this view from three areas of response: toward God, toward others, and toward myself.

The Response toward God

When asked which of the many commandments were the most important, Jesus responded by quoting the fundamental Old Testament admonition, "Love the Lord your God with all your heart, soul, mind and strength" (Mark 12:30). From the creation of the first human, this has been God's desire for man: that he devote his entire being to love his Creator. A biblical view of the self makes the benefits of loving God clear. Our existence, self-concept, and self-esteem are not discovered within ourselves but are derived from God.

What is involved in loving God? We could list attitudes and actions such as obedience, fear, devotion, honor, and commitment. However, let us focus on two areas of personal thinking and living which may be seen to summarize the others: *knowing God* and *worshiping God.*

Knowing God

The Scriptures describe knowing God as the highest of all attainments. For example, the apostle Paul proclaimed, "But whatever things were gain to me, those have I counted as loss for the sake of Christ. More than that, I count all things to be loss in view of the surpassing value of *knowing Christ Jesus my Lord*, for whom I have suffered the loss of all things, and count them but rubbish in order that I may gain Christ, . . . *that I may know Him* (Phil. 3:7-8, 10, emphasis added).

In His prayer before His death, Jesus summarized the realization of eternal life as the knowledge of God, "This is eternal life, *that they may know Thee the only true God, and Jesus Christ whom Thou hast sent*" (John 17:3, emphasis added). The apostle Peter adds, "Seeing that His divine power has granted us everything pertaining to life and godliness, *through the knowledge of Him* who called us by His glory and excellence" (2 Pet. 1:3, italics added).

It is important to understand that the knowledge of God spoken of in the Scriptures is the reflection of an intimate, personal relationship. Such knowledge is not achieved in a momentary rush of spiritual insight or a conversion experience. We grow in our knowledge of God just as we grow in our knowledge of another person: by intimate communication over a period of time. Thus, Scripture reading and prayer are not ends in themselves but means through which we know our Lord better. If communication is not a priority, the relationship suffers and the fellowship is strained.

Knowing about God is a fundamental step in knowing Him, and *doing things for the Lord* is an outgrowth of our devotion to Him, but neither can take the place of a true knowledge of Him that begins with a faith commitment and continues in a growing relationship with Him. Knowing God should be the most cherished relationship is our lives. Nothing this world offers can match the joy, peace, and excitement that comes from knowing Him. Knowing God thus becomes the goal of every person—above every measure of personal gain or glory:

> Thus says the Lord, "Let not a wise man boast of his wisdom, and let not a mighty man boast of his might, let not a rich man boast of his riches; but let him who boasts boast in this, *that he understands and knows Me*, that I am the Lord who exercises lovingkindness, justice, and righteousness on earth; for I delight in these things," declares the Lord. (Jer. 9:23-24, italics added)

A practical question may be asked, How do I know that I know Him? The answer, of course, is that such assurance is based upon the character of God as revealed in the Scriptures. He desires to be known and reveals the means of knowing Him through Jesus Christ. There is also an intangible sense of assurance that comes from the Holy Spirit, "The Spirit Himself bears witness with our spirit that we are children of God" (Rom. 8:16). As we grow in our knowledge of God, our assurance and security in the relationship also grows. Further, we must not forget that "we become like what we love." The longer our affections are set on Him, the more our life will reflect the fruit of His righteousness.

Practically, a biblical self-view draws our deepest emotions upward toward God. Prayer, study, and meditation become privileges, not duties. Our lives become God-centered rather than self-centered. As C. S. Lewis summarizes it, living for the Lord "means that every single act and feeling, every experience, whether pleasant or unpleasant, must be referred to God. It means looking at everything as something that comes from Him, and always looking to Him and asking His will first, and saying, 'How would He wish me to deal with this?'"[28]

Even our leisure time becomes an ultimate concern in light of God's presence. J. I. Packer astutely reminds us, "Living becomes an awesome business when you realise that you spend every moment of your life in the sight and company of an omniscient, omnipresent Creator."[29]

Worshiping God

To love Him is to know Him; to know Him is to worship Him. A truly biblical view of the self compels man to worship (Ps. 96:8). Once we capture even a partial understanding of the true character of God, the

---

[28] C. S. Lewis, "Answers to Questions on Christianity," in *God in the Dock: Essays on Theology and Ethics*, ed. Walter Hooper (Grand Rapids: Eerdmans, 1970), p. 50.

[29] J. I. Packer, *Knowing God* (Downers Grove, IL: InterVarsity, 1983).

response is a mixture of awe, fear, joy, and delight.[30] The following passage from Kenneth Grahame's *The Wind in the Willows* represents an insightful understanding of the attitude of worship. Here, Mole and Rat encounter the "august presence":

> "Rat!" he found breath to whisper, shaking. "Are you afraid?"
>
> "Afraid?" murmured the Rat, his eyes shining with unutterable love. "Afraid of Him? O, never, never! And yet—and yet—O, Mole, I am afraid!"
>
> Then the two animals, crouching to the earth, bowed their heads and did worship.[31]

Since our view of the self must be God-centered, then so must our worship. God's holiness, power, and goodness strike the chord of reverence in the hearts of His creatures. Such an attitude of veneration is an expression of the true order of things: *God*, infinite, all-powerful, and sovereign; *man*, finite, limited, and dependent.

> Ascribe to the Lord, O families of the peoples,
> Ascribe to the Lord glory and strength.
> Ascribe to the Lord the glory of His name;
> Bring an offering, and come into His courts.
> Worship the Lord in holy attire;
> Tremble before Him, all the earth.
> Say among the nations, "The Lord reigns;
> Indeed, the world is firmly established,
> It will not be moved;
> He will judge the peoples with equity."
> (Ps. 96:7-10)

Worship is truly a human activity. It is "that exercise of the human spirit that confronts us with the mystery and marvel of God in whose presence the most appropriate and salutary response is adoring love."[32] Further, Scripture indicates that we are shaped by what we worship (Ps. 135:15-18).

---

[30] For a theological and practical exploration of worship, see Ronald Allen and Gordon Borror, *Worship: Rediscovering the Missing Jewel* (Portland, OR: Multnomah, 1982).

[31] Kenneth Grahame, *The Wind in the Willows* (New York: Scribner's, 1908), p. 134.

[32] Ralph E. Martin, *The Worship of God* (Grand Rapids: Eerdmans, 1982), p. 29.

The expressions of worship are both public and private. In a public sense, praise, prayer, singing, proclamation, and the ordinances are the usual demonstrations of worship. But again, the focus of these activities must be the Person of God, not the worshiper or his actions. Even at a personal level, true worship can be found. The worship of an everyday presentation of ourselves to God ("your spiritual service of worship," Rom. 12:1) is manifested in the practical application of faith and love in daily living (Rom. 12:9-21).[33]

The Response toward Others

A biblical view of the self allows us to cherish what God cherishes. Martin Buber's classic book *I and Thou*[34] points out that we can relate to others in two ways. The first is to see others in an "I/It" relationship, that is, to relate to others as we would to an object. From this perspective, each person is significant only because he plays a functional role in our lives (the grocer, the mailman, the sales clerk, etc.). Tragically, society depersonalizes relationships and insulates individuals from each other.[35] Many lives revolve around personalities experienced through television, videos, radio, compact discs, or other audio-visual media. This impersonal nature of daily living is a true example of the "I/It" relationship.

The second way to relate to others is in an "I/Thou" relationship. This is the more biblical approach. Each person we encounter is not an "It," but a "Thou," a separate human being with thoughts and feelings like myself; a person with a significance that is inherent in his creation in God's image.

As a result of a biblical worldview of the self, we are in a better position to respond to those around us. Many terms are found in the Bible to describe how we should respond to others: love (1 Pet. 4:8), deference (Rom. 12:10; Col. 3:12ff.), encouragement (Rom. 15:5), service (Gal. 5:13). There are times when we must confront, rebuke, or admonish (Luke 17:3; 2 Tim. 4:2; Titus 1:13; 2:15), but even when this is necessary the focus is upon the edification of the individual (Rom. 15:1-2; Gal. 6:1; 1 Thess. 5:11).

---

[33] See E. Kasemann, "Worship in Everyday Life: A Note on Romans 12," in *New Testament Questions for Today* (Philadelphia: Fortress, 1969), pp. 188-95.

[34] Martin Buber, *I and Thou*, trans. Ronald Gregor Smith (Edinburgh: T. & T. Clark, 1937).

[35] See Craig Gay, *The Way of the (Modern) World.*

The Christian is free to respond to others in such a kind manner because of his self-view, which adopts God's perspective on others. He is able to see others through the eyes of God and value them as He does. The Christian will thus stand against all forms of prejudice or racial discrimination.[36] He believes that all people have equal standing in the sight of God regardless of position in society, ethnic background, or physical attributes (Gal. 3:28).

We are to accept others because we have been accepted by God (Rom. 15:7). We are likewise to forgive others because we have been forgiven (Eph. 4:32). Our relationship to others may be summed up in the word *humility*. The humility of Jesus Christ, who condescended to become a man, is the example for us to follow (Phil. 2:5-8). Such an attitude is described by the apostle Paul, "Do nothing from selfishness or empty conceit, but with humility of mind let each of you regard one another as more important than himself; do not merely look out for your own personal interests, but also for the interests of others" (Phil. 2:3-4).

Walter Wangerin, Jr., applies this biblical perspective with these poignant words:

> Every time you meet another human being you have the opportunity. It's a chance at holiness. For you will do one of two things, then. Either you will build him up, or tear him down . . . you will create, or you will destroy. . . . There are no useless, minor meetings. There are no dead-end jobs. There are no pointless lives. Swallow your sorrows, forget your grievances and all the hurt your poor life has sustained. Turn your face to the human before you and let her, for one pure moment, shine. Think her important, and then she will suspect that she is fashioned of God.[37]

The Response toward Self

Having a view of myself is quite a paradox. I am both the subject and object of the observation. Yet once I adequately settle on an understanding of humanity in general, I am free to see myself as a part of the great works of art created by God. Many benefits accrue to those who see themselves through the eyes of God, but we will highlight two here: *purpose* and *peace*.

---

[36] For a good discussion of the various approaches to the issue of racism, see Douglas M. Jones, "The Biblical Offense of Racism," *Antithesis* 1:1 (Jan/Feb 1990):32-37.

[37] Walter Wangerin, Jr., *Ragman and Other Cries of Faith* (San Francisco: Harper & Row, 1984), pp. 129-30.

Purpose: A Reason to Live

The most important personal benefit of knowing who I am is knowing why I am here. All life is potentially governed by two laws: the law of survival and the law of significance.[38] At the natural level, the animals of the wild follow the first law—survival is fundamental to existence. But humanity alone is also driven by the second law—the desire to find meaning and purpose, the motivation to contribute to humanity and life. When individuals equate love with sex, vocation with salary, and value with material possessions, they become less human and more like the lower animals.

As we discussed in chapter 3, nontheistic worldviews founder on the issue of personal meaning and purpose. The naturalist, for example, would encourage us not to think about the question of purpose, or for that matter, about any of the other ultimate questions of life. Either the answers are unknowable or they are so disturbing that they would distract us from enjoying the here and now.

But the human restlessness present in every heart drives us to seek out a reason for our existence. Austrian psychiatrist Viktor Frankl survived the Nazi death camp, Auschwitz. During the terror of his imprisonment, he was struck by the fact that many who endured the death camp were not the most hardy in physical makeup but those who had an internal reason to live. Finding a purpose for life is not an act of faith, Frankl concludes, but a fact of human existence. He goes on further, "I think the meaning of our existence is not invented by ourselves, but rather detected."[39] This meaning is clearly found in a biblical worldview. We have been made *by* God and *for* God (Col. 1:16). True life is given by God to enjoy. True meaning is derived from the reality of God's special creation of me and His never-ending oversight of my life.

Even sociological studies demonstrate that "a worldview constructed around a belief in a Being who personally cares about human life and history may have provided more meaning and direction than a perspective of the world that does not allow for involvement of a personal God."[40] This of course does not mean that a biblical worldview is correct because it gives man a reason to live, but since it does meet the

---

[38] Warren Bryan Martin, *A College of Character* (San Francisco: Jossey-Bass, 1984), p. 116.

[39] Viktor E. Frankl, *Man's Search for Meaning*, trans. Ilse Lasch (New York: Pocket Books, 1963), p. 157.

[40] Carol C. Molmar and Daniel W. Stuempfig, "Effects of World View on Purpose in Life," *The Journal of Psychology* 122:4, pp. 370.

human need for meaning it must be seen as a viable option even by skeptics. The old maxim is appropriate: "Christianity is not true because it works, it works because it is true."

How does God's purpose for me translate into the decisions I make in my personal life? God's explicit will is for my holiness (Rom. 12:1-2; 1 Thess. 4:3), that is, for my character and will to be conformed to His. Once I set my mind to pursue this goal, other lifetime decisions take on a revised priority. I can now see them in the light of pleasing God, and I will be motivated to adopt a biblical set of values rather than those of the people around me. The better I know Him, the easier my decisions will become. The result is a spiritual sensitivity that allows the decisions I make to be guided by an understanding of God's priorities.

Peace: A Freedom for Living

The distress present in modern society has caused a neurosis, both individually and socially. Anxiety permeates the lives of people who seek a relief from their restlessness by an addiction to success, sensuality, or drugs. Our generation is marked by disorder and disharmony, and the result is an alienation from God, others, and even myself.

The anxiety and restlessness of this age are removed by the presence of God, the God of peace (Judg. 6:24). The idea of peace, the Hebrew *shalom*, is a major biblical theme.[41] Peace is the goal for every person, family (Gen. 13:8), and community (1 Sam. 20:42). Strife and disorder are signs of God's absence. Ultimately, when God makes all things new in the age to come, peace will reign (Is. 9:27; Zech. 9:9-10).

Jesus promised His disciples, "Peace I leave with you, My peace I give to you; not as the world gives, do I give to you. Let not your heart be troubled nor let it be fearful. . . . These things have I spoken to you, that in Me you might have peace. In the world you have tribulation, but take courage; I have overcome the world" (John 14:27; 16:33). When we come to Christ, we are restored to peace. We have peace with ourselves (Rom. 14:17; 15:13), peace with others (Gal. 5:22; Eph. 2:14-17; 4:3), and peace with God (Rom.5:1).

The future for the believer is secure. A glorious eternal life is guaranteed for all those who love the Lord. As a result, the present takes on a new dynamic. The difficulties of this life have a new meaning now.

---

[41] See Nicholas Wolterstorff, Until Justice and Peace Embrace: The Kuyper Lectures at the Free University of Amsterdam (Grand Rapids: Eerdmans, 1983). Also, Cornelius Plantinga, Engaging God's World: A Christian Vision of Faith, Learning and Living (Grand Rapids: Eerdmans, 2002).

For the Christian, the certainty of the future should serve as a powerful motivation to live and look beyond the circumstances of this life. A spirit of *hope* reflects a genuine grasp of God's promises.

When my self-concept is God-centered and not self-centered, I have a different perspective on how I approach life. Self-centered philosophies are tantamount to idolatry.[42] Seeking to fulfill myself, my desires, and my pleasures is a never-ending craving for more which is also idolatrous (Eph. 5:5). This in no way is an eradication of my significance as a person, but an expression of that which is truly human. We must start with God, the Creator and Former of man, if we ever hope to be more than "mere men." Johnson concludes, "As our knowledge of [God] and his infinite, transcendent value increases, we will find that our esteem of ourselves as one of his beloved ones will grow as well."[43]

Now we must expand our circle of application and turn our gaze outward. A biblical worldview sets man is his proper place in the world and gives guidance for his relationships to other "works of art" in God's creation. Our next exploration will be the biblical view for the family.

DISCUSSION QUESTIONS

1. "The worship of the self is the new idolatry." Explain this statement. Give several examples where this is illustrated in our society. How is this emphasis seen among Christians?
2. Based on the brief quotation of her thought, how do you think Ayn Rand would view Communism and New Age thinking?
3. Why are people so hesitant to accept personal responsibility for sin? How does this affect both the message and method of evangelism?
4. Think for a moment about the atrocities committed under the Nazi regime before and during World War II (or any of the more contemporary expressions of genocide). How would the various approaches to explaining personal evil (diseased, determined, depraved) interpret these events?
5. How does the concept of "loving God" relate to "knowing God" and "worshiping God"?
6. Describe how a biblical view of the self leads one to respond to: (a) the poor; (b) the mentally and physically handicapped; (c) people of different ethnic backgrounds; and (d) the rich and famous. What is at the root of partiality and bigotry?

---

[42] Paul Vitz, *Psychology as Religion*, p. 91.
[43] Johnson, "Self-Esteem," p. 234.

FURTHER READING

Aeschliman, Michael D. *The Restitution of Man.* Grand Rapids: Eerdmans, 1983.

Gay, Craig M. *The Way of the (Modern) World: Or, Why It's Tempting to Live as If God Doesn't Exist.* Grand Rapids: Eerdmans, 1998.

Gergen, Kenneth J. *The Saturated Self: Dilemmas of Identity in Contemporary Life.* New York: Basic Books, 1991.

Johnson, William A. *The Search for Transcendence.* New York: Harper & Row, 1974.

Kass, Leon R. *Life, Liberty, and the Defense of Dignity.* San Francisco: Encounter Books, 2002.

Lawler, Peter. *Stuck with Virtue: The American Individual and Our Biotechnological Future.* Wilmington, DE: Intercollegiate Studies Institute, 2005.

Lewis, C. S. *The Abolition of Man.* New York: Macmillan, 1960.

McClay, Wilfred M. "The Secret of Self" *First Things* 158. December 2005:29-33.

McDonald, H. D. *The Christian View of Man.* Westchester, IL: Crossway, 1981.

Myers, David G. *The Inflated Self: Human Illusion and the Biblical Call to Hope.* New York: Seabury, 1981.

Niebuhr, Reinhold. *The Nature and Destiny of Man*, vol. 1. New York: Scribner's, 1964.

Packer, James I. *Knowing God.* Downers Grove, IL: InterVarsity, 1973.

Vitz, Paul C. *Psychology as Religion: The Cult of Self-Worship.* Grand Rapids: Eerdmans, 1977.

Wagner, Maurice E. *The Sensation of Being Somebody: Building a Biblically Adequate Self-Concept.* Grand Rapids: Zondervan, 1975.

9
A VIEW OF AND FOR THE FAMILY

The Traditional Family: Back to the Future
The Transitional Family: Backward to the Present
    Family
    Marriage
    Parenting
    Worldviews and the Family
The Transformed Family: Forward to "The Beginning"
    A Biblical View of the Family
        The Divine Metaphors in the Family
        The Creative Prototype for the Family
    A Biblical View for the Family
        God's Blueprint for Marriage
        God's Blueprint for Parenting

Chris Whittle, creator of "Channel One," observes that once we were a nation of parents with 2.5 children; now we are a nation of children with 2.5 parents.[1] Today's family is now characterized by what some have called the three Ds—divorce, day care, and dual incomes.[2] The family values promoted in today's sitcoms and reality shows are quite different than those of a previous time. Many yearn for the elusive dream of a happy home and loving family, but they no longer know what an ideal family is.

The Traditional Family: Back to the Future

Americans who long for the traditional family are pursuing a dream that is all but extinct. In the first place, what we have called the *traditional family* has never existed in many non-Western cultures.[3] Although one of the few cultural universals is a kinship group, family structures are as varied as the cultures they represent.

---

[1] Chris Whittle, *Tennessee Business Roundtable*, March 7, 1990 (Nashville).

[2] Kerby Anderson and Bob McEnany, *Future Tense*, a forthcoming book to be published by Thomas Nelson, Nashville.

[3] Robert L. Munroe and Ruth H. Munroe, *Cross-Cultural Human Development* (Monterey, CA: Wadsworth, 1975), pp. 7-25.

219

In the second place, the traditional family warmly remembered by many Baby Boomers, and idealized on television shows such as "Father Knows Best" and "Ozzie and Harriet," is a recent development in American history. For most of our ancestors, family life included fathers and mothers working side by side in an agrarian setting (the bread grower and bread maker). The children contributed significant labor to the family unit. It has been only since the Industrial Revolution of the late nineteenth century that men go to an office or factory (the bread winner), leaving their wives at home (the homemaker), while the children spend the day at school.

Will the next generation warmly remember their family experiences? A cover story for *Newsweek* concludes, "Our families will continue to be different in the twenty-first century except in one way. They will give us sustenance and love as they always have."[4] But no basis whatsoever was given for such optimism.

What is a normal family? The experts disagree, and when polls are taken, the populace disagrees. The traditional family has a strong hold on the American imagination, but by 1988 fewer than twenty-seven percent of the United States population fit the so-called traditional model.[5]

Former Supreme Court Justice Potter Stewart once remarked that although we may not be able to define a family, we know one when we see it. But do we? The *Oxford English Dictionary* contains twenty definitions of *family*. Legal agencies operate with different meanings, some including or excluding those who regard themselves as "family." A State of California task force defined family by function, such as providing for the physical health and safety of its members, teaching social skills, and creating a retreat from external stresses.[6] In one survey, respondents overwhelmingly rejected the definition "a group of people related by blood, marriage or adoption," and chose as their definition "a group who love and care for each other." Same-sex unions and adoptions are commonplace. Feminist Gloria Steinem declared, "Family is content, not form."[7] The freedoms loudly proclaimed by Steinem and others carry a price tag. Much like Oscar Wilde's description of a mackerel in the moonlight: it glitters, but it stinks.

---

4   Jerrold K. Footlick, "What Happened to the Family?" in *Newsweek*, special
      edition: "The 21st Century Family," Winter/Spring 1990, p. 20.
5   Jean Seligmann, "Variations on a Theme," in *Newsweek*, special edition,
      Winter/Spring 1990, p. 39.
6   Footlick, "What Happened to the Family?", p. 18.
7   "Overheard," *Newsweek*, special edition, Winter/Spring 1990, p. 11.

The Transitional Family:
Backward to the Present

Today, signs of changing attitudes within the family are everywhere. Historian James Hitchcock describes the process of moral worldview erosion within a culture:

> With regard to each previously held absolute a predictable pattern is followed—first unthinkable thoughts are expressed publicly, in the media and elsewhere, justified on the ground of free speech and the need to hear "all points of view." Then certain respectable people—clergy, professors, judges, etc.— announce that such ideas must be taken seriously, even if not approved. The "rigidity" of past beliefs is scored, to the point where those who hold to traditional opinions are made to feel slightly guilty. Finally a few respectable individuals proclaim publicly their acceptance of the new idea. Within an amazingly brief period of time what had been unthinkable becomes quite thinkable, then becomes a new orthodoxy. Those who hold to the old idea are quickly placed in the position of being eccentric and in need of justification.[8]

Hitchcock is correct; those who value traditional family structures in which moral absolutes reign are now on the defensive. The staggering fact is that most of these changes took place within half a generation. To view these transitions and their implications more clearly, we shall focus on the family in general, on marriage, on parenting, and then consider how different worldviews regard the family.

Family

Anthropologists admit that although "the family has been the seedbed of socialization in all heretofore known cultures . . . the signs are now clear that the family is atrophying."[9] Some eagerly await presiding over the funeral of the family unit.

An alternative approach many are adopting is to redefine the family. For example, in September of 1989 the New York State Court of Appeals maintained that the term *family* "should not be rigidly restricted" to husbands and wives, but should include "domestic partners." Thus the lines marking off the family have blurred, and homosexual relationships

---

[8] James Hitchcock, "Competing Ethical Systems," *Imprimus* 120:4 (April 1981):5.

[9] E. Adamson Hoebel and Everett L. Frost, *Cultural and Social Anthropology* (New York: McGraw-Hill, 1976), p. 417.

now claim whatever legal status the *family* affords.[10] This is not a new step; the Board of Supervisors of San Francisco had already taken steps to enact such measures.[11] However, "It is one thing when that argument proceeds from the mouth of a gay-rights activist; it is quite another when the highest court of New York and the governing board of a metropolitan area put their weight behind such distortion."[12] Those who oppose these sorts of measures are labeled bigots.

American society is confused over what the family actually is. This is reflected in the fact that there is less domestic stability in our society than ever before.

Marriage

In my office is a cartoon that pictures a couple before a marriage counselor. He asks them incredulously, "You are monogamous, heterosexual and faithful? How long have you been practicing this alternative lifestyle?" Humorous, yes; farfetched, no. Marriage is in serious trouble. Demographers project that half of all first marriages made today will end in divorce. Most divorced people remarry, but six out of ten second marriages will fail.[13] The concept of commitment to a spouse simply because one is married to him/ her is rare.

Furthermore, traditional roles, which had at least been considered acceptable, are now targets for demolition. Feminists like Vivian Gornick claim that "being a housewife is an illegitimate profession . . . the choice to serve and be protected and plan toward being a family-maker is a choice that shouldn't be. The heart of radical feminism is to change that."[14] The role of the husband and the identity of the wife are no longer clearly defined.

Parenting

Parenting is also in upheaval, struggling for survival in the backwash of divorce and materialism. The changing values and moral standards of

---

[10] Footlick, "What Happened to the Family?", p. 18.

[11] The only thing that stopped its becoming law was a petition of twenty-seven thousand names that opposed it and thus required it to be decided by referendum. It was defeated by San Francisco voters by a margin of 50.5 percent to 49.5 percent. Mayor Art Agnos said, "We are going to come back with it again and again until it succeeds." See Robert Digitals, *World*, 18 November 1989, p. 12.

[12] Timothy K. Jones, "Sort of Married," *Christianity Today*, 8 September 1989: p. 14.

[13] Footlick, "What Happened to the Family?", p. 16.

[14] Vivian Gornick, University of Illinois, *The Daily Illini*, 25 April 1981.

today's children are far more reflective of the entertainment media than they are of the moral standards their parents would prefer them to adopt. Sexual self-discipline is no longer a value among our youth. Those who abstain from intercourse often engage in other sexual practices that do not carry the risk of pregnancy. As George Will describes their philosophy, "The good life is the glandular life."[15]

Some of the upheaval may be traced to demands placed on parents outside the home. The requirements for success in a materialistic society come into unavoidable conflict with the demands of family life, and thus the children become "hindrances to mobility and obstacles to total self-expression."[16] Although the ideal may be *Little House on the Prairie*,[17] the reality is *Little House on the Freeway*.[18] Kerby Anderson comments, "In a culture which values narcissism over compassion, business world success over parenting, children become villains instead of precious gifts from God."[19] Some experts are now advising that "we must take them away from families and communally raise them."[20] Solutions such as leaving children in day care can generate more trauma than help and constantly plague concerned parents.

Worldviews and the Family

Why are these changes taking place? One reason is that as we become more aware of alternative worldviews, new values challenge those of the past. Hoebel and Frost offer the common diagnosis: "With advancing civilization, kinship recedes in relative importance."[21] Some anthropologists would add that we *should* evolve out of the need for families—let family become extinct—since (with the rise in divorce and child abuse) families no longer seem to be performing their societal functions well.

We have said that a worldview is both a view *of* the world and a view *for* the world. The major worldviews we have discussed have implications for each one's view of the family—both for marriage and for parenting.

---

[15] Cited in Carl F. H. Henry, *The Christian Mindset in a Secular Society* (Portland, OR: Multnomah, 1984), p. 15.

[16] Kerby Anderson, "Where's Dad?" syndicated column, January 15, 1985.

[17] Laura Ingalls Wilder, *Little House on the Prairie* (New York: Harper & Row, 1953).

[18] Tim Kimmel, *Little House on the Freeway* (Portland, OR: Multnomah, 1987).

[19] Kerby Anderson, "Where's Dad?"

[20] Dr. Mary Jo Bane (professor at Wellesley College), quoted by the Associated Press in the *Tulsa World*, 21 August 1977.

[21] Hoebel and Frost, *Cultural and Social Anthropology*, p. 210.

A *naturalist* worldview says all creatures evolved and that biological mating accounts for the very existence of the family in history. Animals tend to group in "families," and mankind did the same. Eventually, humans saw that families had social value, and marriage with parenting became an institution. But the family (and the love within the family) has no *intrinsic* value for the naturalist. Because there are no absolutes, any value placed on the family is tenuous and may differ from person to person.

Further, any standards of morality are merely traditional or sociological. Because all consequences arise within this life, mankind fears herpes more than he fears hell.[22] Man's sex life is reduced to "a series of stimulating encounters with biologically differing mates, events with no moral significance or religious answerability."[23]

For example, atheistic philosopher Bertrand Russell advocated only "terrestrial" reasons (i.e., reasons deriving from this life) for marital fidelity. Therefore he saw no problem with "a few temporary extramarital affairs"[24] within a permanent marriage. He stated very clearly, "Agnostics, as such, have no distinctive views about sexual morality."[25] His wife, however, felt differently. This is the naturalist's ethical dilemma: Where are the standards for the standards? Any priority placed on the family by an individual naturalist consists in values brought to his worldview, and not in values derived from his worldview.

Unlike the naturalist worldview, a *transcendental* worldview does not have any defined view of the family that necessarily follows from its premises. It is amorphous, and thus may take whatever form is dictated either by one's culture or by the individual. The result may range from the deification of family in oriental cultures to the desertion of family in Western communes.

Because "God" in this worldview is an impersonal force, there is no reason to promote an institution that focuses on developing personality and relationships. Also in transcendentalism, distinction between masculinity and femininity is blurred. Thus, two of the key reasons for the existence of the traditional family is aborted.

Moral standards are again seen as more *descriptive* of my personal preference than *prescriptive* of moral absolutes. One university student told me, "Maybe Christianity is true for you, but don't force your morality on me." This attitude is extended by anthropologists into a

---

[22] Henry, *Christian Mindset*, p. 15.
[23] Ibid.
[24] Bertrand Russell, "What Is an Agnostic?" in *Bertrand Russell On God and Religion*, ed. Al Seckel (Buffalo, NY: Prometheus, 1986), p. 26.
[25] Ibid., p. 80.

larger question: Because more than half the societies of the world are polygamous,[26] who is to say Christians are right about monogamy? Indeed, the only absolute is that there are no absolutes, and "every man does that which is right in his own eyes" (Judg. 21:25, KJV). And what of Christianity? It is considered a threat to self-fulfillment, according to a growing vanguard of society.

The *postmodern* worldview is antagonistic toward the traditional family. Gender roles and sexual norms are social constructs used as tools of oppression by the dominant social class. Following the lead of Michel Foucault, many postmodernists embrace a nondefined view of family and consider all expressions of sexuality as legitimate.

By contrast, a *biblical theistic* view of the family derives from the character of the personal God in whose image man was made. Family is the place where children are taught spiritual truth, where values and behavior are rooted in divine commands, and where family relationships are to model divine truth. These relationships are anchored outside of man and have eternal value. The remainder of this chapter shall focus on developing a biblical view of the family.

The Transformed Family:
Forward to "The Beginning"

Carl F. H. Henry observed that today's secular *mind*-set rests as never before upon a nonbiblical *will*-set.[27] Sadly, this is true even within Christian circles. The sins of the culture have become the sins of the church—and this is seen no more clearly than in the eroding family. Christians believe what God says, but the ethical gap between our view *of* the family and our view *for* the family is growing wider.

At its best, culture often embraces an *idealistic* view of the family. The biblical view of the family is *realistic* and rooted in the Scriptures. There Christians find both descriptions *of* God-honoring families (and those that are not) and prescriptions *for* what God wants the family to be.

A Biblical View of the Family

The Divine Metaphors in the Family

It is significant that God illustrates divine relationships from the family: Christ is the *Son*, God is the *Father*, we are *born* again, and become *children* and *sons*, *adopted* into His family, with *inheritance* and

---

[26] Hoebel and Frost, *Cultural and Social Anthropology*, p. 201.

[27] Henry, *Christian Mindset*, p. 19.

riches at our disposal. We are *disciplined* as beloved sons. Other family images include Christ as the *bridegroom* and the church as the *bride* of Christ.

God structured human relationships so that the family would serve as a domestic mirror to reflect our eternal relationship with Him. Of course, our understanding of His love will be limited—we are limited beings. I may describe the heat and light of the sun by pointing to the heat and light of a candle; but the reality is infinitely superior to the illustration. Likewise, when the Bible says that God is our loving Father, we must remember that human father-love does not begin to compare with the depths of divine Father-love.

But God did not use family illustrations haphazardly. These pictures show what God intended the family to be. This becomes clear as we examine the direct biblical references to the family.

The Creative Prototype for the Family

The Creator had a blueprint in mind when He built the Christian home. The blueprint toward which Scripture turns for guidance in marriage relationships is found in the creation ordinances, in which God dealt with man as he came from His hand in a state of integrity. Both Jesus (Matt. 19:3-9; Mark 10:3-9) and Paul (Eph. 5:31) appeal to Genesis 2 as the definitive word regarding what God intended marriage to be *before* it became marred by sin.[28] We need to reexamine the blueprint and remodel our homes.

In Genesis 1:27 the fact of man's creation is given; Genesis 2:18-25 offers further detail.[29] Everything God created received His benediction (Gen. 1:4, 10, 12, 18, 21, 25, 31). The first malediction in the Bible is found in Genesis 2:18—it is *not good* that man should be alone. God had placed man in a perfect environment where he enjoyed absolute Divine communion. However, Adam was lacking because God created him to be in *two* relationships: communion with God (Eccles. 3:11) and communion with other human beings.

But not just any kind of communion with other human beings would meet man's need. Companionship is God's design, which includes both comradeship and sexual partnership.[30] Adam recognized the woman as his true counterpart—bone of his bone, flesh of his flesh (Gen. 2:23).

---

[28] See John Murray, *Principles of Conduct* (Grand Rapids: Eerdmans, 1957), pp. 27-81, for a thorough discussion.

[29] K. A. Kitchen, *Ancient Orient and the Old Testament* (Downers Grove, IL: InterVarsity, 1966), p. 117.

[30] God's design was one of *complementarity* (man with woman) rather than one of *identity* (man with man).

The narrative continues, "For this cause"—that is, because of the unique oneness in a husband/wife relationship—a man shall leave his parents (marriage is exclusive) and cleave to his wife (marriage is permanent), and the two shall be "one flesh" (marriage is intimate).[31] Although not a formal definition, Genesis 2:24 offers the clearest description of marriage we have in the Bible. Husbands and wives are to be "one"—physically, emotionally, intellectually, and spiritually.

God imposed both order and priorities on human relationships. God's structure for relationships did not begin after the Fall of man but with the institution of marriage (1 Cor. 11:8-9; 1 Tim. 2:13).[32]

A Biblical View for the Family

God's Blueprint for Marriage

God placed priorities upon relationships. First, our eternal relationship is with God—apparently there will be no marriage in heaven. This does not deny the validity of marriage, or make it God's Band-Aid for loneliness in this world. More likely it reflects man's inability to invest his emotions and passions in more than one being; in heaven, this limitation will be removed and the very best of love relationships will be enhanced and multiplied by as many beings as populate heaven. In other words, the marriage relationship will not be diminished; all other relationships will be enhanced. The marriage of Christ and the church will be a reality, so the need for its prophetic picture will disappear. Even so, the basis for all horizontal relationships is our vertical, eternal relationship with God. "We love, because He first loved us" (1 John 4:19).

Second, our permanent earthly relationship is with our spouse and takes priority over all other earthly relationships. Imagine two circles touching each other at their perimeters—the level of acquaintanceship. As those two circles become more and more entwined—much like orbs in an eclipse—there is greater and greater oneness. Marriage is a covenant toward oneness, and when it is broken by divorce God is deeply offended (Mal. 2:14-16).[33] Idolatry—the heinous Old Testament sin—is God's spiritual analogy for adultery. God's goal for marriage

---

[31] "Flesh" is a metaphor at times for the totality of a person (Gen. 6:17). In other words, marriage is the closest companionship possible.

[32] Susan T. Foh, *Women and the Word of God* (Philipsburg, NJ: Presby. & Ref., 1979), pp. 61-69.

[33] Note that God's relationship to a husband depends at least partially upon how he treats his wife (1 Pet. 3:7).

was, and is, that husbands and wives experience the deepest human companionship possible.

This is directly opposed to modern trends. Husbands are not to hold their wives back—or let their wives hold them back—from total fulfillment, even if their life goals exclude their mates. Today's creedal statements are: "I'm worth it; I've gotta be me; I'm going to grab the success I deserve!" The biblical portrait is drastically different. Our marriages should be an earthly "wedding album" that pictures the future divine union of Christ with His church.

Third, our temporary earthly relationship is with our children; one day they leave our home to establish their own marriages. One major goal for parenting is to teach children about God's blueprint for marriage so that they may build a God-honoring marriage—their own permanent earthly relationship. (All other relationships follow in decreasing priority.)

In the perfect environment of Eden, God made extensive lush provision for man and gave only one prohibition. The couple was not to eat the fruit of the tree of knowledge of good and evil. Satan approached Eve. All of God's positive provision was ignored as Satan focused upon God's single prohibition and reinterpreted God's motives for His command (Gen. 3:5). After Satan enticed her, Adam joined in the sin by partaking of the fruit of the tree under her leadership. The phrase "with her" (Gen. 3:6) carries a nuance that has implications for marital roles: Adam allowed Eve to take "headship" and lead him, which resulted in sin (1 Tim. 2:14).[34] The roles of man and woman were reversed in Adam's disobedience.

Genesis 3:16 records the result of this tragedy. Because of sin, there would now be tension between husbands and wives as they strive toward oneness. This tension was not God's punishment upon man; rather, Genesis 3:16 was God's warning of what would happen with two fallen people in a marriage relationship. In other words, the battle of the sexes began.

Fallen people fall short of God's ideal for oneness. Therefore, God gave guidelines to reclaim the ideal He had designed for the first couple. For the husband, the Bible offers two explicit guidelines for how he is to exercise his headship. One comes from Paul and the other from Peter.

---

[34] Umberto Cassuto, *From Adam to Noah*, trans. Israel Abrahams (Jerusalem: Magnes, 1961), p. 148.

GUIDELINES FOR HUSBANDS

a. Love your wife. Because a wife is commanded to "submit," the symmetrical command for a husband would be, "Rule your wife." Instead, husbands are commanded to love their wives (Eph. 5:25).

Many misunderstand what love is because modern usage is vague: I love Jesus, I love my wife, I love my dog, I love mint chocolate/chocolate chip ice cream (I really do!). Fortunately, the Bible does not simply give a generic command to love; it gives guidelines for how genuine marital love is to be expressed. The divine analogy of Christ with the church (from Ephesians 5—and we will add a final point from the Song of Solomon) is descriptive of the *kind* of love husbands are to have to bring about oneness.

First, Christ's love for the church is *self-sacrificing.* Many have noticed the divine analogy: when Christ "gave Himself up" for the church (Eph. 5:25), He died for her. Thus a husband is to love his wife enough to be willing to die for her. Although this is true, we should remember that death takes one grand decision, and then the act is over. Christ also ever lives for His bride (Rom. 8:26-34; Heb. 7:25). Likewise, husbands are to "give themselves up" in daily decisions to live for their wives. A husband who says he would die for his wife should be willing to put his love into action in smaller ways as well.

Second, Christ's love for the church is *unconditional.* Although His goal is that the church should be without spot and unblemished (Eph. 5:26-27), we were not all that spiritually "attractive" when Christ died for us (Rom. 5:8, 10). Christ's unconditional love would embrace the church, whether or not she had gained weight, or had gray hair, or continued in irritating habits (if I may take a bit of license with these expressions). Husbands are to incarnate unconditional love.

The third and fourth may be taken together: Christ's love is *volitional* and *continuous.* The present imperative verb indicates that husbands are to "keep on loving" their wives. Love is an action that includes man's volition. This does not discount the emotional element of love at all; it simply suggests that decisions can govern emotions, which is an important lesson for a generation that views divorce as a form of spring cleaning. Husbands are to choose—and choose continuously—to behave in loving ways toward their wives.

Fifth and finally, the husband's love for his wife is to be *romantic* love. Romantic love is not infatuation, in which the mind is in neutral and passion reigns. Infatuation has a vision that sees in the other person what we *think* is there—but it is easily self-deceived; it is akin to being in love with love. Infatuation causes a man to forget that, while he sees his wife occasionally at her worst, he usually sees other women only at their best—whether at work or at church. In contrast, true romantic love is realistic; the mind is both in control and focused on creative ways to express love to one's spouse. The pattern for romantic behavior is partially seen in the Song of Solomon, wherein a portrait is painted of the beauty of sexual, romantic love (e.g., 5:11*b*, "Drink and imbibe deeply, O lovers!"). A survey of the Song of Solomon reveals that Solomon enhanced romantic love in three ways. First, he made the Shulamite feel *security* in her position as his chosen bride (1:5-2:2). Second, there was constant *communication* as love was expressed verbally. Third, the husband's *giving attitude* contributed to the mood of romance and desire. The wise husband will give special attention to creative ways to romance his wife.

There is still one crucial element missing from the husband's relationship to his spouse, and this is supplied by Peter.

b. Understand your wife. "Women! Nobody can understand them!" True. Nobody can exhaustively understand any other human being, regardless of gender. But Peter (who was married) supplemented Paul's command to love one's wife when he commanded husbands to "live with your wife in an understanding way" (1 Pet. 3:7). Three implications flow from this command. First, men are not to abuse their position of headship over their wife's *weaker* (submissive) role.[35] Second, akin to the command to love, this command involves a *choice* husbands make when responding to domestic circumstances. Instead of responding sharply or with sarcasm, husbands are purposefully to honor their wives ("grant her honor") in ways that encourage and build. Third, fulfilling this command involves time spent in *communication*, which is a key ingredient in developing biblical oneness. If husbands do not obey this responsibility, there will be serious consequences: their prayers may be hindered. In other words, the husband's horizontal relationship with his wife affects his vertical relationship with his Lord (see Matt. 5:22-23).

But the wife is not passive in home-building. Whether or not the husband responds to God's guidance, God has also given the wife principles she can practice to help remodel her marriage.

---

[35] The verse continues "as with a weaker vessel, since she is a woman." It is interesting that a simile is used; she is not explicitly said to be a weaker vessel, but the husband is to grant consideration as though she were. Furthermore, whatever "weakness" may be in view is likely related to the position a wife has in submission to her husband. The entire context is dealing with submission due to position (2:12-13, 18; 3:1, 5). Because she is in a weaker position, the husband is not to abuse his role as head of the family but is to live considerately with her in all things.

GUIDELINES FOR WIVES. After the Fall, God told Eve, "Your desire shall be for your husband, and he shall rule over you." This is not a description of something that will make life easier for the woman (or else it would be grossly out of place in this context of judgment). Actually her desire will be to dominate her husband; she will struggle in her role as a submissive wife. The Edenic judgment was *not* that the husband now *began* to rule; it simply indicated that headship no longer came easily for either spouse.[36] A paraphrase of the verse might be, "*Your inclination shall be to dominate your husband, but his proper role is to be your head.*"[37] Therefore God gave guidelines to help wives build toward deeper intimacy with their husbands.

a. *Submit to your husband.* Within the context of Ephesians 5:18-33 is the command to be filled with the Spirit (v. 18). This imperative is modified by four participles that describe some ways in which Spirit-filled behavior is manifested. The fourth of these is "being subject to one another in the fear of Christ" (v. 21). Apparently the apostle was concerned lest mutual subjection be both misunderstood and/or distorted, and so he offered specific authority relationships, balanced by corresponding commands for those in a position of responsibility. The structure is as follows·

Headship	*Don't Abuse Headship*
Wives submit (5:22-24) . . .[38]	and husbands love (5:25-31)
Children obey (6:1-3) . . .	and parents do not provoke (6:4)
Slaves be obedient (6:5-8) . . .	and masters rule kindly (6:9)

It is important to note that submission is not absolute but qualified. First, the verb is not causative (*not* "husbands, make your wives submit") but reflexive: submission is a voluntary, self-imposed relationship of a wife to her husband. Second, submission is a husband/wife relationship, not necessarily a male/female relationship. Every command for wives to submit to husbands in the Bible is exclusive; they are to submit to *their*

---

[36] Genesis 4:7 contains exactly the same construction as 3:16. See Cassuto, *From Adam to Noah*, pp. 165-66; Foh, *Women and the Word*, pp. 68-69.

[37] The paraphrase expresses the nuances of three words: desire (in this case, a natural inclination that is not healthy), for (not longing for, but the direction toward which the "desire" will be aimed), and shall rule (the proper rule that will reestablish creation roles; not a rule that is certain but one that rightly should happen).

[38] Verse 22 contains no verb but is dependent upon the preceding verse to supply the verb: "be subject."

own husbands, not to other men. Third, submission is an attitude.[39] It is related in Ephesians 5:33 to "respect" for her husband. First Peter 3:4-5 describes it as a "gentle and quiet spirit," which may win an unsaved husband. We also may make a distinction between *submission* and *obedience*—ordinarily the two overlap, but at times they may not. Although there may be limits to obedience, there are no limits to submission.[40]

b. Love your husband. Surprisingly, the command to love one's husband is not given as the complement to the husband's obligation to love his wife in Ephesians 5. However, Titus 2:4 commands older women in the church to encourage the younger women "to love their husbands." This love is again an act of the will and is to be manifested in loving behavior, as she "rules" her home well. As with the husband's love, this love is to be unconditional. One husband reacted, "It's very humbling to know there is another person who knows what a rat you are, but still accepts and loves you anyway."

God's blueprint for the family does not end with the marriage relationship. Although marriage is mankind's permanent earthly relationship, our temporary earthly bond is with our children, the fruit of the marriage union.

God's Blueprint for Parenting

The challenges marriage is facing may be matched by the task Christian parents face. Christian homes are feeling the impact as the values of a biblical worldview collide with our secular culture. Two major challenges come from outside the family.

First, technology has outrun the ethics that manage the technology. This has resulted in parents having historically unprecedented choices available. Geoffrey Cowley observes, "For the first time in history, people are deciding, rather than wondering, what kind of children they will bear. . . . The whole definition of normal could well be changed. The issue becomes not the ability of the child to be happy but rather our

---

[39] This is in contrast to those who believe submission means that the wife is intrinsically inferior to the husband. Note the implications of this line of reasoning if it were applied to the Trinity (I Cor. 11:3).

[40] If a husband tells his wife to do what is explicitly contrary to God's Word, she cannot obey him, but her attitude can still be submissive and not rebellious. Further, a submissive wife still has biblical responsibilities toward her husband, such as speaking the truth to him in love (Eph. 4), confronting him when he is in sin (Matt. 18:15), and so on.

ability to be happy with the child."[41] If today's parents are unable to meet these challenges, how can their children develop the ethical structure for the decisions they will be forced to make?

A second external challenge comes from education: one major assumption public education makes is that there are absolutely no absolutes. Almost anything else can be taught to our children (or taught to their teachers) with public sanction. For example, Beverly Galyean is a teacher of hundreds of public school teachers (from her federally funded Los Angeles school program). She states her philosophy of education as follows: "Once we begin to see that we are all God, that we all have the attributes of God, then I think the whole purpose of human life is to reown the Godlikeness within us; the perfect love, the perfect wisdom, the perfect understanding, the perfect intelligence, and when we do that, we create back to that old, the essential oneness which is consciousness. So my whole view is very much based on that idea."[42] This is nothing more than the transcendental worldview, expressed in terms that are really quite old (see Gen. 3:5).

Other challenges face parents. Children are maturing earlier than ever physically and later than ever emotionally.[43] Secular authorities are alarmed because this difference is "evident in all areas of youthful development: sex, love, marriage, education and work."[44]

Peer influences are often blatantly anti-Christian. The Christian teen who lives in a home governed by biblical principles often finds his or her outside life continually in conflict with those home values, which produces further stress. The most common way teenagers cope with stress is to put on headphones and escape into entertainment. However, this escape tends to compound the problem of teenage stress because of the major themes that dominate today's entertainment: sex, appearance, rebellion, false religion, and materialism.[45]

Informed Christian parents are concerned. Carl F. H. Henry rightly observes, "Training children in the Way is a matter of parental duty. The rebellious child in your own home who on occasion is tempted to tell you to go to the eschatological unmentionable may be the most important

---

[41] Geoffrey Cowley, "Made to Order Babies," *Newsweek*, special edition, Winter/Spring 1990, p. 94.

[42] Frances Adeny, "Educators Look East," SCP Journal (Winter 1981-82):29, cited in Erwin Lutzer and John F. DeVries, *Satan's "Evangelistic" Strategy for This New Age* (Wheaton, IL: Victor, 1989), p. 137.

[43] Kenneth L. Woodward, "Young Beyond Their Years," *Newsweek*, special edition, p. 55.

[44] Ibid.

[45] For example, see Lutzer and DeVries, *New Age*, pp. 139, 141.

potential leader you will ever direct into the service of Christ."[46] A child is a parent's greatest missionary enterprise. All other goals are temporal, but a child's relationship to Christ is eternal.

As Christian parents, we want our children to be redeemed, and then to think thoughts consistent with and conducive to holy living. We also desire that our children develop biblical wisdom, the Old Testament education principle that demonstrates skill in the art of living. As we attempt to move our children from dependence (upon parents) to independence (from parents), we want them to obey God when we are no longer around. Our desire is that they seek heavenly things first, and then put earthly concerns in their proper place (Matt. 6:33).

To accomplish these goals, Scripture again offers explicit and implicit responsibilities that parents owe their children and children owe their parents.

GUIDELINES FOR PARENTS

a. Love. Children are to be viewed by their parents not as a burden but a blessing (Psalm 127). The nurture parents give is to be gentle and tender (1 Thess. 2:7). No child should feel he or she has to earn parental love (contrast Gen. 25:28). Enacting this principle involves spending time with our children. Charles Francis Adams, nineteenth-century political figure and diplomat, kept a diary. One day he entered, "Went fishing with my son today—a day wasted." His son, Brook Adams, also kept a diary that is still in existence. On the same day he made this entry: "Went fishing with my father—the most wonderful day of my life!"[47] What the father saw as a waste the son saw as an investment. Being a loving parent takes time.

Furthermore, unconditional love will not permit favoritism of one child over another, nor will it withhold love if a child does not meet certain behavior norms or talent expectations (see Gen. 25:28). It will not treat a child's personal problems as insignificant. When an earthly father incarnates heavenly love, the child is drawn that much closer to the heavenly Father.

b. Training. Unconditional love does not, however, mean there are no expectations from the child. Jesus said, "If you love me, you will keep my commandments." Parents are to train their children in the skill of living (Prov. 22:6). A father is measured for spiritual leadership in part by the godly control he exercises within his home (1 Tim. 3:4-5). Overindulgent parents can harm a child when withholding discipline that is needed to help the child mature. The tragic lives of Absalom (2 Sam.

---

[46] Henry, *Christian Mindset*, p. 18.
[47] *Family Happiness Is Homemade* 11:9 (September 1987).

14-18) and Adonijah (1 Kings 1) serve as negative case studies: apparently David loved his sons, but because he did not discipline them they rebelled against him and against God.

Even in discipline, however, unconditional love will attempt to distinguish between those times when a child is simply being childish (which will be outgrown) and willful childishness (which may not be outgrown)—and will respond accordingly.

Children are to be brought up in the nurture (discipline that regulates character) and instruction (training by the Word) of the Lord (Eph. 6:4). This includes encouragement, teaching, exhortation, and discipline.[48] Much of disciplining is common sense; withholding appropriate punishment (Prov. 23:13), equivocating limits (1 Kings 1), and not clarifying expectations may produce improper behavior and insecurity in a child (Eph. 6:4; Col. 3:21).

Deuteronomy 6:6-9 offers guidelines for parental instruction. First, God's words are to be engraved on the hearts of the parents—they are steeped in Scripture and model it ("shall be on your heart," v. 6). The passage proceeds to suggest *how* parents are to teach: there should be opportunities for formal instruction ("teach them") and informal instruction ("talk of them," v. 7). Also *where* to teach and *when* to teach are suggested—at all places where opportunities are present, and at all times. Life is the laboratory in which parents are to instruct their children in wisdom.[49]

c. Modeling. The most effective lessons are more "caught than taught." This was certainly true of the disciples as they observed the priorities of Jesus. Likewise, children are more apt to observe what their parents *do* than to listen to what they *say*. While trying to comfort a young girl who had just wrecked her mother's car, I assured her that when her mother arrived, she would be more pleased that her daughter was safe than concerned about a car. However, as soon as the mother arrived, she never looked at the girl but screeched, "Look at what you did to my car!" No matter how much the mother might have protested later that she loves her daughter, the girl will not believe her, because in the moment of testing the mother did not model godly parental love or priorities.

Second Timothy suggests two deterrents to apostasy in the life of Timothy. The second one is familiar: the Scriptures (2 Tim. 3:16; "sacred writings" in v. 15), which are inspired and profitable for teaching and

---

[48] Prov. 13:24; 19:18; 20:30; 23:13-14; 29:15; 2 Thess. 2:11; Heb. 12:7.

[49] One friend in the military has been posted to a location where he is separated for a year from his family. This creative man is sending back monthly videotapes of guitar lessons for his sons, and devotions for his family.

training (vv. 16-17). The first deterrent, however, may not be as readily noticed: the godly life of the teacher establishes the credibility of the teaching ("knowing from whom you have learned them," v. 14). Although the reference may be to Paul, it is more likely that Lois and Eunice, the two godly women who reared Timothy, are in mind. Parents' lives must match their lips.

GUIDELINES FOR CHILDREN. By definition, children vary in their ability to understand what the Bible says. As they mature, however, they bear greater responsibility and accountability for their choices, including how they treat their parents. The Bible does not hesitate to give clear instructions, which children are expected to obey.

a. Honor. The "first commandment with a promise" was given in the Old Testament (Ex. 20:12) and repeated in the New Testament (Eph. 6:2). The Hebrew concept of honor includes more than just *love* for one's parents; it means to *cherish* one's parents. The Bible uses as a gauge of a decadent society whether or not parents are cherished by their children (Ex. 21:15, 17; Matt. 10:31; Rom. 1:30).

b. Learn. Second, children (when young) are to embrace the instruction of their parents; and when children are older they are to listen to their parents' wise counsel (Prov. 1:8ff.; 17:6). Our day is characterized by the worship of youth; age is considered a disease to be avoided. Yet the Bible describes the wisdom of age as a treasure to be cherished.

c. Obey. Children are told clearly to obey their parents "in the Lord, for this is right" (Eph. 6:1; Col. 3:20). Second Timothy 3:2 includes in its description of apostasy that children will be "disobedient to parents." Indeed, a child's rebellion can disqualify the father from ministry (1 Tim. 3:4-5, 12; see also 1 Sam. 3 and 8).

d. Care. As advances in medicine extend the average lifespan (and Baby Boomers age), the population demographics of the United States will change drastically. Whereas the population used to resemble a pyramid, at present it resembles a barrel. In the next decades it will resemble a hot air balloon.[50] Even traditional families will change: the Census Bureau says that within the next decade four generation families will be the norm. The costs for medical care for the aged are escalating, and the Social Security system is less than secure.

---

[50] In 1960, 55 percent of the population was in the workforce, and 9.3 percent was retired. By 2030, 57.4 percent will be in the workforce, yet those who are retired will number almost 21 percent. See Melinda Beck, "The Geezer Boom," *Newsweek*, special edition, Winter/Spring 1990, pp. 62-66.

One passage (which is often misunderstood) specifically addresses this mandate. Children are to care for their widowed mothers. If a child does not, he or she "has denied the faith, and is worse than an unbeliever" (1 Tim. 5:3-5, 8). This biblical command may become far more relevant to Christian families and to the church than it has been in recent decades.[51]

Conclusion

Over fifty years ago, R. Redfield was prophetic in observing that man used to be bound by the moral order, but now follows the technical order in which "men are bound by things, or are themselves things."[52] This cultural trend has escalated. Christians are to be salt and light in their society. There are few areas of personal need and pain that touch individuals as much as the family. A solid Christian family, anchored in biblical principles, can have tremendous impact as a witnessing force in the community.

As Christians face the next generation, we need to be rooted "in the beginning" with our principles firmly set. Then when our worldview collides with our culture we may faithfully say, "As for me and my house, we will serve the Lord" (Josh. 24:15).

DISCUSSION QUESTIONS

1. Describe the changes in society that you can pick out in your own town. How have these changes affected your family?
2. Discuss: Does the Bible give more good examples or bad examples of godly families within its pages? Why do you think this is so?
3. Discuss how the Christian family can be used as an example of "salt and light" (Matthew 5:16) in your community.
4. Turn to 1 Corinthians 13 and list at least five things or actions love will do. Give an illustration for each of the five: (1) in a husband/wife relationship, and (2) in a child/parent relationship.
5. Where is the earliest place in the Bible that we find God's blueprint for family living? How do you explain biblical examples of polygamy and divorce in light of God's blueprint?

---

[51] Many questions will have to be addressed by Christians. Will stepchildren feel the same obligation to care for their stepparents when such parents get old?

[52] R. Redfield, *The Primitive World and Its Transformations* (Ithaca, NY: Cornell U., 1953), p. 21.

6. For a family project, get a copy of today's newspaper. Have your family scan it for every article that affects (directly or indirectly) God's blueprint for the family. Discuss whether or not any teachings of the Bible apply to the articles, and then pray together about what you can do to keep your family strong.

FURTHER READING

Adams, Jay E. *Christian Living in the Home*. Phillipsburg, NJ: Presby. & Ref., 1972.

_____. *Marriage, Divorce, and Remarriage in the Bible*. Grand Rapids: Baker, 1980.

Craven, Michael. *Where the Battle Rages: The Sexualizing of America*. Available online at www.nationalcoalition.org.

Crabb, Larry. *The Marriage Builder*. Grand Rapids: Zondervan, 1982.

Dobson, James and Gary Bauer. *Children at Risk*. Dallas, TX: Word, 1990.

Hurley, James. *Man and Woman in Biblical Perspective*. Grand Rapids: Zondervan, 1981.

Kesler, Jay; Ronald A. Beers; and LaVonne Neff, eds. *Parents & Children*. Wheaton, IL: Victor, 1986.

Kesler, Jay, and Ronald A. Beers, eds. *Parents & Teenagers*. Wheaton, IL: Victor, 1984.

Mason, Mike. *The Mystery of Marriage*. Portland, OR: Multnomah, 1985.

10
A VIEW OF AND FOR THE CHURCH

The Church in a Changing World: A View of the Present
    The Pulpit and the Pew: Changes
    The Church and Worldviews
The Meaning of the Church: A View of the Past
    Definition of the Church
    Beginnings of the Church
    Description of the Church
    Differences among Churches
The Mission of the Church: A View for the Future
    Intimacy with God (Upward)
    Community among Believers (Inward)
    Mission to the World (Outward)
Conclusion

Christians are related to a Person, but also to a People. The Bible knows nothing of "private" religion; "no one can be reconciled to God without being reconciled to the people of God among whom his experience of God's grace immediately sets him."[1] Unfortunately, while individual Christians may be respected for their faithfulness and moral integrity (such as Billy Graham or Mother Theresa), few people have the same high regard for the Body of Christ. Often people object that "the church is full of hypocrites," which allows the critic to commit the fallacy of generalization (what may be true of some of the parts is true of the whole) and dismiss Christianity altogether.

The public no longer ascribes credibility to the church. Further, as the sins of the culture become the sins of the church, the credibility gap widens. The church is no longer a place of integrity in the eyes of the non-Christian world. Financial "huckstering" has long been a target for late-night comedians. Scandals, moral failures, and continuing media stereotypes of Christian leaders have eroded the confidence of many. Young Christians are disillusioned. Many people wonder if the church hinders more than it helps.

---

[1] Bruce Milne, *Know the Truth* (Downers Grove, IL: InterVarsity, 1982), pp. 209-10.

What has happened to the church today? Are its message and its goals out of touch with our technological society? Is the church no longer necessary? Before we answer these questions, we must ask how modern culture has touched the lives of the people who make up the church.

The Church in a Changing World: A View of the Present

The Pulpit and the Pew: Changes

It is axiomatic that cultures undergo change. In a broad sense, theology is application of the truth of God's Word to the culture in which it is ministered. Ideally, Christians adjust, adapt, and apply biblical truth in light of these changes. When a culture becomes increasingly secular, the task is more difficult. In today's moral and social turmoil, the church has functioned less like an anchor giving stability and strength in the midst of a hurricane, and more like a spider spinning a web on the hands of a clock. Although the church cannot change its message or its goals, three specific areas of change illustrate how the church must adapt its strategy to minister to a new culture.

First, the *sphere of ministry* has changed. We no longer live in a monolithic society with a single ethical system; today's culture is pluralistic, both in morality and religion. "In God We Trust" symbolized the faith of a former generation, but now is simply a slogan. Scientific explanations account for things that had been viewed as evidence of the supernatural. Through technology man is now able to solve many of his own problems that once were matters of faith and prayer; the tendency is to rely on immediate solutions for all our concerns. Today if a woman is barren she takes a fertility pill instead of praying. Others search for chemical imbalance as an explanation for sinful behavior. As a result, there is an inclination to put trust in the visible, the here and now.[2]

Second, the *person in the pew* has changed. The attitudes of our cultural environment have affected the individuals within the church. One anthropologist sermonizes, "The price of man's development of technology, of the standardization of the pattern of living, and of the drive to economic equality among men has been very high. The accelerated pace, the rise of cynicism, the worship of conformity, the commercialization of happiness, and the awesome horror of new

---

[2] Fertility treatments can produce results, and chemical imbalances do occur. The focus here is on an encroaching mindset. See Millard Erickson, *Christian Theology* (Grand Rapids: Baker, 1985), p. 899.

weapons of war are some of the shadows cast by civilization in the twentieth century."[3] Individuals in the pew find themselves in the backwash of many cultural trends.

These trends have caused many to reexamine both the authority and the relevance of traditional church teachings. In past generations, churchgoers were caught up in the same (sometimes irrelevant) theological debates hammered out in seminaries (limited atonement, God's sovereignty and man's free will, tongues, etc); today, many are wondering why Stephanie cannot be the pastor of a church. Still others ask what is so wrong with the New Age movement, or if homosexuality (or simply its abuse) is a sin. Taking firm and unmovable positions on any issue is considered bigotry by our culture (in which intolerance is not tolerated), and this makes many Christians uncomfortable.

Some trends are beyond the control of most church members. There is simply less time today to devote to activities outside the home. In 1973 the average American had 26.2 hours per week of leisure time; by 1988 this had dropped to 16.6 hours per week.[4] People are understandably less willing to become involved in church programs that require much time. For many, church is now a place to "come to" rather than a vital worshiping community.

As we saw in chapter 9, the traditional family is not the normative family. The church is no longer filled with two-parent homes. Now singles, re-singles, and particularly single parents and working women, all of whom have unique needs, fill the pews.

Finally, the *nature of pastoring* has changed. First and foremost, the credibility gap between what the pastor says and how he lives is increasingly suspect. The clergy no longer command respect for the integrity of their position.

Other changes affect pastoral effectiveness. Preaching used to be more didactic; today it must be conversational, relational, and include self-disclosure. The pastor used to "shepherd"; now strategic planning is central to many ministries.[5] Pastoral counseling used to be isolated to crisis circumstances within a family; today many pastors could become fulltime counselors.

---

[3] Walter A. Fairservis, in Foreword to Raymond Firth, *Human Types: An Introduction to Social Anthropology* (New York: Mentor, 1958), p. 1.

[4] Steven McKinley, "Caring for the Cocooned," *Leadership* (Winter 1990), p. 28.

[5] David Fisher, "A New Context in Ministry," *Leadership* (Winter 1990), pp. 24-25. Further contrasts are available in Lyle Schaller, "The Changing Caregiver," *Leadership* (Winter 1990), pp. 26-28.

Jim Petersen identifies three forces in society that have greatly impacted the life of the church: relativism (there are no absolutes, of truth or of morals), privatization (what I do is my own business), and individualism (the center of my fulfillment is *me*).[6] The task of the church, on the other hand, is grounded in God's absolute truth, is corporate, and is God-centered.

What should be the priorities of a church that strives to minister in and to a changing world? Different answers have been suggested, depending upon the worldview of the respondent.

The Church and Worldviews

For a *naturalist* the Christian church is, at best, a group of people who may do helpful social work but who delude themselves, and then encourage each other in their corporate delusion that they have a personal relationship with a Supreme Being.

At worst, some naturalists consider the church a threat because of its biblical roots and values. One credo of naturalism, the *Humanist Manifesto II*, proclaims, "Humans are responsible for what we are or will become. No deity will save us; we must save ourselves."[7] In this view the church is a negative and distracting influence which retards man's social and moral evolution. Sam Harris says, "A glance at history, or at the pages of any newspaper reveals that ideas which divide one group of human beings from another, only to unite them in slaughter, generally have their roots in religion."[8]

For a *transcendentalist* also, the church serves at best a horizontal function. Any ideology that promotes cosmic oneness may be stirred into the spiritual melting-pot with other religions. Because transcendentalism maintains that there are no absolutes and truth is relative, then everything that divides, such as a religion which affirms absolutes and seeks to maintain doctrinal purity, is to be jettisoned. Thus the biblical church is regarded as an enemy of transcendentalism.

For some *postmodernists,* organized religion is guilty of centuries of oppression against women, minority groups and homosexuals. Certainly, the church has perpetrated many evils, but for the postmodernist this requires the abandonment of any absolutist claims of Christianity. Some

---

[6] Jim Petersen, "The Eclipse of the Gospel," *Discipleship Journal* 55 (1990), p. 12.

[7] *Humanist Manifesto II* (Buffalo: Prometheus, 1973), p. 16.

[8] Sam Harris, *The End of Faith: Religion, Terror, and the Future of Reason* (W. W. Norton, 2005), p. 12.

within Christianity have embraced Christian postmodernism as the best path to authentic faith. The most significant expression of this is the "Emerging Church," a loose network of thinkers and pastors who feel postmodernism has great potential to exorcise the church of its modernist demons.

A *biblical theist* who believes God has revealed Himself in the Bible and has given guidelines for corporate life as well as individual life regards the church as the agent through which five crucial needs are met: the function of worship (upward), the functions of nurture and edification (inward), and the functions of evangelism and social concern (outward). Indeed, the church is the extension of Christ in this world. These perspectives are rooted in the biblical view of the church, to which we now turn.

The Meaning of the Church:
A View of the Past

Definition of the Church

The original meaning of the word "church" (*ekklesia*) was "assembly."[9] Although the root idea is "called out," the emphasis of the word is more accurately "called together." The concept is an old one: in classical Greek the word referred to a group of people assembled together for a purpose, often business or political meetings (Acts 19:32, 39, 41). It came to be used of an assembly of Christians.

Biblically, some aspects of Christ's relationship to the church remain mysterious (Eph. 5:32). However, two Christological illustrations demonstrate the most important functions of the church. These two prominent metaphors are "the bride of Christ" (2 Cor. 11:2-3; Eph. 5:21-32; Rev. 19:6-9, 21:9) and "the Body of Christ" (Rom. 12:5; 1 Cor. 12:12-27; Eph. 1:22-23; 2:16; 4:25; 5:23, 30; Col. 2:19, 3:15). As the bride of Christ, the church is to submit to Christ and to remain pure for her husband. The focus of this metaphor is single-minded devotion to Jesus Christ alone, forsaking all other claims on our allegiance.

As the Body of Christ, the church is to demonstrate her union with Christ, to judiciously exercise spiritual gifts, and to grow spiritually.[10]

---

[9] See K. L. Schmidt, "Ekklesia," in *Theological Dictionary of the New Testament*, ed. Gerhard Kittel and Gerhard Friedrich, 10 vols. (Grand Rapids: Eerdmans, 1978) 3:501-36.

[10] For discussions of both metaphors see J. Oliver Buswell, *A Systematic Theology of the Christian Religion* (Grand Rapids: Zondervan, 1963), 2:217-26.

The focus of this metaphor is upon the headship of Christ. Clowney states, "Neither the individual nor the group is primary in the church, because Christ is primary."[11]

Theologically, "the Church includes all persons anywhere in the world who are savingly related to Christ."[12] Corporately, the church is composed of a group of people who are resident aliens in this world, who maintain heavenly citizenship, and thus have a strong bond of fellowship with other resident aliens.[13]

The Jews had a common prayer, "God I thank you that I was born a man and not a woman, a freeman and not a slave, a Jew and not a gentile." In contrast to this, Paul proclaimed that "there is neither Jew nor Greek, there is neither slave nor free man, there is neither male nor female; for you are all one in Christ Jesus" (Gal. 3:28). Only on the basis of Christ's work can cultural barriers be hurdled and so diverse a group be brought together to build up one another in love.[14] For this reason Christian fellowship between believers is rich and immediate, even in cross-cultural settings.

Acts 1:1 fits well with the "body" metaphor: it implies that the book of Acts is a record of what Christ continues to do and teach through the church just like Luke's gospel is a record of what Christ began to do and teach in His physical body while on earth.

[11] Edmund Clowney, *The Doctrine of the Church* (Philadelphia: Presby. & Ref., 1969), p. 48.

[12] Erickson, *Christian Theology*, p. 1034. Erickson continues, "It also includes all who *have lived* and been part of his body, and all who *will live* and be part of his body" (italics added). Many extend the definition of the church to include Israel in the Old Testament. *The Westminster Confession* states, "The catholic or universal Church, which is invisible, consists of the whole number of the elect, that *have been, are,* or *shall be* gathered into one, under Christ the head thereof" (*The Westminster Confession of Faith* [Richmond, VA: The Board of Christian Education, Presbyterian Church of the United States, 1963], xxvii.1 [italics added]). We regard the church as fitting a separate program from the promises God made to Israel, and therefore this chapter will focus on the New Testament church. See the discussion in Charles Ryrie, *Basic Theology* (Wheaton, IL: Victor, 1986), pp. 399-401.

[13] Francis Lyall, *Slaves, Citizens, Sons: Legal Metaphors in the Epistles* (Grand Rapids: Zondervan, 1984), pp. 47-66.

[14] John apparently disciplined a first century church dictator who "loves to be first" above other Christians. Diotrephes also exalted himself above Christ. See *proteuon*, used of Christ in Col. 1:18, compared with *philoproteuon*, used of Diotrephes in 3 John 9.

Beginnings of the Church

Jesus anticipated the beginning of the church and gave Peter its "keys" (Matt. 16:18). He told the disciples to remain in Jerusalem for the coming baptism of the Spirit (Acts 1:4-5). The church began when the Spirit came upon the Christians on the Day of Pentecost. First, Jesus seems to refer to the church as future (Matt. 16:18). Second, Luke does not mention *ekklesia* at all in the gospel, but mentions it twenty-four times in Acts. Third, the function of Christ as Head and the ministry of spiritual gifts awaited His resurrection and ascension respectively (Eph. 1:20, 4:7-12).

Yet there is a sense in which the church is a unique continuation of God's people of all ages. Through his bold witness at Pentecost, Peter exercised the "keys" to open the door of faith to the Jews (Acts 2), later to the Samaritans (Acts 8, the "Samaritan Pentecost"), and finally to the Gentiles (Acts 10-11, the "Gentile Pentecost"). Consequently, the church now includes all nations and peoples in one Body (Eph. 2-3).

Description of the Church

There is one church, and there are also individual churches that make up the church. Three considerations support this conclusion. First, the majority of usages of *ekklesia* in the New Testament refer to a local church.[15] Second, though many churches within a city met in homes,[16] Paul addressed the church (singular, corporate) of any city to which he wrote.[17] John employed the same practice in his brief epistles to the seven churches of Asia Minor (Rev. 2-3). Sometimes the term was used of all believers in a city (Acts 8:1), and sometimes of believers in a broad geographical area (Acts 9:31). Third, even though groups of varying sizes were included within the churches, Scripture is very clear that there is one unified Body and one baptism (Eph. 4:4-5). Jesus did not say, "I will build my churches," but, "I will build my church" (Matt. 16:18). In fact, one focus of Jesus' high priestly prayer was that believers would be united (John 17:21-22). The basis of such unity is the work of Christ on the cross, making diverse groups into one Body (1 Cor. 12:12-27).

This means that all Christians, everywhere, are a part of one another. Of course, there is a distinction between the visible church (local

---

[15] Erickson, p. 1033.

[16] Rom. 16:5; 1 Cor.16:19. See particularly the singular in 1 Cor. 1:2 and 2 Cor. 1:1.

[17] Galatians was not written to a city, but to a cluster of cities in a Roman province (1:2, "to the churches of Galatia").

believers who gather together) and the universal church (all Christians collectively).[18] But all believers have the same mission and message. The church is not fragmented. Rather, "the individual congregation, or group of believers in a specific place, is never regarded as only a part or component of the whole church. The church is not a sum or composite of the individual local groups. Instead, the whole is found in each place."[19]

Differences among Churches

Some have objected that because there are so many different denominations, and only one of them can be right, how do you know which one, if any, is right? Does the existence of groups of Christians who may disagree with each other argue against the truth of Christianity? The major differences in areas of doctrine and church structure are obvious to those outside the church. The answer to this common objection requires both an historical perspective and some insight into the limitations of fallen man.

Doctrine

First, some denominations exist not because they teach some things as true which others teach as false, but because they emphasize certain doctrines or practices differently from other churches. Second, where there are true doctrinal disagreements, most churches agree with each other on about 95 percent of their doctrine. Third, this huge area of central agreement is astounding in light of the fact that we are formulating doctrine about the infinite God with finite minds, and we are sinful people who sometimes distort truth, whether or not we are aware of doing so. Because of human mental and moral limitations, one might expect far more doctrinal disagreement among Christians than actually exists.

Where Christians do disagree they must do so in a spirit of love and concern and must not allow conflicts to become personal. Whenever possible, Christians should join forces and work together. Not only does this offer a good testimony before the world, it demonstrates good stewardship to avoid duplicating efforts both on the mission field and at home (John 13:34-35).

---

[18] This includes all who have been baptized by the Holy Spirit into the Body of Christ (1 Cor. 12:13).

[19] Erickson, p. 1033.

Structure and Leadership

While the church is a growing *organism* (Eph. 4:16), it is also an *organization*, which requires structure for full effectiveness. The New Testament gives ample evidence for various structures that arose to meet immediate needs: the "deacons" of Acts 6, the elders and deacons of the pastoral epistles,[20] and various substructures that helped individual congregations function more efficiently (1 Tim. 5:3-22). From these hints have arisen various forms by which the functions of the church are carried out. Historically, the three most prominent structures are congregational, presbyterian, and episcopal.

CONGREGATIONAL. The chief emphasis in this structure is placed on the local congregation, which elects officers (Acts 6:3-5), ordains ministers, exercises discipline (Matt. 18:17), and is independent of church councils and denominational agencies. While apostolic authority was exercised within the early church, the apostles were foundational (Eph. 2:20) and appointed no successors for after their death. Rather, Christ only is the head of the church (Col. 1:18), and all believers are individual priests (1 Pet. 2:9). Historical support for this form is found in the first century church manual, the *Didache*.[21] Today baptist, congregational, and independent churches reflect this sort of organization.

PRESBYTERIAN. Presbyterians would agree with congregationalists that overseers and elders (Gk. *presbyters*) are one and the same. One term describes who they are (presbyters or elders) while the other describes what they do (overseers).[22] Rather than guidance by congregational vote, the elders of a local church oversee the affairs of that church (Acts 15:1-29; Heb. 13:17; 1 Thess. 5:12-13). Further, the elders are subject to the larger "presbytery" (a collection of congregations) which is in turn subject to the "synods" (regional gatherings of presbyteries) and then to the "general assembly" (the denominational gathering).

Although synods and councils may err (in contrast to the inerrancy position of Catholicism), they do adjudicate church matters. The *Westminster Confession* states:

---

[20] See Titus 1:5-9 and 1 Tim. 3:1-13.

[21] Leon Morris, "Church Government," in *Baker's Dictionary of Theology*, ed. Everett F. Harrison (Grand Rapids: Baker, 1960), pp. 126-27.

[22] The terms "elder" and "bishop" are used interchangeably (Titus 1:5, 7; Acts 20:17, 28).

It belongeth to synods and councils, ministerially, to determine controversies of faith, and cases of conscience; to set down rules and directions for the better ordering of the public worship of God, and government of his Church; to receive complaints in cases of mal-administration, and authoritatively to determine the same: which decrees and determinations, if consonant to the word of God, are to be received with reverence and submission.[23]

Presbyterian, Reformed, and some Lutheran churches adopt this form of organization. The "Plymouth Brethren" function under a simplified presbyterian structure.

EPISCOPAL. The episcopal form distinguishes between elders and bishops, the latter being authoritative over the elders. As the apostles were God's leaders for the New Testament church (overseeing and appointing elders, Acts 14:23), so bishops today exercise the same apostolic function. This ministry includes ordination and pastoral appointment (Acts 6:6, 14:21-23; 1 Tim. 4:14; Titus 1:5). Episcopalian, Methodist (with some "presbyterian" modifications), and Anglican churches follow this pattern.[24]

If one were to use governmental terms, the episcopalian form is closest to a *monarchy*, the presbyterian form much like an *oligarchy*, and the congregational like a *democracy*. No one questions whether or not God has used all of these forms to accomplish His purposes in the world, and no one questions that, at least in some periods of church history, each has been abused. All of these structures were found quite early in the life of the church.

Two crucial issues touch the structure of the church. The first relates to function *vs.* form. *Function* refers to the biblical goals of the church, while *form* refers to how (in terms of structure and programs) those goals are accomplished. Logically, function creates form.[25] The crucial issue

---

[23] *Westminster Confession*, xxxiii.2. Acts 16:4 is cited as scriptural support.

[24] The Roman Catholic church is a variation of this form of government, with the addition of the papacy and the strong priority given to church tradition over Scripture. This discussion has focused upon the Protestant church. We should also note that some groups such as Quakers advocate no form of government.

[25] Forms of evangelism, worship, discipleship, and personal ministry may need to change in order to accomplish the same goals. A common problem for many churches is that once forms have been created, they tend to become indestructible. See Jim Petersen, "The Eclipse of the Gospel," *Discipleship Journal* 55 (1990), p. 12.

for any local church is not what form its programs take, but whether or not it fulfills the function for which God instituted the church.

The second issue is leadership. The qualifications by which Scripture describes elders and deacons are to be taken seriously. These qualities are not necessarily related to popularity or success but to godly character (1 Tim. 3; Titus 1). They do not describe what leaders are to do but rather what they are to be. God clearly requires that Christian leaders be men of integrity and honor, whom even those outside the church will respect and admire (1 Tim. 3:7).

When these two issues are in biblical balance, the goals for the church will be in proper perspective. But what are the goals for the church? We will consider the task for the future as we examine three major goals in the next section.

The Mission of the Church:
A View for the Future

The church can be seen in action in many spheres of our complex culture. Campus ministries, groups of Christian professionals or businessmen, Christian colleges, and missions organizations fulfill different aspects of the church's ministry. These parachurch organizations, which are recent in origin, derive their purpose and function from the local church.

God created the church to accomplish three main goals: first, *intimacy* with God; second, *community* with believers; third, *mission* to the world.[26] These remain constant as the function of the church into the future, regardless of the forms used to reach these goals.

Intimacy with God (Upward)

The goal of individuals within the worshiping church is the same as that of the apostle Paul: "That I may know Him" (Phil. 3:10). The worship of the church promotes experiential and intellectual knowledge of Jesus Christ.

---

[26] Wayne Jacobsen, "Caring for the Overextended," *Leadership* (Winter 1990), p. 33.

Worship

Worship is not defined in the Bible. Different words are used to translate concepts we associate with worship,[27] and they seem to cluster around two ideas: *internal* feelings of reverence, and *external* prostration before Jesus. Both are reactions to being in the presence of a holy God.

Experiences and feelings by themselves, however, do not constitute worship. When the Israelites worked up substantial feelings in their "worship" services and even covered God's altar with their tears, they were not necessarily worshiping God (Mal. 2:13). Rather, worship of God must be done in Spirit and in truth (John 4:24). This includes the teaching role of the church.

Teaching

God the Spirit has given His truth to the church for her instruction and learning. One of the primary functions of the corporate meeting of believers is to receive instruction in God's Word (Acts 6:4; Eph. 4:11-13; 2 Tim. 3:14-4:2). The church is to teach its worshipers to be both hearers and doers of Scripture (James 1:22).

When both worship and teaching are a vital part of the church, Christians are strengthened to cope with earthly challenges. Their eyes are not on the world but on Christ (Heb. 12:2), and their mission as His ambassadors takes priority over all else (2 Cor. 5:15-21).

Community among Believers (Inward)

The most visible pictures of the communion of believers are the two ordinances[28] of the church: the initiatory rite of baptism and the continuing rite of the *Lord's Supper*. Baptism is the means by which believers are publicly associated with Christ and identified with His Body, the church.[29] It is a one-time action that speaks of a decision to accept Jesus Christ as Savior, and is an outward indication of an inward

---

[27] *Leiturgia, latreuo, proskuneo, sebomai, threskeia.* For a helpful discussion of each see Terry Miethe, *The New Christian's Guide to Following Jesus* (Minneapolis: Bethany, 1982), p. 69.

[28] Some prefer the term sacrament. From its original usage, it connotes something of the idea of mystery (it was used in Latin to translate the Greek *mysterion*). Therefore, those groups that view the ordinances as more than a remembrance of Christ tend to use the term sacrament.

[29] For clear examples of association/identification, see Mark 10:38-39 and I Cor. 12:13.

change. All believers are to be obedient to this command and example of the Lord (Matt. 28:19; Acts 2:37-38).

The second ordinance is the Lord's Supper. Jesus commanded believers to partake of the symbolic bread and cup in order to remember the Lord's death until He comes (Matt. 26:26-28; 1 Cor. 11:23-29). This continuous activity represents the ongoing "feeding" upon Christ as believers participate together in true "communion."

There are also other ways the communion of believers may be expressed besides the ordinances. Christians are to meet together regularly for fellowship and worship (Heb. 10:25). The early Christians met at least on a weekly basis (1 Cor. 16:2; Acts 20:7), sometimes more often than that (Acts 2:46), to "stimulate one another to love and good deeds" and to encourage each other (Heb. 10:24-25). A significant part of this communion was mutual bearing of burdens (Gal. 6:2). Sometimes the bearing of burdens was financial (Acts 4:32-35; 11:29; James 2:8, 15-16); at other times this responsibility included confrontation and church discipline (Matt. 18:15-17; 1 Cor. 5:1-5; Gal. 6:1).

The reason for this family intimacy is that believers are members of one another (1 Cor. 12:12-27). Such involvement fulfills God's commandment for servanthood (Phil. 2:1-4), which Jesus said is the defining characteristic of Christian greatness (Mark 10:43-45).

John White points out that as a Christian I have no free will to choose whom my brothers and sisters are, or whether or not I will be committed to them. "They belong to us and we to them. We have no control over the fact that we are to love, care and be responsible for them."[30] I owe Christ everything; He demands that my indebtedness to Him be transferred to my new family, the family of God. Some Christians may attract me; others may seem repugnant, and the feeling may be reciprocal. Even so, "You are not to confine yourself to the favorite few. You are committed to the freaks and oddballs of the lunatic fringe as well as to those Christians about whom you feel highly critical. You belong to people whose views you disagree with."[31]

The basis of Christian fellowship (*koinonia*) is not found within the Christian or his brother; the basis is found in Christ alone. As J. Y. Campbell explained, "The primary idea expressed by *koinonos* and its cognates is not that of association with another person or persons, but that of participation in something in which others also participate."[32] The

---

[30] John White, *The Fight* (Downers Grove, IL: InterVarsity, 1976), p. 130.
[31] Ibid.
[32] J. Y. Campbell, "KOINONIA and Its Cognates in the NT," *Journal of Biblical Literature* 51(1932):353, cited by Clowney in *The Church*, p. 51.

biblical idea of fellowship is not the camaraderie of a social club but keeping Christ central to all thoughts and activities. The fellowship of the church includes the sharing of joys and sorrows (1 Cor. 12:26). Hurt is reduced by being shared; joy is increased by being shared.[33]

There is great freedom here. If the Body of Christ functions as God intended, then we belong to a body of people who should always love and accept us whether or not we are attractive or successful, because their commitment to us is not based on their admiration for us but on Christ's Person and work.[34] This does not happen naturally, but supernaturally. To the degree that Christ is "the Head" of individual Christians, the corporate Body of Christ will follow its Head and will function as a body. And the proper functioning of the Body of Christ (inward ministry) will have immediate results in one of the other tasks of the church, witnessing (outward ministry).

Mission to the World (Outward)

The task of the church is to make disciples (Matt. 28:18-20). Jesus said that those who follow Him are to be His "witnesses" (Acts 1:8). This mandate is rooted in the authority of our Lord, and is encouraged by His continuing presence with His witnesses ("I am with you always, even to the end of the age," Matt. 28:20).

On the individual level, the idea of being a witness has become confused with questions of techniques and methods.

> Some people "witness" by carrying leatherbound Bibles, others by giving tracts to service station attendants or leaving literature in public toilets. Many sport bumper stickers ranging from the ancient fish symbol to "Honk if you love Jesus." Yet others erect roadside billboards. . . . Some older postreformation groups witness by their dress. Amish and Mennonite men of certain groups do not wear ties or shave their beards, feeling that it would be worldly to do so.[35]

Some well-meaning groups teach methods of gospel presentation by "flow chart" or by surveys whose results will never be tabulated. But this is to make abnormal and complex what God intended to be simple. "Witnessing and projecting an image are not the same thing."[36] As a witness a Christian is someone who is "truthful about what he has seen,

---

[33] Erickson, p. 1056.
[34] White, *The Fight*, p. 132.
[35] Ibid., pp. 62-63.
[36] Ibid., p. 66.

heard, or personally experienced"[37] about Jesus Christ. He is to be genuine and not overconfident that he knows the answers to every objection that might be raised. "The task of a witness is not to convert people nor to 'clinch a deal' but to supply them with the data by means of which the Holy Spirit brings conviction to them."[38] Therefore he must respond honestly to questions from a biblical worldview, for he can do no less.

An effective Christian witness is able both to articulate and defend his faith (1 Pet. 3:15) and to incarnate its truth through a consistent Christian life. Christians have been granted the ministry of reconciliation and serve as ambassadors of Christ. Because Christ makes His appeal to the unsaved through individual Christians, the believer's walk must match his talk so that the gospel is not hindered (2 Cor. 5:15-21).

On the corporate level, the fellowship of believers is one of the most effective "tools" for Christian witness.

> The church that convinces men that there is a God in heaven is a church that manifests what only a heavenly God can do, that is, to unite human beings in heavenly love. . . . There is nothing on earth which convinces men about heaven or that awakens their craving for it like the discovery of Christian brothers who love one another.[39]

Even though unbelievers rarely if ever entered the meetings of the early church (1 Cor. 14:23 only hints at the possibility), Jesus was quite specific about the external witness of the church: "By this all men will know that you are My disciples, if you have love for one another" (John 13:35). This served as the church's only advertising campaign in the first century and has continued to be the most effective one it has ever had. God instituted the family and the church to meet our horizontal needs of fulfillment and loneliness. To the people who long for intimacy with others, we say that the Good Shepherd knows His sheep personally (John 10:27), not just by computer code.

The church is to be characterized by openness to all. Distinctions that may matter to government and society are unimportant as individuals stand together under Christ. Whether those differences be racial ("neither Jew nor Greek"), economic and social ("neither slave nor free man"), or gender-related ("neither male nor female"), the fact is that "you are all one in Christ Jesus" (Gal. 3:28). When Christians truly "do

---

[37] Ibid., p. 61.
[38] Ibid., p. 75.
[39] Ibid., pp. 149-150.

nothing from selfishness or empty conceit, but with humility of mind let each of you regard one another as more important than himself" (Phil. 2:3), there is a feeling of belonging and acceptance that is contagious and winsome to people who are hurting deeply.

Conclusion

Individually, Christians are not doing well. As a brief perusal of most Christian bookstores will attest, many more books are oriented toward helping Christians cope with personal problems than ever before. In the first century, Christians were concerned about how to impact their world. Today, Christians seem more concerned about how the world has impacted them.

Corporately, the church is not doing well. I remember the incredible optimism evangelicals had in 1980, anticipating our greatest ever impact over the next decade. That decade is now history. During the last week of 1989, two television networks offered specials summarizing the highlights of the previous decade. The only attention evangelicals received on those hour-long shows was three spots highlighting scandals involving Christian leaders. This was the media summary of the evangelical legacy.

The church has the best news of all for the world. Jesus Christ offers hope for the hopeless. We freely admit that we are sinners; we identify with Isaiah in our intense awareness of both personal and public sin (Isa. 6:1-6). But we proclaim with joy that we are sinners who have been redeemed by the grace of God through faith in our Lord Jesus Christ. Hours before He was arrested and crucified, Jesus prayed for the future church. Of all the things He could have mentioned, He really prayed only for one thing—unity (John 17:20-23). His reason was not just that believers would meet the needs of each other (though this is important) but "that the world may believe . . . [and] know that Thou didst send Me" (John 17:21, 23).

As we seek to obey the Lord corporately and individually, we are to be salt and light in our society (Matt 5:13-16). Although salt enhances the taste of foods (Job 6:6), the function of a preservative is in view. The believer is to be an agent in the world that helps delay moral decay by living a consistent Christian life. The danger is in losing one's saltiness. Technically this is impossible, for sodium chloride is not like a battery that can eventually lose its charge. The point, however, is that foreign elements can be added to salt; it is then no longer useful. The danger for the Christian is that we will become double-minded. With so much of the world in us that we cannot enjoy Christ, and so much of Christ in us that we cannot enjoy the world, we become totally ineffective and unstable (James 1:8).

Light is another common metaphor in the Bible, found twenty-one times in John's gospel alone. Collectively, believers are to be a spiritual beacon in the world. Individually, we are to serve as lights in the world (Phil. 2:15), not because of our intrinsic glow but because of our connectedness with the unique Light (John 8:12), Jesus Christ (Eph. 5:8; see Rev. 2:5).

Both of these metaphors make the point that for the church and its impact on the world, actions do speak louder than words. We are to fulfill our upward, inward, and outward ministries faithfully, adapting our methods, though not our message, to the changing needs of our culture. We are to function as salt and light, both individually (as members of a local church) and corporately (as "the church"), so that as a watching world observes our good works our Father will be glorified (Matt. 5:16).

DISCUSSION QUESTIONS

1. If you had an unsaved friend and wanted to show him the Body of Christ in action, where would you take him? To a worship service, an all-church picnic, or a church basketball game? Why?
2. What are the ordinances of the church, and how do they contribute to the ongoing life of a local church?
3. Describe the inward, outward, and upward ministries of the church.
4. What does it mean for Christians to function as salt and light in this world? What are some ways in which we have failed in our task? What can we do, as individuals and as local churches, to close the "credibility gap" and fulfill this responsibility?
5. If, on a personal level, you simply do not like an individual in your church, what is your responsibility toward him or her? (See Eph. 4:11-5:1.)
6. Read the following passages and list specific responsibilities God has given Christians toward each other: Philippians 2:1-4; Galatians 6:1-5; Ephesians 4:11-5:1; Romans 14:1-15:13; 1 Corinthians 12:12-31.

Further Reading

Allen, Ronald B. and Gordon Borror. *Worship: Rediscovering the Missing Jewel*. Portland, OR: Multnomah, 1982.

Beasley-Murray, G. R. *Baptism in the New Testament*. Grand Rapids: Eerdmans, 1962.

Coleman, Robert E. *The Master Plan of Discipleship*. Old Tappan, NJ: Revell, 1987.

Erickson, Millard. *Christian Theology*, vol. 3. Grand Rapids: Baker, 1985, pp. 1025-1148.

Kane, J. Herbert. *Understanding Christian Missions*. Grand Rapids: Baker, 1974.

Martin, Ralph P. *Worship in the Early Church*. Grand Rapids: Eerdmans, 1964.

Moore, T. M. *Culture Matters: A Call for Consensus on Christian Cultural Engagement*. Grand Rapids, MI: Brazos, 2007.

Pearcey, Nancy. *Total Truth: Liberating Christianity from its Cultural Captivity*. Wheaton, IL: Crossway, 2004.

Schaeffer, Francis A. *The Church at the End of the 20th Century*. Downers Grove, IL: InterVarsity, 1970.

Strauch, Alexander. *Biblical Eldership*. Littleton, CO: Lewis & Roth, 1986.

Vanhoozer, Kevin J., ed. *Everyday Theology: How to Read Cultural Texts and Interpret Trends*. Grand Rapids, MI: Baker, 2007.

Wells, David. *God in the Wasteland: The Reality of Truth in a World of Fading Dreams*. Grand Rapids, MI: Eerdmans, 1994.

Wells, David. *No Place for Truth: Or Whatever Happened to Evangelical Theology*. Grand Rapids, MI: Eerdmans, 1993.

Wells, David. *Above All Earthly Pow'rs: Christ in a Postmodern World*. Grand Rapids, MI: Eerdmans, 2006.

11
A VIEW OF AND FOR THE WORLD

Living in Two Worlds
The Natural World
    The Environmental Situation
    Roots of Indifference
    A Biblical Perspective
    A Biblical Response
The Social World
    Children of Our Culture
    Issues of Our Culture
    Attitudes toward Our Culture
        Separation
        Reconciliation
        Transformation
    Challenge of Our Culture
        The Working Life
        Media and Entertainment
    Morality of Our Culture

Living in Two Worlds

The 1985 scene is now famous: forty-five rock musicians linking arms and swaying to the steady rhythm of the song "We Are the World," a piece which expressed universal solidarity. Bob Geldof, a performer with the British rock group Boom Town Rats, organized the event after seeing television reports of the devastating drought in parts of Africa. Famine, disease, and death ravaged the population, particularly that of Ethiopia, and little was being done to help them.

Today, "save the world" conscientiousness takes the form of concerts, protests, campaigns, and documentaries. The global awareness captured by these events is a remarkable reminder that the world is no longer out there—it is right here. The plight of people halfway around the globe has become as important as the concerns of our next door neighbor. But it does not stop there. Often, it extends beyond the human needs of starvation and disease to include rescuing dogs and cats from biomedical research, snail darters (fish) from dam-building, the air and rivers from pollution, the land from development, and the planet from fossil fuels.

Amid the clamor, what does a biblical worldview have to say? In other words, What is a biblical worldview in this context? The term *world* is generally used with a dual focus: the natural world and the social world. The Bible also refers to the "world" (Greek, *kosmos*) in these two ways.[1] The first is the *kosmos* of the created, physical realm (Matt. 24:21). This is the natural world—the world of mountains, seas, plants, and animals. The second is the *kosmos* of the created, personal realm (Matt. 4:8; John 3:16). This is the social world—the world of people, cultures, and societies.

Applying a biblical perspective to the broader concerns in the world has not always been an integral part of Christian thinking. A biblical worldview is usually applied to personal regeneration, personal decision-making, family, and church. Any reference to the world is usually a plea for evangelism and missions. For many, the social world and the natural world seem extraneous to the personal religion of the Christian. How does the Bible address these concerns? We shall look in turn at a biblical view for the world from the perspective of the natural world, and then from the perspective of the social world.

The Natural World

Responding to the needs of the natural realm seems to be the purview of rock stars and "whole-earth" activists. Hollywood personalities invest their talents and dollars to preserve the environment and save the animals. Environmental organizations force campaigning politicians to take a stand on ecological issues and promise government funds for preservation and cleanup. Membership and financial support for groups such as Greenpeace USA and the World Wildlife Fund are some of the biggest gainers among non-profit organizations. The ecological bandwagon takes on riders at a dizzying rate. What in the world has caused this environmental clamor?

---

[1] The complexities of the various meanings of *kosmos* are explored by Hermann Sasse in *Theological Dictionary of the New Testament*, ed. Gerhard Kittel and Gerhard Friedrich, 10 vols. (Grand Rapids: Eerdmans, 1964-76), 3:868-98.

The Environmental Situation

First we must try to make sense out of all the current claims. To gain a perspective, the present concern for ecological integrity is a relatively recent phenomenon. At one time there were no environmental institutes or popular movements to preserve nature. Today, most nations have some governmental arm to monitor environmental concerns.

Ecological awareness, at least as we are experiencing it today, began to develop in the early sixties as part of a larger concern for humanity and the global quality of life. As technology began to dominate the social life of Americans, the producing, using, and discarding of products seriously affected the natural environment. As a result, many conclude that the current state of affairs is a crisis, with "nature" as the hostage in danger of extinction.

Actually defining the environmental situation is difficult. The natural world may be divided into four interrelated spheres: air, water, plants, and animals. The interruption of the natural environmental processes results in any number of ecological crises. Man's intervention with technology and industry has produced many concerns about the future of planet earth. Air and water pollution threaten the basic sources of nourishment for life. The elimination of many species of animals for commercial purposes affects the biological cycle in ways that are yet to be measured. The destruction of forests, especially the tropical forests of South America, damages the earth's ability to replenish oxygen in the atmosphere. Further concerns arise from offshore oil drilling, the use of pesticides, and the frantic rate of residential and commercial development.

An even graver problem is seen when the combination of several of these factors is considered from a global perspective. The release into the air of carbon dioxide (from burning fossil fuels), chlorofluorocarbons (from refrigerators, air conditioners, and aerosol spray cans), and methane gas (from coal mining, livestock, and landfills) forms a barrier trapping the sun's heat in the earth's atmosphere. This phenomenon, known as the greenhouse effect, is said to result in global warming, rising sea levels, changing climates, and even temperatures too high to sustain human life. Alarmists argue that the potential effects of this will be devastating and that it may be too late for responsible action. Others argue that humans are not able to have that level of impact on the planet, and that the results of warming will bring more good than harm.

When we survey the array of environmental dysfunctions, the most sobering thought is that often little regard has been given to the effect certain activities will have on the environment. Further, a naive belief pervades Western society that if a crisis endangers human existence, science will find a way to overcome the problem. The underlying attitude toward the natural world is indifference—we use anything that is "not-man" to increase our comfort and quality of life.

Roots of Indifference

Such a view toward the environment is a long way from the world-views that see nature as divine or at least a partner in the cycle of life. Many experts point to Christianity as the culprit in the ecological crisis. Lynn White, professor emeritus of history at UCLA, claims that Western society's destructive attitude toward nature lies in the Judeo-Christian tradition: "By destroying pagan animism, Christianity made it possible to exploit nature in a mood of indifference to the feelings of natural objects."[2] White considers science and technology so "tinctured with orthodox Christian arrogance toward nature"[3] that there is little hope for our environment in the present.

Even though many share White's conclusions,[4] his analysis is seriously flawed. Animism's worship of nature had long subsided before many cultures adopted an indifference to the environment. Ecological problems also threaten non-Western societies where the Judeo-Christian tradition has little influence.

However, the attack on a supposed Christian view of nature is not limited to those outside the faith. Christian writer Wesley Granberg-Michaelson charges, "Western Christianity has been quick to stress humanity's role to 'rule and subdue' the earth, providing a godly rationale for the onslaught of modern technology and offering few if any safeguards against the desecration of the earth."[5]

Admittedly, Christian response to environmental issues has been slow, limited, and for the most part obscured by the secular response. There seem to be at least two reasons for this.

The first is found in the spirit of the times leading up to the modern ecological heyday. Spiritual and doctrinal issues overwhelmed any social agenda, and Christians were so theologically preoccupied with man's relationship to God and far-reaching (eternal) spiritual concerns that the

---

[2] Quoted by Paul R. Ehrlich, Anne H. Ehrlich, and John P. Holdren, *Ecoscience: Population, Resources, Environment* (San Francisco: W. H. Freeman, 1977), p. 809.

[3] Ibid., p. 810.

[4] See, for example, Arnold Toynbee, "The Religious Background of the Present Environmental Crisis," in *Ecology and Religion in History*, ed. D. and E. Springs (New York: Harper & Row, 1974).

[5] Wesley Granberg-Michaelson, ed., *Tending the Garden: Essays on the Gospel and the Earth* (Grand Rapids: Eerdmans, 1987), p. 2.

natural (temporal) world was ignored. A new heaven and earth are promised in the Bible, so why devote time and energy to a world that will be destroyed?

Second, the recent association of environmental movements with certain streams of naturalistic and transcendental thought, particularly the New Age movement, makes evangelicals uneasy. New Agers preach that we must save the universe because we are all a part of the single fabric of existence. To preserve the environment is to preserve ourselves. Some see a New Age conspiracy in certain responses to ecological concerns,[6] and the result is that many evangelicals shy away from environmental pursuits to avoid the New Age label.

However, many evangelicals have begun to respond to environmental matters. The rationale is found in a careful understanding of the scriptural perspective of God's purpose for man and the earth.

A Biblical Perspective

A biblical worldview certainly does not present an attitude of indifference toward the natural world. The many passages that describe God's concern and care for His creation are difficult to ignore. From a biblical perspective, the earth belongs to the Lord and is the physical sign of His glory and power (Ps. 19:1; 24:1; Rom. 1:19-21). Living things are dependent upon God for "the breath of life" (Gen. 6:17; 7:15), while the sea, land, and trees are said to offer praise to their Creator (Ps. 96). Psalm 8 is God's invitation to wonder at what He has made: "O Lord, our Lord, how majestic is Thy name in all the earth, who hast displayed Thy splendor above the heavens!" (Ps. 8:1).

The psalmist continues by proclaiming that man has been appointed by God "to rule over the works of Thy hands" because "Thou hast put all things under his feet" (Ps. 8:6). Indeed, the physical world is created "for" mankind (Gen. 1:28; 2:7ff.) but not for the purpose of exploitation. Man was given the mandate to "cultivate and keep" the garden (Gen. 2:15), not to worship or abuse it. Man's "dominion" over the earth is *derived*, that is, he cares for the earth by the authority of God and should treat it as God would.

However, some are not convinced that environmental concerns are necessary for the Christian agenda. Is it not true, they argue, that the physical world is subject to decay and will be transformed when God recreates a new heaven and earth? If so, then why worry about the environment? It will all be changed by God anyway.

---

[6] Constance Cumby, *The Hidden Dangers of the Rainbow: The New Age Movement and Our Coming Age of Barbarism* (Shreveport, LA: Huntington House, 1983), pp. 155ff.

The argument may seem persuasive, yet it falls apart when we apply it to other aspects of God's creation. For example, why take care of our physical bodies? Why exercise or eat the right foods? After all, our bodies will be transformed at the resurrection. Admittedly, the differences between the natural world and our natural bodies are great; yet, an attitude of indifference toward a natural creation of God cannot be justified at any level.

Imagine a prominent artist creating a work of art "for" a group of people he dearly loved. How would the recipients respond to the gift? Would they not care for the work of art as the precious gift that it was? Further, consider if the art was necessary for the very survival of the group and its posterity. Would they not make painstaking efforts to preserve, protect, and enjoy the work?

While Christians may be guilty of focusing attention only upon spiritual matters, it is often forgotten that all creation is included in God's plan of redemption (Rom. 8:18-25). The Lord has total claim of the world: He created and will redeem the physical realm. Christians, of all people, should raise the loudest voices against the abuses foisted upon God's creation.

What may surprise many is that Christians have not been silent. Thousands are motivated to respond to ecological problems on the basis of theological principles and biblical injunctions. For example, the Christian Nature Federation in southern California seeks to re-establish within the natural sciences "the Christian worldview which acknowledges a transcendent, personal, caring God who created the natural world out of nothing, who is sovereign over the affairs of men, and who provides redemption from the effects of the Fall through the Savior, Jesus Christ."[7] Also, the AuSable Institute, located in Michigan, is a resource for Christians to learn about their relationship to the environment. The philosophy of the AuSable Institute is to "confess that God is owner of all. Humankind is not the owner of that over which it has authority. Human authority is more that of trustee than owner. The scope of this trust is global. Since all creatures depend on the earth for life, health, and fulfillment, stewardship is the responsible use and care of creation. This is a clear and repeated testimony of Scripture."[8]

---

[7] Quoted in *World*, 28 October 1989, p. 16.
[8] Quoted in Granberg-Michaelson, *Tending the Garden*, p. vii.

A Biblical Response

A biblical worldview demands some response to environmental issues. Several principles must guide.

First, humanity does take the prominent place in God's plan for His creation. Redemption history is the single thread weaving together God's revelation in the Scriptures. However, we cannot ignore the fact that environmental dysfunctions are the result of man's sin in two developing contexts. Initially, the natural world was subject to corruption because of man's fall (Gen. 3:17-19; Rom. 8:19-22). Current exploitation of the environment arises from man's arrogance and indifference toward God's work.

Second, man's prominence in God's plan in no way justifies an indifference to environmental concerns. Certainly given the biblical passages and themes noted above, God has a high view of His creative work. We must seek to have God's perspective on the natural world.

Third, science and technology cannot completely answer the environmental questions or solve ecological dilemmas. They are tools or, at best, servants to be guided by the moral decisions of humanity. Science did not cause the ecological problems we now have, man's exploitative attitude toward the environment and his misuse of technology is the root cause. Whatever course of action is taken by humanity will also arise from moral considerations.

Fourth, whatever approach we take toward environmental issues must arise from a biblical view of the natural world, not cultural or societal trends. For too long Christians have reacted to public issues with undisguised surprise and emotion. Christians should have been demanding a biblical approach to the environment long before it became fashionable to do so.

A time is coming when God will renew His handiwork. The groanings of creation will never be allayed by mankind's efforts, but tending the garden God has given us can provide a world that preserves the witness to His glory. The old saying is quite true: "We do not inherit the earth from our parents, we borrow it from our children."

The Social World

The natural world seems passive to man. It responds to man's initiatives; it declares God's glory and serves as a constant witness to God's power and presence. Man's confrontation with the created world of nature should be one of reverent, nurturing stewardship. The natural world does not cause wars, it does not tempt man to sin, nor does it pressure him to conform.

Confronting the social world is more problematic: it fights back. The world of people, with its social pressures and conflicting values, frequently sets the agenda for Christian response. Within the social world, Christians have the unique dilemma of living in two different realms: the realm of God and the realm of the world. The guidelines for living in God's realm are spelled out in Scripture. However, the realm of the world follows the rhythm of an uncertain drummer. Most often it places social demands upon each person to live in such a way that fosters harmony and happiness. Sometimes those social demands conflict with the biblical design. How should Christians apply a biblical worldview to the pressures of the social world?

Children of Our Culture

As we briefly discussed in the first chapter, we are all products of our culture, our immediate social world. In the social environment in which we are reared, a whole world of values and accepted behaviors is taught and confirmed. Society determines and conserves what is good and bad, what is right and wrong, and what is beautiful and ugly. These values may be received from an external authority (i.e., the Bible), or they may be self-derived (i.e., social customs, mores, etc.), but they are always present and serve to conform the members of the society to similar patterns of believing and behaving.

The social world includes many avenues of personal expression and relationships. The intangible patterns of cultural behavior seen in daily interactions, family life, and community values are the soul of one's culture. These elements of life shape the thinking and valuing of the members of the society. The expression of these values is usually seen in the creative arenas of a society: art, music, and literature. The proliferation and existence of various kinds of entertainment both express and shape the values of a people. The more formal institutions of society, such as the educational systems and economic structures, determine on a broad scale how the society functions as an integrated whole and how personal needs are met.

The most unique facet of culture is the government. Government alone has the authority to determine behavior (by making laws) and to enforce adherence to that behavior (by punishing lawbreakers). Many of the problems related to modern government are not explicitly addressed in the Bible. For example, the Bible does not commend democracy over autocracy or socialism over communism. However, biblical teachings have led many to favor one form of government over another.[9] What the Bible does dictate is that the purpose of government is to restrain evil and preserve order (Rom. 13:1-7; 1 Pet. 2:13-14). The many forms of government in biblical times, which were present as a background to the writing of Scripture, indicate God's concern for justice over structure.

The social world is neither a friend nor an enemy of God. Biblically, human society is not in itself evil, that is, there is nothing inherently evil about customs, government, art, or literature. However, the Bible speaks often of the "world" as evil and antagonistic to the reign of God. This is true for two reasons. First, society is made up of humans, and humans by nature are depraved (Jer. 17:9; Rom. 3:10-11; Eph. 2:1-3). Therefore, the reality of evil in the heart of every person spoils the aggregate of social structures as well.

Second, beyond man's personal evil is the reality of the spiritual world that influences social systems. Satan is called "the god of this age" (2 Cor. 4:4) and "the ruler of the kingdom of the air" (Eph. 2:2) who continually works to bend the course of the world toward his direction (Eph. 6:12). The apostle John states emphatically that "the whole world lies in the power of the evil one" (1 John 5:19), and James warns Christians to avoid sympathetic association with the world (James 1:27; 4:4). Theologian Robert Webber concludes, "Satan works through the structures of society to distort, pervert and disfigure that which is good. No part of the created order can escape the influence and power of Satan."[10]

Does this mean the social world is totally godless? Are there any aspects of the social world God has salvaged for His purposes? Should Christians ever involve themselves in the affairs of the social world or should they write it off as destined for destruction?

Issues of Our Culture

There is no question that Christians are to guide their lives by the authority of God mediated through the Scriptures. Questions arise, however, when the Christian must "go public." Do the biblical mandates for godliness and moral purity apply only to the Christian's personal life,

---

[9] See, for example, the essays and bibliographies in Richard John Neuhaus and Michael Cromartie, eds., *Piety and Politics: Evangelicals and Fundamentalists Confront the World* (Washington, DC: Ethics and Public Policy Center, 1987); also Ronald H. Nash, *Poverty and Wealth: The Christian Debate Over Capitalism* (Westchester, IL: Crossway, 1986).

[10] Robert Webber, *The Church in the World* (Grand Rapids: Zondervan, 1986), p. 27.

or should they be extended to all of society? This conflict between private and public morality is at the heart of the Christian's dilemma.

Should Christians (and their churches) concern themselves with social issues? Many contemporary evangelicals have answered yes. The current evangelical social agenda is to confront "the tide of moral decline in American culture."[11] Key moral and public concerns in the immediate American society include the following:

Life/Death Issues

>   Reproductive technologies
>   Medical ethics
>   Genetic enhancement
>   Abortion
>   Euthanasia
>   Capital punishment

Individual Rights Issues

>   Women (equal rights)
>   Homosexuals (personal rights)
>   Minorities (civil rights)
>   Poor (welfare rights)
>   Human trafficking

Public Education Issues

>   Place of religion in public schools
>   School choice
>   Teaching creation/evolution
>   Teaching sex education, including gender and sexual orientation

National Defense Issues

>   Confronting global terrorism
>   Place of United Nations
>   Nuclear weapons/power
>   Military spending

---

[11] James Davidson Hunter, *Evangelicalism: The Coming Generation* (Chicago: U. of Chicago, 1987), p. 125.

These do not include the many issues involved in the broader questions of economic and governmental reform. There is little agreement in American culture concerning the "right" position on each of the above issues. Many evangelical writers are attempting to address these and many other issues from a biblical perspective for the purpose of setting out a biblical response. But even evangelical Christians disagree on what view is the right (i.e., "biblical") view and what agenda the Christian should follow.[12] Declarations have attempted to address social issues with a united Christian front (for example, "A Declaration of Evangelical Social Concern" of November 1973 and "The Oxford Declaration on Christian Faith and Economics" of January 1990), but mobilization of Christians has been fragmented and inconsistent.

Attitudes toward Our Culture

A biblical worldview may lead one to a specific position on an issue, but should a Christian work to conform society to this moral stance? If so, by what means should one's culture be changed? Historically, the answer has been worked out from three different perspectives with differing agendas: separation, reconciliation, and transformation.[13]

Separation: The Christian Avoiding the World

From a separatistic perspective, the "world" is fundamentally antagonistic to God and the spiritual realm. There is no hope for its transformation, and therefore engaging society or the government in any form of interaction is futile for the Christian. Christians are to live by the norms of God's kingdom, as described in the Scriptures. Secular society is to be ignored. Although Christians cannot always escape some influence of the world, they must respond to the call "'Come out from their midst and be separate, says the Lord" (2 Cor. 6:17). Christians are "aliens and strangers" (1 Pet. 2:11) in this present world, which is epitomized by spiritual darkness and evil (1 John 2:15-16; 5:19).

---

[12] A survey of contemporary books and periodicals by evangelicals demonstrates the diversity of thought. For the views of "the coming generation" of evangelicals, see Hunter, *Evangelicalism*, pp. 130-54.

[13] Webber points out that these three approaches follow a chronological development of church history. The separation approach was reflected in the early church; the reconciliation approach has antecedents in early Constantinianism; and the transformation approach is rooted in Augustine and elaborated in the early medieval period. It is interesting to note that all three approaches were utilized by the Reformers: the Anabaptists, Luther, and Calvin respectively. See Robert Webber, *The Church in the World*, p. 81.

How this separation from the world is carried out has varied. Some physically disassociate themselves from the influence of the world, as did the medieval monks, the modern Amish, and similar traditions. Because a complete physical separation is difficult in contemporary society, some groups take a social and philosophical approach to "coming out from among them." While maintaining employment in the "world," the rest of the individual's life revolves around the local church. Government and society are attacked from the pulpit and in daily conversation as being godless and anti-Christian. In many cases, alternate institutions are set up to shield the Christian from social interaction with the world. The only accepted engagement with secular society is for the purpose of evangelism.

A somewhat similar separatistic approach to cultural engagement dominated the agenda of post-Depression fundamentalists. Armed with the expectation of Christ's imminent return, fundamentalist Christians focused on personal evangelism, usually ignoring involvement in social issues. Christianity was counter-cultural in the extreme, not a part of culture.

This view of Christianity and the world grows steadily weaker. With minor exceptions, most mainline and fundamental evangelicals agree that interaction with the world is not only inevitable but necessary to accomplish the will of God. The gospel of Jesus Christ has social implications, as do God's calls for justice and compassion on the part of social institutions.

However, the separatist approach does have positive features. It gives a helpful insight into the distinction between God's will and the ways of the world. The antagonism is real, not imagined. Further, many who have practiced a separatistic approach have demonstrated that the secular pressures to conformity can be overcome.

On the other hand, the separatist approach is somewhat impractical in its application to daily life. Although some persons may be able to withdraw from worldly influences, most Christians have neither the resources nor the opportunity to disengage completely from the world. Then, of course, there is always the problem of degree: where are we to draw the line in the separation? Further, the separatist approach runs counter to the pattern of godly servants in the Bible who were very much *in* the world but not *of* the world. Joseph, Nehemiah, and Daniel are but a few such examples of outstanding individuals who are highly praised for their application of godly principles to their social world.

Reconciliation: The Christian Befriending the World

The mention of Joseph, Nehemiah, and Daniel reminds us of the biblical accounts of those who maintained a commitment to God's principles while spending most of their lives in what believers today would consider "secular" service. This social and spiritual détente recognizes the superiority of God's law while acknowledging the legitimate place and authority of social institutions.

The reconciliation approach appeals to Paul's affirmation that Christians are to obey the governing authorities and be in subjection to them (Rom. 13:1). Paul follows this admonition with the pronouncement that all authority (including social authority mediated through the government) is established by God. In light of the social and political context in which Paul wrote these words, his command is even more striking. Lest there be any doubt concerning the authorities that were to be respected, Peter adjures Christians to "honor the king" (1 Pet. 2:17).

The reconciliation approach is not a capitulation to secular society but rather the recognition of the biblical role that social structures play in God's plan. Thus, at most points, what the government ordains, God ordains (Rom. 13:2). Government may be God's servant (Rom. 13:4), not His enemy. It is the necessary means by which order and peace are preserved among men.

However, because the Christian lives in two realms, conflict is inevitable. There are limits to the obedience a Christian must exercise toward social authorities. When such an authority conflicts with a command of God, Christians have no other option but to "obey God rather than men" (Acts 5:29). Biblical examples of such conflicts clearly represent the pattern to follow (Dan. 3:6; Acts 4:5). Today it is illegal in some countries for Christians to worship and evangelize; yet, like the apostle Peter, many continue to "break the law" in order to obey the higher authority of God's law.

Those involved with the Operation Rescue program appealed to this conflict as the rationale for their obstruction of abortion clinics. The secular law permits abortion, they argued, but God's law does not. Therefore, they feel justified breaking the immoral worldly law in order to promote the law of God. It is debatable whether or not this reasoning is a correct application of the principle of appealing to a higher authority;[14] nevertheless, their approach was one form of reconciliation.

---

[14] For differing perspectives on the legitimacy of the Operation Rescue agenda see Randall Terry, *Operation Rescue* (Springdale, PA: Whitaker House, 1988) and J. M. Connors, "Operation Rescue" *America* (29 April 1989), 160:400-402.

Most evangelical groups would fall into this category. The moral agenda of the reconciliation approach is not to change or "Christianize" the structure of society or government, but rather to ensure that morality and justice prevail. How morality and justice are advanced in society is currently worked out with different programs among Christians. On the one hand, the fundamentalist right seeks for a return to "traditional values" and less government involvement in the affairs of everyday life. Politically, the fundamentalists lobby for "laws promoting morality," that is, laws against abortion, illegal drugs, pornography; laws for school prayer and the like. The most obvious example of this approach is the now-defunct Moral Majority.[15]

On the other hand, the evangelical radical left equates a moral government with a system that ensures justice for all people, help for the poor and needy, and care for the ill. They argue for *more* government involvement in the affairs of everyday life to carry out the biblical mandate to meet the needs of our brothers. They claim that our current system has resulted in the exploitation of many who cannot afford health care, job training, and adequate housing. The moral failure of individuals (including Christians) who ignore these needs places the burden upon a "government of the people" to promote biblical justice in society. This approach is advanced by such groups as Evangelicals for Social Action and periodicals such as *The Other Side* and *Sojourners*.[16]

A reconciliation approach that shuns political involvement is the resurgence of the Anabaptist tradition which urges the church to allow the Christian community to mold social ethics.[17] The life of Jesus is the pattern for all Christians to follow. Neither He nor His followers possessed genuine political authority, yet Jesus and the Christian movement were agents of radical social change.

---

[15] For a full description of the agenda for the fundamentalist right, see Jerry Falwell, Ed Dobson, and Ed Hindson, eds., *The Fundamentalist Phenomenon: The Resurgence of Conservative Christianity* (New York: Doubleday, 1981).

[16] Good sources for an exposition of the evangelical radical left are the periodicals mentioned above and Ronald J. Sider, *Rich Christians in an Age of Hunger*, 2d ed. (Downers Grove, IL: InterVarsity, 1984); and Jim Wallis, ed., *The Rise of Christian Conscience* (San Francisco: Harper & Row, 1987).

[17] See John Howard Yoder, *The Politics of Jesus* (Grand Rapids: Eerdmans, 1972); *The Priestly Kingdom: Social Ethics as Gospel* (Notre Dame, IN: U. of Notre Dame, 1986); and James William McClendon, Jr., *Ethics: Systematic Theology* (Nashville: Abingdon, 1986).

Jesus acknowledged the believer's responsibility to governing authorities ("Render unto Caesar. . . . "), but also forged a path of nonviolence and peacemaking. In this way, Christians intimidate worldly powers by the sheer force of their moral authority. For example, Queen Mary feared the prayers of John Knox more than the fire power of the Spanish Armada. Entire nations have been influenced toward social change by the nonviolent approaches of Dietrich Bonhoeffer, Martin Luther King, Jr., Mother Teresa, Dorothy Day, John Wesley, and a host of other social activists.

Christians are to recognize that their social ethics and agenda are peculiar in the eyes of the world and will be the object of scorn and even attack, yet the Lord Himself will vindicate a godly, uncompromising confrontation with the social world. The Anabaptist approach will engage society with nonpolitical, nonviolent means of overcoming discrimination, pornography, abortion, and other outward manifestations of moral disease. The life-changing message of the gospel must be at the heart of any efforts of social change.[18]

Whether fundamentalist right, radical left, or Anabaptist, the reconciliation approach accepts God's authority as primary while acknowledging the biblical legitimacy of secular social institutions. A pluralistic society is not only accepted but expected. In many ways, modern society is a great deal like the pluralism of the first century when Christianity was born. The Christian community, however, will not allow the prevailing social ethos to dictate the church's agenda for spreading the truth of God into society.

The most difficult problem faced by the reconciliation approach is, again, where to draw the line. There is a wide range of possible areas of agreement and disagreement in the application of this view. Some Christians will adopt a laissez faire attitude toward social issues while at the same time seeking to be good citizens and Christians. Others zealously involve themselves in political or social action groups in order to call secular society into account for its unbiblical tendencies.

Transformation: The Christian Renewing the World

The zealous involvement of some Christians mentioned above is an extreme position for the reconciliation approach but characteristic for those who adopt the transformation approach. The goal of the transformationists is to bring the "secular world" into obedience to the "sacred realm" of God. For the transformationist, there is no distinction

---

[18] For an excellent exploration of the practical application of the Anabaptist approach, see Stanley Hauerwas and William H. Willimon, *Resident Aliens: Life in the Christian Colony* (Nashville: Abingdon, 1989).

between sacred and secular. All is God's. Some elements of God's reign have rejected Him and continue in a state of rebellion, but the Lord is still the authority in all affairs of life.

The work of Christ, it is believed, is more than merely a spiritual pardon for sin, but it is "cosmic in scope."[19] Christians are to involve themselves in the process whereby all creation "will be set free from its slavery to corruption into the freedom of the glory of the children of God" (Rom. 8:21). Then, and only then, will Christ "have first place in everything" (Col. 1:13-18). The very structure of society must be reformed under the lordship of Jesus Christ. All civil magistrates must bow the knee to God who grants them authority.

Unlike the reconciliationists, those who hold to a transformation approach have no room for a legitimate pluralistic society. All authorities are commanded by God to "worship the Lord with reverence . . . [and] do homage to the Son" (Ps. 2:11, 12). Therefore, all aspects of society— government, economics, law, education—must be under the singular authority of God's law. There is no latitude for alternate views.

How this transformation is accomplished is not always clear. Different representations of this approach have been seen historically, for example, in the Holy Roman Empire and in some of the early Puritan societies. In these cases, the state bowed to the dictates of the church. There was not a state-church, rather there was a church-state. The law of God (as understood by the church leaders of the time) determined the moral foundation for civil legislation.

The most obvious form of modern transformational thought is seen in the theonomist movement. Theonomy (from *theos*, "God," and *nomos*, "law"; also known as Christian reconstructionism) seeks a radical reform of American society to bring it into conformity to God's laws. God's law is defined as the moral and civil teachings of the Old Testament. This excludes those aspects of the ceremonial law that were specifically fulfilled by Christ or abrogated by the New Testament.[20] In other words, the civil law code of ancient Israel is accepted as the God-ordained pattern for a biblical view of society and government.

The transformationist approach will always be fraught with questions. At the heart of the problem is the idea of superimposing the Old Testament law onto modern society. Was God's specific legislation

---

[19] Richard Mouw, *When the Kings Come Marching In* (Grand Rapids: Eerdmans, 1983), p. 63.

[20] For a full explanation of the teachings of theonomy, see the writings of R. J. Rushdoony, Gary North, and Greg Bahnsen. The most succinct description of the application of theonomy can be found in Greg Bahnsen, *Theonomy in Christian Ethics*, 2d ed. (Phillipsburg, NJ: Presby. & Ref., 1984).

for Israel intended to be the only acceptable pattern of civil government? Not everyone agrees that the Old Testament civil law should be enforced in modern society. Theonomists often criticize those who disagree by claiming that they "only accept part of the Bible as valid for our age,"[21] an unusual charge because even theonomists do not live by the details of the Mosaic law. When the Bible does describe guidelines for government, the form it outlines is a totalitarian state governed by rulers in a family succession (Deut. 17:14-20). Such a form is arguably unworkable in modern Western society.

In addition, the distinctions made by theonomists among the civil, moral, and ceremonial laws of the Old Testament are somewhat artificial. These distinctions may be helpful in categorizing the various spheres of application of the law for Israel, but to use such nonbiblical categories as a means for accepting some for today (civil and moral) and rejecting others (ceremonial) is inappropriate.

There will always be difficulty in understanding the discontinuities between the Old Covenant and the New. However, the New Testament is clear that the law served as a "tutor" until Christ came (Gal. 3:18-19, 23-25). Jesus Christ came and fulfilled the whole law (Matt. 5:17-19), not merely the ceremonial aspects of Israel's ordinances. Jesus is "the end of the law" to all who believe (Rom. 10:4).

What can be accepted by all is: the lordship of Jesus Christ over all the earth; the sole source of morality located in the revelation of God; and the legitimacy of civil authority as a servant of God. The Christian faces the challenge of holiness in the personal sphere and wholeness in the public square.

Challenge of Our Culture

Our day is besieged with moral and social difficulties. Abortion and pornography are allowed by the government; how should the Christian respond? The judicial system is riddled with inequities; should a prophetic voice be raised? Prejudice and discrimination against minorities continues; should Christians take a stand?

Everyday life oozes with unbiblical and antitheistic values: the sensuality and violence of television and other forms of media; the "God-neutral" approach to learning in public education; the societal partiality toward the rich, the powerful, and the young; the pragmatic ethics that justify lying and cheating in the pursuit of "having it all." How does the Christian determine the correct response?

---

[21] Kevin L. Clauson, "The Christian America Response to Theonomy" in *God and Politics*, p. 64. Clauson is not a theonomist but is sympathetic with this aspect of their teaching.

The three approaches described in this chapter all reflect a biblical response to the pressures of the world. Separation will one day be a reality; social institutions will one day be reconciled to God's standards; and the world will one day be transformed. Until the perfect has come, however, Christians are left with the responsibility to make a difference. A biblical worldview will not allow a passive approach toward the social world. Francis Schaeffer reminded us that Jesus Christ is Lord of all: "He is our Lord, not just in religious things and not just in cultural things . . . but in our intellectual lives, and in business, and in our relation to society, and in our attitude toward the moral breakdown of our culture."[22] Although we do not have an abiding city on earth, we do have duties that constrain us. Writer Madeleine L'Engle admits, "It is impossible to listen to the Gospel week after week and turn my back on the social issues confronting me."[23]

The goal is to be Christ-centered in all things. For this reason, Christians cannot sit by idly as culture squeezes the soul and mind out of its people. Carl Henry sums it up best, "The divine mandate is to beam light, sprinkle salt, and knead leaven into an otherwise hopeless world."[24] Social engagement must take place at every level of the Christian life. Let's look at several examples: our work life, media and entertainment, and public social issues.

The Working Life

The Christian's greatest intensity of time and involvement with the world is usually found in the workplace. The role of work in society has been changing. The alienation of one's work from the family and neighborhood reflects a tremendous shift in the social life of America. At the personal level, although we remain convinced that our work is an important element of a meaningful human experience, the paycheck usually becomes the focus of our significance.

For the Christian, *how* one works is more important than *what* one does. Referring to the work of servants, Paul admonished: "Whatever you do, do your work heartily, as for the Lord rather than for men; knowing that from the Lord you will receive the reward of the

---

[22] Francis A. Schaeffer, *The Great Evangelical Disaster* (Westchester, IL: Crossway, 1984), p. 39.

[23] Madeleine L'Engle, "What May I Expect from My Church," in *Churches on the Wrong Road*, ed. Stanley Atkins and Theodore McConnell (Chicago: Regnery, 1986), p. 260.

[24] Carl F. H. Henry, "The New Coalitions," *Christianity Today*, 17 November 1989, p. 26.

inheritance. It is the Lord whom you serve" (Col. 3:23-24). Excellence, integrity, and honesty should be the marks of the Christian's work.

Unfortunately, many employers are more concerned with profits than with any other aspect of their business. The bottom line determines the direction of the company and personnel decisions. The company uses people to produce things or services.

Biblically, companies have the responsibility to practice sound financial principles and hold employees accountable for the quality of their work. People are far more important than products, programs, or projects. Because this is true, the work of a company should be designed to produce and develop the people who are employed. However, not all employers see the development of their employees as even a peripheral goal of their operations. If an employer is abusive and takes advantage of employees, the worker still has a responsibility before God to work with integrity (1 Pet. 2:18-20).

The Christian worker will also be concerned about the spiritual status of those with whom he works. Meeting the social, physical, and spiritual needs of those around him is a priority as he seeks to implement a biblical worldview in the work place. Excellent resources are available for the Christian who desires to explore a biblical perspective of work.[25]

Media and Entertainment

Western society is driven by its entertainment. Personal schedules, public functions, and even government and church programs conform to the entertainment itinerary. Entertainers are arguably the most powerful and well-paid individuals in our culture.

The Christian dilemma arises from both the content and value of the current types of entertainment in the media. Unfortunately, a great deal of media entertainment is both wicked and worthless. A biblical worldview calls for the Christian to guard what he sees, thinks, and hears. The psalmist echoes this admonition when he declares: "I will set no worthless thing before my eyes" (Ps. 101:3). "Worthless" is the Hebrew *belial*, a term that indicates both degradation as well as

---

[25] Among these are: Calvin Redekop and Urie A. Bender, *What Am I? What Am I?: Searching for Meaning in Your Work* (Grand Rapids: Zondervan, 1988); Richard C. Chewning, John W. Eby, and Shirley J. Roels, *Business Through the Eyes of Faith* (San Francisco: Harper & Row, 1990); John A. Bernbaum and Simon M. Steer, *Why Work? Careers and Employment in Biblical Perspective* (Grand Rapids: Baker, 1986); and Judith Allen Shelley, *Not Just a Job: Serving Christ in Your Work* (Downers Grove, IL: InterVarsity, 1985).

worthlessness.[26] The designation, "children of Belial," occurs sixteen times in the Old Testament in reference to people who were "wicked and good for nothing." The term "Belial" eventually became a personal reference for Satan. It is no wonder that when Paul charges Christians not to allow the wickedness of the world to influence them, he asks "What harmony has Christ with Belial?" (2 Cor. 6:15).

Obviously, Christians should avoid all forms of entertainment that appeal to prurient interests. Movies, television programs, and songs that flaunt sensuality and promiscuity are never appropriate for the Christian. Fleeing immorality is always the best and wisest course of action. This is not merely a prudish view of morality but a recognition that the vivid imagery of entertainment heavily influences values and can desensitize our moral convictions.

But even beyond avoiding the obvious immoral forms of entertainment, Christians are called to discern that which is *excellent* (Phil. 1:9-11). Not everything that is harmful is necessarily evil. The writer of Hebrews admonishes believers to "lay aside every encumbrance . . . and run with endurance the race that is set before us" (Heb. 12:1). The "encumbrance" described is not necessarily that which is evil or sinful, but rather that which "hinders the runner." Habits, hobbies, avocations, and other activities that are substitutes for biblical responsibilities or that compromise spiritual values obviously weigh down those running the race. A biblical worldview forces the Christian to think just as seriously about his leisure time as he does about his prayer time.

Christians must honor that which is good and true, and this may involve speaking out against forms of entertainment that are immoral or antibiblical. At the same time recognizing that non-Christians will disagree, the follower of Christ has no alternative but to stand up for that which is right. This is not advocating censorship, rather it is a proclamation of truth that must serve as the moral conscience of society.

Morality of Our Culture

The "salt and light" venue of the Christian's confrontation with the world is most clearly seen when dealing with issues of public morality. Abortion, pornography, discrimination, and a host of other moral questions are not the problem but rather *symptoms* of a greater problem. The problem is rooted in a conflict of worldviews: *Who* is the authority? Is it God or is it ourselves? The challenge to God's standards cannot be met merely by turning moral issues into political positions.

---

[26] See Philip E. Hughes, *The Second Epistle to the Corinthians*. New International Commentary on the New Testament (Grand Rapids: Eerdmans, 1962), pp. 248-52.

Christians must speak from a base of moral authority and personal compassion. They should be marked by a desire for justice, a drive toward righteousness, and a concern for the individual. True transformation can take place in society from the inside out. Attacking social problems at the root may do more than legislative reform to stem the further growth of immorality. For example, if Christians targeted the causes for widespread abortion and helped to relieve the social and economic hardships that often lead a woman to choose abortion, many of the pro-choice utilitarian arguments would be voided. The sheer moral authority of an uncompromising stand on principles, coupled with a sincere understanding and compassion, would make an impact on society that would be difficult to overcome.

The Bible lays out principles to guide human relationships. How these relate to forms of government and a social agenda is not always clear. But what is clear is that Christians are called to care for the needs of the poor (James 2:15-16; 1 John 3:17-18) and to do good to all (Gal. 6:10). Loving one's neighbor includes loving those who have different beliefs and backgrounds (Luke 10:25-37). Like the apostle Paul, we must seek wisdom in relating to outsiders (Col. 4:5-6), even going as far as accommodating their lifeview (1 Cor. 9:19-23) in order to communicate the word of truth to them. Naive isolationism and social withdrawal cannot fulfill the biblical mandate to influence the world. Christians must visibly stand out as those who walk after different goals for different reasons. Richard John Neuhaus delivers this challenge: "There should be a Christian distinctiveness, a Christian way of being out of sync, a Christian uncomfortableness, which we feel and which others feel about us, with all of the positions one can take in the political, cultural, and ideological debates in our society."[27]

The work of Jesus Christ provides the basis for the Christian's response to the world. Now, the natural world rots, rusts, and decays; the social world corrupts, fights, and dies. What began through His death and resurrection shall continue until He returns. Jesus reminded His followers of their ultimate hope: "In the world you will have tribulation, but take courage; I have overcome the world" (John 16:33).

---

[27] Richard John Neuhaus, "Advancing the Rose of Religion in Public Life," in *Christian Allies in a Secular Age*, ed. Kevin Perrotta and John C. Blattner (Ann Arbor, MI; Servant, 1987), p. 50.

DISCUSSION QUESTIONS

1. What do you think are the various motivations for the many people involved in the "save the world" programs? Should Christians be at the forefront of those benevolent activities? Why or why not? Do such relief initiatives "fit" with a biblical worldview?
2. How would each of the three approaches to Christian social engagement in this chapter confront the following issues: embryonic stem cell research, civil rights for minorities, euthanasia, teaching creation/evolution in public schools, military action?
3. Writer Madeleine L'Engle claimed: "It is impossible to listen to the Gospel week after week and turn my back on the social issues confronting me." In your opinion, what aspects of the gospel message led her to make such a statement? Do you agree or disagree? Why? What social issues are particularly related to the message of the gospel?

FURTHER READING

The Natural World:

Beisner, E. Calvin. *Where Garden Meets Wilderness: Evangelical Entry into the Environmental Debate.* Grand Rapids: Eerdmans, 1997.

"The Cornwall Declaration." Interfaith Stewardship Alliance. Available online at www.interfaithstewardship.org.

Miller, Darrow. *Discipling Nations: The Power of Truth to Transform Culture,* 2d ed. YWAM, 2001.

Wright, Richard T. *Biology Through the Eyes of Faith.* San Francisco: Harper & Row, 1989. See especially chapter 9, "Stewards of Creation."

The Social World:

Gay, Craig M. *The Way of the (Modern) World: Or, Why It's Tempting to Live as If God Doesn't Exist.* Grand Rapids, MI: Eerdmans, 1998.

George, Robert P. *The Clash of Orthodoxies: Law, Religion and Morality in Crisis.* Wilmington, DE: Intercollegiate Studies Institute, 2001.

Godawa, Brian. *Hollywood Worldviews: Watching Films with Wisdom and Discernment.* Downer's Grove, IL: InterVarsity Press, 2002.

Mielander, Gilbert. *Bioethics: A Primer for Christians,* 2d ed. Grand Rapids: Eerdmans, 2004.

Mouw, J. Richard. *When the Kings Come Marching In.* Grand Rapids: Eerdmans, 1983.

Nash, Ronald. *Social Justice and the Christian Church.* Lanham, MD: University Press of America, 1990.

Neuhaus, Richard John. *The Naked Public Square.* 2d ed. Grand Rapids: Eerdmans, 1986.

Niebuhr, Richard H. *Christ and Culture.* New York: Harper & Row, 1951.

Postman, Neil. *Amusing Ourselves to Death: Public Discourse in the Age of Show Business.* New York: Viking Press, 1985.

Vanhoozer, Kevin, Charles A. Anderson, and Michael J. Sleasman, eds. *Everyday Theology: How to Read Cultural Texts and Interpret Trends.* Grand Rapids: Baker, 2007.

Webber, Robert E. *The Church in the World.* Grand Rapids: Zondervan, 1986.

Wolterstorff, Nicholas. *Until Justice and Peace Embrace.* Grand Rapids: Eerdmans, 1983.

APPENDIX

CASE STUDIES FOR EACH CHAPTER

Chapter One: Case Study

A Worldview Smorgasbord

The array of worldview options present in Western culture is astounding. From movies, music, television, print media, games, and the internet the typical consumer of the Information Age confronts more worldview ideas on a daily basis than those living in other centuries would have seen during the course of their entire lives. Also, the speed at which information (and people) can travel means that worldview expressions from other cultures become part of ours as well.

For example, from a naturalistic perspective, audiences are bludgeoned with an approach to life that borders on nihilism from "blood and guts" slasher films, from the "get rich or die trying" lifestyle celebrated in much of the hip hop industry, and from the popular "shoot 'em up" games that now outrank movies in overall sales. The focus is on personal profit, revenge or pleasure at any cost, even wholesale slaughter. Somewhat tamer in action, many teenage movies and prime-time sitcoms poke fun at authority and locate ultimate concerns in immediate sexual experiences and relationships.

Concurrently, the complete spectrum of religious beliefs is at the fingertips (and therefore the whims) of any internet user. As the world continues to get smaller, religions that were historically non-western can be found in nearly any western city. This sort of open access fuels the popular idea that the focus of religion is the individual rather than truth. This can especially be seen in contemporary portrayals of the afterlife which avoid any reference to judgment.

A theistic view of life and the world is rarely treated as credible. Many discussions of moral, political, or academic issues by mainstream media outlets dismiss religious perspectives in favor of those that are thoroughly secular. Christians who truly believe the Bible are unfairly lumped together with Islamic extremists as having the same tendencies toward naïve credulity, herd hysteria, and the potential for violence. Often, the public place of the Christian is as a tool of political manipulation or for a box-office boost.

In the midst of many cacophonous and conflicting voices clamoring for their views, how do people decide which truth-claims merit their attention, even their allegiance? Even if the average person approaches worldview ideas according to the current postmodern ethos of "anything goes," he cannot avoid consequences of the worldviews that the internet, videos and popular culture bring into his living room.

The condition of the world (post-Christian and postmodern) and of cultural shifts away from "absolute" truth accentuate the importance for Christians to think "worldviewishly." At the least, we need to know our worldview and have the ability to evaluate alternate views.

Chapter Two: Case Study

Ideas Have Consequences: Europe, Secularism, and Islam

Is Europe headed for extinction? Many think so. For years, the birth rate in European countries has been in steep decline. The birth rate in every member nation of the European Union is below the 2.1 average (meaning 2.1 children for every woman) that is needed for a country to maintain its national population. In fact, many European countries are far below that magic number of 2.1. As of 2005, Germany's birth rate was only .085, which means that the largest European country also had the lowest birth rate of any European country.

This situation has been the subject of much commentary and government planning due to the projected impact on the European work force and national economies. Several local and national governments in Europe now financially reward couples who have children. Russia has attempted to deal with a decline in birth rates by instituting a new holiday: "National Conception Day." Exactly nine months before their major national holiday couples are given the day off work, and are given financial incentives if they give birth exactly nine months later!

The potential consequences of these falling birth rates extend beyond the economy. While European countries face a population decline, there is not a single Islamic country that is *below* the 2.1 birth rate. In fact, in many Islamic countries the fertility rate is above 6.0! It is also probable that the Islamic population embedded within European countries is mostly responsible for the birth rate being as high as it is. According to the Brookings Institute, the Muslim birth rate is three times higher in European countries than the non-Muslim birth rate. In other words, there will be a tremendous increase in the percentage of the Muslim population in Europe in the coming years. In late 2007, newspapers in Great Britain reported that Mohammed would soon become the most popular name given to male babies.

From a worldview perspective, both the causes and the consequences of this are worth examining. Clearly, naturalism dominates the European ideological landscape, and has for many decades. In this secularist view, morality is determined by the individual. In particular, sexual freedom has been a hallmark of secularist values. Contrary to a theistic view, sexuality is not tied to marriage for its context; nor is it tied necessarily to procreation as its consequence. In a world without God-given design, sexual freedom is valued as a right while marriage and child-bearing are reduced to mere personal choice. Among non-Muslims in Europe, cohabitation is preferred to marriage, no-fault divorce laws are common, and access to contraception (including abortion) is considered an issue of personal rights. With these values so deeply embedded, an increase in population is highly unlikely. Russia is a case-in-point. National Conception Day, though creative, has little chance of succeeding since in Russia there are annually more abortions than live births.

Thus many researchers believe that signs point to a drastically different demography in the coming decades: either the "Europeanization" of Islam or the "Islamization" of Europe. Will Europe become Muslim by default?

For Christians, there are two challenges in light of these developments. First, we must have *insight* and understand how naturalism has impacted our culture's (and our own) values when it comes to marriage, family, and procreation. Second, we must have *foresight* as to how currently embedded ideas are shaping our culture as we seek to live and communicate the Gospel here and now. "Western civilization" may not survive the twenty-first century. To handle these challenges, we must be more Christian than western.

Chapter Three: Case Study

Where the Evidence Leads: The Case of Anthony Flew

On December 9, 2004, an Associated Press headline announced a worldview shift so drastic that it shook the world of philosophy: "Famous Atheist Believes in God: One of the World's Leading Atheists Now Believes in God, More or Less, Based on Scientific Evidence." Perhaps the most prominent atheist of the latter half of the twentieth century, who was responsible for the most "systematic, comprehensive, original, and influential exposition of atheism that is to be found"[1] was no longer an atheist.

Flew, who often debated his theistic philosophical counterparts in public settings prior to his "conversion," has also been public about his new belief in God which, according to Flew, was the inevitable result of being consistent to the principle he had tried to live by his entire career as a professional philosopher: follow the evidence, and arguments, wherever they lead.

For Flew, the arguments of Christian philosophers such as Richard Swineburne, (on the coherence of theism), Alvin Plantinga (on theism as a proper basic belief), William Lane Craig (on human freedom), and Gerry Schroeder (on refuting the possibility of life arising by chance) were compelling.[2] Also, when asked if recent discoveries about the origins and makeup of life offered evidence of a Designer, Flew replied:

> Yes, I now think it does.... Almost entirely because of the DNA investigations. What I think the DNA material has done is that it has shown, by the almost unbelievable complexity of the arrangements which are needed to produce (life), that intelligence must have been involved in getting these extraordinarily diverse elements to work together. It's the enormous complexity of the number of elements and the enormous subtlety of the ways they work together. The meeting of these two parts at the right time by chance is simply minute. It is all a matter of the enormous complexity by which the results were achieved, which looked to me like the work of intelligence.[3]

For many, the news of Flew's change of mind brings to mind the conversion of another prominent British atheist of a generation ago, C. S. Lewis. For Lewis, the move from atheism to theism was a step in his journey toward Christian theism. Christians should be encouraged by Flew's move and reminded of the role that argument, reason and evidence can play in the battle of worldviews. However, at the same time, Christians should not forget that argument, reason, evidence, and our lifestyles are also to be employed (in dependence upon the Holy Spirit) to point people to the person of Jesus Christ, the full revelation of God.

---

[1] Roy Abraham Varghese, "Preface" in Anthony Flew, *There Is a God: How the World's Most Notorious Atheist Changed His Mind* (New York: Harper-One, 2007), p. ix.

[2] See Flew, *There Is a God*, pp. 48-78.

[3] Ibid., p. 75.

Chapter Four: Case Study

The Primacy of Scripture

As an outspoken atheist, Sam Harris is typically not known by Christians for things they hold in common. For example, his book *The End of Faith: Religion, Terror and the Future of Reason* argues that theistic beliefs, and Christianity in particular, is antithetical to and actually obstructs societal progress. He is particularly scathing in his comments about the Bible which, he writes, "was the work of sand-strewn men and women who thought the earth was flat and for whom a wheelbarrow would have been a breathtaking example of emerging technology."[4]

Interestingly, however, he also criticizes religious moderates in his book—those who claim that the Bible can be believed in some areas but not others; or those who embrace religion for personal reasons, but are not dogmatic about it.

Harris writes:

> In America, religious moderation is further enforced by the fact that most Christians and Jews do not read the Bible in its entirety and consequently have no idea just how vigorously the God of Abraham wants heresy expunged. One look at the book of Deuteronomy reveals that he has something very special in mind should your son or daughter return from yoga class advocating worship of Krishna . . . (see Deuteronomy 13:7-11). The above passage is as canonical as any in the Bible, and it is only by ignoring such barbarisms that the Good Book can be reconciled with life in the modern world. *This is a problem for "moderation" in religion: it has nothing underwriting it other than the unacknowledged neglect of the letter of the divine law.* (Italics added)[5]

Harris's main critique of religious moderation is that it makes no sense; it has no authoritative foundation other than personal opinion. Christian theists should agree with Harris at this point.

However, for the Christian, the Bible is the authoritative source for developing their worldview, and thus should hold a primary place in their thought and their ethics. The lack of a Christian worldview that is endemic to much of contemporary Christianity is the result of our own "unacknowledged neglect" of the Scriptures.

---

[4] Harris, *End of Faith* (New York: Norton, 2005), p. 45.
[5] Ibid., p. 18.

Chapter Five: Case Study

Resolving a Contradiction: How Did Judas Die?

The accounts of the death of Judas are among the passages of Scripture that appear contradictory. Did Judas die by suicide or by accident? Matthew 27:5 describes the death of Judas as suicide by hanging: "And throwing down the pieces of silver into the temple, he departed, and he went and hanged himself." On the other hand, the account in Acts 1:18 mentions different details: "Now this man (Judas) acquired a field with the reward of his wickedness, and falling headlong he burst open in the middle and all his bowels gushed out." How might these accounts be reconciled? (Hint: consider following the procedure described near the end of chapter five.)

Chapter Six: Case Study

Comforting the Grieving as Christ Did

Nicholas Wolterstorff's book *Lament for a Son* is a first-hand account of his grieving the death of his son, Eric. In it, he reminds us of the depth of loss that accompanies death:

> There's a hole in the world now. In the place where he was, there's now just nothing. . . . Only a gap remains. . . . Only a void is left. . . . A person, an irreplaceable person, is gone. Never again will anyone apprehend the world quite the way he did. Never again will anyone inhabit the world the way he did. Questions I have can never now get answers. The world is emptier. My son is gone. Only a hole remains, a void, a gap, never to be filled.[6]

Wolterstorff then advises the one who is trying to comfort the grieving.

> But please: Don't say it's not really so bad. Because it is. Death is awful, demonic. If you think your task as comforter is to tell me that really, all things considered, it's not so bad, you do not sit with me in my grief but place yourself off in the distance away from me. Over there, you are of no help. What I need to hear from you is that you recognize how painful it is. I need to hear from you that you are with me in my desperation. To comfort me, you have to come close. . . .[7]

---

[6] Wolterstroff, *Lament for a Son* (Grand Rapids, MI: Eerdman's, 1985), p. 33.
[7] Ibid., p. 34.

In a biblical worldview, this is precisely what Christ did: He came close. He entered the depths of the pain and despair of this world and our own hearts. Yes, He died *for* us; but also He was *with* us. The apostle John reports that though He knew He would soon raise Lazarus from the dead, Jesus still wept with his grieving sisters (John 11). The apostle Paul expressed it this way: *"He made Him who knew no sin to be sin on our behalf, so that we might become the righteousness of God in Him"* (2 Corinthians 5:21, NAS). Long before, the prophet Isaiah anticipated that the "suffering servant" (the Messiah) would be one who bore not only our sins, but also "our griefs and our sorrows" (Isaiah 53:4). In the incarnation, God came close; in the crucifixion, God took our hurts into Himself.

Chapter Seven: Case Study

The Intolerance of the Tolerant

Colleges and universities pride themselves on their tolerance as places where any ideas and contrary beliefs may be examined objectively, not defensively. With their anti-hate speech codes, departments devoted to the study of diverse cultures, spotlight on the historical oppression of minorities, and general acceptance of morally questionable behaviors, they appear to be havens of open-minded discussion. When it comes to Christianity, however, they are often havens of anti-religious bias.

That many professors disdain Christianity is not an alarmist myth. In fact, a 2007 study published by Gary Tobin of the Institute for Jewish and Community Research[8] found that fifty-three percent of college and university faculty held "unfavorable feelings" toward evangelical Christians while at the same time holding favorable opinions of most other religious groups. Interestingly, the intent of Tobin's research was to uncover bias against Jews, but the only other group found to face a significant level of bias was Mormons, though the level was not really comparable to what Christians face.

Tobin also found that college and university faculty were far less likely to identify themselves as Christian than the general public, and are far more likely to refer to themselves as secular or liberal than as conservative or religious. Perhaps even more startling was the finding that while a strong majority of the faculty believed that fundamentalist

---

[8] Gary A. Tobin and Aryeh K. Weinberg, *Profiles of the American University,* vol. 2: *Religious Beliefs and Behaviors of College Faculty.* Institute for Jewish and Community Research, 2007.

Christians should keep their beliefs out of politics, they were undecided as to whether Muslims should keep their beliefs out of politics.

Tobin's conclusions echo the results of an earlier survey of college faculty summarized in a March 2005 issue of the Washington Post. The article revealed that seventy-two percent of professors and instructors in colleges across the U.S. are liberal.[9] This was a marked increase from just twenty years earlier, when the number of those who identified themselves as liberal was only thirty-nine percent. By contrast, the Harris poll found that only nineteen percent of the general public describe themselves as liberal.[10] The Post article also reports that fifty-one percent of college faculty rarely or never attend church or synagogue, eighty-four percent are in favor of abortion, and sixty-seven percent accept homosexuality.

Chapter Eight: Case Study

Emerging Technology and the Human Being

In 1910, G. K. Chesterton observed: "The huge modern heresy is to alter the human soul to fit modern social conditions, instead of altering modern social conditions to fit the human soul."[11] False worldviews victimize people by redefining the term human. Many if not most of the battles in what have become known as the "culture wars" (the major social challenges facing western culture) are rooted in a basic disagreement of what it means to be and live as human. One example is the transhumanist movement.

In 1998, philosophers Nick Bostrom and David Pearce founded the World Transhumanist Association, a group dedicated to the use of emerging technologies as a means to control and advance human evolutionary progress. The term transhumanist refers to those who want to initiate the transition from being a non-enhanced human toward becoming "posthuman." In the transhumanist view, we can control and move beyond our humanity, enhancing human nature through mechanical and cellular technological integration. Transhumanists view human nature as

---

[9] "College Faculties a Most Liberal Lot, Study Finds," by Howard Kurtz. *Washington Post*, 29 March 2005, C01.

[10] *The Harris Poll*, #8. 13 February 2002. Online article: http://www.harris interactive.com/ harris_poll/index.asp?PID=285.

[11] Quoted in Craig M. Gay, *The Way of the (Modern) World: Or, Why It's Tempting to Live as If God Doesn't Exist* (Grand Rapids, MI: Eerdman's, 1998), p. 237.

non-fixed, a work-in-progress, and improvable through science, technology, and reason.

Clearly, this movement reflects a naturalistic worldview. As is the case with every worldview, transhumanism offers a) an understanding of human nature, b) a theory of humanity's problem, and c) an idea of human salvation—all of which compete with the biblical worldview for our allegiance. For example, a recent conference sponsored by the World Transhumanist Association was entitled "Transhumanity Saving Humanity," and boasted that "emerging technologies will give society the ability to solve the greatest challenges facing humanity." For the transhumanist, the challenge is remaining trapped in our current human form when future technologies could potentially offer so much more. Topics of the conference included life extension and longevity, bionics, colonizing outer space, future civilizations, and future humans. Appropriately, the conference featured an appearance by actor William Shatner, who played Captain James T. Kirk in the original *Star Trek* television series.

Chapter Nine: Case Study

Marriage, Family and Society

"The triangle of truisms, father, mother, and child cannot be destroyed; it can only destroy those civilizations which disregard it," wrote G. K. Chesterton.[12] Historically, this has proven true. "No society has ever survived after its family life deteriorated," warns Dr. Paul Popenoe, co-director of the National Marriage Project at Rutgers University.[13]

What's the state of the family today? Consider the following scenario: Bill and Martha married then divorced, with Martha taking custody of their three children. Bill began a homosexual relationship with Jim, and the couple adopted a son who now calls his "parents" Daddy and Poppa.

Martha met Eric (who had children by a former marriage) and they married, which gave her three children a stepbrother, a stepsister, a stepfather, two sets of stepgrandparents, plus the previous relatives on their father's side.

Eric and Martha desired children, and when they were unable to have them they decided to have Martha impregnated by artificial insemination. While Martha was pregnant, tests showed that the baby had

---

[12] *Family, Society, Politics*, vol. 4 of *The Collected Works of G. K. Chesterton* (San Francisco, Ignatius Press, 1987), p. 237.

[13] Quoted by Rita Thaemert in "The American Family: Future Uncertain," *Time Magazine* (December 28, 1970). Archived at: http://www.time.com/time/archive/printout/0,23657,944265,00.html.

Huntington's disease which, although always fatal, is usually dormant until after age forty. Eric and Martha must decide whether *some* life is better than *none*. If they keep the baby (who will be the only one without a stepparent), at age eighteen he will be able legally to have the identity of his "real" father—the one who donated the sperm, that is. Perhaps by then, a cure will be available for his condition.

Babies can be born through a surrogate mother, an embryo transfer, or from an artificial womb. Lesbian and homosexual couples may legally adopt children. The traditional definitions of Daddy and Mommy no longer describe many who rear children. (Gay and lesbian activists suggest that the terms Mother and Father on birth certificates discriminate against same-sex couples and should be replaced with terms such as First Parent and Second Parent or even Progenitor A and Progenitor B.)

According to Harvard Professor Emeritus Carle Zimmerman, the signs for our civilization are not positive:

> The extinction of faith in the familistic system is identical with the movements in Greece during the century following the Peloponnesian Wars, and in Rome from about A.D. 150. In each case the change in the faith and belief in family systems was associated with rapid adoption of negative reproduction rates and with enormous crises in the very civilizations themselves.[14]

Chapter Ten: Case Study

The Church and Its Image Problem

Is the church its own worst enemy? Decades ago philosopher Bertrand Russell offered this diatribe against Christianity:

> You find as you look round the world that every single bit of progress in humane feeling, every improvement in the criminal law, every step towards the diminution of war, . . . every mitigation of slavery, every moral progress that there has been in the world, has been consistently opposed by the organized churches of the world. I say quite deliberately that the Christian religion, as organized in its churches, has been and still is the principal *enemy of moral progress* in the world.[15]

---

[14] Ibid.

[15] Bertrand Russell, "Why I Am Not a Christian," in *Bertrand Russell on God and Religion*, ed. Al Seckel (Buffalo, NY: Prometheus, 1986), pp. 69-70 (italics added).

Russell's charge may not always be repeated openly, but the erosion of public confidence in institutions, especially religious institutions, has resulted in a "worst case" interpretation of the Christian church. According to David Kinnaman, president of the Barna Group, and Gabe Lyons, "Christianity has an image problem."[16] This was their primary conclusion from an extensive three-year research project of the perceptions contemporary young adults hold about Christianity. Here is how they described their findings:

> In our national surveys with young people, we found the three most common perceptions were that Christians were anti-homosexual (ninety-one percent), judgmental (eighty-seven percent) and hypocritical (eighty-five percent). These "big three" were followed by the following negative perceptions, embraced by a majority of young adults: old-fashioned, too involved in politics, out of touch with reality, insensitive to others, boring, not accepting of other faiths, and confusing. When they think of the Christian faith, these are the images that come to mind. *This is what a new generation really thinks about Christianity.*

These perceptions persist despite the impressive historical record of contributions that Christianity has made to society, which include the founding of hospitals and other institutions to care for the sick and elderly; the founding of relief organizations to care for the poor, disenfranchised and abused; the founding of modern science; influencing the founding of democracy and the free-market; and confronting slavery, human trafficking, and the sexual exploitation of women and minors.[17]

Kinnaman and Lyons also reported on the positive perceptions they found, though from a Christian worldview, not all of these perceptions should be considered positive:

---

[16] David Kinnaman and Gabe Lyons, *UnChristian: What a New Generation Really Thinks about Christianity.* (Grand Rapids, MI: Baker, 2007), p. 11.

[17] For a full account of Christianity's contributions to society, see Alvin Schmidt, *Under the Influence: How Christianity Transformed Civilization* (Grand Rapids, MI: Zondervan, 2001); Rodney Stark, *For the Glory of God: How Monotheism Led to Reformations, Science, Witch Hunts, and the End of Slavery* (Princeton, NJ: Princeton, 2003); Ibid., *The Victory of Reason: How Christianity Led to Freedom, Capitalism, and Western Success* (New York: Random House, 2005); Vincent Caroll, *Christianity on Trial: Arguments against Anti-Religious Bigotry* (Encounter, 2002); M. Stanton Evans, *The Theme is Freedom: Religion, Politics, and the American Tradition* (Washington, DC: Regnery, 1994); and Dinesh D'Souza, *What's So Great about Christianity* (Washington, DC: Regnery, 2007)

The most common "favorable" impression is that Christianity teaches the same basic idea as other religions: *more than four out of every five young outsiders embrace this description* (italics added). Three-quarters believe that Christianity has "good values and principles" and most outsiders indicate that present-day Christianity is "friendly."

Clearly, there is more to the Christian worldview than being "friendly" or useful, or offering the same ideas as other religions. The following statement by Kinnaman and Lyons makes it clear that our culture is missing much of what the Christian worldview has to offer:

Outsiders were split down the middle when it came to the following images: a faith they respect, a faith that shows love for others, something that offers hope for the future, and people they trust. Only a small percentage of outsiders strongly believe that the labels "respect, love, hope, and trust" describe Christianity. A minority of outsiders perceives Christianity as genuine and real, as something that makes sense, and as relevant to their life.

Certainly, perception is not always reality. Still, it is worthwhile to investigate *why* they are *what* they are.

Chapter Eleven: Case Study

Christian Environmentalism amid Ecological Panic

Times have changed: the global cooling alarm of the 1970s has been replaced with the global warming alarm of the early twenty-first century. One case in point is the Gaia Napa Valley Hotel and Spa in California. This eco-friendly establishment was constructed using recycled materials, utilizes solar panels for twelve percent of its electricity, and features low-flush toilets and low-flow showerheads. Even the contents of the nightstand drawer reflect their ecological commitments:

Visitors to the Gaia Napa Valley Hotel and Spa won't find the Gideon Bible in the nightstand drawer. Instead, on the bureau will be a copy of *An Inconvenient Truth*, former Vice President Al Gore's book about global warming.

They'll also find the Gaia equipped with waterless urinals, solar lighting and recycled paper as it marches toward becoming California's first hotel certified as "green," or benevolent to the environment. Similar features are found thirty-five miles south at San Francisco's Orchard Garden

Hotel, which competes for customers with neighboring luxury hotels like the Ritz-Carlton and Fairmont. . . .

The Gaia and Orchard are seeking to be the first hotels in California certified by the U.S. Green Building Council, which has authenticated 800 buildings across the U.S. and has about 6,000 in the process, including thirty hotels. San Francisco and other cities offer financial incentives to lessen water and energy use and reduce carbon dioxide emissions. . . .[18]

Different approaches to important issues often result from different worldview starting points. The theistic mandate to care for the world God created and entrusted to humanity serves as the basis for a pro-active Christian response. As discussed earlier in this chapter (chapter eleven), the derived authority mankind possesses over the environment does not permit despoiling nature for the benefit of humanity's personal luxury.

From a naturalistic worldview, the urgency to respond to the environmental crisis is often based on evolutionary assumptions. In an evolutionary paradigm, there are razor-thin margins in the fragile saga of human survival. Because no divine hand guides the history of the world, we are here by chance. In fact, we beat the odds—we shouldn't be here at all! This pragmatic concern for the survival of the human race creates a utilitarian ethic (in which the end justifies the means). If the environment is exploited, we could be responsible for the destruction of planet earth.

The rise of environmental consciousness also coincides with the growing influence of popular transcendental thought. Although a connection between the two may not be a cause-and-effect, there is no doubt that ecological concerns are an integral part of the New Age worldview. If humanity is one with the environment, then the need to care for the earth is obvious. Less mystical is the call by some in the educational wing of environmental activism for a new "ecological ethic" by which decisions governing environmental issues can be guided. Even though such a "moral ecology" is not strictly transcendental in nature, it adds support to a New Age, whole-earth interpretation of life.

Many factors contribute to the current confusion regarding ecological care and protection. The most obvious is the conflicting data about the causes, extent, and consequences of global warming. The biblical worldview offers the true account of the story of the world—including creation, stewardship, redemption, and renewal—and therefore offers a framework for understanding our present and future situations.

---

[18] "California Hotels Go Green with Low-Flow Toilets, Solar Lights" by Ari Levy and Carole Zimmer, *Bloomberg,* 27 April 2007.

INDEX OF SUBJECTS

Abortion, 266, 269-71, 273, 276-77, 283, 288
Agnosticism, 27
Animal rights, 37, 258-59
Atheism, 10, 23, 26, 58, 71, 283-84
Authority, of Bible, 17, 47, 50, 63n, 108, 112-124, 130-31, 134-37, 139-43, 190, 269

Baptism, 245, 250
Biblical worldview
    biblical perspective, 15-17
    explanation of, 93-108
    as "touchstone proposition," 95-96
    view of God, 96-101
    view of man, 101-104
    view of nature, 104-106
Buddhism, 32, 34, 66, 173, 185

Canonicity, 116-124, 139-143
Children, 221-22, 232-37. *See also* Family
Church, 239-56
    and baptism, 245, 250
    and cultural changes, 240-42
    beginnings of, 245
    congregational form, 247
    defined, 243-44
    denominations, 247-49
    Episcopal form, 248
    and fellowship, 251-53
    form/function of, 248
    and hypocrites, 239
    and Lord's Supper, 250-51
    mission of, 249-54
    and missions, 252-54
    Presbyterian form, 247-48

and worldviews, 242-43
and worship, 249-50
Cosmological argument, 77-78. *See also* God, existence of
Culture
    ancient cultures, 11-13
    definition of, 14
    and worldview, xi, 14-15, 37

Deism, 2, 23, 32, 45-46, 64
Denominations. *See* Church, denominations

Empirical data, 84, 115
Enlightenment, xii, 50-52, 145
Entertainment, 19, 199, 233, 264, 275-76
Environmental crisis, 37, 258-63
    biblical response to, 261-63
Errors, in Scripture, 113-15, 129-38. *See also* Inerrancy
Ethics, 23-29, 34, 232, 266, 270-71, 273
Evil, problem of
    defined, 149-50
    and emotions, 150-51
    and fideism, 156-57
    and finitism, 157-58
    and Free Will Defense, 161-63
    and illusionism, 152-53
    and Islam, 154-55
    and logic, 149-50, 162-64
    and mixed evil, 148
    and moral evil, 148
    and natural evil, 147
    and naturalism, 151-52
    and postmodernism, 153-54

and transmoralism, 158-60
Existentialism, 21n, 23, 31

Faith, 2, 27, 52, 70, 81, 84, 112,
    117, 129, 133, 135, 137-38,
    156, 172, 174, 178, 186, 196,
    209, 212, 214, 240
Family, 219-238. *See also*
    Husbands; Parenting;
    Wives
    and children, 232-37
    and creation, 226-28
    definition of, 220
    and marriage, 222-23, 232-
        37
    metaphors for, 225-26
    and parenting, 222-23, 232-
        37
    traditional form of, 219-220
    and worldviews, 223-25
Fellowship, 209, 244, 251-53
Finitism, 23, 45-46, 157-58

God
    confronting, 10, 24-27, 33-
        34, 41-43, 96
    existence of, 10, 25, 41, 44,
        50, 57, 64, 66, 76-83
    naturalistic view of, 24-27
    transcendental view of, 33-
        34

Hedonism, 23, 31
Hinduism, 32, 152, 173, 185
History, 6, 9, 11, 21, 28, 37, 48-
    51, 74, 82-83, 92, 97-98,
    123, 125, 135, 137, 142, 155,
    242, 248, 293
Holy Spirit, 95, 97, 100-01, 114,
    118-19, 121-22, 134, 210,
    231, 245, 250, 286
Humanism, 31, 84

Humanist Manifesto, 31, 136,
    242
Humanity
    biblical view of, 101-04,
        197-216
    confronting, 10-11, 27-29,
        34-36, 43-44, 56, 101
    depravity of, 101-04, 204-07
    naturalistic view of, 27-29
    transcendental view of, 34-
        36
Husbands, 229-30. *See also*
    Family

Inerrancy, 115, 129-38. *See also*
    Errors, in Scripture
Infatuation. *See* Love
Islam, x, 46-48, 59, 90, 97, 107,
    150, 154-62, 171, 173-74,
    178, 180, 185, 281-83

Jesus Christ
    deity of, 98-100
    humanity of, 98, 99
    uniqueness of, 100
Judaism, 46-48, 97, 150,
    174, 177-78, 185

Lord's Supper. *See* Church
Love
    infatuation, 229-30
    in marriage, 229-32. *See also*
        Family

Manuscripts, of Scripture, 125-
    27
    Old Testament, 125-27
    New Testament, 127-29
Marriage. *See* Family; Love
Masoretes, 126
Missions. *See* Church
Monism, 21n, 33-34

Moral argument, 77, 80-81. *See also* God, existence of
Moral Majority, 270

Naturalism, 13, 22, 24-32, 49, 58, 95, 151, 242, 283
    expressions of, 30-32
    evaluated, 67-72
    view of God, 24-27
    view of man, 27-29
    view of nature, 29-30
Nature. *See also* Environmental crisis
    confronting, 11-13
    biblical view of, 44, 78-79, 104-06
    and environmentalism, 258-63
    naturalistic view of, 29-30, 81
    theistic view of, 44-45
    transcendental view of, 36-37
New Age, 5, 32, 38-39, 58, 74, 100, 241, 261, 293
Nihilism, 30-31, 87, 281

Parenting. *See* Family
Pluralism, 171-93
    defined, 172-73
    and exclusivism, 173, 179, 181, 189
    and inclusivism, 172, 189
    and selectivism, 172
    and universalism, 173, 182-83
Postmodernism, 48-58
    evaluated, 83-88
    view of man, 56-58
    view of reality, 53-56

Revelation, 42, 45, 50-52, 94, 96, 113, 116-24
Roman Catholicism, 50, 120, 185, 247

Salvation, 35, 37, 47, 91, 100-03, 135, 174-77, 179-91
Science, 12-13, 25-27, 38, 52, 67-72, 76, 84-85, 95, 105, 115, 164, 260-63, 291
Secularization, 58, 196
Self, 197-217
    biblical view of, 202-16
    naturalistic view of, 200
    transcendental view of, 201

Talmud, 46, 126, 140
Teleological argument, 77-80. *See also* God, existence of
Terrorism, 82, 266
Text. *See* Manuscripts, of Scripture
Theism, 39-48
    evaluated, 76-83
    expressions of, 45
    view of God, 41-42
    view of man, 43-44
    view of nature, 44-45
Transcendentalism
    evaluated, 73-75
    expressions of, 37-39
    view of God, 33-34
    view of man, 34-36
    view of nature, 36-37
Trinity, 48, 97-98

Values, xi, xiii, 1, 8, 11, 20, 80, 87, 198, 215, 219, 222-25, 232, 242, 264, 270, 276, 283, 292

Wives, 231-32. *See also* Family
World
    natural world, 257-63
    social world, 263-277
Worldviews. *See also* Biblical
     worldview
    and culture, 13-15
    definition of, 7-8
    elements of, 9-13
    evaluation of, 61-66
    organizing, 21-23
Worship, 42, 87, 157, 186, 210-
    12, 243, 249-51